MW00475710

Burdened

Burdened

Student Debt and the
Making of an American Crisis

Ryann Liebenthal

DEYST.

An Imprint of WILLIAM MORROW

BURDENED. Copyright © 2024 by Ryann J. Liebenthal. All rights reserved. Printed in the United States of America. No part of this book may be used or reproduced in any manner whatsoever without written permission except in the case of brief quotations embodied in critical articles and reviews. For information, address HarperCollins Publishers, 195 Broadway, New York, NY 10007.

HarperCollins books may be purchased for educational, business, or sales promotional use. For information, please email the Special Markets Department at SPsales@harpercollins.com.

Portions of this text (parts of chapters 10, 11, and 12) have been previously published in *Mother Jones* and *The New Republic*.

FIRST EDITION

Designed by Jennifer Chung

Library of Congress Cataloging-in-Publication Data has been applied for.

ISBN 978-0-358-35396-6

24 25 26 27 28 LBC 5 4 3 2 1

To A. and E., my greatest teachers,
and to Jean Z., the first author I ever met

CONTENTS

Introduction

Jordan Long should have graduated from Morehouse College on May 19, 2019. But instead of sitting beside his friends in the Atlanta sun with a yellow-and-green kente stole draped across his neck, Jordan was back at his mother's house in Oakland, California, where he'd been living for the past two years. At the end of his sophomore year, he had taken stock of his financial situation and come to a startling realization. He had already racked up $65,000 in student debt, and he was on track to graduate with $150,000 or more, an almost unimaginable sum split among him and several family members who had taken out loans on his behalf.

Jordan had been excited to go to Morehouse, an all-male historically Black college whose alumni include Martin Luther King Jr. and Spike Lee, and he'd thrived there, enrolling in business courses and serving on the board of Safe Space, the campus LGBTQ organization. But he just couldn't see how any of that justified saddling his family with six figures and an interest rate. He emailed the financial aid office to see if there was anything they could do to help. He'd already received grant money and a small scholarship, but the well had dried up. The school's resources were limited, and yearly costs were edging toward $50,000.

Together Jordan and his mom, a health-research coordinator, decided that the situation was unsustainable. He took a few days to reflect, then let the school know he wouldn't be returning. In tears, he wrote his resignation letter for Safe Space. When he came back to Oakland that summer, he enrolled at a local community college and began working at a Best Buy. Eventually, he earned his associate's degree and transferred to the state university in Hayward to continue working toward his bachelor's.

On the day Jordan should have graduated from Morehouse, he

watched from home as a man named Robert F. Smith stepped up to the dais to deliver words of advice and encouragement to his classmates. Smith, a graduate of Cornell, had founded his own private equity firm and become a billionaire—the wealthiest Black man in America—so he was well poised to offer his counsel on life after college.

"We all have the responsibility to liberate others so that they can become their best selves," Smith said as the sun beat down on the nearly four hundred young men in front of him. "We need you to become the elected leaders," he said. "We need you to become the C-suite executives." He told the graduates to gather themselves. "Take a moment, stand up, give each other a hug." Then he dropped the bombshell. That day, he announced, he would be making a gift to the graduating class—he would pay off their student loans.

Joyous surprise spread across the faces of the professors and administrators behind Smith as the crowd in front of him erupted in elation. Back in Oakland, Jordan Long couldn't believe his bad luck. He'd dropped out of his dream school to save money, and now he was the odd one out of his classmates with student loan debt—and unlike them, he still didn't have a degree.

The higher education lottery had chosen its winners, as it does every year, and Jordan Long was not among them. There was nothing particularly unusual about this. If Jordan's loss felt especially poignant—garnering attention from *People* magazine and the *New York Times*—perhaps that was just because his choice had seemed so *responsible*, such a sensible rebuttal to a system that rarely rewards the Jordan Longs of this world. Who could ever have guessed that Jordan was actually throwing away his golden ticket?

Jordan had been caught in the crosshairs of a system that has for six decades offered conflicting guidance to its supposed beneficiaries, teenagers who want nothing more than to enter the world with their best foot forward. College students like Jordan—with the talent but not the wealth to make their way through America's elite institutions—are urged to follow their dreams as far as they can go. To take out student loans if they must; it's "good debt," after all. But at the same time, they must never for an instant forget that they're on the hook for it, even if their degree, in spite of all the lofty rhetoric, doesn't land them in the C suite. In that case, the choice was irresponsible, the debt is no good, and it will never, ever go away.

The system is broken, all the way to its core, and it will take a lot more than one benevolent billionaire to fix it.

THIS BOOK IS AN INVESTIGATION INTO THAT BROKENNESS, AN ATTEMPT TO make sense of how it came to pass that some 45 million Americans now hold IOUs in addition to their diplomas, at a cost of $1.7 trillion, more than any other debt but home mortgages. It's a story of lifetime ambitions and legislative minutiae, wrongheaded presumptions and disregarded prognostications, racists and radicals, extortionate profiteers and institutions led astray by the need to exist at all costs. In it we see boom-time excess wasted through small-minded dismissals of human potential—and opportunities for solidarity and change arise from moments of social crisis. More than anything, we see how political infighting, moral failure, bigotry, militarism, and usury, alongside manifold accidents and missed opportunities, form a byzantine system that almost no one can understand or navigate—but which afflicts one in six American adults.

We didn't invent student debt in America. That honor goes to twelfth-century Bologna, where the first university students pooled their ducats for a loan fund to pay their tutors. But we have made of that rudimentary system a fine art.

Of course, student debt is not the only, or even the most pernicious, burden American society has placed on its members. But it is a big one, and it offers a shocking and instructive example of how America manages to take good ideas and turn them bad. The history of the student debt crisis is the story of how something that hardly existed a century ago has become a barricade to the financial futures of roughly one in six American adults—keeping them from buying homes, starting families, saving for retirement. It's the story of how American inequity will always find a way: of how women hold two-thirds of all debt and earn 26 percent less than men do from their degrees; of how Black students start out with one-eighth the wealth of white students and leave school with double the debt; of how bankers and businesspeople have made billions off the misery of American students. And it's the story of how the American government made it all possible.

My hope is that telling this story demonstrates that student debt is a problem worth fixing—and one that's within our power to fix. For this, it's useful to look not only at the ways in which the student debt system is wrong, but also at how it's wrongheaded. It's simply not a very good way to go about solving the problem of how to make a higher education system function for a large portion of the population. We know this because many other places have done just fine—better, even—without it.

Research shows that when a society pays for its members to be educated, everyone benefits. And there are a few moments in our history where we came tantalizingly close to making education into a common good rather than an obscene and nearly unwinnable gamble. Instead, at each of these junctures, we reified the idea that education is a commodity delivering benefits to individuals, who must also bear its costs. The student debt crisis is the inevitable result of that ideology, and so to reverse the crisis we must not only revolutionize the structure and funding of higher education; we must also understand the ingrained, fundamentally American way of thinking that brought us to this point.

I set out in these pages to demonstrate not only the degree to which the student debt system rests on a morally vacuous origin—but also the ways in which that system is simply not efficient or functional in accomplishing even its stated aims, which in many ways it actively subverts.

The story begins with the GI Bill, which solved a domestic labor problem by expanding educational opportunity to the masses. Yet even though the GI Bill involved no loans, it set up the conditions and ideology that paved the way for the student debt crisis. It treated education as an individual commodity, the main purpose of which was to respond to market needs. And it was designed and implemented by Southern racists whose principal objective was excluding the "undeserving."

In the years that followed, presidents and legislators set out to expand educational opportunity for the civilian population. From the beginning, their main concern was how to pay for it. Liberals pushed for scholarships, while conservatives, indisposed to social welfare programs, opted for tuition tax credits or nothing at all. The rival factions landed on loans as a budget-friendly compromise. From these humble origins, they built student loans into a behemoth. To keep the program off the US Treasury's books, they farmed it out to commercial banks. With officials' go-ahead, the financiers, like foxes let into the henhouse, remodeled the whole framework of student aid in their image.

From roughly the 1970s to 2008 and the onset of the Great Recession, politicians mostly viewed their role not as protecting students' interests, but rather preserving bankers' profits. Under the careful tending of Republicans and Democrats alike (but especially Ronald Reagan), the student aid system was transformed into an instrument of market logic. Education became a means not to expand horizons and develop new ways of thinking, but, simply, a way to make money. In the process, how students funded their educations became a question of who would profit, and how much. By the twenty-first century, the system that legislators had built up over decades enabled public and private institutions, for- and nonprofit entities, to collectively take advantage of students under many different names and mission statements.

In 2008, the crash came, and everything changed. From the era of the student, we moved into the era of the student debtor. With the emergence of Occupy Wall Street, student debt was elevated from a source of shame to the basis of a new class identity. In the years since, student debtors have organized, protested, and persisted. Remarkably, they have made tremendous strides, upending notions of responsibility and winning significant material gains for the most exploited among them. In the time since I began writing this book five years ago, they almost knocked over the whole apple cart—successfully pushing the idea of student debt cancellation to the forefront of political discourse. Under their pressure, President Biden moved to cancel a portion of every federal debtor's load. The gesture was less than many wanted but more than anyone thought possible only a decade ago.

But, alas, even this was more than six conservatives at the Supreme Court could brook. They shot down Biden's cancellation program and left the rest of us back at square one. So here we are, perched on the threshold of a new era, one in which the future of student debt, and higher education itself, hangs in the balance. It is from this perch that I look back at the system we have created over the past century.

A CENTRAL QUESTION THREADS THROUGH THIS INVESTIGATION: WHAT AND who is education for?

This is a question we no longer tend to ask of elementary or even secondary schooling: we take it for granted that education is a necessary part of a child's development into young adulthood. It is for everyone—not only a right but a requirement. At the same time, it is not *for* anything in particular, beyond the general responsibility to provide children with the knowledge, skills, and values necessary to grow into functioning adults.

That, at least, is how it used to be.

As high school became compulsory in the middle of the twentieth century, the high school diploma lost its edge. Employability shifted up the educational bracket. Whereas a college diploma had once conferred elite status, the mark of nobility and prestige, it became a quotidian acquisition. By the end of the twentieth century, a degree was a prerequisite for most white-collar positions. As such, it became a precondition for entrée into the middle class, transformed from a laudable achievement into a social expectation.

This attitude has begun to corrupt the lower grades as well. Elementary school was once about learning to read, tally figures, and engage with others. Now it has become a key component in the race to become a valued member of the workforce. Education officials, obsessed with international competitiveness, have pushed punishing testing regimes on ever-younger children. Parents in high-status zip codes fret and game their way into prestigious public schools, or pay Ivy League prices for private options, lest their young prodigies fall off the long and winding track to Harvard or Yale. Children in down-market areas, on the other hand, may never learn to read.

As long as public schooling continues to exist, education through high school is nominally everyone's problem—a community responsibility. Beyond that point, the responsibility is cut short. Upon graduation, the eighteen-year-olds are on their own. Having gotten them to the threshold of higher learning, we wash our hands of any duty to get them through the door, much less see them to the finish line. We may toss them a grant or two, though we know it will prove woefully inadequate at all the institutions we have spent two decades telling them they must prepare themselves to attend.

Instead we tell them to go out, get a job, make a good living, and don't come calling if it doesn't work out. No one made you go to college, we say. No one made you take out that loan. I paid mine off; why should I pay yours off too?

This book shows how flawed that perspective is, by examining the ways in which, starting in the middle of the twentieth century, our notion of education became fatally impoverished. We allowed the market to poison the well, and it came to determine nearly every aspect of our educational system: who and what education was for (people who can use it to make money), how much it would cost (a lot), how it would be paid for (debt), and who would benefit (schools, the government, and above all, finance).

I start with the premise that it is immoral to require young people either to immiserate themselves for a credential or to ply a trade unlikely to raise them above the station into which they were born. Many of the people I spoke with during the research and reporting that made this book share this perspective. They insist that higher education ought to be a right, one to which our government should ensure affordable, if not free, access.

But what is a "right" exactly, and who gets to claim it? To me, it is a way of defining what we mean by society—its functions, its obligations, its parameters. When I say that it is immoral to put young people into debt in order to obtain college degrees, I mean that it is a society-wide failure—of political will, yes, but also of imagination and compassion. We have abdicated our collective responsibility to provide for one another. We signed our rights over to the market, and in return we received only a bill.

I too am someone burdened by student loans. In pursuit of a bachelor's degree from Reed College and a master's from NYU, I accrued six figures of debt. So I make this argument with something more than pure journalistic objectivity.

I began researching the history of the student loan program in 2017. That year, a George W. Bush–era program for public servants—Public Service Loan Forgiveness—was about to reward its first set of participants, people who had spent ten years working in often low-paying jobs with the promise that their debts would eventually be canceled. I'd had experience in the program myself and sensed that it was about to crash and burn. I started reporting a feature article on this impending failure for *Mother Jones*. My prediction bore out—in the first full year of forgiveness, twenty-eight thousand people applied, and only ninety-six received relief, a success rate of less than 1 percent.

What I uncovered in my reporting and research for that article was so much more than I had imagined. I'd found a story of a well-intentioned federal program defined by mismanagement and riddled with private-sector negligence bordering on fraud. But as I delved into the history of student debt, I realized that the problem went far beyond one failed forgiveness program. At its heart, the issue was that legislators and presidents had founded the student loan system on a misguided vision of what education was for. Then they compounded that error over decades of political compromises, private-sector giveaways, and disregard for the people who were the supposed beneficiaries of their failed program. The student loan system, I came to understand, was rotten through and through.

This was both an enraging and heartening revelation. I realized that my own "failure"—and that of every other unsuccessful borrower like me—was the result of decades of bad decisions made by people much more powerful than me. I became convinced not only that student debt should be eliminated, but also that we must overhaul our education system to make it unnecessary in the first place.

With this revelation came a desire to learn more about how we got here. I kept researching, and my scope widened. I started writing this book in 2019 with the belief that to really change the way we do things, it's useful to see how our systems went wrong in the first place and observe the ongoing mechanisms by which they conduct their harm. Only by taking the whole thing apart can we see how to put in place something more humane, more functional, more in line with what the most generous notions of society posit as our collective responsibilities and rewards.

This book is an attempt to perform that dismantling—to understand the actions and ideology that led us to where we are today, $1.7 trillion in debt for pursuing education. And to imagine how we might repair to a more equitable system.

PART 1

The Era of Missed Opportunities (1941–1971)

IN LATE 1941, AS THE United States danced around its role in a rapidly mushrooming global conflict, the country's leaders were positioned, for the first time in history, to make a massive direct investment in Americans' pursuit of higher education. In December, an influential New Deal agency dropped a colossal report on public welfare that urged the president to provide federal aid to help the country's youth continue their studies. This aid was to be delivered in the form of "educational grants," allocated "as needed to assure educational opportunity for all young people," or at the very least all those "who desire and can benefit by continued schooling." This was a radical and unprecedented proposal—all but guaranteeing the option of a college education for millions of citizens, an offering with the potential to lift an entire generation into the middle class.

But, alas, the recommendation went unheeded. Three days later, Japanese bombers ambushed a naval base on Oahu, killing nearly twenty-five hundred, and the following day Congress declared war. The report by the National Resources Planning Board (NRPB) was shunted to the side of President Franklin D. Roosevelt's massive war desk, not to be released to the public for another year. The NRPB suffered a similar fate, dismantled in the summer of 1943 by a hostile Congress. With it died many of the groundbreaking proposals outlined in its report of more than six hundred pages, covering everything from social security to assistance for the blind, as well as the program of aid for education addressed on page 461. As the country mobilized for war, higher education as a right of citizenship simply was not on offer.

Unfortunately, what we got instead, a little less than a year later, was the GI Bill.

CHAPTER 1

The GI Bill of Goods

There's one thing everybody knows about the GI Bill: it was great. After Franklin D. Roosevelt signed the bill—formally, the Servicemen's Readjustment Act—into law in June 1944, just months before he died, millions of returning GIs began taking advantage of its basket of benefits. An unemployment provision offered $20 a week (about $350 today) for up to fifty-two weeks. A home-loan subsidy gave veterans the chance to buy houses with no money down. There were farm and small-business loan programs, on-the-job training, and expanded medical care. But what most people remember is that the GI Bill sent America to college.

The legislation provided up to $500 per year for tuition at any eligible school the veteran got into, along with a living subsidy of $50 a month (more if the vet had a wife and family).* This was an extremely generous benefit—at the time there was no university or college, public or private, that charged more than $500—and meant that even the poorest veteran could make his way to Harvard or Yale or anywhere else that would have him, all free of charge.

The education and training program was successful beyond anyone's wildest imaginings. Its price tag of $14.5 billion—whopping for its time and more costly than the Marshall Plan—paid for schooling at all levels, and its effects on higher education were remarkable. Between 1940 and 1950, the number of men graduating from colleges in the United States each year tripled, from 100,000 to 300,000. By the time the bill expired in 1956, another 5.6 million vets had gotten vocational, or "subcollege," training. All told, the GI Bill increased the number of

---

* Female veterans with spouses, however, did not get additional living subsidies.

white-collar professionals—engineers, teachers, accountants, health-care workers, scientists, lawyers, and clergy—by more than 1.5 million. One 1998 study found that more than half of World War II veterans who went to school on the GI Bill considered the experience a turning point in their lives. These men undoubtedly lifted the economic status of their families and of the country, contributing to an unprecedented midcentury period of prosperity. "This legislation created middle-class America," wrote Columbia University political scientist Ira Katznelson in 2005. "No other instrument was nearly as important."

And America as a whole benefited. Those lucky graduates exhibited their gratitude by making more money (and thus paying more in taxes), living healthier lives, and becoming more engaged in civic affairs, in particular the civil rights movement. In 1988, a congressional study on the GI Bill found that the government's investment in education likely created immense economic benefit. Paying for 2 million vets to go to college after World War II had cost $7 billion. But it had produced an "extraordinarily large payoff for the nation"—generating as much as a twelvefold return on that investment, including $12 billion in extra tax revenue.

In short, the bill was the apex offering of a midcentury era of expansion of American higher education. It singlehandedly moved the country into an age in which a college education was an aspiration for the masses, not merely an achievement for the elites.

This was a big shift. Even by the 1940s, a high school education was still something of a lofty aspiration. Mississippi had become the last American state to compel school attendance through the eighth grade only two decades earlier. Colleges had been around far longer: Harvard had planted the first college flag on American shores in 1636 as a training ground for the colonies' political and religious leaders. But although tuition was low in those early days, none but the wealthiest colonial subjects could afford to spare their sons from the family farm or business. With women and ethnic minorities more explicitly excluded, just a tiny percentage of the burgeoning American population could even consider the option of pursuing an advanced education.

Although access expanded gradually over the next four centuries, on the eve of the GI Bill, America's institutions of higher education were still excluding far more people than they let in. In one fell swoop, the GI Bill broke down the walls.

And yet, as generous as the GI Bill was, it harbored the seeds of the student debt crisis. Nestled in the distance between the ideal and the reality of the bill's offerings, those seeds germinated and grew over the next several decades, vining and embedding their way deep into the American educational landscape.

For those who were able to benefit from it, the GI Bill transformed a college degree from an elite privilege into a mass opportunity. But its success doomed its successors. In focusing goodwill on veterans, the bill's authors squandered momentum for sustained support of civilians.

Even the bill's lauded basket of goods bore rotten fruit, as racism, sexism, and political compromise plagued it from the start. And this trio of deficiencies stood in the way of truly inclusive education funding. After the GI Bill enshrined higher education as an aspiration for all, a decades-long era of missed opportunities magnified its flaws and mitigated its accomplishments. We still live today within the broken, compromised system the GI Bill created. "One important reason there is no strong welfare state," writes historian Kathleen Frydl, "is because of the World War II GI Bill itself."

THE GI BILL BRAIDED TOGETHER THREE ROOTS OF THE PRESENT CATASTRO-phe. First, the bill initiated a system of financial aid focused entirely on the individual, whose merit would be forevermore measured against his own personal investment in his education. Second, and more nefarious, while expanding opportunity for millions of young men, the bill excluded untold numbers of other citizens. Its crafters and proponents intentionally left out women and most nonwhite Americans, a dishonor that set them back generations and still holds them down.

Women, pushed out of college in the 1940s to make way for returning GIs, have long since regained their ground on campus, but at a significant cost: today women make up 57 percent of all college students but hold two-thirds of total student debt. Black college students, whose ancestors were largely prevented from accessing the GI Bill's wealth-building benefits, today start out with one-eighth the family wealth of the median white student, and they leave school with twice the debt.

Third, the bill, drafted to forestall a postwar labor crisis, designated the market as the ultimate arbiter of what and who an education should be for. This bred a long, insidious slide to a careerist vision of education, the value of which is tallied not as an end in itself but solely as a factor of its future monetary potential.

Foregrounding market needs also fed a festering pool of educational fraudsters and opportunists out to make a buck off students—and the federal government. The General Accounting Office calculated that fully one-third of the money spent on education via the GI Bill went to frauds and scams. These too targeted Black Americans, who continue to be disproportionately preyed upon by for-profit educational frauds.

How did this happen? It's a tale as sordid as it is infuriating.

Supporters of the GI Bill never intended to send America to college. They merely hoped to avoid the disastrous aftermath of World War I, when twenty thousand unemployed veterans had marched on Washington at the height of the Great Depression to demand overdue bonus payments, a drama that ended when President Hoover dispatched General Douglas MacArthur—Major Dwight D. Eisenhower by his side—to storm the veterans' camp, which burned to the ground. It was a "bad-looking mob," MacArthur declared of the marchers, "animated by the essence of revolution." The vets were dispelled—by the tip of the saber and the tear-gas canister—but Washington took heed. The menace of the World War I Bonus Marchers still loomed large more than a decade later.

In 1944, as World War II neared its end, education offered a solution to two potential challenges: reintegration of veterans into society and manpower needs. By diverting returning veterans to schools or job-training programs, the government could relieve pressure on the labor market, prepare future employees for pivotal industries, and hopefully prevent another embarrassing bonus scandal.

Yet Roosevelt himself was not a big proponent. He didn't support singling out veterans as an especially deserving class. Instead, in January 1944, as Congress was just beginning to debate the omnibus package that would come to form the GI Bill, FDR gave a State of the Union address calling for a vast expansion of the welfare state. Among other things, his "second Bill of Rights" would have provided to *all* citizens the right to a home, to medical care, to a job and a basic income, and to a "good education." This generic offering was a big ask: because education was not included among the Constitution's enumerated federal powers, it had generally been considered a matter of state and local concern.

By then, however, FDR's power had waned; Congress had become indisposed to the New Deal and conservatives were not keen on expanding the federal role in education. Veterans, on the other hand, were a demographic almost everyone could get behind. Republicans supported the idea of a bill focused on veterans, and New Dealers believed that privileging veterans in the short term might create an opening wedge for universal programs down the line. If the liberals had succeeded, the GI Bill might have been the start of an even greater moment of social program expansion—a movement more in line with the social democracies soon to emerge in war-battered Europe.

But where it could have been a base for expansion of America's higher education system writ large, instead, the GI Bill stopped short.

As Congress was hashing out the veterans' legislation in early 1944, multiple versions of the education title floated through the halls of the Capitol. But instead of selecting an option that would have created a federal machinery of aid distribution offering a foothold for a future expansion of benefits to civilians, legislators chose a bill written by a powerful veterans' group, the American Legion, which was constructed to preserve exclusivity for veterans. The Legion's version vested power in the decentralized Veterans Administration (VA) to distribute benefits through local chapters. The New Dealers lost their opening wedge, and

the dream of a Rooseveltian "citizens first" model of education aid cer-
emoniously died.

Because it was tied to individual military service, the GI Bill made
education into something one literally had to "fight for." Only those
individuals who had risked their lives were thought worthy of this special dispensation. As such, even though the GI Bill did not require that
recipients pay back the cost of an education, it in fact operated less like
a benefit program and much more like a loan—military service was its
(pre-) payment.

This focus on the "deserving" individual had the effect of excluding
most Americans. Women in particular were generally left out. Though
they had not served in the armed forces in significant numbers, some
women had done so and were indeed eligible for GI Bill programs. Yet
these female veterans participated on a largely incidental basis—they
represented a mere 2 percent of the bill's beneficiaries. Most were not
informed of the benefits available to them at all.

After the GI Bill was passed, colleges and universities openly applied
quotas for female applicants, rejecting them in favor of (male) veterans
with guaranteed tuition money. At Cornell, only 50 places out of 350
were set aside for women in the class of 1946; medical schools limited female enrollment to 5 percent; and Penn State stopped admitting
women altogether. Overall, women's share of undergraduate enrollment
dropped from 41 percent in 1940 to 24 percent in 1950.

Additionally, the defeat of a national aid program distributing money
to states and facilities had gone hand in hand with Southern Democrats'
unyielding commitment to funnel benefits through each GI. Instead of
granting states money to build up public institutions or focus on particular areas of study, these legislators insisted that each student designate
his funds for the school of his choosing.

But why such dogged commitment to the individual GI? The answer
is that the American Legion's victory was due not only to well-cultivated
political connections. It was also a triumph of compatible aims. The
Legion's biggest proponent in Congress was also one of the South's most
avowed upholders of white supremacy.

John Elliott Rankin was born in remote Itawamba County, Mississippi, in 1882, just a few years after the conclusion of the Civil War
returned that state to the Union. He had gotten his start as a prosecutor
in Tupelo, then won a seat in Congress in 1920. He took with him a
fanatical commitment to white supremacy. One of the first bills he introduced in Congress proposed outlawing intermarriage in DC. He was
unabashed in his hatred not only of Black Americans but also Japanese
Americans and Jews—anyone who wasn't a white Christian—and was
known to hurl racial epithets (and even his fists) on the House floor.

Rankin's well-known prejudice did not diminish his popularity, or
his power, in the halls of Congress. When it came to veterans' benefits,
Rankin called the shots in the House. For the American Legion, this
made him a powerful ally, and the group cultivated his favor assiduously.

But while Rankin had been a strong champion of veterans in the past,
his foremost concern now wasn't enriching them—it was diminishing
Black veterans. Rankin feared that the segregationist social order would
be upended by giving Black veterans unemployment provisions higher
than what most Black Southerners could earn through wage labor.

The Senate and the House worked up different versions of the bill—
and Rankin's was decidedly stingier. He had wanted to cut Black veterans out altogether, and his draft legislation ensured that they had a more
difficult time accessing benefits. When the Senate and House conference
committees met in June to reconcile the two versions of the GI Bill,
Rankin gleefully threatened to throw the whole thing out rather than
preserve the Senate's more generous provisions. He failed, and many of
his starkest exclusions did not make it into the compromise bill. But he
ensured that it was built on a racist scaffolding. Fortunately for Rankin,
much of that work had already been done for him.

Because the GI Bill was tied to military service, it could be no more
equitable than the draft boards, and society itself. Even during a nationwide draft, the military's recruitment criteria, including literacy requirements and physical health screens, disadvantaged Black Americans.
(Educated in segregated schools, they graduated from high school at less
than one-third the rate of white Americans.) Draft boards disqualified

41 percent of Black men, versus 28 percent of white men. Even married white recruits were often drafted before single Black recruits. At the start of the war, the army had only six units designated for Black soldiers—a capacity of fewer than five thousand men.

This was all intentional. In spite of the considerable risks, wartime service offered significant benefits, and segregationists were desperate to keep Black Americans from reaping them. Black recruits were likely to earn five times, or more, what they would as civilians. And—the source of Southern racists' greatest anxieties—through service they might cultivate a strengthened citizenship status, deserving of all that America had to offer. This was a privilege of which Black Americans were systematically deprived.

Eventually the need for soldiers grew so great that the military was forced to admit more Black draftees; in 1943, at the peak of their recruitment, Black soldiers made up 11 percent of the force. By the end of the war, more than a million Black men had served in some capacity.

Systemic racism meant only a small proportion of the Black population was able to enter military service and thereby become eligible for the GI Bill; it also meant that among those who did serve, a yet smaller proportion actually benefited from the bill. Those Black Americans who were able to pass through the gauntlet of military recruitment found themselves in segregated units, confined mostly to service roles. Black soldiers slept in separate barracks, ate in separate mess halls, and were treated in separate hospitals, which used different (Black) blood in medical treatment. Black troops were aghast to observe that even German captives were treated better than they were—allowed to eat in white mess halls, ride in train cars designated for white people, and even fraternize in officers' clubs.

And whereas white servicemen might gain the opportunity to develop skills—as pilots or machinists, say—that would benefit them upon their return to the civilian workforce, Black soldiers were generally limited to jobs as stewards, cooks, and janitors.

John Rankin had ensured that this discriminatory treatment followed Black veterans home as well. By insisting that the VA distribute benefits,

Rankin and his supporters had succeeded in subjecting Black veterans to racist policies that aimed to diminish or outright deny them access to what the GI Bill could offer them. White employment officials in the South fielded even highly skilled Black veterans into almost exclusively menial jobs. In Rankin's Mississippi, 86 percent of the VA's white-collar job placements went to white veterans, while 92 percent of blue-collar jobs went to Black veterans.

Not only did racist VA officials overwhelmingly steer Black job seekers into dead-end blue-collar positions; they also aimed to steer prospective Black students away from all but the most labor-oriented educational programs, almost invariably at the poorly maintained, segregated institutions established during Reconstruction. Because the GI Bill had been constructed in a way that preserved segregation, it did nothing to help Black veterans expand the extremely limited options to further their education. By insisting that the bill treat benefits as vouchers tied to each individual veteran, who could choose to attend any school to which he was accepted, Rankin ensured that the South's network of segregated schools need not change their policies and accept Black students. On the other hand, the cash-strapped Black-serving schools of the South suffered shortages of qualified teachers, space, and supplies and were largely limited to vocational curricula. Few Black institutions conferred bachelor's degrees, and not a single Black college at the time offered an engineering or doctoral degree. By the start of fall classes in 1947, these institutions had turned away 55 percent of Black veterans seeking admission—a total of about twenty thousand prospective students.

This inequity, along with the deeply rooted ecosystem of discrimination and the fact that Black veterans were significantly less likely than their white comrades to have completed high school, ensured that Black Americans aspiring to a college education were often simply out of luck. A mere 12 percent of Black veterans were able to attend college on the GI Bill, compared to 28 percent of white veterans. That missed opportunity gave them less than half the chance to get a college degree, reach a ladder rung to a better job, and make a better life for them and their families.

Even the most dauntless Black veterans—those who managed to persuade racist VA officials to approve their matriculation into four-year programs—exited school into a workforce that continued to view them as second-class citizens. White Americans with some college education in 1960 earned $1,300 more on average than those with only high school diplomas; for Black Americans the wage benefit was $300.

Thus, what had been sold as a "double V" for Black soldiers—victory against fascism abroad, with a corresponding victory against discrimination back home—was in many instances a double loss. Where the GI Bill brought millions of white Americans into the middle class and kept them and their descendants in it, Black Americans fell farther behind. They were blocked from furthering their educations, ascending career ladders, and building transferable wealth through home ownership. This unequal legacy has trickled down to the current day, and its effects also feed into the student debt crisis.

Once they returned stateside, Black vets found that their well-earned sense of civic pride stoked even greater hatred from white Americans. They were lynched for voting; for challenging Jim Crow; even, and perhaps especially, for daring to wear their uniforms in public. "I spent three-and-a-half years in service of my country and thought I would be treated as a man when I returned to civilian life. But I was mistaken," said Isaac Woodard, a Black veteran from South Carolina. In 1946, Woodard returned from the Pacific and, still in uniform, boarded a Greyhound bus in Augusta, Georgia. Eventually, he had to take a leak and asked the driver if he had time to go during a planned stop. "Boy, go on back and sit down," the driver responded. "God damn it," Woodard replied, "talk to me like I'm talking to you. I'm a man just like you." In response, the driver called the local police. At the next stop, an officer greeted Woodard at the bus doors, then took him around the corner and rammed a billy club into each of his eyes, permanently blinding him. A jury acquitted the officer after twenty-eight minutes of deliberation.

Woodard's story was shocking but not unique. Many other Black veterans were targeted just for demanding the dignity they had fought for. After daring to draw water from a white drinking fountain at a bus station in Americus, Georgia, Hosea Williams was beaten to a pulp by a white mob and left for dead. Only after he had been loaded into the hearse did the local Black mortician notice a faint pulse and rush him to a nearby veterans' hospital. "Goddamn it," Williams said to himself later. "I fought on the wrong side."

But the war changed Williams's fortunes in other ways. When he came back to his small Georgia hometown, his grandfather persuaded him to seek out an education. Eventually, Williams used the GI Bill to obtain a degree in chemistry from Atlanta's Morris Brown College, a historically Black college. While there, he joined a local chapter of the NAACP and became involved in civil rights organizing—his passion driven by his experiences in the army and subsequent return stateside. After college, between stints as a high school science teacher, he earned a master's degree in chemistry at Atlanta University, also historically Black. His credentials gave him a ticket to a professional, comfortably middle-class life as a research chemist. His struggle to get there propelled him into the highest ranks of the civil rights movement, changing America for the better.

But Williams had been phenomenally lucky. Few other Black veterans, even those who were able to make good on the promise of the GI Bill, achieved the level of education he did. His is a success story that proves the exception rather than the rule. In demonstrating what a nationwide commitment to education might have offered in a more equitable society, it reveals just how profoundly the GI Bill fell flat.

The vast majority of Black GI Bill beneficiaries did not even make it to college, but instead found their way to trade schools or vocational-training programs. And here they came head to head with yet another of the GI Bill's rotten roots: its unrelenting obsession with the market. This increasingly pernicious aspect of the GI Bill also targeted its Black beneficiaries, and it too would only metastasize in the decades to come.

BECAUSE IT WAS INITIALLY ENVISIONED AS A MEANS FOR MANAGING THE DO-mestic workforce, the GI Bill redirected education to a path more in line with market forces. After the bill, higher education no longer necessarily denoted the kind of self-exploration and canonical well rounding of the liberal arts college that had dominated throughout America's history. By the 1950s a college degree had become, at least for the masses, a way of obtaining a career.

This was by no means the desire of university officials, who in 1944 viewed the impending invasion of their campuses with a haughty, scornful eye—they considered the GI Bill a crass way to keep vets "off the bread line." University leaders worried, with undisguised classist panic, that unwashed hordes of veteran students would storm America's schools, forcing them to lower their standards and cater to vocational-training demands, thereby turning them into "educational hobo jungles," as the president of the University of Chicago sneered.

This blue-blood hysteria initially seemed rather overwrought. Surveys conducted before the bill's passage had suggested that at most 10 percent of the 16 million returning veterans wanted to go back to school full-time after the war. And in the first year, that seemed to bear out. Only 15,000 veterans had enrolled in college by the beginning of the fall 1945 term.

But by 1946, 200,000 veterans had enrolled; more than a million in 1947 (half the total national student body); and by 1949 more than 2 million had availed themselves of the GI Bill's higher education benefits, more than double even the most capacious projections.

The veteran masses outperformed traditional students academically and eschewed the schoolboy hijinks (panty raids and the like) common before the war. In so doing, they proved that higher education was not merely the domain of America's wealthy elites, but could be an equalizer for the (white) masses as well. The veterans, Harvard president James Conant recanted in 1946, "are the most mature and promising students Harvard has ever had."

But the market impulse also opened the door to unscrupulous opportunists. Of the 800,000 veterans enrolled in so-called subcollege programs in 1949, about three-quarters were receiving their "education" at proprietary institutions. These were career or vocational training schools, for-profit entities founded to enrich their owners. Of the 8,800 for-profit schools in operation in the fall of 1949, 5,600 had sprung up in just the five years since the GI Bill's enactment. In fact, more GIs enrolled in for-profit vocational schools than in public and nonprofit colleges and universities combined.

The roughly one-third of these for-profit endeavors that were scams and fly-by-night operations were designed to bilk soldiers—and the government—out of their $500 a year. By 1948, an estimated $200 million was being pilfered annually for lessons in horseback riding, ballroom dancing, photography, TV repair (free TV included!), piccolo, glass engraving, mixology, and the like.

Veteran students, who collected a living subsidy in addition to their tuition and fees, were apparently not much bothered by being taken in like this. "Veterans, come to Florida," advertised one of the nation's nearly four thousand new flight schools. "Enjoy the sunshine. Enjoy the breezes. Bathe in the ocean while you learn to fly. Exercise your rights under the G.I. Bill and we will refund $30 of your travel expenses after one week of training."

The shams that targeted Black veterans, on the other hand, were generally more focused on exploitation than beaches and sunshine. With significantly fewer options, Black veterans were often stuck with the most exploitative of these fraudsters—for instance, a shoe shop owner who made recruits pay *him* to train in his store—because the meager GI Bill living stipends they received were up to double the wages they had received before.

A 1951 investigation by the General Accounting Office found that of the 1.7 million veterans who used their GI Bill funds to attend for-profit schools, four out of five never completed their programs, and two-thirds of the schools were overbilling the government. Those findings led to a rule prohibiting the VA from giving funds for attendance at institutions whose student bodies comprised more than 85 percent veterans, which became known as the 85–15 rule. This helped stem the tide for a couple of decades. But for-profits quickly found cracks in the sealant and grew to become a multi-billion-dollar grift that would ruin the lives of hundreds of thousands of unwitting attendees.

This scandal—and the exploitative industry it nurtured—could have been prevented had the GI Bill instead built up a national system of public vocational schools and job-training programs. Such legislation might have thereby avoided the proprietary school scandal and preserved the distinction between higher education and workforce preparation.

Instead, by its combined flaws—its focus on the market and the individual, and its exclusion of whole classes of people—the GI Bill opened the door to for-profit charlatans, offering a template that they would follow over future decades to leach free federal money from downtrodden Americans looking for a better life.

The only difference was that in 1945 or 1946, that free money came at no cost to the student beyond the legitimate opportunities he missed when a huckster took those funds and gave nothing back. In future decades, this money would also come with a hefty interest rate.

EVEN BEFORE THE GI BILL EXPIRED, IN 1956, THERE WAS ONCE AGAIN A BRIEF moment of possibility—as in 1941—to create a better system, one wherein higher education was made a right of citizenship that all could access. The veterans had shown that a diverse mix of students from different backgrounds could thrive in an academic setting, and universities had refashioned their programs to fit the veterans' needs and interests. But the schools needed help accommodating a surging student body. Broadening the GI experiment by helping schools expand their services to the civilian population was a logical next step for the federal government. But it was both too early and too late for such a radical transformation.

Harry Truman, who ascended somewhat fortuitously to the presidency after FDR's death in 1945, inherited a country on the mend but still wounded by war and the years of economic hardship that had preceded it. Often well-meaning, Truman lacked his predecessor's popular devotion, political savvy, and sheer force of personality. Although he proposed a variety of radical surgeries to improve the overall health of the nation, he was ultimately limited to superficial interventions. This was particularly true in the intertwined arenas of education and race.

Truman had been so disturbed by the story of Isaac Woodard's blinding that he ordered the creation of a commission on civil rights. Its blistering report, *To Secure These Rights*, urged an end to segregation throughout America. "The United States can no longer countenance these burdens on its common conscience, these inroads on its moral fiber," the commission declared.

The report shook the nation, but it did not move Congress.

Instead, dozens of Southern Democrats responded by threatening to bolt from the party. Faced with an uncooperative Congress, in 1948 Truman signed an order desegregating the military. Theoretically, this meant that future veterans would not be subject to the inequities that Black veterans had faced after World War II. In practice, however, military leaders undertook the process with a patent lack of urgency, delaying full integration until 1963.

Truman's efforts to broaden the reach of higher education were even less fruitful. In 1946, he assembled a commission of more than two dozen prominent education experts. A year later, the group, known as the Zook Commission, declared a crisis in American education. Inequality of access had not been reduced but rather more deeply entrenched. The commission urged an immediate course correction. Its recommendations would still be considered radical today.

Among the commission's most revolutionary proposals was to offer free higher education to all by extending public education to the first two years of college, through the "fourteenth grade," and providing students a stipend for living expenses. This was to be achieved through a vast expansion of a recent innovation in public higher education: the community college. This undertaking, the group urged, was necessary to prepare Americans for the future and to show the world the equalizing potential of democracy.

Through the Zook Commission, Truman was pushing for an approach to higher education that was more generous and democratizing;

with *To Secure These Rights,* he was urging society itself to be more inclusive and equitable. Had he succeeded in achieving these two objectives, America might have entered a new, more just era, with the promise of higher education truly available to all, including those it had most often left out.

But free college, like civil rights, was politically unpalatable. The powerful network of private colleges and universities naturally opposed this threat to their revenue, and it was further doomed by the intransigence of Southern Democrats, who would never go along with a system that so thoroughly eviscerated segregation. And because it would have been tremendously costly, the idea of free college was easy to shelve.

For the second time in history, higher education for all had come within reach. But the crisis of war had passed, and with it, the impetus for change. The spirit of generosity underlying the GI Bill had dimmed to a broad complacency, as postwar prosperity lifted just enough boats to make further reforms seem less urgent.

In the end, one of the only real takeaways from the Truman education report to gain immediate traction was the recommendation to offer more courses meeting the professional needs and ambitions of a growing non-elite population of students. Yet again, in the battle between the rights of the citizen and the needs of the market, the market won out.

And so did the GI Bill's insidious legacy take shape over the following eight decades.

Even before it was enacted—before it was larded up with racism and charlatans came to feed at its trough—the GI Bill subtly changed the national understanding of what education was "for," mostly for the worse. Predicated on a logic of usefulness, it inaugurated an era of higher education that privileged manpower and national security needs—vocation and commerce above learning and civic engagement. Most important, it set the boundaries for what we consider politically possible and socially desirable in the debate over who should get to go to college—and it placed the majority of Americans outside the gates. In essence, the GI Bill represented the last great stop in America's journey toward a caring, holistic democratic socialism—and it had already fallen far short of the goal.

Because it focused on the individual, rather than the educational system as a whole, the bill set us on the course to today's crisis. Over the next eight decades, virtually every major aid program would focus not on educational systems or schools, but on the student, required to prove their worth on an individual basis. No future program would surmount the notion of individual personal investment that the GI Bill had instilled in the public consciousness.

The GI Bill of 1944 was meant to be temporary. But the United States soon found itself entangled in the Cold War, a conflict during which education came to be seen as the primary battlefront. And the enemy's advances in that arena inspired another piece of legislation with consequences even more far-reaching than those of the GI Bill. No longer would students receive benefits enabling their education. Instead they would be made to pay. As the anxieties of the nuclear age ignited a national clamor for more widespread aid, legislators made literal the GI Bill's metaphorical "loan" of military service. Instead of fighting, students took on financing.

CHAPTER 2

Reading, Writing, and *Sputnik*

T he vital question that everybody is thinking about," announced CBS's correspondent on the network's news broadcast of October 6, 1957, was this: "Why and how did the Russians beat us to the draw?" Two days earlier, the Soviet Union had launched the world's first artificial space satellite, a 184-pound sphere called *Sputnik I*. Americans were propelled into a frenzy over this question and its unspoken corollary—Is an atomic bomb headed to *my backyard*?! Many began to focus special interest on education, especially the ways in which the American system was lagging behind the Soviets'. CIA director Allen Dulles noted that the USSR was graduating a vast number of scientists and engineers: over a decade, Dulles warned, this would add up to 1.2 million new Russians working to advance the Soviet system, 300,000 more than would be lending their talents to the American side.

How *were* the Soviets getting so far ahead? Americans wondered. The answer did not exactly offer a rocket boost to our national self-esteem. Russian high school graduates had taken five years of physics, four of chemistry, and five of advanced mathematics. The average American teenager didn't take any hard science classes at all. Unlike the USSR's youth, focused with military discipline on the essentials, America's students were prancing in a field of frivolity. For more than half a century, America's education system had been dominated by the Progressive movement, spearheaded by the philosopher John Dewey, which emphasized "life adjustment"—the holistic molding of children according to their interests, group cooperation, and extracurricular activities. But this, national sentiment now held, had failed to build up the cadre of hard-nosed scientists, engineers, and mathematicians necessary to keep the United States competitive. And this failure, critics posited, had become an issue of national security. "What has long been an ignored national problem," the editors of *Life* magazine lamented in early 1958, "*Sputnik* has made a recognized crisis."

More than a decade after the GI Bill's shock wave had hit higher education, *Sputnik* offered a new opportunity. It would take nothing less than a total reconceiving of the education system, from elementary school through the highest grades, to accomplish the turnaround politicians and pundits were urging. At the college level, the possibility of systemic change again arose—a chance to build up America's mental might by extending the GI Bill's largesse across larger swaths of the population, with fewer restrictions, from a greater sense of national responsibility and right. After all, if the country was going to ask its young people to develop themselves on its behalf, it was only natural to expect the government to have some skin in the game.

But this argument failed to convince the protectors of the national budget. Instead, the *Sputnik* crisis led to the introduction of the first federal college loan program—an ignominy that would form the core of our current crisis.

It started with a pair of Democrats from Alabama.

ON AUGUST 12, 1957, TWO MONTHS BEFORE *SPUTNIK*, CONGRESSMAN CARL Elliott was doing something he'd done many times before: making the case for increased federal investment in education. That morning, the brawny Alabama legislator lifted his broad frame up to the dais in room 429 of what was then known as the Old House Office Building to speak to the education subcommittee he chaired.

As he spoke, he zeroed in on the intertwined concerns of manpower and national supremacy. "For decades, we in this land have exerted every possible pressure to guarantee the preservation and proper utilization of our natural resources," he declared. The effort had come "at a cost of billions of dollars." But more recently, America had neglected an even greater resource: personnel. And now the scarcity was acute—even "desperate": already the media was sounding alarms over shortages of scientists, doctors, nurses, and librarians. Of even greater concern, an official

in the Department of Health, Education, and Welfare reported that
Russians were outpacing the United States in production of engineers
by a ratio of three to two. If America did not begin watering these fields,
its human resources would soon wither and wilt.

To address this issue, Elliott gathered up his band of education-
policy legislators and went on the road, aiming to conduct a national
temperature-taking on the notion of a federal college scholarship and
loan program.

"Everywhere we went, everyone agreed something needed to be done
about education," Elliott would later recall. As in the run-up to the GI
Bill, manpower and national defense concerns were at the heart of what
Elliott called the "vague uneasiness" mounting in the American psyche
in the early years of the Cold War. "But those fears had been simmering
for a decade," he said. And he would know—he'd tried to introduce an
education-aid bill in every session of Congress for the nine years he'd
been there. None had ever stuck, each one buffeted by the destructive
crosscurrents of religious strife and racial animus that divided the country and its politicians.

Elliott refused to give up. For him, education was *the* issue. Born
in 1913, he had grown up in Alabama hill country, the oldest of nine
children, his parents tenant farmers. But Elliott was a natural student.
From an early age, he was a nut about books, despite having little access
to them; his reading material was limited to the family Bible and a small
"library" an uncle lent out from a trunk in his bedroom.

After Elliott earned his high school diploma, he headed to Tuscaloosa
to enroll at the University of Alabama, carrying a hometown benefac-
tor's $25 tuition check, a cardboard suitcase, and the $2.38 in savings
he had left to his name. To pay his way through school, he worked as a
gardener, a waiter, and a coal stoker, and for lodging he squatted in the
campus observatory. Against such long odds, he emerged with his law
degree in 1936, and twelve years later he was in Congress.

Elliott was a genuine populist, and a lifelong believer in the power of
education, which he credited for his own rise out of poverty. "Education
[. . .] had always been like a religion to me," he wrote in his autobiog-

raphy. In his first year in office, he introduced a bill to provide federal college scholarships. It died.

As Elliott put it in his memoir years later, his efforts had been thwarted by "a politically paranoid version of the three R's." The first of these was religion. Education-aid bills were routinely stymied by a controversy over parochial schools: whether to offer benefits to Catholic private schools, for instance, or suffer the potent wrath of "the monsignors" for shutting them out. Even more than this religion debate, however, it was the second *R*, race, that had put up an impassible roadblock to legislation on education. Any measure funding segregated schools would alienate Northern liberals, but Southern Democrats would never support a bill that upended segregation.

Now, in the third *R*—the Reds—Elliott saw a game-changing advantage. The threat of Soviet spacecraft offered a bogeyman so visceral and profound that it had the power to defang even the most rabid anti-Catholic or states'-righter. "Sometimes people can be persuaded to do something," Elliott would later write. "But most times they have to be *frightened* into it."

On October 4, 1957, *Sputnik* whizzed onto the horizon, flying at five miles a second and heralded by a faint "ping, ping, ping" of radio waves dropping like rain from the sky. Many viewed it as a harbinger of doom. But to Carl Elliott the satellite appeared as a long-awaited deus ex machina. "While most of the nation saw *Sputnik* as an evil shadow," he would recall, "I saw it as an opportunity."

Elliott was not the only Alabama Democrat who saw kismet cross the sky. Around the globe, the air was cool and breezy in West Berlin as the little Russian moon circled over a night thick with clouds. Down below, Lister Hill, the chair of the Senate's committee on education, was on a European vacation with his wife. Unlike Elliott, Hill had been born into a wealthy family in Montgomery. His father, Luther Leonidas Hill Jr., was a famous surgeon who had performed the first successful open-heart surgery in the country. (The procedure was performed in the home of a Black boy stabbed with an ice pick, and a kerosene lamp was Hill's only light.) In spite of his privileged upbringing, Hill, like Elliott, was an ardent New Dealer who had been gunning for an aid-to-education bill for years. And also like Elliott, he saw the rare opportunity that *Sputnik* had just delivered to make it happen.

Stewart McClure, the chief clerk of Hill's committee, saw it too. McClure typed up a memo, telling the senator that the time was ripe for a bill. He marched his memo across the capitol, to Hill's office, and handed it to the senator's executive secretary. "John, I want this put on the top of the spike," he said. "I want him, when he comes in here tomorrow morning, to see this *first*."

The next morning, McClure got a call. "Come on over here," Hill said. "Let's see what we can do."

Lister Hill was also one of Carl Elliott's first calls. "It's time to pass the bill," Elliott told Hill when he got him on the line. Hill, a more cautious politician, was tentative. "You know I've been down this road a few times before, old fellow," he replied. "But this time I believe you're right."

A few weeks later, another Russian rocket went up, this one— "Muttnik"—carrying a live dog in its cabin. (Poor, sweet Laika died within hours.) The national uproar hit a fever pitch, and Elliott and Hill got to work. After Congress broke for Christmas, they met in Alabama and posted up in a Birmingham hotel to hash out a draft of an education-aid bill. They put it to rest one night just before midnight. "Just then," Elliott recalled, "the bells across Birmingham began ringing. It was midnight, New Year's Eve, the beginning of what I hoped would truly be a new year." Before that new year could bear its fruits, however, a few questions remained to be settled. The real crux of the issue was what manner of student aid Hill and Elliott would actually propose— and, more important, what they could pass through Congress.

John Perkins, an official in the Department of Health, Education, and Welfare, had other ideas. The country's recent personnel shortages, he argued, had occurred "because we are harvesting what I call the small crop of youth of the Depression period." But the "large baby crops" of the postwar period, growing every day, were soon to ripen on the vine.

With this in mind, Perkins told the subcommittee, it was the educational institutions, rather than students, that really needed financial aid. As is still the case, the actual cost of educating students—what we refer to today as the "net price"—was in 1957 much higher than the "sticker price" charged by colleges. "Thus," said Perkins, "in a sense all college students are receiving a scholarship." Meanwhile, the colleges, bombarded with GIs after 1944, were already financially strained. Handing out even more scholarships, in Perkins's view, would only exacerbate the problem. As more students entered schools, the gap between what they paid and what it cost to educate them would multiply.

But a federal college-funding bill was a nonstarter, and everybody knew it. Any bill that gave money directly to institutions would raise a debate about whom those institutions let in and whom they served. Such a bill would simply never make it past the one person in the House who refused to compromise with the segregationists.

ADAM CLAYTON POWELL JR. WAS A COMPLEX AND, TO HIS FELLOW LIBERAL Democrats, consternating presence in the House of Representatives. A son of Harlem, Powell was New York's first Black representative, elected in 1945. And his early years were spent repaying his constituents by making a stand against racial injustice.

In the realm of aid to education, this was a double-edged sword. By the 1950s, Powell had made his way onto the House education committee. But he was not afforded the degree of power or dignity enjoyed by his fellow representatives. Powell was not permitted to use the same restrooms or even eat lunch alongside his white colleagues. But he was not an accommodationist, and he made sure that every one of his fellow congressmen was forced to take note of his influence. Up against the crushing weight of entrenched racism in Congress and throughout American society, Powell used the one tool he had: obstruction.

Whenever legislation proposing an injection of public funds into a social issue emerged from his or any other committee, Powell would insert a seemingly innocuous proviso. His colleagues referred to it, with disdain and despair, as the "Powell amendment." It stated simply that no federal funds be given to any institution—be it a school, hospital, or otherwise—that practiced racial segregation.

Given the intransigence of the Southern delegation, this emendation was the kiss of death for any bill that bore it. It meant that a bill proposing federal funds for America's schools would never make it through the House. And thus had education-aid legislation been summarily doomed for more than a decade.

By 1958, Carl Elliott and Lister Hill had learned how to tailor legislation to steer clear of the Powell amendment. Their proposed federal scholarship program would not attempt to upend the dominant segregated order. Instead, the two Alabamians came up with a workaround. To get past Powell's kiss of death, they proposed delivering aid not to institutions but to students, who could take it to any school they chose, segregated or not. After all, Elliott and Hill *were* accommodationists. Hill regularly led filibusters against civil rights legislation, and Elliott felt that integration was moving "too fast, with too much force."

It's tantalizing to imagine what Elliott and Hill might have come up with if they'd been free of their personal and political limitations. Without segregation's sword of Damocles hanging over their heads (and their hearts), perhaps they might have ushered in a state-federal partnership to fund public universities, or a significant boost to the numbers of community colleges, as had been suggested under Truman. Perhaps a systemwide, institutionalist approach could have hit at just the right moment to break through.

Things in the country were, after all, changing. Even President Eisenhower had to admit it.

Eisenhower, a stolid military man and the prototypical fiscal conservative, had been steadfast that the federal government's role in education was "merely to facilitate—never to control." But this position became untenable in late September 1957, after segregationists in Arkansas blocked nine Black students from entering a public school. Reluctantly, almost three weeks after the crisis had begun, Eisenhower sent the army's 101st Airborne Division to enforce the peace.

Then came the *Sputnik*s. After the first Soviet satellite launched,

Eisenhower tried to persuade the public to calm down: secret spy-plane evidence had convinced him the Russian threat was not so great, certainly not urgent enough to sacrifice a balanced budget. "I'd like to know what's on [the] other side of the moon," he confessed to his cabinet, "but I won't pay to find out this year."

The public wasn't assuaged. Eisenhower's failed attempt to launch a rival rocket, the *Vanguard*, later that fall was a resounding "Flopnik." Then *Time* magazine declared Nikita Khrushchev, "Russia's stubby and bald, garrulous and brilliant ruler," its Man of the Year. Eisenhower went on the defensive. Hoping to win back eroded trust, he grudgingly increased defense spending—and opened the door to a long-stalled education-aid program.

Hill and Elliott were in.

Now that the Eisenhower administration had come around, even some of the president's foot soldiers trekked down to Lister Hill's Senate hearings to make the case for education funding. Eisenhower's science-and-technology adviser James Killian noted that up to a hundred thousand of the nation's top high school students did not go on to college. When they were asked why, as many as half said they just didn't have the money.

Other witnesses expressed support for federal education aid in terms of the Cold War. The president of the American Council of Learned Societies testified that "not six people in this country can read a newspaper in Telugu," a language spoken by 13 million people in India. "But when a Soviet delegation arrives in that country, its members can speak and read Telugu." Columbia psychiatrist Joost Meerloo spoke of a "turncoat" in each uneducated American. This was based on news that twenty-one American POWs who had been brainwashed by Chinese captors in Korea and subsequently chose not to be repatriated were high school dropouts. To combat this apparent crisis in civic literacy, education would have to become its own battlefront.

The legislation that Hill and Elliott drafted in the wake of these testimonials focused on scholarships, awarded on a mix of need and merit. Perhaps recognizing that scholarships alone would be too heavy a political lift, they rounded out these funds with complementary work-study

offerings and low-interest loans. Even so, the bill was meager. The initial draft of their legislation included only forty thousand scholarships
a year, at $1,000 apiece, and a $40 million fund for loans, given out at
2 percent interest.

There was a further compromise. While Hill and Elliott had wanted
to offer aid to all students, they knew that to win over less enthusiastic
legislators, they would have to narrow their bill to address the current
crisis. They decided to prioritize funds to science, math, engineering,
and foreign language students—leaving out nearly all the "less valuable"
students of the humanities.

To seize the opportunity provided by *Sputnik* and the specter of
Soviet power, Hill and Elliott's bill also needed to harness the hawkish
lexicon of the moment. Thus was born the National Defense Education Act (NDEA). "I invented that god-awful title," Stewart McClure
recalled years later. "If there are any words less compatible, really, intel-
lectually, in terms of what is the purpose of education. [. . .] It was a
horrible title, but it worked."

In other words, Hill and Elliott were negotiating in bad faith but
with good intentions. They were not actually committed to propping up
science and math fields; their top priority was breaking the logjam. They
believed that if they could get an education bill through the Senate and
especially the House, more funding, better bills, and expanded access
would all eventually follow.

But as the compromise bill snaked its way through Congress, concession after concession stripped away many of its best elements. The
number of scholarships was whittled down from forty thousand to ten
thousand (to be spread among a college-going population of more than
3 million). Then Republicans insisted on adding a loan provision—
despised even by Eisenhower.

As legislators debated the bill on the floor of the House, Republicans
made a snap decision to ax the scholarship provision altogether and use
its funds to bulk up the loan program. This was a huge blow to Elliott,
who saw the scholarships as the capstone to his political career. But with
an education bill finally within reach, he had to let them go.

Elliott's long-dreamt scholarship bill was now essentially a program of low-interest loans. (In the first full year of the NDEA's implementation, 115,450 students received loans of up to $1,000, which they would pay back over eleven years at 3 percent interest. Those who became teachers would have them forgiven altogether after five years.) The focus was on subjects deemed useful to the nation. It bore little resemblance to what Elliott and Hill had drafted as the bells rang out over Birmingham.

But for the two Alabamians, it was still a reason to celebrate. After decades of false starts, Congress had finally passed a civilian education-aid bill.

THE NDEA WAS SIGNED INTO LAW IN LATE AUGUST 1958, NEARLY A YEAR after the launch of *Sputnik I*. Even without the scholarships, even with the loans, it remained a substantial aid bill, and it would soon help thousands go to college. Although it was intended only as a four-year program, Hill and Elliott had correctly predicted that it would have longer legs; it was repeatedly extended, and its signature loan program, later renamed the Perkins Loan, persisted into the twenty-first century. And long-term supporters of federal aid were correct to see in the bill an opening for a more general and generous education funding bill. In less than a decade, the Higher Education Act would enshrine the notion of federal aid to education and significantly expand on the NDEA's offerings.

But while the NDEA represented a significant step forward for the premise of federal aid to education, it didn't address the field's most significant problems. As members of the foretold baby boom began arriving on schoolhouse steps (by fall of 1958, there were almost 43 million students in American schools, an increase of 30 percent over just five years), educators warned of severe shortages in buildings and teachers. But school construction was difficult to frame in the language of national defense—and was a guaranteed target of the dreaded Powell amendment—so it had fallen by the wayside. Instead of focusing on systemic fixes, the NDEA, like the GI Bill, had set its sights on individuals.

In the end, while *Sputnik* could have inspired a thoughtful revision of public education from the early grades through the PhD, legislators instead doubled down on the worst elements of the GI Bill. Their bill reaffirmed education as a commodity acquired almost exclusively for the benefit of the domestic workforce and the national defense. It skewed our education system toward certain subjects, deemed profitable for industry and defense, and away from those more concerned with the study of humanity and ethics. And because it was constructed to preserve segregation, it privileged only those individuals considered worthy of the country's investment.

This might all have been, if not entirely anodyne, at least not actively harmful—if Elliott and Hill's initial dream of a scholarship program had remained intact. But by converting that free money into a loan, the NDEA subjected higher education to a cost-benefit analysis in which, in the final tally, the nation reaped the benefits and its eighteen-year-olds were asked to assume the cost.

One final irony of the NDEA was that in its quest to rescue the American education system from its Dewey-era deficiencies, it had set the Soviet system as the ideal to be aped. The National Student Association warned that the United States was at risk of reducing its pedagogical program to "a satellite of the Russian system, spinning in an orbit dictated by Russian scientists." And in offering up the NDEA as the means of remaining competitive with the Soviet Union, legislators planted an ideological flag that still stands today: the point of higher education is not to become a better person or citizen or to be enriched and soothed by the balm of knowledge, but rather to fill the needs of the state (and producers of capital) for productive workers and militarily valuable minds.

This focus could have profound impacts on an individual's course of study. Education historian Joel Spring was in high school in Southern California when *Sputnik* exited the atmosphere. After the NDEA was passed, teachers pushed him into advanced math and science courses, emphasizing the need to compete with the archetypal "Ivan" over in St. Petersburg. Lacking funds but hoping to avoid the draft as war erupted in Vietnam, Spring declared a major in mathematics to benefit from the new federal aid program. After a year, he dropped out and reenrolled as a history major, paying his way by working as a railroad conductor. Later, he entered the University of Wisconsin's teacher-training program and began taking out NDEA loans. Spring eventually earned his PhD and became a professor, but he retained a dim view of the educational priorities fostered during his adolescence. Schools, he concluded, were not in it for the betterment of society, or even their students. Instead, they existed "to serve the interests of the business community by selecting and educating workers."

This ethos can be seen today in the iron grip STEM fields hold on the minds of university administrators and politicians, to say nothing of students. Institutions that spent decades building up their STEM offerings now disingenuously lament that the humanities are too "expensive" and staff them with grad students and adjuncts living on poverty wages. No longer even nominally committed to the enrichment of their students, they focus almost exclusively on churning out busy worker bees keyed to the needs of the labor market and devoted to amassing capital.* Meanwhile, headlines appear every week lamenting the crisis of the humanities, on the one hand, and the depredations of scammy coding bootcamps on the other.

By setting up a system that offered a broadly accessible financial means for rendering productive, highly skilled workers, the NDEA laid yet another paving stone on the path to today's student debt crisis. It cemented student loans as a key source of education funding, enshrining the notion that higher education was a privilege rather than a right—a

---

* Although it has become a truism that liberal arts studies are a drain on institutional resources, Christopher Newfield, an emeritus professor at the University of California Santa Barbara, argues persuasively that this is false. In his 2016 book *The Great Mistake*, he contends that the relationship between STEM fields and the humanities is actually reversed: English, history, and philosophy departments in fact *subsidize* the sciences, whose research and equipment needs cost far more than the federal and industry grant funding they take in. The money to pay for these pursuits invariably comes out of tuition revenues generated by the humanities, which typically require only a well-lit room and a professor (or graduate student).

purchase made by consumers rather than citizens—and a source of material gain for all involved: the school's endowment, the well-employed graduate, and even the state.

In sum, the federal student loan program owes its existence to a supposed postwar manpower crisis whose solution took on an almost feudalistic cruelty: from behind a rhetoric of "no handouts," Congress and the president chose to finance society's advancement and security on the backs of young Americans—mostly men, mostly white—who were asked to continue their studies primarily for the benefit of the American government, not to fulfill their own aspirations. Their reward for this patriotic effort would be a hefty bill. In this way, the cost of education became a regressive tax levied against a subset of the working and middle classes for having done everything asked of it. Not only were American students becoming consumers of their own edification, they were asked to make the purchase as a gift for their country, and be grateful for the opportunity to do so.

NO MATTER ITS FLAWS, CARL ELLIOTT CONSIDERED PASSING THE NDEA A PERsonal high-water mark of his achievements in Congress. He had made it his mission to help poor young Americans access the education for which he had fought so hard, and he believed that his bill had moved the needle considerably toward that goal. And in many ways, he was not wrong. But the changes he and his colleagues effected in classrooms would ricochet across the decades in ways he surely didn't anticipate. They would also seal his own fate.

Back in August 1957, when he'd convened his subcommittee's hearings, Elliott had opened with a rousing declaration on the importance of education to America's domestic prosperity and international supremacy. "America's future success at home and abroad, in peace or war," he said, "depends on the education of her citizens. Democracy is based on that foundation. Whatever happens in America's classrooms during the next fifty years will eventually happen to America."

He almost certainly couldn't have predicted the portent embedded in those words.

In the Alabama of 1964, the Alabama of George Wallace's "segregation today, segregation tomorrow, segregation forever," a nominal commitment to states' rights was not enough. A Southerner also had to snarl. Elliott did not snarl, and he became the rare Democrat to lose his seat during Barry Goldwater's landslide loss to Lyndon Johnson in 1964. After an unsuccessful bid for governor against George Wallace's dying wife, Lurleen, Elliott slinked back to his home in Alabama's northern hills. He attempted to return to his law practice, but he never managed to earn a proper living. He tried to find honorary lectureships in politics at schools that he had helped fund—but no one would have him. Having cashed out his congressional pension to fund his 1966 governor bid, he whiled away the rest of his days surviving on a Social Security check in an increasingly decrepit Alabama home, which, once his, he had been forced to sell and then rented back from his creditors.

Thus had the idiosyncratic, racist politics of the South returned one of its most ardent champions back to his humble roots—to the town that named a street after him and then forgot him. His legacy was a bill that introduced federal loans to America's college students. He remained, even in retirement, more than half a million dollars in debt.

CHAPTER 3

The Education President

Lyndon Baines Johnson came barreling into a windowless West Wing conference room where several of his aides had assembled, waiting. Glaring down at them was a giant lacquered billfish—a honeymoon catch of the previous head of state, John F. Kennedy, who had been shot down in Dallas a year earlier. It was 1965 and LBJ had just been inaugurated president, again, after winning a landslide reelection that also delivered a total of 295 Democrats to the House and 68 to the Senate. "Look, we've got to do this in a hurry," the president said. He was determined to learn from the lesson that had doomed FDR, his political hero. The Democrats had captured 16 million votes from the Republicans in November, but those, Johnson knew, would slip away like sand between his fingers. "It doesn't make any difference what we do. We're going to lose them at the rate of about a million a month." His lackeys would need to move quickly to implement the Great Society, the ambitious policy agenda that the president had announced the week before. "Get your subcommittee hearings going," he ordered. "Get [your bills] through the subcommittee and through the full committee and past the rules committee and on to the floor of the House just as fast as you can." As the meeting wrapped up, Johnson turned and left the group with a parting exhortation. "I want to see a whole bunch of coonskins on the wall!" And with that, the meeting was adjourned.

In the weeks and months that followed, Johnson's footmen did their best to carry out his wishes. To a remarkable degree, they succeeded, shepherding a bevy of watershed social policy legislation through the chambers of Congress. This was LBJ's banner moment, when his star burned brightest, before he irreparably quagmired himself—and the nation—in Vietnam, when he was still able to harness to maximum effect his political skill and the goodwill bestowed on him by the circumstances under which he entered office. Over the next ten months, he oversaw the enactment of the Voting Rights Act, the creation of Medicare and Medicaid, and an overhaul of federal education financing from kindergarten through graduate school.

Johnson was successful where others had failed not just because he'd benefited from a surge of national goodwill in the wake of his predecessor's horrific death, though that couldn't have hurt. He'd also been blessed with an unmatchable force of will and political acumen that left even his allies squirming. When congressmen wavered, they were subjected to the famous Johnson "treatment." The operation involved this hulking force of a man almost literally browbeating his opponent: according to reporters Rowland Evans and Robert Novak, he would bear down on his interlocutor with all his charm and bulk, "his face a scant millimeter from his target, his eyes widening and narrowing, his eyebrows rising and falling." They called the treatment "an almost hypnotic experience" that "rendered the target stunned and helpless." After Alabama governor George Wallace left a session with Johnson over the beatings of civil rights protesters in Selma in 1965, he expressed relief that it was over. "Hell, if I'd stayed in there much longer," he said, "he'd have had me coming out *for* civil rights."

And that was the other, and perhaps most crucial, reason Johnson was able to win the bulk of his domestic policy agenda. The summer before, he'd fulfilled one of Kennedy's signature goals—one that had eluded everyone who'd cared about it since Lincoln—and knocked over one of the last big dominoes standing in the way of real social change in America. On July 2, 1964, after a predictably brutal fight with his party's Southern delegation, Johnson signed the Civil Rights Act, which finally outlawed segregation in public spaces, including schools. Paired with the Voting Rights Act, passed the following summer, these two laws at last put an end, at least in writing, to the dreadful practice of Jim Crow.

Now that the great barricade was gone, possibilities abounded. For a visionary president like Johnson, who was, as his vice president, Hubert Humphrey, put it, "a nut on education," this was a huge gift. Finally, the field of education was open to groundbreaking progress. All the long-sought financing solutions, shelved or compromised to steer clear of the racists' ire—bills to send general aid to colleges, to partner with states on federal matching programs, to build a national network of community colleges—could be dusted off and brought back to life.

But of course that's not what happened. In the twenty years since the GI Bill had created, whole cloth, a new notion of what and whom higher education could be for, an entire consumer market had been born and shaped for this product. The number of eighteen- to twenty-one-year-olds increased by 50 percent over the course of the 1960s—and college enrollment followed suit. In the last year of Eisenhower's administration, there were 3.6 million young people streaming through the ivied gates of America's universities. By the time Johnson's second term was over, that number had shot up to 7.5 million.

The boom babies had grown up absorbing the new gospel of education, of what it had done for their families (their fathers) and for the country (its industry and military). They emerged into a society newly rich with material comforts and were encouraged to continue on the road to greater prosperity. That's what education was becoming centrally about—prosperity, and how to achieve it. Questions concerning rights or citizenship or democracy were fading, despite the protestations of a few lone voices for equity. The parameters were solidifying, the constraints were tightening, the no-handouts people were winning. From here on, it would be harder and harder to go up against the idea that education was a good that had to be paid for. The Great Society shapers of midcentury American education were concerned mostly with how to construct the perfect financing plan.

Yet, as Johnson entered the Fish Room that day in January 1965, there was still a chance to turn the tide. He was stepping up to the last great precipice of opportunity, the last real opportunity to beat a path back to a vision of education that put students and society over the market.

There was reason for optimism. From the start Johnson placed education among his top priorities. Like Carl Elliott, he credited it with his rise out of a life of poverty and obscurity. "He just believed in it," Humphrey would later recall, "just like some people believe in miracle cures."

LBJ had begun his professional life in education, in fact, far from national politics, as a teacher of mostly Mexican American children in a tiny, desolate town in South Texas. The nine months he spent in Cotulla in 1928 and 1929 were a break from his studies at Southwest Texas State Teachers College (now Texas State University)—a break he took because he'd run out of money to pay his next year's attendance, and because the $75 student loan he'd borrowed from Blanco State Bank was coming due in September. Nevertheless, he applied himself to his teaching role with characteristic maniacal energy, gaining the respect and admiration of the children he taught and installing appreciable improvements in a school that, according to Johnson mythologizer Robert Caro, had been neglected by its "five other teachers [. . .] Cotulla housewives who treated the job with the contempt they felt it deserved." Lyndon Johnson, on the other hand, "arrived early and stayed late—and he was a teacher like Cotulla had never seen."

After he returned to San Marcos and earned his diploma, Johnson took a position as a high school speech teacher in Houston. He was similarly driven in this new role—leading what had been an unremarkable debate team to a second-place finish in the state championships. But when Johnson's Texas political connections netted him a job as a congressional secretary in Washington, DC, the next year, he quit his teaching job on the spot. Johnson arrived in DC at the height of the Great Depression and rose through the ranks of Congress, becoming Senate majority leader two decades later. That's where he was in 1960, when John F. Kennedy chose him to be his running mate.

Kennedy had gotten the ball rolling for Johnson's big schools push. The handsome young president had also come in hot on education, even though, unlike Johnson, he was a privately schooled blue blood. When he announced his campaign, he had listed improving education among his top six priorities. After his election, Kennedy assembled a set of task forces to hash out solutions for his domestic and foreign policy priorities, including education finance and student aid. But he made little headway toward these goals during his time in office.

As Johnson took on the Oval Office after Kennedy's death and began to prepare his candidacy for a term in his own right, the new president assembled his own set of task forces. On education he populated a group with academics and state officials, along with some businessmen (the inventor of Polaroid film, for instance, and the editor in chief of Time Inc.). The task force included one Black man, Dr. Stephen J. Wright, president of Fisk College, and no women. At their first meeting, in July, Johnson urged the members to "roam imaginatively" and think big. He made it clear he wanted to generate transformative education policy, not merely fill in gaps. He asked them to set their sights not on "what is possible, but what is needed," and not just in the short term, but "for the long, long pull."

After Johnson won the election in November 1964, he outlined plans to achieve "a national goal for Full Educational Opportunity." (The phrasing, evocative of his former mentor, FDR, was but one of many bread crumbs indicating LBJ's commitment to achieve the unfinished ends of the New Deal.) The demands of a modern, urban, technological society, he declared, required that Americans learn more and continue doing so, throughout their lives. The uproar inspired by *Sputnik* had cemented the dramatic notion that educational attainment was integral not only to a student's professional future but also to the very success of the country's economy and its national defense. Johnson doubled down on this idea. "Every child must be encouraged to get as much education as he has the ability to take," Johnson proclaimed. "We want this not only for his sake—but for the nation's sake."

It was as if the president of the United States were telling America's youth that going to college was not just a personal investment but also their patriotic duty. Young people all across the country absorbed the message that education was something to be pursued as far as it could take them, no matter the cost.

Most of the money Johnson earmarked for education was directed at children and teenagers, in what would become the Elementary and Secondary Education Act, the pinnacle of his educational program. Presidents and congressmen had been unsuccessfully attempting to patch up the ailing public schools (and their underpaid teachers) for decades, but, as in higher education, they were perpetually stymied by the two *R*s of race and religion. Having effectively neutralized the first of these with the Civil Rights Act, Johnson found the solution to the second by directing aid not to schools but to poor children, whether in public or private schools. It was, like the GI Bill and the National Defense Education Act before it, yet another continuation of the long-standing emphasis on aiding the individual rather than the institution. But it worked like magic—the long-elusive legislation sailed through Congress with barely a comma changed.

With that down, aid to higher education should have presented itself as something of a lighter lift, even perhaps a bit of an afterthought. Yet it ended up being among the more protracted of Johnson's 1965 agenda items.

By 1965, the college-bound population was booming—the number of students had doubled, from 2 million to 4 million, in the previous decade, and the proportion of college-age Americans going to school had risen from 22 to 40 percent since the GI Bill. But the schools were in trouble. The tuitions they charged were less than it cost them to educate all these students, yet still too expensive for large portions of the population to shoulder alone. To meet the demands of growing masses of students, institutions were desperate to find resources to expand their facilities and faculties. In the 1960s, schools, and the Americans who wanted increasingly to attend them, were begging for help. In response, Johnson's education task force proposed providing financial support to struggling colleges, increasing the availability of grants to needy students, and expanding work-study programs. And, asserting that "the Federal Government alone cannot meet all needs," they recommended a third source of aid: more loans.

The man chosen to mold these recommendations into a policy proposal was Douglass Cater, the education president's "education man."

Born in Alabama and educated at Harvard, Cater had come to the White House by an unconventional route: he had met Johnson in 1953, as a journalist on assignment to write a story about Johnson's "Rising Democratic Star" in the Senate. Eleven years later, the president called Cater down to Washington to join him for a nude swim in the White House pool, alongside aides Jack Valenti and Bill Moyers. While the four men splashed about, Johnson quizzed Cater on his policy savvy. A few weeks later, Johnson's national security adviser, McGeorge Bundy, called to offer Cater a job.

Cater incorporated the task force recommendations into a legislative framework already assembled by the Office of Education and the Bureau of the Budget. The administration's initial bill contained four titles: Title I was aimed at developing a system of "urban extension" education. In the early part of the twentieth century, the land-grant universities (schools founded in exchange for gifts of land from the federal government to the states) had done this for agriculture, taking research and methodologies for improving crops straight to farmers. The new extension program would apply the idea to urban environments, bringing university acumen to the problems of inner cities and making professors foot soldiers in the War on Poverty, enlisted to eliminate housing and employment discrimination, bring "culture" to the slums, and help housewives earn degrees.

Title II of the higher education bill was directed at academic libraries: they were to get $50 million a year through 1968 to upgrade their resources. Title III addressed itself to supporting "developing institutions," which was code for historically Black colleges and universities, notoriously overlooked and underfunded. They would get $55 million in the first year.

But the real meat of the bill was in Title IV: financial aid to college students.

BY THE END OF THE 1950S, FAMILIES WERE UNDER INCREASING FINANCIAL strain to put their children through college, in spite of the various scholarships, school-based loan funds, and work-study programs available to them. "All of these help, but they fall far short," Elmer O. Cappers, the president of a Massachusetts bank, had written in an industry magazine in 1957. "Many, many incomes are stretched to the breaking point." The crisis only grew over the next decade. By the time the Baby Boom generation began finding its way into the halls of the nation's colleges and universities in proportions never seen before, the price of education had risen dramatically—up sixfold since 1930. Cost, and not ability, was turning a large portion of students away. Nearly one-fifth of low-income men and two-fifths of low-income women in the top 25 percent of their graduating classes eschewed higher studies—versus just 6 percent of wealthy men and 7 percent of wealthy women. Overall, almost 80 percent of wealthy students went on to college, while only a third of poor students did. "It is clear that many well-qualified young people," commissioner of education Francis Keppel told House legislators in March 1965, "simply regard higher education as totally out of not only reach but even of dream."

To remedy this situation, legislators now looked to Massachusetts, where Cappers claimed to have found the solution to students' financial woes. In 1956, the state legislature had incorporated the Massachusetts Higher Education Assistance Corporation, a quasi-governmental agency of which Cappers was board president, which had come up with a pioneering plan to help college students by putting them into debt.

The Massachusetts scheme worked like this: after completing their first year of college (absolutely no one wanted to loan to the unreliable freshman), students applied for funds from their local banks. If a bank decided that a student was a good risk, it would offer up to $500 toward their studies, at 4.5 percent interest, quite a bit lower than the going rate. If the student failed to repay within three and a half years after leaving school, the corporation would reimburse the bank up to 80 percent of the loan balance. The loans were less expensive to the state than grants—since theoretically they'd be repaid, with interest—and the government didn't even have to provide the upfront capital, which came from banks. Win-win.

By 1957, the corporation had guaranteed the loans of three hundred

Massachusetts students. The following year, its balances totaled almost $1 million, and officials in New York and Maine took notice, putting together guarantee corporations of their own. In 1960, a nonprofit corporation, United Student Aid Funds (USAF), followed suit and formed its own loan guarantee fund. In time, more would join the field, and these guarantors would grow, becoming not just stopgaps in the funding stream but major players in the business of student debt. And as the federal aid kitty grew larger, their own interests and incentives—revenue—strayed farther and farther from the students they had gotten into the business to help.

But none of that was apparent yet. In the 1960s, a guaranteed loan program seemed like a clever (if convoluted) solution to an intractable budgetary conundrum. In 1964, Vince Hartke, a Democratic senator working on an education-aid bill, drafted a small guaranteed-loan provision, just $1 million annually to insure student loans made by commercial banks. The Hartke proposal was soon taken up, largely unchanged, to form the bulk of the Higher Education Act's Title IV.

There was just one problem with the Guaranteed Student Loan Program (GSLP): nobody really liked it.

The GSLP was an urgent compromise intended to head off what the administration considered a far more dangerous option. The Johnson administration addressed its program to the poorest of students, those for whom college was a pipe dream, hoping its financial aid "package" would fill in the gaps. Title IV expanded both the NDEA's loan program and a new work-study program modeled on a Depression-era offering. Its most important achievement was a goal that had escaped legislators for decades, the same one that Carl Elliott and Lister Hill had been forced to abandon in the 1950s. For the first time, the federal government would provide no-strings-attached scholarships to students who demonstrated "exceptional financial need." The bill authorized $70 million in funding for these scholarships, which would go to needy students in chunks of up to $1,000 a year. At the time, this was roughly equivalent to total yearly charges at the average public university.

But while the Johnson administration focused its attention on the poor, an increasing number of legislators had begun to highlight the plight of the middle class, a potent electoral constituency already shouldering high tax burdens. "I am worried about the people who are really forming the productive end of our society today," Florida Democrat Sam Gibbons said during hearings over the Higher Education Act. "This goose can only lay so many golden eggs." The NDEA had limited loan availability to families making under $3,000 a year. But with public university tuitions at $1,500 or more a year, a family of four making the median annual income of $6,000 could not be expected to put two kids through school simultaneously on just their savings.

Legislators courting middle- and high-income voters had come up with an alternative. They proposed offering tuition tax credits for families with children in college. This would win them big points with voters, but it would not do much to achieve Johnson's goal of evening the educational playing field. The credit would go disproportionately to the wealthy and middle class, while low-income families, exempted from income taxes, wouldn't benefit at all.

The administration rejected the tax-credit scheme, but not just because it was regressive. It would also have cost a fortune. One plan popular in Congress was estimated to cost $750 million in the first year. If passed, it would balloon to $3 billion within a half decade. Taking so much money out of the federal budget would sap the administration's ability to fund its own priorities. And officials worried that it would give institutions carte blanche to raise tuitions, since parents, less burdened, would no longer balk at the cost.

But the idea wouldn't die, and it was gaining steam in Congress. The administration had to come up with something to stem the tide or risk undermining its own education-aid proposals. Its counterproposal would need to have the same basic appeal to the middle class as the tax credit but leave enough money on the table for scholarships and work-study and NDEA loans, the cornerstones of the Johnson program. In

other words, it would have to be budgetarily attractive enough to make
tax credits seem unreasonable.

BY 1965, LOAN-GUARANTEE PROGRAMS HAD SUCCESSFULLY SPREAD TO SEV-
eral states. Following the Massachusetts example, their legislatures created agencies that had the imprimatur of the state—and access to its
coffers to ensure that banks could recoup losses if students didn't pay.
This was important because then, as now, college students do not represent a low financial risk. Without a guarantee, most banks in the 1960s
either would not loan to them or hedged their bets by charging usurious
interest rates, running as high as 26 percent. A guaranteed loan program
was one way a state government could help middle-class families acquire
the out-of-pocket costs of paying for college without having to take on
the full financial liability.

The state prototypes presented an appealing model for a national
financial-aid program to steal thunder from tuition-tax credits, and the
Treasury Department pressed to have a loan-guarantee measure inserted
into the administration's bill. Under the plan, banks would loan up to
$1,500 annually to each student. The federal government set the rate
for students at 3 percent, and it sweetened the pot for banks by providing them with a 2 percent interest subsidy. As a result, even though the
Treasury was on the hook for the full loan, the only costs reflected in
the federal budget were the interest subsidies and any eventual default
payments—projected at just $15 million in the first year. All students
would be eligible, regardless of family income, so long as they could
find banks willing to lend to them. And with the risk now removed,
surely banks would be willing. The administration envisioned the plan
spawning a whole new industry, which would operate largely without
government involvement.

This last point proved a tough sell. Although we think today of the
student loan program as an enterprise mostly benefiting financial institutions, in the beginning they did not find it a very enticing venture. As
Congress opened hearings on the student aid bill in February 1965,

representatives from the banks lined up to denounce it. The bankers claimed that even with the government's subsidy, the loans' fixed interest rate would leave them breaking even at best. And they bristled at the operational burden of administering a federal program. Instead, the banks wanted the opportunity to create their own educational loans at more lucrative rates, like, say, 7 percent.

The American Bankers Association also admonished the government for trying to fix something that, they claimed, wasn't actually broken. A federal guaranteed loan program, the association argued, was unnecessary since there were already loan programs in fifteen states, serving 40 percent of the nation's college population, with more in the works. And even if those expansions didn't pan out, USAF, the nonprofit loan guarantee company, was making great strides in advancing its own nationwide loan program for college students.

USAF had also taken the Massachusetts loan program as its model. For every dollar deposited into its guarantee fund by colleges and private donors, USAF would insure $12.50 loaned by a bank. By 1965, it was on the hook for almost seventy thousand loans, a total of nearly $40 million. USAF's president, Allen Marshall, testified that the program was successful, even though it was not for profit, because banks saw in students the potential for a lifelong customer base. The bank, he said, "has made a friend and customer of a future community leader— perhaps an attorney [or] a garage owner." But if the program were expanded too much, the banker would no longer be able to give so generously, and it was the poorest students who would be left out. Marshall urged the subcommittee to relegate the proposed GSLP to one of "last resort," in the rare instance in which a state plan or USAF's own guarantee program was not available.

The bankers had another bone to pick with the government's guaranteed loan proposal. Because the federal program would be more liberal in its offerings—with higher borrowing limits and longer repayment terms—students would likely pick it over existing guarantee programs. This would generally seem to be a good thing—the federal government filling a need not served either by the states or by private enterprise. But the bankers argued otherwise, claiming that these *benefits* of the GSLP were actually bad for students, because they would allow them to incur greater debt and pay interest over a longer period. And subsidizing such loans to students, they added, would discourage parents from continuing to contribute to educational expenses.

In all, the bankers' arguments added up to a mess of incoherent quibbles: they did not want the program because it was not profitable, yet it would take away business from other programs that were also not profitable, which would hurt students by benefiting them too much. But without their capital, the federal program would never work, so legislators had to court the banks, no matter how ridiculous they found their arguments.

Other stakeholders argued against the loan program on more reasoned philosophical grounds. These idealists warned that relying on loans was a risky endeavor, and inherently inequitable. In hearings before the House, the American Council on Education, the primary lobbying group for colleges and universities, reminded legislators that for the average high school graduate, the barrier to entering college was most often the means to pay. "Reliance on loans as the primary solution to this problem," the council warned, "means that the heaviest indebtedness is incurred by those who can least afford the obligation of repayment." A director of student financial aid at George Washington University concurred: "Recently I have talked with two students—seventeen years old—who are borrowing $2,000 a year," he said, worrying about the "staggering indebtedness" of $8,000 (equivalent to about $80,000 today) they would face at graduation. "Only through expanded scholarship funds," he added, "can this situation be arrested."

Some witnesses took their critique further and argued that higher education should be publicly funded, just as high school and kindergarten were. Ralph Mansfield, on the board of Americans for Democratic Action, the liberal political organization cofounded by Eleanor Roosevelt, argued that college should ultimately be made free. Even the chair of the House education committee, an often contrarian Oregonian named Edith Green, noted that the legislation she had introduced and was championing was not what she considered an ideal system. "I hope someday that we will have free education at the college level," she mused offhandedly in one hearing, "because I think it is as necessary as high school education was a generation ago."

By far the most passionate call for free college came from an official of the AFL-CIO, who proposed a system that sounds radical even by today's standards: "The best way to make higher education available to young Americans," he said, "is through tuition-free junior colleges, colleges, and universities within daily traveling distance of their homes. We believe the time has come when free public education must break the twelve-year time barrier and be limited only by the ambition and talents of the student."

In short, plenty of imaginative leaders in the 1960s sensed that free higher education was the right (and smart) thing to do—for students and for the country. They argued that raising the population's level of education for the nation would boost national income and bring untold tax revenue back to the government (as had happened after the GI Bill). That it would help relieve urban misery and give people something to hope for. That it would make Americans healthier, happier, and better citizens. But theirs was not the overriding sentiment. That, instead, was a desire to keep federal costs down, to ensure that private enterprise still had a role to play, and to prohibit students from getting a "free ride." That is and always has been the American way.

There was, however, still the problem of Edith Green, herself a former schoolteacher, who also disliked the administration's plan for more pragmatic reasons. She worried—presciently—that a guaranteed loan program would become a "boondoggle" and instead preferred expanding the NDEA loan program, whose funds came directly out of the government's coffers. "I must say," she declared skeptically in one 1965 House hearing, "I have not had a single letter [. . .] from any college or university in the United States which has asked for the Federal guaranteed loan program. [. . .] I am just wondering where this demand comes from."

In fact, Green was so persuaded by the various arguments against the guaranteed loan program that she managed to strike it entirely from the bill her subcommittee advanced in May. The administration, having failed to woo Green with a sweet-talking lunch and a "treatment" session with the president earlier that year, began to panic, worried that the loss of guaranteed student loans might scuttle the entire program of the Higher Education Act.

Desperate for a solution, in July Johnson's aides invited the American Bankers Association to the White House to make a deal. To get the bankers on board, they offered to authorize the GSLP as only a three-year standby program. The revised Higher Education Act finally passed the House, with the GSLP intact, in mid-August, and the Senate in early September. An amended bill was ready for the president's signature on October 20. Student loans were about to become a major facet of America's higher education landscape, with repercussions that grew from a small ripple into a massive riptide.

PRESIDENT JOHNSON SIGNED THE HIGHER EDUCATION ACT ON NOVEMBER 8, 1965, in a stage-crafted ceremony in the gymnasium of his Texas alma mater: Johnson was seated at a stately desk, his feet resting on a Persian rug laid atop the wooden planks of the gym floor, the bleachers packed with applauding onlookers. The desk was symbolic: it was the one he'd sat at when he worked as a secretary in the university president's office, one of the many ways he'd funded his education, along with mopping floors and selling socks door to door. The act he was signing would ensure, he declared, "that a high school senior in this great land of ours can apply to any college or university in any of the fifty states and not be turned away because his family is poor."

As he concluded his remarks, Johnson waxed personal. "I shall never forget the faces of the boys and girls in that classroom at that Mexican school," he said, as torrents of rain filled the San Marcos River that flowed around the campus. "And I remember even yet the pain of realizing and knowing then that college was closed to practically every one [. . .] because they were too poor." Johnson had vowed then, he said, to someday wrest open the "door to knowledge" to *all* Americans.

His audience of thirty-five hundred students and faculty burst into applause. It must have seemed then that something truly transformational was at hand—something that would forever alter how Americans thought about and paid for college.

Instead, what Johnson enacted on that day mostly reinforced the utilitarian, market-pleasing pilings on which it was built.

The first three titles of the Higher Education Act were indeed expansive, even utopian. In envisioning the urban extension program outlined in Title I, for instance, the Office of Education painted a picture of the university as a tool not just for the enhancement of the wealthy elites' financial portfolios, but also for the betterment of society in general. It was not only a benefit, the administration's cheerleaders argued, but also a responsibility for the academy to share its wisdom with the rest of society. Doing so would make citizens more democratic and generate a "far-reaching effect on our industrial efficiency, our national economy, and the economic and social health of the American community."

Yet Title IV, where most of the bill's money was lodged, hardly hinted at such populist ideals. It was in some ways even less progressive than the status quo, a fact not overlooked at the time. Critics took issue in particular with the guaranteed aspect of the loan program, worrying that, contrary to the direct loans of the NDEA, taxpayers would now be subsidizing banks rather than students.

The Higher Education Act, with its funny math that looked good only on paper, dashed any hopes of escaping the debt cycle. From the GI Bill's focus on student grants, we had moved to loans under the NDEA, and now to even more loans. For all his charisma and political vigor, Johnson was unable to stare down that one great barricade to real American social uplift: cost. By the warped logic of American budgeting, instead of funding schools directly, it was somehow less politically costly to pay banks to pay teenagers to pay schools—sums that wouldn't cover the costs of educating the students, loaned at interest rates that wouldn't even cover the costs to the banks of loaning the money in the first place, paid by students who couldn't afford any of it.

From here on out, higher education would be a commodity, not a right, and it would not come for free. The menacing storm clouds of global and domestic politics would make sure of that. Johnson's first hundred days were up. Whatever remaining hope the idealists might have had that the tide could still be turned on education—that something revolutionary was yet possible, however expensive it might seem— had even then begun to evaporate.

By the end of 1966, the Democrats' party was over. Urban unrest, which had begun making headlines just as Johnson was unfurling his Great Society programs, continued to bedevil the president and his administration. In the summer of 1965, as Congress was hashing out the Higher Education Act, a largely Black and working-class bedroom community of Los Angeles erupted in protest following the arrest of a Black resident on suspicion of drunk driving. Six days later, the riots that began in Watts had consumed forty-six square miles. Police arrested thousands of Black Angelenos and killed nearly two dozen. As the Johnson years came to a close, the neglected and abused populations of cities like Chicago and Detroit and Newark simmered with rage, frequently boiling over. The pervasive sense of urban chaos that reigned in these years rendered a large portion of the white middle-class population increasingly unsympathetic to the plight of the people the Great Society was trying to uplift.

But the Johnson administration had little time to focus on its compounding domestic crises, because another crisis was brewing overseas, and it began sucking up almost every available national resource.

In August 1964, the US military claimed, North Vietnamese boats had twice attacked American naval patrollers in the Gulf of Tonkin, along the Vietnamese coast. Johnson's decision to retaliate with a bombing campaign began an escalation that quickly spiraled out of control. (When it was revealed that the second supposed attack had never actually happened, it was too late to correct course.) By the end of 1966, there were nearly 400,000 American soldiers on the ground on the Indochinese peninsula, and college-age men were being drafted by the tens of thousands every month. "Thus," wrote political scientist Larry Berman in 1983, "did Lyndon Johnson commit slow political suicide."

Pundits began referring to Johnson's "credibility gap" in Vietnam, and for good reason. Johnson had waffled his way into the war without ever asking the American people for their approval or preparing them for what was to come. In the November midterms, Republicans regained forty-seven House seats and three Senate seats, and increased their control of governorships to twenty-five, half the country. On top of that, inflation was up to 4.2 percent, from an average of 1.3 percent between 1960 and 1964. Even members of Johnson's own party were now balking at the president's budgetary asks.

In late 1966, Johnson's top domestic policy aide, Joseph Califano Jr., assembled a new task force for education policy. The all-white, all-male group of fifteen drafted a 149-page list of proposals and submitted them to the White House in the summer of 1967. Among the recommendations were some bold measures for higher education, including increases in federal aid across the board and, significantly, an allotment of general aid to institutions that amounted to 10 percent of their instructional costs plus $100 for every student. The task force also proposed creating a pilot program to make students' freshman year tuition-free, providing additional services to minority students and pairing the historically Black colleges with neighboring white colleges to improve their resources.* But when the group met with the president to discuss its recommendations, its chairman reported, "We talked about the report for maybe five minutes, and then he spent the next forty-five minutes talking about Vietnam."

Johnson's best bet for continued policy success was to impose a tax increase, but he stubbornly resisted this idea, instead hoping to thread the

---

* This rather patronizing idea perhaps derived most from the committee's demographic uniformity.

needle on Vietnam and his domestic programs by trimming the Great Society budget down to the bone (while increasing Vietnam funding by $3 billion). His 1969 budget proposed holding most Great Society programs steady or even decreasing their funding. For instance, Johnson refused his staff's recommended $99 million increase in funding for student aid programs to accommodate the needs of incoming freshmen. "Disapprove any increase," he scrawled on the aides' pleading memo, and so the number of poor freshmen eligible for grants in 1969 had to be cut nearly in half, from 105,000 the previous year to 63,000. Overall, Johnson's budget request reduced funding for higher education from $1 billion in 1968 to $700 million in 1969, to the consternation of Great Society supporters in Congress, like Texas firebrand Ralph Yarborough. "I happen to believe it is more important to build America," the senator declared, "than it is to destroy some other countries." Oregon Senator Wayne Morse, the longtime chair of the Senate subcommittee on education, responded to Johnson's budget request with a sharply defiant note back. "I do not intend to let the Bureau of the Budget determine the educational policy of this country," he railed. "Congress is going to determine it. If the president wants to veto it, let him veto it." But in the end, Congress appropriated $10 million less than Johnson asked for.

Johnson finally asked Congress for a tax increase in August 1967. But he didn't get it until June 1968, after he'd announced that he wouldn't be running for reelection, when the extra revenue was too late to do him or his programs any real good. Congressional conservatives used the tax increase as a cudgel to cut 1969 spending by $6 billion (a decision Morse referred to as a "political LSD trip") and eliminate 245,000 employees from the executive branch. Disillusioned with the abandonment of their ambitious project of societal renovation, prominent Johnson officials and aides began announcing their resignations.

As legislators met to reauthorize the Higher Education Act in 1967, higher-ups in the Office of Education admitted that low-income students were not benefiting as much as they should be, and that truly equalizing opportunity would require "vastly greater funding of the grant program and the work-study program." Nearly a third of GSLP funds—by that point totaling just under $700 million—were going to low-income students, even though the program had been designed so that these students should not have needed to rely on the GSLP in the first place. The loan program had, even by then, spun out of control.

That year, John Oswald, a representative of college and university lobbying groups, appeared before Edith Green's committee. Oswald testified that proposed budget reductions in the first three titles of the Higher Education Act would imperil the administration's goal of increasing educational opportunity and equity. The reason, he said, was that by reducing aid to institutions while focusing even more heavily on loans to students, the administration was ensuring that college costs would go up and that the only way to meet them would be to increase student charges. The course was set for an interminable spiral that would defeat the entire premise of the Higher Education Act—to make higher education an attainable goal for all Americans, regardless of income.

"Helping disadvantaged students meet the increasing costs of going to college is necessary and desirable," Oswald testified, "but in a sense it is a case of treating the symptoms rather than the disease." What institutions really needed, he argued, was general aid so they could keep costs at a minimum and offer assistance to students merely as a bridge to meet basic needs. Federal aid, the schools emphasized in a pamphlet Oswald presented to the committee, was a two-way street, since the government was asking institutions to support *it* in fulfilling national priorities and using *their* facilities to accomplish those goals. "Indeed," they claimed, most of the time "colleges and universities are supplying fiscal aid to the national government rather than the reverse." But Congress, faced with escalating costs in Vietnam and increased antipathy toward seemingly expensive federal programs, ignored them. The budget cuts proceeded; the GSLP grew; student costs rose and were increasingly discharged by a growing reliance on privately funded credit.

IF THE GI BILL AND NDEA TAUGHT US ANYTHING, IT'S THAT IT TAKES A CRISIS to open the lockbox on big social change. And if the stars don't align—as was the case when a politically vulnerable FDR proposed a program of civilian education aid—the crisis will simply pass you by. Or, worse, your opponents will harness it to achieve their own ends—as the American Legion did with the GI Bill. Once a precedent is in place, it's hard to shake. It shapes what is politically possible for the next crisis, and that one shapes the next one, and so on down the line.

The GI Bill had gotten the ball rolling; it kicked off the association between higher education and manpower, tightly linking school to work. Where legislators might have used the foreseen labor crisis to create a New Deal–style education funding program, they instead settled for an incentive program, making education primarily a tool of capitalist enterprise. The NDEA cemented the bond. With it, education became a solution not just to a manpower crisis but to a national security crisis as well. With the stakes raised, the government began actively encouraging students to go to school and take on debt to do so.

But the Higher Education Act really sealed the deal. It was the biggest, and most damaging, of the midcentury missed opportunities in education. By introducing a permanent loan program that was concerned more with enriching banks than helping students, it ensured that any future revisions to higher education financing would have to contend with powerful actors whose self-interest rarely, if ever, aligned with the goals of societal uplift. This all but guaranteed that the future of financial aid would be not a revolutionary overhaul but an incremental tinkering that served to placate demands for change rather than actually enact it. It was, in other words, the death knell for the notion that higher education is a right rather than a commodity.

Why did the most savvy political operator ever to hold the White House fail so spectacularly? Was it merely that the precedents he inherited were already too entrenched? Or that, unlike the return of troops after World War II or the Russian *Sputnik*s, the dual crises that Johnson inherited and stoked—assassination and war, both a shock to presidential power and stability—were not specifically focused on an issue that education could fix? Or was it simply that even when all the other constraints—race, religion, national apathy—had been lifted, the budget still reigned supreme?

Perhaps Johnson's program was, like much else, doomed by his own ambition. Like Carl Elliott before him, Johnson was so intent on getting a win that he didn't always focus on what exactly he was winning. This was, perhaps, the greatest of his many Achilles' heels. His political skills meant that in the domestic realm, he was often successful, but on the international stage, outside the warm waters of congressional backbiting that he was used to, he floundered. His desperate need for a win in this wider realm led him to reckless, hideous ends. Vietnam sank him and, with him, any hope of a truly great society.

Among those cast aside in the process were America's young people. In the many hearings before Congress in the 1960s about the need to provide help for college students, one demographic remained curiously unrepresented: college students. Apart from a few targeted invitations to students from a representative's or senator's home state or a veteran, student voices did not get a hearing on this or any other matter that concerned them. Legislators seemed far more interested in hearing college administrators talk about what students needed than in seeking input from those personally affected by their policies. But outside Congress, students were angry, and they were making themselves heard in whatever way they could.

PART 2

A Market Is Born (1972–1995)

A NEW CHARACTER EMERGED IN the American college student of the 1960s. By 1965, the silence of the previous generation was replaced by a utopian vision expressed with resounding fury. The new generation possessed a seemingly boundless will to speak out on the world's ills and agitate against them. As this character flowered, academia was opening its doors to greater and greater numbers, and to previously excluded and underrepresented groups: to Black, Asian, and Hispanic students, and to women. In places like California, the new matriculants were ushered in on the taxpayer's dime, at virtually no cost to them. This, of course, made them lightning rods for reactionary rage.

Over the course of the next decade, the avatars of an ascendant conservatism, embodied by Ronald Reagan in California and Richard Nixon in the White House, amplified that rage into a virulent attack on the supposed failures of Great Society liberals. The conservatives' weapon of choice was money—or rather, the lack of it. The taxpayers revolted, and won. In the university, that meant clawing back the jewel of public subsidy and leaving on its pedestal a great heap of nothing. Free gave way to fee.

In Congress, opposing legislators offered two options for those who could no longer pay their way. The road they built was but an extension of the one constructed by Roosevelt, Eisenhower, and Johnson, and they paved it with the same materials—a fixation on the individual, exclusion of the "undeserving," the primacy of the marketplace. But here the path bifurcated: liberals proffered grants; conservatives loans. They would jostle and vie for dominance. At the start, it appeared as though the liberals might win—for a brief, shining moment, their avenue of free money was long enough to carry students to graduation from one of the country's many venerable public institutions that state funds had recently built up.

But the din of the supposedly silent majority drowned out the students' outcry. Slowly an ideology of "human capital"—of individuals themselves as investments in which they must commit the funds to be earned in their futures—carried the day. States began reducing their subsidies to schools, diverting them into ventures like health care and prisons. Institutions compensated by raising fees. Grants could not keep pace—they were too expensive, and the political will was no longer in students' favor. Soon grants were eclipsed by loans, a market that expanded and, for those who controlled it, became exceedingly profitable, as it buried more and more students under debt.

By the end of the 1970s, students did as they were told. They relented to the market. On the ruins of utopia they built an edifice of retail, of which they were the product.

In 1980, Nixon was long gone, but his brand of conservatism had not trailed on his disgrace. In fact, it had grown only more rigid and entrenched. And its high priest, the man who nurtured and exploited Nixon's great white backlash to his own glorious ends, had assumed a new perch in the White House, ready to rain down his vacuous creed of the self onto the masses below.

CHAPTER 4

Market Actors

Between 1964 and 1970, a storm raged over the whole land-scape of American higher education. Schools across the country erupted in protest—over racism, the Vietnam War, even the impersonal alienation of the university. Tens of thousands of students marched, went on strike, sat in. Thousands were arrested. Several were killed.

At the cyclone's leading edge, preceding and predicting its path across the country, was the San Francisco Bay Area. In that single metroplex, student fury rained down on every part of California's three-tiered system, from the prestigious university in Berkeley to the state college across the Bay, and back again to Oakland's community colleges, which spawned the Black Panthers. Doing his best to seed the storm was the state's governor, the onetime actor and future president of the United States, Ronald Wilson Reagan.

Reagan had no obvious reason to view college students—even the rowdy, protesting sort—as the enemy. As a young man in the 1920s and '30s, he had attended Eureka College, a Christian liberal arts school in Illinois with a student body of 187, receiving financial aid to cover his $180 yearly tuition. He graduated with a 1.37 grade point average, a D-plus, and described his time there as "four years on a campus with red brick walls and you leave with a tear in your eye." But even the consummate conservative had cut his teeth as a young rabble-rouser; as a freshman he had helped lead a student strike in protest of cuts to faculty positions.

By the time the 1960s rolled around, Reagan was no longer the striking type. The chimp's costar in *Bedtime for Bonzo* campaigned for Nixon when he ran for governor of California in 1962 (Reagan's candidate lost) and was co-chair of California Republicans for Goldwater in 1964 (his candidate lost again). Just as Reagan was considering a run of his own, the University of California Berkeley exploded with student unrest. And Reagan correctly saw that explosion as his ticket to the majors.

Reagan used California's student uprisings to generate and harness a potent backlash against students, which spread across the nation. He capitalized on the voters' reactionary rage to catapult himself into the governor's mansion and then the White House. And in the process he turned California from a state with a world-class public university system into the leading edge of a nationwide spree of runaway tuition and debt-financed higher education.

THE STORM BROKE OVER BERKELEY. ONE MORNING IN OCTOBER 1964, A UC Berkeley alumnus set up a table on a little patch of red brick at the edge of campus and began distributing leaflets for the Congress of Racial Equality (CORE), in violation of recent administration policy. A campus official told the former student to stop, but he refused. Administrators called city police, who drove onto the plaza to arrest him for trespassing. As the alumnus was dragged limp into the squad car, a group of students sat down, blocking it; then one of them, Mario Savio, climbed onto the roof and began to speak. The Free Speech Movement (FSM) had just begun.

A brilliant yet melancholy twenty-one-year-old philosophy student from Queens, New York, with a short billow of brown curls and a debilitating stutter, Savio was an unlikely movement leader. But after enlisting as a "Freedom Summer" volunteer with the Student Nonviolent Coordinating Committee (SNCC) in 1964, he returned to Berkeley more committed than ever to the pressing political issues of his time. While in Mississippi that July, working to register Black voters and teach children at an outdoor "freedom school," Savio and two of his colleagues (one white, one Black) were attacked on a road in Jackson. The experience—and the lack of concern it inspired in the local white community—had a profound effect on him. Having just spent a summer trying to persuade

Mississippians to risk their lives for civil liberties, he could not sit by quietly as his own university restricted his basic rights.

The Berkeley students on the plaza "occupied" the police car for more than twenty-four hours. The afternoon after the protest began, five hundred officers arrived on campus and began brandishing their billy clubs. By that point, there were seven thousand people on the plaza. At the last minute, UC president Clark Kerr negotiated an agreement with Savio and others for the students to relinquish the squad car. He hoped the trouble was over, but it had just begun.

Ronald Reagan was just starting to dip his toes in the political waters when the Berkeley movement began, and he saw in the FSM protests an emblem of liberalism gone amok. It became clear that his antipathy for mass higher education went deeper than a classic conservative phobia of bureaucrats and a desire to slash government spending. As he began his campaign for governor of California in 1965, he railed against the "beatniks, radicals, and filthy speech advocates" who had brought UC Berkeley to shame, all in the name of "academic freedom."*

At the time of the FSM protests, California was at the forefront of American higher education. In 1960, a group of California officials and university administrators, including Kerr, had published the Master Plan for Higher Education, a document outlining policies to coordinate the state's universities, state colleges, and two-year junior colleges amid a projected surge in enrollment. It ensured that any California high school graduate could attend some form of public higher education at no tuition cost, with the state colleges and universities restricted to the top tier of graduating classes. Even before the Master Plan, California spent more than any other state on higher education, and by 1965, annual support for colleges and universities consumed almost $500 million— one-sixth of the state's general fund.

---

* Reagan wasn't opposed to singling out other campuses. In 1969, he seemingly fabricated a bizarre racist claim about thirty-five "Negro students" attacking a dean at an unnamed institution "with switchblades at his throat" until he agreed to admit forty students from a list they had drawn up.

Most students were not as lucky as those in California; nationwide, college costs were rising far faster than the cost of living. As a result, in 1970, Californians were about 50 percent more likely to attend college than Americans in general. California's college enrollment had more than doubled in the 1960s, to nearly 1.15 million in 1970.

In California, the university system swung open its doors to a host of new matriculants, permitting a sweeping expansion of access to previously excluded groups, such as Black Americans and women. The rise of the student protest movement, exemplified by the bra- and draft-card-burning Berkeley hippies and the Black Panthers just a few miles away, shone a spotlight on these groups. These young people, so newly welcomed into the hallowed sanctums of American academic privilege, were evidently unimpressed with the policies that had gotten them there.

Freed from the bonds of tuition, students, conservatives claimed, had lost respect for the authority of the family, the state, and, perhaps most troubling, the free market. Galvanized by their newly democratized exposure to higher education, the era's youth began making revolutionary demands on society as a whole. They wanted to tear down the canon rather than absorb it. To destroy the system, not learn to make napalm.*

In focusing animus on college students, Reagan tapped in to the anxieties of a white populace convinced that young reprobates were taking them for a ride. Just as college was becoming a necessity—yet no longer a guarantee—for entry into the middle class, a significant proportion of the population began to question who really "deserved" the benefits of a college education.

Every night on the news, the common (white) man was reminded that his tax dollars were paying for hairy-armed women, political radi-

---

* The president of Brandeis University related a telling anecdote. One student there had decided to denounce his chemistry major because, he told a professor, he didn't "want to learn to make napalm." "Who is asking you to do that?" asked the professor. "Why don't you plan to use your chemistry in cancer research?" Yet, the president was forced to acknowledge, the student did have a point: "Billions of dollars are consumed by war, while funds for cancer research dwindle."

cals, and militant Black revolutionaries to prance around an ivied campus for four years and possibly commit some casual arson. As the culture wars percolated, Johnson's Great Society began to sink under the attack of Nixon's "silent majority," and the university fed a rising sense of outrage.

Yet again, the liberals had given the undeserving a handout, and now these interlopers had forgotten their place. Resentment brewed.

No one knew how to cultivate that resentment better than Reagan. "The hall was entirely dark except for the light from two movie screens," he intoned on the California campaign trail, describing a 1966 Berkeley antiwar "Peace Trip" dance. "On these screens the nude torsos of men and women were portrayed, from time to time, in suggestive positions and movements. Three rock and roll bands played simultaneously. The smell of marijuana was thick throughout the hall."*

To clean up this behavior, Reagan vowed to instigate a "moral crusade." He would call in a former chief of the CIA to hold faculty to account as "examples of good standards and decency," and he would fire the chancellors, something that wasn't within the governor's power. No matter—it won him the election.

And it turned out that getting rid of the university's leadership *was* within his power, after all. After his inauguration, Reagan pressured the state's regents to fire the University of California's president, Clark Kerr. Then he began holding press conferences before and after meetings of the board.

Once in office, Reagan set out to put the students back in their place: he compared campus radicals to the Viet Cong and asked the army to

---

* In fact, by all accounts, the dance was pretty wild. Seth Rosenfeld cites the "bug-eyed" reports of campus cops, who lamented that the crowd of four thousand "was very unruly, loud, dirty [. . .] and the body odor was terrible." As the bands, including Jefferson Airplane, performed, strobes flashed across the room, and dancers in various states of undress contorted in apparently sexual poses. Couples danced suggestively, and some in the bleachers seemed to be having sex. A lot of people were tripping on acid, many were stoned, and erotic movies were projected, with added psychedelic special effects, onto the walls. "The people on the dance floor were acting very funny," the janitor later testified.

spy on them. And he was not afraid to use violent means to suppress student demonstrators. Amid a 1969 protest over People's Park, a vacant lot that students had reclaimed and occupied, Reagan called in twenty-five hundred members of the National Guard. The encounter quickly turned violent. The guards' rifle fire left hundreds injured and one innocent bystander dead. "Once the dogs of war are unleashed," Reagan responded, shruggingly, "you must expect that things will happen."

Yet the public largely supported his militancy. Reagan's approval ratings *increased* after the People's Park incident; meanwhile, 82 percent of respondents in a 1969 Gallup poll favored expelling protesters and 84 percent wanted them cut off from student loan money, which was seen as a liberal benefit enabling bad behavior.

Reagan found another way to get to students' pocketbooks. He lambasted the property taxes that helped fund schools as government overreach. The cost of operating a tuition-free system that was "subsidizing intellectual curiosity" for elites and providing a platform for radicals, he indicated, came at the expense of hard-working blue-collar Californians who hadn't had the opportunity to get to college.

His solution was to cut university budgets by 20 percent and introduce a tuition fee of $180 to $250, depending on the institution. This, the governor said, would make "those who are there really not to study but to agitate [. . .] think twice about paying a fee for the privilege of carrying a picket sign."

The public overwhelmingly supported the tuition hike, but the university system's regents reacted with horror. They correctly predicted that this would set the universities on a slippery slope, encouraging future governors to cut further from appropriations in times of crisis because they knew that tuition could provide a budgetary escape valve. As it turns out, they were more than right: California's governors have done this not just in times of crisis but in boom years as well. They managed only weakly to push back on Reagan's tuition proposal by turning it into a "student charge" of nearly the same amount.

But the damage was done. Thus ended California's grand experiment with tuition-free higher education. And as they say, as goes California, so goes the nation.

BY THE TIME THE HIGHER EDUCATION ACT WAS UP FOR REAUTHORIZATION again in 1971, the campus crises had spread far beyond California's borders. In April 1970, Nixon had ordered ground troops into Cambodia, Vietnam's western neighbor. College students exploded in protest. In California, Reagan was intent on restoring order. "If it takes a bloodbath," he said, "let's get it over with." Three weeks later, the bloodbath washed up in the Midwest. At Kent State in Ohio, members of the National Guard were called to campus after demonstrators burned its ROTC outpost to the ground. The soldiers shot unprovoked into a crowd of students, killing four. President Nixon blamed the students. "When dissent turns to violence," he said, "it invites tragedy." Eleven days later, Mississippi highway patrolmen fired more than four hundred rounds of buckshot into a dormitory at Jackson State, a historically Black college, killing two. A nationwide student strike spread to more than eight hundred schools.

In response, America's leaders sought to punish the youth. Among those agitating for a crackdown was Edith Green, the chair of the House higher education subcommittee. She was not alone. By 1970, more than thirty states had enacted some kind of campus unrest legislation. Most made it illegal to cause a disturbance on a public campus. In California, that included "unusual noise" and "indecent language," and perpetrators were barred from receiving state aid for two years. Gallup registered "youth protests" as among the nation's major issues. President Nixon convened the national Commission on Campus Unrest. In the eyes of many Americans, the university had shifted from a beacon of universalist liberalism to a symbol of the dissipated mores and ungrateful insubordination of an entire generation. The ivory tower had lost its gleam.

Although Nixon had campaigned on "law and order" to discipline student protesters, whom he called "bums," his aides had persuaded him to back off on enacting punitive measures. But Green was dogged. A former schoolteacher and education lobbyist who had been told that her dream of becoming an electrical engineer was a "silly" aspiration for a girl, Green was considered one of the most expert legislators on American education. Initially a die-hard liberal, at this late stage in her career she came to espouse the American West's "small government" conservatism, and she began to depart from her past stances.

She insisted on advancing a measure—against the objections of her aghast liberal colleagues—that would cut off protesters from federal student aid for up to five years. "Wanton destruction by the beneficiaries of higher education," she said, had made it difficult to go soliciting more money from "tax-paying constituents." But in fact, she was the one gumming up the works. Her bill failed on the House floor, but fighting over it had consumed a great deal of time, and her subcommittee failed to put together an education-finance bill in 1969 or 1970. "If she doesn't get her own way," said a former Johnson aide of her contrarian attitude, "she takes out her hatchet and chops down trees just as they start to bloom."

This left colleges and their students on the defensive when they appeared before Congress in 1971, essentially hat in hand, to beg for more funding.

Colleges and universities had responded with gusto to the federal government's mid-'60s invitation to be its on-the-ground partner in the quest to increase opportunity and expand the country's technological prowess and military capabilities. They'd built out campuses and hired scores of faculty in anticipation of the crush of students. But now the flow of students began to taper, and as the war in Vietnam consumed ever more of the national purse, the government began to renege on its part of the deal. Federal support to institutions, which had grown by up to 40 percent a year in the mid-1960s, flatlined. State appropriations to colleges and universities had soared in the 1960s, but as competition for resources stiffened, they peaked and began a steady decline. Foundations and alumni cut back on donations to private institutions.

Amid this nationwide economic downturn and shifting political

priorities, universities found themselves on the brink of financial catastrophe. They'd gone into debt to fund their expansions, and now
the gushing oil well they'd expected to tap indefinitely had dried up.
They had no certainty year to year about their funding streams, which
were largely out of their control. A Berkeley economist estimated that
more than two-thirds of American institutions were either struggling or
headed onto shaky financial ground by the early 1970s. Private schools
like NYU and Columbia, whose tuition covered only a fraction of actual
costs, had started eating into endowments and running large annual
budget deficits. Gone were the fears of a previous era about government
control of higher education. Schools were now desperate for help from
wherever they could get it. "The only place the money can come from,"
said Nathan Pusey, the president of Harvard, in 1967, "is the federal
government."

But the institutions' pleas for help fell on deaf ears. Nixon had entered office with a commitment to "fiscal responsibility"—which did
not bode well for domestic spending.

Presenting the Higher Education Opportunity Act of 1970, Nixon
emphasized the need for a "financing floor" of grants, loans, and work-
study income for poor students. But cloaked in this egalitarian rhetoric
was Nixon's primary focus: to further convert university finance into a
function of the market. In addition to low-income programs, he wanted
to expand the loan program by adding new, unsubsidized options and
creating a special government-chartered corporation to buy loans from
banks and sell them on a secondary market.

The administration's bill hit the floor of Congress with a resounding
thud. Neither the House nor the Senate education subcommittees were
impressed with its emphasis on loans. Democrats, who still held the majority, were also wary: the supposed concern for low-income students,
they suspected, was merely a ruse to eliminate other streams of student
aid funding. With little buy-in, subcommittee members essentially ignored Nixon's bill. Finally, a year later, facing a summer deadline to
reauthorize the Higher Education Act or allow students to go without
funding, legislators felt compelled to act.

Meanwhile, as Edith Green tied up her subcommittee in attacks on student miscreants, the Senate gave shape to the higher education bill's two most significant aspects: grants and loans.

WHILE SKIING IN THE ALPS IN THE WINTER OF 1969, SENATOR CLAIBORNE Pell devised a way to solve the education funding crisis. What if we offer *all* students a grant, he thought. Give them each $1,200, minus whatever their parents paid in income taxes. That way the poorest students receive the full benefit, and the wealthiest none. At lunch, he wrote up his idea on a ski-lodge placemat and instructed his staff to figure out the details.

Unlike Edith Green's discordant operation in the House, the Senate's education subcommittee reflected the congenial, patrician mien of its members. There, second-term Rhode Island senator Pell, a wealthy diplomat's son descended from colonial royalists, had recently taken the reins. Bipartisanship ruled, and the mostly liberal and moderate senators on the subcommittee rarely disagreed openly.

But when his subcommittee invited institutional representatives to discuss his grant proposal, which he termed the Basic Educational Opportunity Grant (BEOG), Pell was dismayed by the reaction. They were hardly more enthusiastic than they had been about the administration's bill, which had offered them nothing. In fact, Pell's proposal was not fundamentally different from the administration's "financing floor," although he intended it to supplement rather than supplant the existing package of grants, loans, and work-study. Peeved that educators weren't taking his BEOG more seriously, Pell ignored their calls for federal support for institutions. Instead, he sided with Frank Newman, a public relations director at Stanford University. Newman had authored a report arguing that institutions had brought their financial woes upon themselves by excessive spending and resistance to reform and innovation. Rather than giving them a blank check to waste, Newman proposed offering a stipend for every needy or disadvantaged student they admitted. Pell agreed, and wrote Newman's idea into his bill.

After two months in conference, culminating in a final knock-down negotiating session that dragged on until five in the morning, the Senate and the House reconciled their versions of the bill, which had more than four hundred points of disagreement. Green had fought Pell's university stipend, which she viewed as elitist. "Inherently we are saying all poor students are stupid and have to have special assistance," she argued, in her characteristically blunt way. At the same time, she wanted to downplay aid to poor students, whom she believed responsible for all the ruckus on campuses. (In fact, it was largely middle-class white students who were responsible for campus unrest.)

In the end, Pell got his grant (which had grown to a maximum of $1,400), and universities got virtually nothing. The Pell Grant (so named in 1980) was a high-water mark for student aid, and it made the 1972 reauthorization into the most momentous higher education bill of the century—surpassing in impact even the bill it amended, the Higher Education Act. The bill was estimated to cost $19 billion in new spending, with $1 billion of that going to Pell's BEOG each year. For a few years, it did actually make college more affordable. By 1975, there were nearly 2 million recipients, and the grant supplied them with five times the amount they took out in loans, enough to cover more than full tuition at public institutions and a third of that at private ones.

But in many ways, the grant was less revolutionary than it seemed. It was in essence the GI Bill writ large—a way of sealing the leaks in the academic financing boat, one individual student at a time. Cast as a bulwark against the forces of economic woe buffeting college students, it did almost nothing to slow the rise of college costs. Pell's effort was a well-meaning and hard-fought attempt to even the playing field for nonwealthy students. But whether through the hubris born of senatorial power, mistrust of educators' incentives in demanding institutional aid, the desire to put his own mark on the system, or sheer pragmatic realism, Pell was unwilling to consider more systemic solutions. In many ways, as a number of educators had warned, the student-centered approach to federal aid embodied by Pell Grants and the guaranteed loan program only ensured that college costs would increase: as federal and state support to schools dwindled in the Reagan recession of the early 1980s, institutions substituted students' government aid for their own. In that decade, public college costs, which had actually declined relative to inflation in the 1970s, effectively doubled.

And to get his grant, Pell had been forced to make a concession that would prove even more consequential.

Although it had come from Nixon, the idea for a secondary student-loan market attracted bipartisan enthusiasm. An entity that could buy and warehouse loans would increase banks' liquidity and—its proponents argued—encourage them to make yet more loans. Colorado Republican Peter Dominick, doing the administration's bidding, had inserted the proposal into the 1972 amendments to the Higher Education Act.

At the time, the student loan program had begun to flounder. Less than a decade after its creation, default rates were rising steadily, and banks remained reluctant to loan to financially risky lower-income students and families. Although the guaranteed loan program had not initially been intended for poor students, the rise in college costs had outpaced other forms of aid, and not even Pell's grant could plug the hole.

The legislators who developed the 1972 Higher Education Act amendments envisioned higher education as a realm operating on the principles of the free market: if students were furnished with funds, they would select the institutions most attractive to them, encouraging colleges to compete for students and tailor their services to student needs and desires. And for conservatives, consumerism ensured that students, who needed to graduate and get jobs to start paying back those loans, would stop making waves.

More than that, loans were the conservatives' riposte to Pell's largesse, born of the belief that students did not deserve a "free ride."

This was Milton Friedman's era. The famous conservative economist was known for his abstemious view of government's role in society—believing that Social Security should be privatized and public school funding replaced with government-issued tuition vouchers. In the 1950s and '60s, he peddled a new concept that had emerged among his colleagues at the University of Chicago: human capital theory, which treated "education as an investment in man and [. . .] its consequences as a form of capital." In this line of thinking, Friedman wanted government higher-education spending to be focused only on loans. Students should borrow against their future selves and repay the IRS over the course of their working lives. The phenomenal student indebtedness such a system would engender was justified, he argued, on the grounds that education really only benefits the individual receiving it, through boosted income.

Friedman's ideas, which had lain dormant during the era of the Great Society, experienced a reflorescence under Nixon. As the American economy cratered under a Middle East oil crisis and persistent waves of stagflation, Americans became less tethered to the notion that education was a benefit to all. "Higher education is a virtuous activity. It is also an expensive activity," the *New York Times* declared in 1978. "Since most of the benefits—status, income, personal satisfaction—accrue to the students themselves, it seems that they should bear most of the burden."

This was not true. As data from the GI Bill has shown, society at large benefits in myriad ways from investments in higher education. But rather than responding to reality, Friedman spoke to the discontented biases blooming within white America. A celebrity economist with a weekly *Newsweek* column, Friedman acknowledged that it was natural for "campus rebels" to be militant about tuition-free education, for, "after all, their pocketbooks are at stake." But "low-income taxpayers and youngsters not in college" were not so effectively vocal. Thus, "'free' tuition is highly inequitable to them." Like Reagan, he was arguing that subsidizing the educated would come at the expense of the blue-collar taxpayer. This line of attack was as spurious then as it is today. In (nearly) tuition-free California, fully 80 percent of high school graduates were attending some form of higher education in 1970—as compared to

50 percent nationwide. If these were not the students Friedman was pretending to speak for, who were?

Yet even the government officials charged with administering student aid programs were in thrall to the Friedman doctrine. In 1968, President Johnson tasked labor economist Alice Rivlin with generating an education-financing plan for the Department of Health, Education, and Welfare. A year later her report was transmitted to the president, two weeks before he was due to leave the White House. "Should higher education, like secondary education, be provided free of charge to all?" the department secretary asked in his headnote. But he cast this thought aside. The increased income students reap from their education means they should pay. And anyway, "present public resources" made a tax-funded higher education system an impossibility, at least "for the foreseeable future."

To help students make an adequate contribution to the investment in themselves, Rivlin's team suggested more grants—and more loans. Unfortunately, however, people, "unlike houses and cars," she wrote, "cannot be mortgaged." Not even a government guarantee had proved enough to induce banks to loan to all "low-income students who might be willing to borrow." At no point did she acknowledge that the banks might be on to something—that, in fact, it *is* a bad idea to lend to low-income students, despite their willingness. Instead, to "correct the loan market," she suggested replacing the GSLP with a government-sponsored "nonprofit private corporation" that could lend to students—a so-called national student loan bank. This was precisely the idea Milton Friedman had originated in 1955.

But the market-oriented Nixon administration did not want to cut banks out of the deal, and so it offered a tweak. Instead of a national student loan bank, Nixon proposed creating an entity that could buy and sell the loans that commercial banks made, thereby increasing their liquidity.

Legislators in Congress bought the Friedman line and adopted the Rivlin plan, with Nixon's tweak. They called their new loan market the Student Loan Marketing Association, or Sallie Mae.

Milton Friedman had won the day, to the detriment of college-going students everywhere.

SALLIE MAE BEGAN AS A GROTESQUE MARRIAGE OF GOVERNMENT AND FREE enterprise. As a government-sponsored enterprise, or GSE—a quasi-public quasi-private hybrid conceived in the mold of the housing-market entities Fannie Mae and Freddie Mac—it benefited from special perks, like access to funds at a super-low interest rate tied to the US Treasury rate. As a privately held corporation overseen by a board of directors (with fourteen members chosen by shareholders and the other seven appointed by the president), it was given a degree of autonomy not permitted to other government entities and allowed—indeed, encouraged—to turn a profit on its student loan business. To raise money for its operations, the government offered more than $100 million in stock in the corporation, underwritten by such financial behemoths as Lehman Brothers, Merrill Lynch, and Morgan Stanley, to a variety of interested shareholders: colleges, universities, and lenders. But few were enticed by the prospect, and the company had to put off its planned initial public offering. "When we first started out," the company's first CEO, Edward Fox, later recalled, "we were sort of held together by wax and tobacco juice."

After the failed IPO, Sallie Mae doubled back. George Putnam, an investment banker who was the treasurer of Harvard, believed so fully in the agency's mission that he personally took on the task of persuading universities to get on board. After he committed $400,000 of Harvard's funds to the fledgling loan market, the pitch was an easy sell. "If Harvard thinks it's a good investment," Putnam said, "that's all they wanted to know." In 1974, Sallie Mae raised $24 million from educational and financial institutions. Shortly thereafter, the company benefited from an infusion from the Treasury-supported Federal Financing Bank, another new financial mutant created to take pressure off private markets. For the rest of the decade, Sallie Mae procured all its funding from this metabank to the metamarkets. By the end of the 1975 school year, the corporation had found its footing. It had purchased or warehoused

$340 million in student loans from banks and schools and was turning a $1.8 million annual profit. A few years later, it began taking steps to become independent of the federal government—announcing that it would start raising all its funds on the open market.

This was it, the big turn. With Sallie Mae in the fray and gobbling up ever larger portions of the student loan kitty, the company's sense of purpose completed its mutation—from serving students to extracting revenue from them on behalf of shareholders. In those days, Sallie Mae's leadership bought into the fiction that they were operating in the public interest, and that making money was their most philanthropic act. They repeated a mantra: "Do good by doing good." But the profit motive was not on college students' side. And in propping up Sallie, the federal government had sent the message that protecting the market—and not the students who provided its capital—was the greatest priority.

While Sallie Mae's fortunes blossomed, students were left to wither on the vine. Skepticism and concern were even then growing about the ballooning loan program, which was racking up a tremendous number of defaults. In 1978, diagnosing students as "The New Debtor Class," the *New York Times* cited higher education experts worried that growing and unmanageable indebtedness would kneecap new graduates or push them to chase only high-paying careers—jobs, in other words, "which clearly do not benefit society."

Others worried about the special burden student loans would present to women, saddling them with a "negative dowry" that would keep them from finding good husbands. All the way back in 1971, New York Democrat James Scheuer (an advocate of free public college) had feared that the loan program was "going to create a whole generation of unmarriageable women." Informed that students were on track to someday graduate from college owing as much as $100,000, he quipped: "I wouldn't touch a girl with that kind of debt with a large pole."

Even the bankers recognized the writing on the wall. They had seen the default crisis coming and presciently warned that the loan program could soon spiral out of control. "If [students] are unable to repay us because the burden is so severe," a representative of the American Bankers Association had testified to the House in 1971, "then we have placed a tremendous stone around the necks of our citizenry."

By the end of the decade, that premonition had borne out. As high inflation took hold in the 1970s, the interest rates students paid on their federal loans crept into the double digits. By the early 1980s, some loans in the GSLP were up to a staggering 12 percent. For many, the hardship was indeed unbearable. In 1978, 17 percent of NDEA loans and 14 percent of guaranteed loans were in default. Millions of students had taken on debt to go to school, just as everyone, from presidents to their parents, had told them to, and what they had received in return was a massive, government-sponsored millstone.

But it wasn't just students who were paying the price. The government's yearly bill for covering defaults came to more than $200 million. On top of that, the overall cost of the loan program was rising sharply—thanks to the new occupant of the White House.

After Nixon resigned the presidency in 1974, his veep, Gerald Ford, had neither the time nor inclination to leave much of a stamp on higher education policy before his abridged two-year term was up. When Ford ran for reelection in 1976, the electorate instead chose Jimmy Carter, a folksy moderate Democrat from Georgia.

In his four years in office, Carter greatly expanded the federal role in education, elevating the Office of Education to a cabinet-level department, and ran up a huge tab on the student loan program. Just as they had a decade earlier, tuition tax credits once again crept into the GOP's platform in the 1970s, and with Carter's support, in 1978 Democrats in Congress once again slapped together a less expensive alternative. The impact of their Middle Income Student Assistance Act was to eliminate the means test for subsidized student loans. In response, middle-class families practically made a run on the banks. Over the next four years, the number of borrowers rocketed up from 1 million to 3.6 million.

The increased loan volume naturally raised the cost of government subsidies to banks. On top of this, in 1969, Congress, hoping to entice reluctant lenders into the program, had authorized a system of "special allowance payments" to top off lenders, bringing them closer to market returns. In 1979, when the House held hearings in advance of another reauthorization of the Higher Education Act, students were paying 7 percent interest on their GSLP loans, and Congress was sweetening the deal with an additional 6.25 percent to the banks. By then, fourteen years into the guaranteed loan program, students had taken out $14 billion, at a cost to the government of $4 billion. Anyone with eyes could see that the program had become a boondoggle, exactly as Edith Green had predicted. "The time is here," a University of Pennsylvania economist urged in 1978, "to dismantle the existing system."

But, of course, that's not what happened. In less than two decades, the loan program had grown so large and necessary to the functioning of American higher education that there was almost no hope of doing away with it. In 1979, students took out $5 billion in guaranteed and NDEA loans—and the government's share of that accounted for more than 60 percent of annual federal student aid. Overall, the yearly cost to the government of subsidizing banks was $280 million. More than $200 million of that came from default payments. Over the life of the loans, the cost to government was expected to rise to about $2.5 billion, roughly half the original amount borrowed.

Alfred Fitt, general counsel of the Congressional Budget Office, called the loan program a "gigantic business" beset with "disturbingly high" default rates. What had started out as "an ingenious and inexpensive way to attract private sector capital to the student loan business," Fitt concluded, had been transformed "into a system much more costly than a direct federal loan program." Moreover, those costs were "not redounding to the benefit of student borrowers, but rather to the benefit of the financial institutions that make the loans." For every $1,000 that banks loaned out, he estimated, the government paid $35 more in subsidies each year than it would cost the Treasury to make that loan directly.

As for Sallie Mae, "It has become a way of laundering federal money," argued William Ford, chair of the subcommittee Edith Green had left in 1973. "In the process everybody who touches it makes something off of it"—except for the student. Meanwhile, "the system is so complicated that everybody forgets that we started these programs for the purpose of buying education." Even after Sallie Mae came on the scene to induce banks to lend more generously, the loan program still wasn't even really working for those who needed aid most. Banks were generally more interested in making large loans to existing customers—that is, the children of their middle- and upper-class patrons, who were more likely to attend high-cost private schools—than they were to lower-income students looking for the last few hundred dollars to get them over the hump at a state or community college.

Everyone was gradually, iteratively losing sight of one fact: the point of the whole endeavor was to expand educational opportunity—not make a buck off students. Instead, the program was becoming more about turning profits and minimizing losses, with little concern for the students who were saddled with the bill. Rather than reading the rising levels of loan defaults as an indictment of the program—a sign, perhaps, that the linkage between education and financial security might not be as firm as the optimists had predicted—those who shepherded the program insisted that the students had failed it, not the other way around.

Gone were the impassioned calls for tuition-free higher education that had crept into the public and political discourse earlier in the decade. By now, almost everyone acknowledged that, whether they originated from the Treasury or from commercial banks, whether their paper remained in bank vaults or turned a profit on the secondary market, loans were here to stay. The best anyone could do at this point was tinker with implementation: one representative from Iowa introduced a bill to make loans interest-free; another proposed loan consolidation and a plan administered by the IRS that calculated payments based on income. The American Council on Education, the lobbying association for schools that had fruitlessly begged Congress for institutional support earlier in the decade, now proclaimed that the loan program had "served the nation well" and offered only a few "technical proposals" rather than "radical surgery" to improve it.

Congress responded by expanding Sallie Mae's charter—and helping the company make a tidier profit in the process. In the 1980 reauthorization of the Higher Education Act, Sallie Mae was allowed to start buying borrowers' loans and consolidating them into one longer-term loan at 7 percent interest, with a choice between repayment plans that either held that rate steady or gradually rose over the years (as, presumably, did the borrower's income). The company could also start making loans directly to students if they lacked access to other lenders. By the early 1980s, it had $8.3 billion in assets and arranged an IPO, underwritten by Goldman Sachs.

Sallie Mae was on its great rise, with annual profits that would soon balloon from a paltry few tens of millions into the billions. Under the spell of such fortunes, and with students' appetite for education apparently limitless, Sallie Mae stopped peddling the myth that it was doing good for anyone but itself. In the coming decades, the company would grow so powerfully profitable that it would become one of the central forces guiding student aid policy, rather than a mere arm of that policy. For students, unfortunately, its direction led not to increased opportunity but greater and greater indebtedness. Despite a 1979 proclamation that it existed to "support vital national goals," this supposedly "public purpose institution" was now in it purely for the money.

INCREASINGLY, SO WERE THE STUDENTS. THE 1960S HAD SEEN A SHIFT IN THE prevailing view of college as an elite privilege to one of a mass benefit, even a universal right: by the end of that decade, 7 million Americans, more than half of all high school graduates, were enrolled in a college or university. Community colleges doubled in number, from 315 to 603, with one new school opening roughly every week, and state college enrollments more than doubled. Higher education had not quite reached its pinnacle, but it would never again grow so fast. In this heady, idealistic time, the liberal arts carried the day: in the 1960s, the proportion of degrees in the humanities and social sciences rose from 30 to 41 percent, the highest they had ever been, while math and the sciences lost 5 percent. Students were drawn to fields that promised to change the world. But this era also saw the emergence of that new term, *human capital*, which described the economic value to a student in obtaining a degree. The value of the credential itself would soon arguably overtake any intrinsic benefit students gained from their educations.

The curve had peaked and soon would flatten. As college graduates flooded the market, their value began to wane. Idealism lost its edge. College was becoming just another way to get ahead.

Starting in 1972, the year of the momentous reauthorization of the Higher Education Act, students evinced a waning interest in high ideals, both academic and personal. Inflation was surging; wages were stagnating, even for college graduates, who had lost much of the "wage premium" they'd built up in the 1960s; and liberal arts graduates were facing double-digit unemployment levels. In the 1970s, money was at the front of pretty much everybody's mind.

Thereafter, the popularity of the liberal arts plummeted, while that of vocational and business studies skyrocketed—increasing by 92 percent by 1985—and colleges expanded their offerings accordingly. The number of students who headed off to school in search of "a meaningful philosophy of life" fell from 82 percent in 1969 to 43 percent in 1985. In their place came students who felt it key to become "very well off financially"—71 percent of them, up from 40 percent at the end of the 1960s. No longer beacons of a liberal, humanist society, students had become consumers of the product of education.

This turn to the market came right as the Great Society expansion of higher education was reaching its pinnacle. But just as schools began opening their doors in greater numbers to women, ethnic minorities, and poor people, a powerful backlash was turning the tide. Little more than a decade after Reagan brought student-financed tuition to California, the 1970s fiscal crisis did the same to New York. In 1975, Gerald Ford refused to bail out a deeply indebted New York City, and as a result, CUNY, the tuition-free jewel in New York's college crown, became the last public institution to lose the battle for free tuition.

Across the country, white citizens could not understand and did not support the protests and unrest erupting in Black neighborhoods and on college campuses. The idea that the gains of the 1960s had not been enough to quell Black Americans' rage was itself enraging to these conservatives, who saw their share of the pie beginning to shrink. The Great Society eroded; states across the country cut appropriations to university systems; schools continued to raise rates; and students were left holding the hot potato, and forced, more and more, to pay for it.

Into this breach had stepped Sallie Mae, which bought federal loans from commercial banks and then marshaled government benefits to turn a profit on them, to prop up a government-sanctioned system of private finance that saw students simply as market actors like any other. Since they were going to have to pay anyway, why shouldn't someone at least make a killing off them? As the retrenchment of the 1970s blossomed into the staunch conservatism of the 1980s, the financiers proliferated, and a killing they did make.

CHAPTER 5

Profits and Loss

B y the letter of American tax law—if not always in its spirit—
most of the schools that came begging for money in the student
aid wars of the 1970s were nonprofit and public institutions.
These were the stately quadrangle campuses most people envision when
they hear the word "college"—the red-brick foundations of higher education, tasked with shaping 90 percent of America's educated elite.

But alongside the Harvards (private nonprofit) and the Berkeleys
(public) lay sporulating a whole other class of institution, one that
aimed for something less transcendent than a liberal, classical canon—
something purer. These schools were in it for the profit to be made from
imparting skills, knowledge, or whatever their students would pay them
for. And glimmering within the floodwaters of student aid that began
flowing in the early '70s, they saw a shining new opportunity to cash in
like never before.

IN 1970, JOHN SPERLING WAS AN ACTIVE PARTNER IN THE CALIFORNIA MAS-
ter Plan. A professor of humanities and economics at San Jose State—
one of California's new cadre of state colleges, at the southern end of
San Francisco Bay—he was a typical academic liberal. He had pedigree:
undergrad at Reed College, thence to University of California Berkeley
for grad school, and recipient of a prestigious fellowship to write his dissertation across the pond at Cambridge University. After he got to San
Jose State in 1960, he found his calling—union organizing. Sperling
built the school's first faculty union, and when the professors up in San
Francisco joined their school's student strike in 1969, Sperling organized a sympathy strike down the Bay.

But it was a disastrous failure—"Almost no one has sympathy for a sympathy strike," he later rued—and Sperling was soon deposed from his union leadership role. Crushed though he was to be dethroned, he credited the experience with giving him wiles and verve. "The lesson was simple," he wrote in his memoir decades later. "Ignore your detractors and those who say that what you are doing is wrong, against regulation, or illegal."

Sperling's ouster had also freed up his schedule so he could work on other ventures. By that point, he had squirreled away a $26,000 nest egg, and he believed he had found the perfect cause for which to put it to use.

Three years after the failed sympathy strike, Sperling had been selected to run a federally funded program for police officers and schoolteachers who worked with juvenile delinquents. His assignment was to help the teachers and cops become "change agents" to reduce rates of delinquency. But he soon discovered that what his students really wanted was more education—master's degrees for the teachers, bachelor's for the cops. Because they had day jobs, traditional coursework was out of the question, and night school offerings were sparse and time-consuming. What his students needed, Sperling realized, was "a product that was equivalent in learning outcomes to traditional campus-based education, yet could be delivered at times and places and in a format that adults found desirable." He wanted to create a new kind of school within the college, where professionals could work on an accelerated track toward a degree. He began calling it the Institute for Professional Development (IPD).

Sperling brought his idea to the administration at San Jose State, but they balked. So he took his talents elsewhere. Sperling was friends with Frank Newman, the Stanford University PR official whose views had influenced the 1972 authorization of the Higher Education Act. By 1974, Newman had some advice for Sperling as well. No school in good financial condition, he told his friend, would have the motivation or will to "innovate" in the way Sperling wanted. Instead, he made a suggestion that would change American education, very much for the worse. What Sperling needed, Newman advised, was to introduce the profit motive. "Find a school in financial trouble," he counseled, "and convince the people running it that your adult education program will generate a profit."

Fortunately for Sperling, Newman knew just the school.

That spring, Newman introduced Sperling to the head of the University of San Francisco, a financially troubled Jesuit institution, and he was eager to get onboard. The following September, Sperling began running his courses—for bachelor's degrees in "public service" and master's degrees in education—out of the university. But by focusing IPD's educational offerings purely on vocational utility, Sperling soon ran afoul of the Western Association of Schools and Colleges, USF's accreditor, which apparently considered IPD a diploma mill. Because of the association's threat to pull USF's regional accreditation (and thus imperiling its access to federal aid), the university terminated IPD's contract.

So Sperling packed up and moved it to Arizona, a state, he noted, that "had never gotten around to writing any regulations." In 1976, from the ashes of IPD, his school was reborn. He called this new incarnation the University of Phoenix, a reference not only to the city in Arizona where it was headquartered but also to the mythological bird of Greek and Egyptian lore, continually resurrecting itself from within its own funeral pyre. To a large degree, this is how Sperling approached running the company. He was constantly changing, adapting, growing.

But Sperling was perfecting a profit-making formula that had been built up over centuries.

IN THE BEGINNING, AS WE ALL KNOW, THERE WAS HARVARD. WITHIN A FEW years, newcomers to the Atlantic shores had their pick of nine institutions of higher learning, including the College of William and Mary, Rutgers, and all the Ivy League schools except Cornell (a land-grant school founded in 1865). By the time of the Revolutionary War, there were about a dozen more. These schools preached a classical curriculum, aimed at raising an American political and religious elite. But even before the colonies became states, entrepreneurs saw an opportunity to educate the less worldly. "The earliest form of vocational education in colonial America was provided by the apprenticeship system," notes a 1925 history of private schooling. This remained a fine option for the enterprising farmer or artisan, but the arrival of commerce changed the game. "The successful book-keeper, and accountant, for example, had to be well-grounded in commercial arithmetic, and the various forms of book-keeping. Surveying and navigation presupposed instruction in geometry and trigonometry, as well as special courses in surveying, and navigation, geography, 'the making of Maps,' and astronomy."

Schools sprang up to educate these new would-be entrepreneurs. As early as 1709, less than a century on from Plymouth Rock, an educational pilgrim by the name of Owen Harris was advertising lessons in navigation, writing, and "Arithmetick," as well as "The Projection of the Sphaere," at his school in view of Boston Harbor, where, he avouched, he "Teaches at as easie Rates, and as speedy as may be." Others instructed merchants in the art of the quill pen, as well as "Bookkeeping after the Italian Method of Double Entry" and "the Doctrine of Curves."

The reading and writing schools of the 1700s became the business and commercial colleges of the 1800s, and they were extremely popular. By century's end there were as many as two thousand of them across the United States and Canada, with nearly a quarter million students, all told.

Many of these schools were ruthlessly competitive and overpriced, their advertisements full of puffery and false promises, and their educational offerings slim to worthless. Profiteers established franchises, committed hostile takeovers to corner the market, and even stooped to fly-by-night schemes to relieve the aspiring indigent of his American dream money. One such school, the Cleveland-based Bryant and Stratton, which offered courses in penmanship, "Commercial Arithmetic," and "Detecting of Counterfeit Bankbills at sight," proclaimed itself the "greatest educational enterprise in the world."

Present-day proprietary school apologists point to the fact that these early commercial "colleges" expanded educational access to excluded groups. And it's true, they did—offering Black students entry to medical schools and providing coeducation at a time when traditional institutions offered neither. But access alone isn't worth a whole lot. The legal and medical professions learned this lesson in the early twentieth century. The two major legal societies, the Association of American Law Schools and the American Bar Association, banded together in the 1920s to publish a list of schools that met the standards they established. Most for-profits didn't make the grade, and their enrollments plummeted. A landmark report by the physician Abraham Flexner in 1910 had gone further, declaring the profit motive simply incompatible with a quality medical education. That heralded the end of for-profit medical schools, which Flexner had found to be riddled with fraud.

The game of whack-a-mole has continued since. The early-century lull in the growth of for-profits was undone by the GI Bill, which heaped fertilizer on the stagnant industry. Then followed further reform to rein the industry back in. At the same time, the rise of new technologies and defense production needs were generating a nationwide demand for vocational training in areas like computer programming and TV repair. This spurred state governments to make substantial investments in public vocational schools and community colleges, then known as junior colleges—two-year institutions that generally focused on career-oriented training. The number of US community colleges, standing at just eight at the turn of the twentieth century, quadrupled between 1920 and 1980. By 1998, there were sixteen hundred. Their growth also put a strain on the for-profit industry, which struggled to compete.

With for-profits' GI Bill excesses still sharply in focus, Congress was careful to tailor subsequent midcentury student aid bills to exclude proprietary institutions. The NDEA's loan program, for instance, explicitly defined an "institution of higher education" as either a public or non-profit entity. The NDEA also expanded a 1946 act funding vocational programs, but these again were designated for "courses conducted under public supervision and control." And for all the talk of student choice as the driver of the Higher Education Act, students were not allowed to take their new Title IV government-guaranteed loans and grants to for-profit schools. But perhaps that was just for show, because the industry had in fact already found a way back in.

ON A FRIDAY NIGHT IN 1965, JUST A COUPLE OF WEEKS BEFORE HE SIGNED the Higher Education Act at his alma mater, President Johnson quietly enacted a number of much less conspicuous bills in the East Room of the White House. Tucked into the schedule and virtually unheralded was the National Vocational Student Loan Insurance Act, passed after much lobbying by for-profit proprietors. Its terms were identical to those of the Higher Education Act, except that it included accredited for-profit schools. "Fewer than half of our young people go to college," said Johnson in his short introductory remarks on the bill. "The quality of life in our country—and the strength of our economy—cannot depend solely upon this minority." The vocational loan bill, he said, would encourage "capable young people who need training to become useful and productive citizens."

By funding loans for vocational training under a banner separate from the Higher Education Act, Congress could theoretically keep better track of where the money was going and turn off the spigot entirely if need be. But just three years later, legislators axed the vocational loan bill and extended the privileges of the Higher Education Act to for-profit vocational schools as well. For-profits were now eligible for *all* Title IV funds, including loans and, after 1972, Pell Grant monies. This virtually unrestrained revenue stream touched off a novel period of explosive growth for the sector.

In fact, when Sperling opened the University of Phoenix for business in 1976, he was already somewhat late to the game. By 1975, for-profit enrollment was up by 112 percent, 80 percent above higher education overall. For-profit cheerleaders, buoyed by the support, started to get boastful: "Public educators think of a school as a pile of bricks and mortar, a piece of real estate," said a vocational-schools accreditor in 1975. "The proprietaries start at the other end of the chain—what do the students want and how can I provide it for them?" John Sperling made the self-congratulatory claim that "being for-profit removed the siren song of soft money, it forced upon us the discipline of the market, and it left us no alternative but to produce a service for which customers were willing to pay a price high enough to sustain a going concern."

This was not exactly accurate—in fact the reverse was mostly true. Critics had already begun sounding the alarm about the near-total reliance of for-profits on the federal aid program, noting the industry's penchant for "sophisticated advertising and unfulfillable promises." In the November 1973 issue of *Washington Monthly*, reporter Sylvia Kronstadt warned, "A new breed of proprietary school has evolved—schools at which nearly every student, and thus the school itself, is dependent upon government aid." In the three previous years, Kronstadt reported, correspondence schools—in which students complete their coursework through the mail—had increased their federal loan volume by 2,000 percent.

And while the University of Phoenix aimed to disrupt the traditional model of education by providing bachelor's degrees in a fraction of the time, most proprietary schools were focused instead on short-course certificates in electronics, auto repair, or other skilled labor fields. At this moment the American economy was in crisis and rapidly shifting away from its agrarian and industrial past. For-profit schools took advantage of Americans' mounting anxieties about advancing technologies that threatened to put them out of a job. As the students of the 1970s leaned in to their role as market actors, they presented themselves as especially easy marks for entities seeking to exploit the changing landscape of work. By explicitly opening the federal-aid door to proprietary schools in 1965, and then more fully in 1972, Congress had allowed market logic—that extractive and opportunistic force—to permeate higher education. A new entry point had appeared for the unprincipled.

By 1970, about a thousand "computer schools" were offering courses in programming and data processing. Even giant corporations were getting in on the action, launching their own technical school franchises. Among them was International Telephone and Telegraph, which spun off ITT Educational Services (later rebranded ITT Tech) in 1968. Regardless of their proprietors, most of the new technical and computer schools were in it primarily for the student aid booty. One federal official estimated that three-quarters of the schools were either functionally worthless or downright frauds. "Computer schools," lamented a Massachusetts consumer protection watchdog, "have become the latest version of the old shell game."

"Because the government turned on the money without watching where it was going," wrote Kronstadt, "roving packs of charlatans and con men moved in to fill the gaps in the educational system. Not only are these hustlers tolerated as they grow fat at their victims' expense, but they are actually abetted by government policy. The secret of their success is the knowledge that the federal government will bail them out when they need help, serving as the collection agency of last resort."

One of those charlatans was a man by the name of Fred Braneff, who rode a meteoric rise to the top of a California diploma-mill empire known as West Coast Schools, then brought it crashing down just as quickly, taking thousands of students and a sixteen-term US congressman with him.

Braneff had begun working at West Coast Schools, a chain of computer schools based in Southern California, as a job counselor in 1970, and the company's CEO was so hypnotized by his charm and charisma that in little more than a year he appointed Braneff president. Unfortunately for everyone involved, Braneff—who went by the pseudonym Fred Peters—was a known scam artist.

"He talked a beautiful game as to helping his fellow man, helping the downtrodden, helping the minority groups," one of Braneff's employees later testified to the Senate. "But it was strictly for money." Braneff was very pleased that the school's student body was primarily Black and Hispanic, his wife recounted, "because that is where the gravy was." Braneff wasn't the only one. Between 1976 and 1990, the share of minorities in proprietary career schools nearly doubled, to 25 percent of enrollment.

One of Braneff's victims was a married father of four named Enrique Ponce. In 1972, Ponce decided to look into an electronics school he'd seen advertised on TV. Having dropped out of school in the eighth grade, Ponce hadn't been able to advance beyond a career in manual labor. The admissions officer at the West Coast Schools branch near his home in a working-class suburb of Los Angeles gave him a simple test and persuaded him to enroll in a TV repair course for $1,280. "She told me that I could obtain a federally guaranteed loan for the cost of the course," Ponce testified at a 1975 Senate hearing, "which I would not have to begin repaying until nine months after I finished the program." He'd even get some money back on the $1,500 loan he was taking out.

The extra money never came, but Ponce started the program anyway. But "the subject matter was highly technical, involving ohms and volts and wiring schematics," he said, and the classes were held at night. After working a full day on a job site, Ponce struggled to follow three-hour lectures on electronics delivered in a rundown old garage. (Another student at the school testified that he thought his instructor was drunk.) After ten exhausting days, Ponce threw in the towel. He came to an arrangement with the school to pay back $50.49, the amount he owed for his time in class, and assumed the rest of his loan would be canceled.

But three years later, in 1975, Ponce started getting letters from the Office of Education. "Unless you make these arrangements promptly, your loan will be assigned to the United States of America for collection," they read. "Protect your credit reputation and contact your lender immediately." Unable to pay the bills, he simply ignored them. But he remained worried that any day, federal agents would come knocking at his door.

He was right to be concerned. As the hearings continued, Office of Education employees revealed that their workplace had essentially placed a target on the backs of student debtors.

As proprietary schools got in on the student aid grift, their students' loan default rates started going through the roof, hovering between 25 and 35 percent through the 1970s. By contrast, those at nonprofit and public four-year institutions never topped 20 percent. At that point, estimates placed proprietary schools as the recipients of about a quarter of all student loans—yet they generated roughly half of the defaults. In

1972 alone, the reporter Sylvia Kronstadt revealed, Congress had spent
$12.8 million to cover losses on defaulted loans and hired fifty-eight
collection officers to go after deadbeat borrowers. Just a year after the
1972 amendments, Senator Pell noted a startling rise in loan defaults
by students of proprietary schools, which were at $55.2 million, an
amount, he said, of "epidemic proportions." He urged Commissioner of
Education John Ottina and his fellow members of Congress to take action. As it happens, the Office of Education took his words to heart—a
bit too sincerely.

Instead of cracking down on proprietary schools or limiting their
funding streams, the Office of Education planned to direct its habitually
scant resources toward hiring two hundred more collection agents. And
if a school went bankrupt or committed fraud? That was of no consequence. "We can't be held responsible for what the salesman said or how
good the course is," said Jeffery Rathensburger, an Office of Education
official, in 1973. "Our obligation to the taxpayer is to collect in full on
every loan." The office was dead set on making its lenders whole, even if
it meant sending students to the poorhouse—and then following them
there. "The only way you can get out of it," said Rathensburger, "is to
die."

"Default rates soared. And what did the Office of Education do?"
testified an official from the Texas attorney general's office at the 1975
Senate hearing. "It compounded its initial error—of failing to enact regu-
lator safeguards—by escalating its collection efforts toward the victims of
its own negligence, while at the same time ignoring nearly altogether the
real source of mounting defaults, the unscrupulous proprietary school
owner. The natural result," he added, was that a borrower "in a very real
sense became victimized twice: first at the hands of a promoter masquer-
ading as an educator, and then at the hands of her own government."
Even the American Bankers Association called the problems students
faced in the program "quite disturbing."

The Texas official was part of an investigation of a Dallas regional
outpost of the Office of Education, where seven employees had been
fired earlier that year for, among other things, impersonating cops and

illegally threatening to take away delinquent borrowers' houses and cars, or throw them into jail. These were full-time federal employees, most of them hired away from private collection agencies, where the tactics were ruthless. Over tear-filled phone calls with defrauded proprietary school enrollees, these self-identified "US marshals" were known to browbeat and threaten borrowers, shouting warnings like "You better get your kids off the streets." The scandal ended only when actual US marshals came to shut down the office. "Of course we knew what the hell was going on with a lot of these schools," testified one former collector from the Dallas office. "But my job was to collect money, period."

Some critics in Congress suggested that such stunning problems had revealed the student loan experiment to be faulty, and they recommended doing a clean sweep and replacing all the loans with grants.

But the Department of Health, Education, and Welfare demurred. "We can't throw out the baby with the bathwater," said its lead investigator. From the enactment of the Higher Education Act, Congress had identified one of the bill's priorities as promoting state guaranty agencies, to relieve the federal government of its burden in insuring the debts. In the years since, the push had worked. By 1975, twenty-six states had their own agencies. Perhaps to avoid getting ensnared in other embarrassing collection scandals, the Office of Education began relying more heavily on these agencies, which served as intermediaries in cases of default. As a result, the guaranteed loan program took on a more stable, three-legged structure: banks made the loans, the federal government guaranteed those loans, and state guaranty agencies ensured that the other two legs were made whole. Then, if students failed to pay, the government could send its hired guns after them and wipe its hands clean. At this point, the end goal of the loan program—ostensibly to provide opportunity for students—had been suborned to the appearance of government efficiency and fiscal responsibility, especially where for-profit schools were concerned. "The government and the proprietary schools," said one Texas attorney, "have never cared much about the problems of the students themselves."

As for Fred Braneff, he wasn't just bilking the poor and downtrodden.

He was also stealing from the federal purse and bribing members of Congress and federal officials to ensure continued access to the student aid gravy train. In 1971, Braneff started paying off a sixteen-term US congressman by the name of Dan Flood, who sat on the powerful House Appropriations Committee. In exchange, Flood procured temporary access to student aid as West Coast Schools sought accreditation, a status that would ensure a permanent flow of funds. Flood resigned in 1980 after this and other payoffs were made public, following investigations into the federal loan program.

Sure to cover his bases, Braneff also entered into an agreement with an official in the Department of Health, Education, and Welfare: in exchange for favorable attention and inside information, the official would get $1,000 a month and a 60–40 split on money the school made off his tips.

But then Braneff got really reckless.

On June 11, 1973, he and two of his associates walked into a bank branch in Phoenix. Opening a large briefcase, they asked the teller if he wouldn't mind converting its contents—some $280,000 (the equivalent of nearly $2 million today) in $100 bills—into cashier's checks. Finding this request highly irregular, the bank manager excused himself to the back office. He made some phone calls to determine if the bills were legit. To his surprise, it all checked out, so he did as he was asked.

Unfortunately for Braneff, however, a Los Angeles radio reporter by the name of Gene Ferguson had caught wind of this strange activity while reporting on a dispute between West Coast Schools and one of its clients, a lender it had burned. The whole thing was so redolent of fraud that Ferguson decided to report it to the San Francisco office of the Department of Health, Education, and Welfare. Although the feds affected surprise, in recent weeks the department's office had also received a letter from a private auditor for West Coast's accounting firm. Company employees, the auditor reported, were claiming that $425,000 in federal student loan money had recently been diverted into executives' personal bank accounts. The auditor was stunned, but he was unable to get anyone at Health, Education, and Welfare to return his phone calls.

The officials in San Francisco, on the other hand, were moved to act by the information they received from Ferguson. Finally, they avowed, they were ready to perform their own audit of West Coast Schools.

But they were too late. The school had closed its doors on May 24, 1973, having apparently run out of funds in the four weeks since it had finally lost its years-long bid for accreditation, and with that, access to federal monies. When it folded, it still had $6 million in federal loans outstanding, and as of January 1974, it was still billing the federal government for interest subsidies on those loans—which the Department of Health, Education, and Welfare had continued to pay.

But the West Coast Schools debacle was, if scandalous, not particularly exceptional. In fact, it turned out to be just the very colorful tip of an iceberg that ran as deep as the pile of promissory notes strewn about the floor of the Office of Education.

IT WAS PERHAPS NO COINCIDENCE THAT THE GUARANTEED LOAN PROGRAM was set up as a three-cornered hat. The Department of Education loves threes: it's a number large enough to ensure that the federal government is not seen as solely responsible for a program or its failures, but small enough that at least somebody (one hopes) knows what is actually going on. Or perhaps it's because it allows the department to turn a blind eye to abuses by third-party opportunists (like state collection agencies) while tacitly endorsing their predatory actions.

In higher education circles, there's a particular setup that bears a term with an almost occult feel: the Triad. To be sure, there's an obscure power to the union of federal, state, and independent regulatory agencies that turns the gears of American higher education. The first in the threesome is the Department of Education, which determines who gets the cash. The second is state education agencies, which are tasked with licensing schools to operate within their borders and enforcing state consumer protection standards. And there is a third, more wriggly entity—accreditation agencies.

Accreditation began at the end of the nineteenth century as a way to standardize curricula and requirements for student admissions and transfer credits. Accreditation agencies were voluntary, peer-based membership organizations for colleges and universities. In other countries, state ministries of education performed this function, so accrediting bodies were a uniquely American upstart. But the general American squeamishness about involving the federal government in education policy meant that we never developed a robust oversight mechanism. During the era of the GI Bill, states were required to vet and keep lists of qualifying institutions, but "it was common knowledge among school operators that it was customary to pay inspectors and give them gifts," noted a 1951 Senate investigation. Among the offers tendered to one inspector were porch furniture, a meat block, ham, and liquor.

In 1952, as the Korean War dragged toward a close, legislators passed a new veterans' aid package that made some amendments to the original GI Bill. In an attempt to avoid a repeat of the proprietary schools' scandal of the 1940s, this new legislation conditioned a school's eligibility on accreditation by an agency approved by the federal government. The Office of Education, wary as ever of getting its hands too deep into the muck of state politics, did not *itself* accredit the schools its grants funded, but it did agree to maintain a list of accrediting agencies it recognized to do the job for it. To receive funds, a school had to be approved by its state and accredited by one of these twenty-eight approved organizations.

This byzantine arrangement found its way into the student aid legislation that followed in later decades. But Congress continued to leave the details up to states and accreditors, even as the number and complexity of US institutions ballooned. And that left quite a lot of room for new accrediting agencies, formed by for-profit administrators with no substantive experience in education, to pop up without any real quality-control mechanism to vet them. Some states, like California, had relatively strict standards in place. Others, like Arizona, did not. One major regional agency, quipped an education scholar, would reputedly "accredit a ham sandwich"—and "with cheese it could grant a master's degree."

The overarching problem was that nowhere in the Triad's structure was there any real place to mitigate the incentive to make money off students—in whatever way possible. The Triad's hands-off approach to accreditation and licensing sent the message that the federal government was not committed to protecting students. And that message sang like a siren calling out to opportunists to get in on the bonanza.

"A pile of money, like a pile of compost," said Dr. Harold Orlans, "can nourish a lot of worms." This was 1974, and Orlans, a longtime researcher at the National Academy of Public Administration, was addressing the House during an investigation of proprietary-school accreditation. He called the reliance on third-party accreditors an "abdication" by government. Even many accreditors agreed, practically begging the Department of Health, Education, and Welfare to take the reins for adjudicating educational quality. The department resisted, insisting that education remain a subject of "local control."

While the Triad had been established to create overlapping checks on school quality and stability, its components were clearly falling down on the job. For instance, state licensing requirements were often extremely lax, in some cases requiring only a nominal fee. Many accreditors would then rubber-stamp a school once it was licensed. So, in spite of all this regulation, a school could sink a tap into the gushing pipeline of federal aid merely by paying a small fee. By 1972, there were already two thousand proprietary schools that qualified for student loan funds.

Articles soon splashed across the pages of major newspapers, detailing the ways unethical schools manipulated the system to cheat students out of their federal money. "Consumers may predictably assume that all accredited profit-seeking schools will treat them fair and square," wrote the *Washington Post*'s Eric Wentworth. But that was unfortunately not the case. "For thousands," Wentworth concluded, "accreditation has spelled deception."

In response, the federal government was remarkably slow to act on the problem. In 1974, two years after amendments to the Higher Education Act gave the Office of Education the authority to suspend or revoke a school's loan eligibility, the office still hadn't published regulations detailing how it would go about doing so. And although the office also had the power to revoke an accreditor's recognition, it had never actually done so. The for-profits were, like dogs off a leash, mostly free to do whatever they wanted.

"Some recruiters," noted Orlans, "have gone systematically through housing projects, slum high schools, and military bases—stirring the hope of simple and gullible people for glamorous jobs they will never get. Some proprietors are modern snake-oil salesmen, who, cornered by the law, decamp to another State and hawk their oil again. Others are smooth corporate men who tack carefully around every law and regulation, which they know better than the Ten Commandments."

Orlans might as well have been describing Fred Braneff, with his predatory focus on minorities and the poor, or John Sperling, who had sought a more welcoming environment in Arizona. What made one a success and the other a failure was that Sperling, unlike Braneff, had been savvy enough to play the Triad to his advantage: moving not merely his money but his whole operation into the loosely regulated confines of the Grand Canyon State. As a result, one of these men wound up in prison, and the other built a billion-dollar stock-market darling.

Another, more profound, problem with the Triad was that, by subcontracting regulatory enforcement out to third parties, it attenuated the link between government and the citizens it was supposed to represent. Instead of taking direct charge of accreditation standards for the schools that benefited from federal money or investing more heavily in community college and vocational-training programs, the federal government abandoned young people to exploitive, overpriced private alternatives. In the process, it turned students from constituents into customers. Government began to take on a marketized, businesslike mien, which was reflected in its rhetoric and actions. Now debtors were akin to securities. Their role was to juice the loan program's value for the mythical taxpayer—as the nation's shareholder, he was now paramount.

At this time consumerism itself became the primary currency through which citizens could effect change. In 1965, Ralph Nader had written a book about auto safety called *Unsafe at Any Speed*. Its impact was explosive. A whole cadre of consumer protection advocates formed around him. They called themselves "Nader's Raiders." By the early 1970s, Nader and his posse were celebrities of consumer do-gooderism. In response to their gnatting, in 1972 the Nixon administration grudgingly formed the Consumer Product Safety Commission—which became responsible for regulatory action such as recalls of unsafe cribs and toys.

Without the power or resources to crack down on bad actors and reform the system themselves, consumer advocates often resorted to disseminating information—correcting falsehoods and creating consumer guides. As federal officials finally began to address the scourge of fraudulent proprietary schools in the 1970s, they took a cue from this movement. Lawmakers and officials insisted that student consumers, armed with information, would be able to choose the market product best suited to them.

But shopping for education is not like shopping for a crib or a car. It is characterized by what economists call *information asymmetry*. Students have no foolproof way of judging the quality of the product from the outside: only those within the field, experts and professionals, can adequately assess the quality of a particular school or program. By abdicating its role in this process, the federal government weakened the value of its own touted method of quality control. Assessments of schools were subcontracted through corruptible third-party accreditors, who were liable to be in cahoots with the proprietors they were supposed to be regulating.

In relegating education to the market, legislators thus combined the worst of both worlds: they paired a privatized, profit-seeking education model given virtually no regulatory oversight with a government mode of debt financing backstopped by unrivaled federal enforcement mechanisms. Fundamentally, in education as in other realms of commerce, the American government chose business over people: it renounced its role of protecting citizens and providing for their general welfare. This, more than almost any other policy action, ensured that students would be exploited and driven into debt in the years to come. Yet fraudulent schools, accreditors, and even federal officials were essentially given a pass when revealed to be bilking millions from students and taxpayers; student debtors, by contrast, found no sympathy.

In 1973, the Federal Trade Commission (FTC) launched a campaign to rid the country of what one California member of Congress called the national "curse" of fraudulent trade schools. To do so, the agency would run an ad campaign. The commission dedicated 6 percent of its budget that year to distributing nearly 100,000 copies of a consumer education booklet, placing bus ads in thirty-two cities across the nation, and running national TV spots featuring such celebrities as Della Reese and Raymond Burr.

As a secondary action, the FTC also began filing complaints against malicious schools. So, asked Washington state representative Joel Pritchard, was the campaign working? Was anyone in jail because of it? The response was not encouraging. "I do not happen to know whether anybody is in jail," answered Joan Bernstein, a representative of the agency's Consumer Protection Division. "I bet they are running correspondence courses out of the jails if they are."

SAM NUNN, A CONSERVATIVE GEORGIA DEMOCRAT, WAS IN 1975 A JUNIOR member of the Senate's powerful Investigations Subcommittee. As he and his colleagues undertook an investigation into the Guaranteed Student Loan Program (GSLP) on the occasion of its tenth anniversary, the young senator emerged as a sharp and outspoken critic of the program's failings. Frustration and fury oozed from his commentary at the Senate hearings, which had revealed a stunning amount of dysfunction at the Department of Health, Education, and Welfare.

Along with the out-and-out fraud, witnesses testified that loan records were kept loose on top of filing cabinets, windowsills, and even the floor, and were, unsurprisingly, often lost. A sampling of claims on default payments to banks found that 10 percent of the files were missing their master promissory note, so there was no way to determine if the loan—which the government might already have paid off—was even valid. Perhaps more troubling, the whole department seemed to harbor an unwillingness to admit that anyone involved in education might be in it for less-than-humanitarian reasons. It had no program to audit monies going to institutions and instead relied on "faith in the integrity of the schools." As late as 1973, in this 130,000-employee agency with a budget bigger than the Defense Department's, there was only one fraud investigator for the entire student aid program—which distributed more than $1 billion a year. The Department of Health, Education, and Welfare didn't know what schools did with the money, or when or whether students withdrew from their courses; it didn't even have a record of how much it had paid for each of its programs.

"A good many officials feel that the program should be operated on the basis of trust and faith," said a congressional investigator for the committee. Additionally, he said, these officials felt "that the people in the education field should not be subjected to criminal penalties or restrictions or rules and regulations which are enforced." As a result, the department stood to lose about 14 percent of its student loan portfolio to default just in the following year. Senator Nunn was enraged. "If the Government loses $1 billion because of this program," he thundered back, "it can only be described as bureaucratic bungling at its worst."

But instead of imposing meaningful statutory reforms on proprietary schools, or appropriating more money to staff up the Office of Education, Nunn's colleagues again took cues from the consumer protection movement. They inserted into the 1976 amendments of the Higher Education Act a requirement that schools provide information on costs and refund policies, the job market, and student retention rates. "Students will make comparisons," said the chairman of the newly established National Task Force on Better Information for Student Choice. "Where there's a glaring lack of responsiveness in providing information, students will be discouraged from attending that school." In other words, instead of directly taking aim at bad actors, the senators opted to grease the wheels of the free market and trust it to do their work for them.

To the student victims caught in the crosshairs, on the other hand,

Congress showed no mercy. After promising to chase deadbeat debtors to the grave, the government decided to go a step further and eliminate the one option left to those who could not pay—filing for bankruptcy.

Even though a General Accounting Office study indicated that only 1 percent of federal loan borrowers wound up in bankruptcy, amounting to just 5 percent of the overall losses in the student loan program, the secretary of Health, Education, and Welfare, Caspar Weinberger, called this a "substantial loophole," and Congress apparently agreed, or perhaps merely viewed going after delinquent students as easier than taking on trade schools. The 1976 amendments to the Higher Education Act included the caveat that students wait five years after graduation before they could seek to have their student loans discharged in bankruptcy. It seemed like a minor tinker in the scheme of things, but it was a harbinger of much worse to come.

For the time being, however, this satisfied the critics. By the end of the decade, thanks to "more effective management of the program," said a preening Weinberger, proprietary default rates were back in the low twenties, and overall default rates were down from their high of 13 percent in 1977 to a much more palatable 8 percent.

The good news didn't last long.

In 1981, Ronald Reagan moved into the White House, bringing with him a penchant for slashing domestic spending. Reagan extended the debt-financing of education into previously unimagined realms, transforming students into flashing neon dollar signs beckoning to institutions—both legitimate and fraudulent—that were desperate for cash.

CHAPTER 6

The Reagan Regression

David Stockman was still something of a hayseed when he rounded the corner of the ornate marble-checkerboard hallway in the Old Executive Office Building and pulled open the mahogany doors to room 252. The sheer size of his new workspace, which he compared to a school gymnasium back in his rural Michigan, left Reagan's thirty-four-year-old budget "whiz kid" agape. Previously a two-term backbencher in the House of Representatives, the new director of the Office of Management and Budget (OMB) now presided over an agency of more than six hundred employees and an annual federal spending program of half a trillion dollars.

Against all odds, Ronald Reagan, the Plasticine, smooth-talking governor from California, had bested a pack of hidebound Republican establishmentarians to defeat the incumbent Democrat and win the presidency. In 1980 the electorate booted Carter for failing to tame the twin headwinds of inflation and low productivity, and now Reagan—with Stockman at his side—intended to reverse the tide. Setting price controls hadn't worked, fiddling with the money supply hadn't worked, honestly nothing had worked—and by January 1981 unemployment was up to 7.5 percent and the prime interest rate was over 21 percent. What was a dyed-in-the-wool conservative budget wonk to do?

Reagan had wooed the electorate with a political hat trick of absurd dimensions. Defying the basic principles of even the newest math, he had promised to cut taxes, increase defense spending, *and* eliminate deficits. There was no arithmetic in the world that could make his numbers add up, but the rabid adherents of a newfound economic theory known as "supply side" insisted that the circle could be squared. With an across-the-board 30 percent tax cut on personal income, they argued, Americans would be incentivized to work and invest, and their increased productivity would flow magically back to the Treasury vaults. They had gotten Stockman in at the OMB as their man on the inside to keep the administration in line. It was a genuine coup.

But when Stockman fed Reagan's numbers into the OMB's computer system, it spat out dire predictions. Gobsmacking annual deficits of $100 billion or more would be de rigueur by the middle of Reagan's first term. Stockman knew this would make it impossible to sell Reagan's economic program to the public—or, at a minimum, to the Republican Party. So, to make Reaganomics compute, Stockman simply revised the computer model, changing its baseline assumptions about inflation and productivity until he got the outputs the president wanted.

Stockman had convincingly dressed himself in the garb of the supply siders to get into this room, but now that he was here, he shed his woolens. Unbeknownst to his benefactors, Stockman had retreated to more classically conservative economic principles—namely, a bottom-to-middle dismantling of the American social safety net. What America needed, he decided, was to cut its fat, and everywhere he looked he saw fat. As far as he was concerned, the whole postwar welfare state was a "coast-to-coast soup line," a shameful transfer of "productive private investment to wasteful public sector expenditures."

Reagan's new wonk was ruthless. Former mentors and friends began to question whether he had any sense of compassion at all. "White House aides, the joke goes," relayed one *Washington Post* columnist, "huddle around his heart during summers to keep cool." Like a McKinsey consultant on a layoff spree, Stockman spared no corner in his slash-and-burn cost-cutting orgy.

Well, almost no corner. There was, unfortunately, the matter of defense. To Stockman's dismay, Reagan had left a huge carve-out in his fiscal conservative bona fides. The Gipper was delighted with Stockman's plan to cut social services to the bone, but he was unrelenting on defense: he insisted on enhancing military funding to levels that made even the generals blush. To make America mighty again, he asked for an extra $100 billion over his first term, a defense budget increase of more than 25 percent, to Vietnam War levels. By 1985, the cumulative bill for Reagan's proposed defense spending would come to $6,000 (about $20,000 today) out of the pocket of every American citizen.

The budget simply could not bear it.

Stockman worked prodigiously to fill the hole, and by February, he had presented the president with a whopping $64 billion in spending cuts. Yet no matter how much he chipped away at Medicaid, food stamps, or school-lunch subsidies, he remained $44 billion short of a balanced budget. But no worries, he had a solution for that too: a kind of fantasy math that involved siphoning off unhelpful data and insisting its impact would be resolved, somehow, at some indeterminate point in the future. Republicans started calling it the "magic asterisk."

"The idea that's been established over the last ten years," Stockman said in defense of his asperity, "that almost every service that someone might need in life ought to be provided, financed by government as a matter of basic right, is wrong. We challenge that. We reject that notion."

In the final tally, Reagan's first budget, passed with vigorous Democratic approval in August 1981, cut federal spending by more than $35 billion. On the chopping block were public housing programs, free school lunches for poor children, and of course welfare—all the social services that actually aided Americans.

Defense spending had, naturally, been spared the ax. It jumped up 50 percent over two years. Corporations benefited handsomely as well, from the massive tax cuts that trailed on the new president's heels. The poor received fewer benefits, and the wealthy even more. Their prosperity did not trickle down—poverty levels increased during the Reagan years to heights not seen since 1965. By the end of Reagan's presidency, 3.2 million Americans had dipped below the poverty line, and income inequality reached its highest level in four decades. If Johnson had been the general in the War on Poverty, Reagan was the Benedict Arnold fighting for the other side, and in the 1980s the turncoat won. As one critic put it, Reagan "pulled the revenue plug on the federal government."

Education was by no means an exception. In fact, just as he had done in California, Reagan seemed to want to make an example of it. Among his most adamant campaign promises was a vow to shutter the Department of Education—which Carter had given cabinet status only the year before—and more or less eliminate aid to students in higher education. So it was no surprise when student aid made it into the Stockman shredder's first round. Like his boss, the budget master harbored no sympathy for American students. Reagan had promised to maintain a bare-bones social safety net to cover the "truly needy," and as far as Stockman was concerned, most college students did not make the cut.

When Reagan had presented Stockman's first budget to Congress that February, he'd proposed cutting student aid by $1 billion, a 20 percent reduction. But the pain was not spread equally around. It was much easier, both procedurally and politically, to cut from Pell Grants: as a discretionary spending item, they appeared to Stockman as a giant glowing target. And they helped the children of the poor, that group most despised by the administration, and who generally lacked organized advocates in Washington. The Congressional Budget Office estimated that the Reagan 1981 budget proposal would cut $725 million from the grants and require all but the most destitute recipients to cough up a $750 "self-help" contribution. In 1982, Stockman went even further. That year's budget request slashed Pell Grants by 40 percent.

Student loans could not be so easily dispensed with. Not only was the loan program politically "inexpensive," but unlike Pell, it was not discretionary: it was guaranteed for anyone deemed eligible. But Stockman found a way to squeeze some blood out of the stone, by reducing eligibility for middle-class families. After all, Stockman asked, "Why should some steelworker pay taxes to help his plant manager send his kid to a private school out of state?"

And then, as if on cue, came a scare-mongering bogeyman: the student welfare queen. "If any of your children are in college," began a 1980 investment column in *House & Garden* magazine, "you would be wise to have them take out a federally guaranteed student loan." Parents of means, the author suggested, were sleeping on a "once-in-a-lifetime opportunity" to turn "a substantial profit" by depositing their children's student loans into high-interest investments. Although the article provided no evidence that anyone was in fact gaming the system in this way, it was soon cited in Congress, and the profiteering student loan borrower became the avatar of a loan program that had spun out of control and desperately needed tightening up.

Reagan exploited the notion of the unscrupulous and unimpoverished borrower to get his requested $1 billion in student aid cuts. He reversed the benefits that Carter had signed into law in 1978 under the Middle Income Student Assistance Act, subjecting middle-class students once again to a needs test before giving them loans. Up to a million students, most of them at public universities and from families making between $30,000 and $45,000 a year, were to be cut off from the loan program.

Reagan went after poor students as well. After much negotiation, he succeeded in effectively reducing spending on the Pell Grant by $500 million, first by cutting the maximum grant award by nearly 18 percent, when adjusted for inflation. He also decreased maximum income limits, which had the effect of throwing a quarter of a million students off the rolls. By 1985, the number of eligible freshmen was down by half.

In another perverse turn, Reagan explicitly favored upper-middle-class private school students over poor public-university matriculants: the new rules on subsidized-loan eligibility took into account "demonstrated need" as demonstrated, in part, by the cost of the institution. So while most public college students coming from households with incomes above $30,000 were cut off, some students from households making more than $100,000 would still qualify for subsidized loan money—if they went to super-expensive private schools. "People who pay three times the cost of a public university to go to Harvard will still get the same proportional benefits as those who opt for a less-expensive institution," said Reagan's director of financial assistance programs. He meant it as a feature, not a bug.

Stockman's budget cuts took effect on October 1, 1981. That day, the House Budget Committee invited him to testify. "I do not accept the notion that the Federal Government has an obligation to fund generous grants to anybody that wants to go to college," he told the members of Congress. "It seems to me that if people want to go to college bad enough, then there is opportunity and responsibility on their part to finance their way through the best they can." Ironically, Stockman had himself just paid off an interest-free student loan made to him by a church group thirteen years earlier—and only after the *Boston Globe* made the loan public knowledge by publishing an article on it.

In the end, total federal aid to students dropped by $2 billion in the two years after Stockman started cutting, a 21 percent decline after inflation. Over Reagan's first full fiscal year as president, the deficit hit $111 billion, almost two and a half times higher than the administration had predicted. It was the largest ever recorded. Yet the Reagan administration would never again produce a deficit so small.

The Reaganomics phantasm of growth and investment ended up delivering something quite different: a deep recession that brought the highest unemployment rate since the Great Depression, casting 4 million more Americans onto the dole by the end of 1982. Reagan then did an abrupt about-face. After effecting the largest tax cut in history, he swiveled to the largest tax hike, similarly required, he argued, to increase productivity and grow the economy. But what he did not change was his position on cuts to government programs.

IT WAS NO ACCIDENT THAT RONALD REAGAN TOOK AIM AT HIGHER EDUCATION. Not only did Reagan's beef with students go back nearly two decades; the aging actor had also come into the executive branch on the heels of a decade-long coordinated campaign of Republican intellectual resurgence. In 1971, a lawyer named Lewis Powell wrote a "confidential" memo for the US Chamber of Commerce, urging an immediate broadside offensive to counteract what he called "the assault on the enterprise system" by "Communists, New Leftists, and other revolutionaries," to say nothing of tenured intellectuals and the literati. It was time for a change. The downtrodden American business executive, whom Powell called the "forgotten man" of American politics, should unite with his brethren, just as Ralph Nader had united American consumers. "The time has come," Powell wrote, "for the wisdom, ingenuity, and resources of American business to be marshaled against those who would destroy it."

Among the gravest threats Powell identified was the American university, which was resolutely liberal and traditionally set the terms of American intellectual discourse. To counter this malign influence, Powell, who would soon find a seat on the bench of the Supreme Court, recommended cultivating a whole shadow class of conservative intellectuals, who would then be fed to the media, government, the courts, and graduate schools of business, to push a pro-market curriculum. These presumed thinkers would be gathered and nourished not at the university but at the conservative think tank.

Powell's memo did not stay confidential for long, and corporate bigwigs quickly heralded it as the master plan to achieve conservative dominance. In its wake, Pennsylvania Avenue started sprouting right-leaning think tanks as fast as the wind could carry their benefactors' tax-deductible seed money. The oil-rich Koch brothers donated their excess millions to the libertarian Cato Institute, Joseph Coors (of beer fame) gave generously of his to a new outfit called the Heritage Foundation, and the billionaire oil-and-banking heir Richard Mellon Scaife spread his money around, using several millions to reinvigorate the decades-old American Enterprise Institute. The think tanks' "scholars" produced rah-rah reports on the wonders of capitalism, then fed them onto a shiny new conveyor belt of conservative media outlets such as the *National Review*, the *Public Interest*, *Commentary*, and the *American Spectator*, to say nothing of the hundreds of credulous national and local newspapers to which they hand-delivered their contrarian findings.

Suddenly, conservatism was deemed, if not cool, at least respectable again.

It was in this heady atmosphere that Reagan had taken the reins of the Republican Party, and he entered the White House with *Mandate for Leadership*, a three-thousand-page blueprint for his first term, in his presidential knapsack. It had been produced by the resident fellows of the Heritage Foundation, the hops-funded intellectual repository with just seven years to its name. The Reagan administration adhered to it as if it were a shooting script.

Legislators had mostly capitulated to Stockman's butchery in 1981, overwhelmed by the sheer scope and complexity of the budget transformation, which had been rammed through Congress at a speed that left little time for reflection. But by the following year the politicians had wised up. The budget director's mystique dissolved overnight in December 1981, when the *Atlantic* published a loose-lipped profile of him in which he revealed that he had basically no faith in his own economic policy. "None of us really understands what's going on with all these numbers," he admitted. Even worse, Reagan's much-vaunted across-the-board supply-side tax cut, Stockman said, was in fact merely a "Trojan horse" to reduce top tax rates for the wealthy. AKA: trickle-down, the old liberal whipping boy.

Slashed by his own scythe, Stockman found that his influence was waning. In a rare spirit of bipartisan defiance, Congress began to rebuff Reagan's requests for massive budget cuts.

But Reagan remained undeterred.

In all but one annual budget proposal of his two terms, Reagan requested massive cuts to education funding.* Year after year he demanded the total elimination of programs like the Pell Grant, work-study, and in-school interest subsidies. In 1983, Reagan requested cuts to student aid of more than $1.75 billion—amounting to a 50 percent reduction overall. In 1988, he requested a 26 percent cut in spending on domestic programs. Education represented 20 percent of the total to be shaved off, even though education spending took up only 2 percent of the overall budget. Over two terms, wrote a pair of education scholars in 1988, Reagan had "chipped away unrelentingly at federal aid to education."

Congress may have been uncooperative, but they were not immune to the siren song of deficit reduction. Although they refused to cut as

---

* Although his 1984 budget proposal held funding mostly steady, this too represented a cut, relative to inflation.

far as the president desired, legislators usually insisted merely on maintaining funding levels without taking account of inflation, which was at 10 percent in Reagan's first year in office and dropped below 3 percent only once, in 1986. And while Reagan was unsuccessful at eliminating in-school interest subsidies on student loans, he did manage to persuade Congress to introduce a 5 percent "origination fee" instead—meaning a student taking out $2,500 would receive only $2,375. It was an interest charge by another name, and even worse; since interest would be calculated on the full amount, students would end up paying interest on the origination fee itself.

Reagan also cut off the 750,000 students who received funds because their families were recipients of Social Security benefits. And he succeeded in undoing the extension of subsidized loans to middle-income students made by the Middle Income Student Assistance Act. Subsidized loans not only paid students' interest while they were in college but also capped it at 9 percent once they entered repayment, at a time when market interest rates were around 15 percent. For every percentage-point increase in the interest rate on Treasury bills, the federal government doled out an additional half billion dollars in subsidy payments to the banks that made the loans.

By offering the subsidy to more students, Carter had effectively put the federal government on the hook for an added $2 billion a year, making it an obvious target for Stockman's knife. In 1982, federal loan applications dropped by 30 percent—yet even as middle-income families were kicked out of the subsidized program and into more expensive loans, needier students who'd seen their Pell Grants slashed migrated to borrowing. The loan program quickly recovered and began to swell again.

ACROSS THE COUNTRY, COLLEGE STUDENTS WERE COMING TO TERMS WITH their new financial straits. "If you're paying $7,000 already," said a Yale junior named Patricia in 1981, "when they start tacking on the extra thousands, you don't feel it—you just lose track." Two semesters at Yale had gone up by 13.5 percent that year, to $10,340. A decade earlier, they had been less than half that. Patricia had hoped to avoid taking on debt, but she'd resigned herself to the idea of graduating with a $5,000 balance. "The cost is outrageous, but what can I do?" asked a freshman at Brandeis, which was up to $9,824. That year, private colleges lost 2 percent of their freshmen, while public universities gained a percentage.

Others were coming to grips with being *cut off* from the loan program. In April 1981, twelve thousand students marched on the capital to protest the cuts. At the next year's Student Solidarity Day, there were seventy-five hundred, their placards reading "Brains, Not Arms" and "Books, Not Bombs." The president of a national community-college association lamented that an administration "that wants to invest so much in machinery and weapons" had so little regard "for the development of human beings." On student aid, he gave the president an F. The chancellor of the University of North Carolina at Charlotte concurred: "We're eating up our seed corn."

The president did not heed their objection. In the end, over Reagan's two terms, federal spending on education fell by $15 billion relative to inflation (about a quarter of the reduction sought by the administration). Over the same period, the Defense Department budget grew by 43 percent. Budget deficits soared, doubling as a percentage of GDP, from 2.5 percent to more than 5 percent, in Reagan's first term. In 1986, Reagan's budget proposal created a deficit of $180 billion. By the end of his two terms, the national debt had gone up by $2 trillion.

But it wasn't just the federal government that was going deeper into debt. In 1988, the Joint Economic Committee of Congress released a report showing that, in only a decade, the volume of federal student debt had tripled, while grants and scholarship aid had declined by almost two-thirds. For the first time since 1972, American students were borrowing more than they were getting in grants.

The scale had tipped.

"STUDENT LOANS: ARE THEY OVERBURDENING A GENERATION?" ASKED A novella-length College Board report in 1986, and the answer was maybe.

One thing that was certain: Black students and women in particular paid the price. Because of "continuing disparities in income," the report found, loans were more onerous to these groups. Nearly half of all students at historically Black colleges and universities came from families living below the poverty line, and more than 80 percent of them relied on student aid, which had tilted sharply in favor of loans since Reagan took office. This, among other disappointing developments, had presumably led to the recent decline in enrollment of Black students.

Between 1965 and 1977, the number of Black college students had increased from 274,000 to 1.1 million and doubled as a portion of the overall college population, to 10.8 percent. But now the peak had been crested, and the numbers were falling. In the first three years of the 1980s, the number of Black freshmen fell by 7.5 percent. At Harvard, the portion of Black freshmen in 1983 fell by a quarter. Meanwhile, eight thousand more Black students graduated from two-year vocational programs, an increase of almost a third. Up against budget cuts, schools were quietly reducing their commitment to diversity. "There is a lot of evidence that we are losing ground," said the head of a consortium of presidents of historically Black colleges and universities. As if on cue, the US Commission on Civil Rights canceled a study on the impact on minority students of cuts to student aid.

The falling tide sank other boats as well. Poor students of all ethnicities languished. For working- and middle-class students, the elite schools became, again, just that, hopelessly out of reach. By 1982, only 16 percent of Harvard's freshmen had fathers who had not gone to college, down from 26 percent in 1979. While rich legacy admits could still coast through the Ivies on gentlemen's Cs, the deserving but unremarkable poor were now relegated to community colleges, or pushed into vocational training, or found themselves simply out of luck. Ironically, the decades-long build-up of public higher education had supposedly been aimed at benefiting them. Nonetheless, "the path to higher education," lamented the president of Swarthmore College, "seems to be closing to the poor."

The only other choice was debt. Frank Newman, the Stanford

University public relations official and author of the 1969 report lambasting colleges and universities as spendthrifts, had become a scholar at
the Carnegie Foundation. By now he realized that the fixes of the 1970s
hadn't fixed much. In a much-cited report, Newman warned that students were taking out "excessive loans" destined to make them choose
careers based on self-interest, reduce their ability to buy homes, and
make them less civically minded.

Newman's caution went unheeded. The pervasive national psychology of markets and investment was having a marked effect on those
hard-up students—Black and white—who made it to college. They
became obsessed with money. In 1970, one-sixth of American college
freshmen planned to major in business; by Reagan's second term, more
than a quarter did. Business, already the most popular major, became a
monolithic force. And that made sense, because everything was business now—everything judged by the corporate dictums of efficiency
and productivity and profit. With the economy down and social welfare
practically abandoned, this was a time for yuppies, not yippies.

Reagan's gambit in California—that if students had to pay, they
would start playing by the rules, since their own money was on the
line—had paid off in spades. College students no longer had the latitude to lark about in the theater and French literature departments.
Now, to cover their debts, they would have to become corporate lawyers
and investment bankers and engineers. According to Reagan, it was "the
age of the entrepreneur."

But the freshly minted entrepreneurs were not always happy to be
pawns of the market. A future lawyer in Boston said he was forgoing his
dream of public interest law in light of his debts, and another said that
to tackle his he would have to self-impose "an eight-year moratorium
on doing good." "We certainly won't be rural general practitioners," said
a medical student who, with his wife, was set to rack up $334,000 in
debt. They anticipated paying over $1 million before the balance was
cleared. For students, this was the new reality.

College students' dreams for the future were becoming smaller, meaner, and their attitudes more complacent. "They prefer safe classes," one professor remarked. "Lectures where they can just sit."

The culture wars became a war on the cultured. In 1982, doing PR for a Stockman-led proposal to cut federal student aid by 47 percent over two years, Secretary of Education Terrel Bell said the federal government could no longer foot the bill for "posh student aid." When criticized, he dug in. "These are not draconian cuts," he said. "We think we're still a bit too generous."

A few years later, Bell's successor, William Bennett, was even harsher. When Reagan proposed cutting federal aid by a quarter in 1985, Bennett admitted that students might have to engage in some "divestiture": "stereo divestiture, automobile divestiture, three-weeks-at-the-beach divestiture." To parents, he was no more sympathetic. "Do your family planning a little better," he advised, "or find other means."

The colleges, for their part, were not amused. Reagan's yearly budget proposals sent them into a frenzy as they scrambled to reimagine their student aid packages. Wisconsin's Beloit College decided to replace lost aid with "moral obligation scholarships" that students would be asked to repay in the form of tax-deductible "gifts." Mary Holmes College, in Mississippi, set up a local "adopt-a-student" program. Some colleges pooled money for complementary student loan funds; others loaned out their endowment funds. In 1986, Yale collected IOUs on $1 million. The parents of wealthy students, meanwhile, could beat inflation by prepaying all four years at once, or, if they had a special place in their hearts for Pittsburgh, by buying baby futures: put down a few thousand now, then pack your kids off to Duquesne University at no extra charge in the next millennium.

Financial aid departments grew in size and complexity. At Wellesley College, the office began educating parents on how to benefit from tax shelters and trusts. The University of Minnesota instituted a "differential tuition" policy, charging more to those studying expensive subjects, like biology. "I've never seen anything so chaotic in my life," said an administrator at Wesleyan.

The government's abdication of its commitment to support college students could not have come at a worse time for America's colleges. The baby boom was over, and its passels of children had grown up and graduated into the workforce. On their heels, Gen X was markedly runty. The number of American eighteen-year-olds maxed out in 1980 and then began a steady twenty-year decline. For the business of higher education, that meant fewer customers. This was not necessarily a problem for the public institutions. Because of their state-subsidized tuitions, they actually benefited in one way from federal student aid cuts: with less money available to middle-class families, the kids started picking budget options. Stony Brook instead of Barnard, Rutgers over Yale. Suddenly faced with a glut of options, these onetime patrons of open enrollment found themselves with an irresistible new latitude to be choosy. At the University of Michigan, for instance, the portion of freshmen who were in the top tenth of their graduating class rose to three-fifths.

For private schools, the loss of customer purchasing power (that is, federal funds) was a five-alarm fire. Their enrollments dwindling, expensive private schools played into the new business logic and started emphasizing their value. They compared themselves to luxury cars. Why get a Buick, after all, when you could have a Cadillac? This was the only way they could compete for top students—the kind who would enhance their profiles, thereby attracting yet more students, and possibly some future donors—and the only way they could justify urging parents to take out second mortgages on their houses to pay for four years at Vanderbilt. "With inflation, the value of a family home has risen," said that school's director of financial aid, "and if a family really wants to send their child to an institution such as Vanderbilt" . . . well, perhaps they ought to just suck it up and borrow.

Meanwhile, the schools were increasing their prices by as much as 14 or 15 percent a year, way above even the most hyper of inflationary jumps. A college that had charged around $6,000 in 1980 was by 1988 asking for roughly double that. A year at Bennington College topped the charts at $20,590. Sarah Lawrence College took second, at $20,360, and Brandeis University third, at $20,186. Family income, on the other hand, had gone up only about 50 percent over the Reagan years. The schools said they couldn't help it—their main cost was labor, and unlike, say, businesses involved in manufacturing, they couldn't markedly offset that cost by increasing productivity. A professor's reach, after all, was limited by the size of the lecture hall. And that lecture hall had to be heated, by ever-more-costly oil and gas, and new equipment purchased to keep students and researchers at the cutting edge of rapid technological advancement, and the buildings maintained, and so on and so on.

It was all very expensive.

Facing an exodus of middle-class students and their money, private schools started vying for them, treating them like the customers they had become. They ran up budgets on the kinds of attractive amenities and high-prestige scholars that would put them ahead of their competitors. And then, one by one, they abandoned a core mid-century principle and began accepting students based on their ability to pay. First up was Wesleyan University, which warned that instead of "aid-blind" admissions, it would have to begin denying acceptance to some needy students outright. "No one likes the idea of taking out people without money and putting in people with money," said the school's dean of admissions. But, alas, there was no other way: because of cuts to federal financial aid, Wesleyan's compensatory scholarship budget was set to double in five years. Other schools—perhaps more cruelly—practiced "admit-deny": they accepted the poor kids but offered them no aid at all. "We always get tears in the guidance office," said a New Jersey high school counselor in the spring of '82. "This year it's from the kids who are getting accepted."

Then another mass transgression: the schools began diverting the aid they *weren't* giving to poor students to those who didn't need it at all—offering merit scholarships to academic high achievers, who skewed wealthy, to enhance the "quality" of their student body. "It's like a sailing race," said the dean of admissions at Lewis and Clark College, in Portland, Oregon. "When everyone else tacks, you have to tack to cover the fleet." The dean of admissions at University of California Santa Cruz put it in terms more intelligible to the unpedigreed: "We're now in the frenzied period of the bribe."

Schools began referring to their "sticker prices," which were significantly higher than "net costs." They affected magnanimity by offering discounts—grants, scholarships—to those who couldn't afford the sticker. They called this scheme "high tuition/high aid." "It's like buying a car," said a professor at Penn State. The sticker price, he said, was just the starting offer. "Everybody knows that this is only the basis for negotiating." But not everyone did seem to know—least of all poor and minority students. "Even though the money eventually shows up," said a House education staffer, "they've gotten the message: Higher education is not for you."

To the middle-class losers of the college-aid haggle the schools suggested extreme measures to bridge the price gap. It would be worth it, they said, because an elite education was an investment that couldn't help but pay off. "You can't put a price tag on a Yale education," said one admissions recruiter in 1982. The price tag for two semesters at Yale that year ran to just shy of $12,000.

As news of these skyrocketing tabulations piled up, the public began to realize that paying for college was no longer the proposition it had been a decade or two earlier, when an enterprising youngster might take out a small loan and work summers for tuition money. By 1986, when the minimum wage was $3.35, students would have to flip burgers twenty-three hours a week all year long to pay their way through the average public university, and upwards of forty-five hours a week for a private school. This was apparently of no consequence to Reagan, who wanted to pay them even less. In 1983 he proposed creating a "subminimum" wage of $2.50 an hour for people under the age of twenty-two. He wished he could go farther and get rid of the youth minimum wage altogether. It—and not his policies—he suggested, was the cause of an almost 40 percent unemployment rate among Black youths, an all-time high.

Parents and students began to avail themselves of new financial sources and services: companies like Scholarship Search and the National Scholarship Research Service that, for a fee, promised to root out a bevy of private scholarships for them. "People ought to cultivate their grandparents," urged one financial adviser. The summer sleeper of 1986 was *Big Trouble*, John Cassavetes's directorial swan song, about an insurance salesman (played by Alan Arkin) who gets embroiled in a double indemnity scheme to put his triplets through Yale. "Education has become a free market, with the best surviving," said Leon Botstein, the president of Bard College.

On the other side of the ledger, at the very top of that market, was Sallie Mae, which not only survived but thrived in the '80s. In 1984, it was listed as a publicly traded company on the New York Stock Exchange. And then its profits began to explode—between 1982 and 1986, they nearly quadrupled, from $37.8 million to $144.6 million. By 1988, Sallie Mae logged $28.6 billion in assets. Opening up the shareholder pool to the public had the additional benefit, the company's board chairman explained, of making the company "less vulnerable to government tinkering." Soon the public-private chimera started engaging in bewilderingly complex financial transactions, expanding its reach into state guaranty agencies and savings and loan banks; investing more than $1 billion in commercial leases of aircraft, rail cars, hydroelectric power plants, and offshore drilling rigs; and selling its wares on the international markets, to investors in Europe and Japan.

As the 1980s beat on, Sallie Mae continued to grow, reaching its tentacles into every haunted corner of the student loan industry. Changes in the 1986 reauthorization of the Higher Education Act had reduced the number of lenders in the program, concentrating loan volume in a few behemoths; Sallie Mae was quickly becoming the biggest. Soon the company was gobbling up other lenders. Meanwhile, a General Accounting Office report on government-sponsored enterprises like Sallie Mae, conducted in the wake of widespread savings-and-loan-bank failures at the end of the Reagan era, concluded that the company had no real federal oversight to ensure "the safety and soundness of its financial activities"; its finances had never even been audited by its putative overseer, the Treasury Department.

This warning, like all the rest, went unheeded as Sallie Mae continued its conquest. By the dawn of the 1990s, Sallie Mae alone held half the federal student loan market. The free market had won out yet again.

Indeed, looking back at the education policymaking of the Reagan White House, you can almost see Milton Friedman, the great free-market carnival barker, talking through the so-called Great Communicator as if through a ventriloquist's dummy. Reagan was known to carry around Friedman's *Capitalism and Freedom* on the campaign trail back in his California governor days. And when he became president, most of Friedman's ideas about education found expression in his administration, which made crippling the public foundations of higher education a primary objective and justified it on the basis of the "human capital" returns to be reaped by the individual student.

Reagan and his second-term secretary of education, William Bennett, rationalized their cuts to student aid by invoking what's known as the college wage gap—the extra amount college degree holders are believed to earn relative to their uneducated peers—then estimated (by them) at $640,000 over a lifetime. "It is only sensible and fair that that beneficiary pay the cost, rather than the taxpayer," Bennett said in 1986, in discussing his proposal to eliminate in-school interest subsidies on guaranteed loans. Indeed, "switching the interest burden from the Government to the recipient," he offered, "would make it possible to offer large loans with longer repayment periods."

Bennett even resurrected an idea from Milton Friedman for forming a national student loan bank to make loans out of the federal Treasury, then require students to repay them as a percentage of their income over a few decades of their working years. In 1986, Congress authorized a pilot program of the Income Contingent Loan, which would charge students the Treasury rate plus 3 percent (then totaling 8.6 percent) on loans up to $17,500, then make them repay at up to 15 percent of their income over an indefinite period. Others suggested eliminating subsidized loans altogether—and replacing them with unsubsidized ones. "The prospect of heavy debt after graduation would no doubt discourage some students from borrowing," offered Peter Passell, a Yale-educated economist, in a *New York Times* op-ed. "But that may be the wisest form of restraint."

In the span of a single presidency, the logic of two decades of federal aid had gradually, mostly silently, yet inexorably turned on its head. No longer was every young person encouraged to get "as much education as he has the ability to take," as Johnson had urged in 1965. Rather, kids these days, the conservatives seemed to be saying, needed to tone it down a bit. Forty years after the blue bloods of Harvard and the University of Chicago recoiled at the thought of unwashed masses of GIs descending on their ivied grounds, the tables had turned sharply. The university officials of the 1980s were aghast at the suggestion, made by Bennett, that in fact, not everyone even *ought* to go to college. And, scandalizing them further, he intimated that students certainly didn't need to be subsidized by the federal government to go to elite, expensive private colleges when there were perfectly good public options available. Following this logic, he proposed limiting the annual amount of federal aid to $4,000—the average cost of tuition at a public university.

And why not? After all, private colleges, whose prices were double or even triple those of the public ones, were making up for their lack of state appropriations with indirect federal subsidies, brought to them by student grants and loans. Fully 36 percent of private schools' income came from federal and state sources, and a growing portion of that comprised student loans. Rather than distributing this cost among local taxpayers, to whom institutions would be at least in theory accountable, it was concentrated in individual students, who were taking on unmanageable levels of debt to cover the spread. "More loan money does not make it easier for families to meet college costs," Bennett said; instead, it "makes it easier for colleges to raise college costs."

As with many Reaganite sound bites, Bennett's suggestion to put limits on aid to expensive private schools had an aura of reason, even an undertone of progressivism. It was a striking reversal from an administration

that had previously spared private schools the worst of its austerity measures, and whose student-aid white whale was tuition tax credits.

In fact, one of Bennett's strongest critics was his predecessor, Terrel
Bell, who argued that an abdication of private colleges, pushing stu-
dents into public institutions, would merely shift the burden onto state
taxpayers. This was practically socialism. It "flies in the face" of the very
Reaganite notion that "government policy should encourage the private
sector to do more so that government can do less," Bell raged in the
New York Times, from his post-government professorship at the (public)
University of Utah.

But perhaps that was just a testament to how far the situation had
degraded. The war on higher education could no longer afford to spare
the innocent private-sector institution. The surface of Bennett's seemingly leftist proposal hid a sinister, cynical core—a desire, it seemed,
to raze the whole liberal, free-thinking structure of American higher
education and return the masses to the factories and the mines, where
they belonged. If there was anything uniting these discordant policy
trajectories, it was disdain.

After all, Reagan and Bennett weren't proposing anything else. They
offered no corresponding program of expansion for the public universities that were to absorb the private-college losses that their policies generated. They did not propose partnering with the states to fund education
at higher levels in order to keep tuitions from skyrocketing, as naysayers
warned they inevitably would. In fact, Reagan wanted to fold all the cat-
egorical grants that the federal government made on the state and local
level—for things like special education and civil rights enforcement—
into one block grant to each state. And then, gradually, he wanted to get
rid of the block grants. He called it a "new federalism."

PERHAPS THIS WAS THE BIGGEST JOKE REAGAN PLAYED ON AMERICA—AND
certainly the biggest he played on California. Here was a man who, as
governor of the most populous state, the state with the best university

system in the country, had set out to systematically destroy that system, then had the audacity to tell the states that education was their burden.

Just before Reagan entered the White House, the home-state revolt he kindled finally consumed the nation. In 1978, a California business-man named Howard Jarvis began railing against property taxes. Because of inflation, homeowners would be priced out of their homes in a matter of years. "Even the Russians don't do that," he said. "It is a goddamned crime." Enraged, Jarvis (and his political ally, the local real estate agent Paul Gann) took advantage of California's unique citizen initiative sys-tem to pass a measure that effectively set the rate of property taxes in stone. In the year after it passed, with more than 60 percent of the vote, property tax revenue in California dropped by three-fifths. Spending on education began a steady decline, and over the next decade, the net price of attending a California public institution rose by 420 percent, more than it did in any other state in the nation.

But it wasn't just California. The tax revolt swept the nation, and likely swept Reagan into office. The states, said Walter Heller, a former chairman of the Council of Economic Advisers, had just committed "fiscal hara-kiri." On average, state spending on higher education dur-ing the 1980s fell by 4 percent of an institution's total revenue. And reduced state spending led to reductions in federal matching funds, a double whammy.

With the economy in freefall, thanks to Reagan's fiscal policies, states were getting less from the federal government *and* their tax revenues were declining. They were also spending more on Medicaid and prisons, whose populations shot up in the 1980s—both mandatory areas of spending. Higher education, the states' largest discretionary item, became the great budget "balance wheel." As states cut appropriations to public univer-sity systems, student costs went up. It was a fairly simple formula. "If the states put in a dollar less," one expert noted, "colleges get a dollar more from tuition."

Public university systems faced a major conundrum. Even as demo-graphics shifted, their enrollments were stabilizing or even going up, thanks to increased recruitment and retention efforts. Yet funding wasn't keeping pace. To maintain some level of parity, state systems began to ape the tactics of the private schools. They expanded their financial aid and fundraising operations. At the start of the decade, not a single development officer could be found on any of the sixty-four campuses of New York's state university system; by 1986, there were fifty. Running a state system became increasingly complex, with ever more offices and people needed to staff them. The budget for administration swelled.

And just like the private schools, the state schools turned to a high tuition/high aid model, which they claimed would allow them to continue admitting low-income students while reaping much-needed cash from higher-income and out-of-state students. But despite officials' hand-wringing, for poor students the figures just weren't tabulating. Over the course of Reagan's two terms, the cost of attending a public college or university rose by 83 percent. In that time, the value of the maximum Pell Grant grew by just 5 percent. The institutions by and large weren't making up the difference. Only thirteen states kept their need-based grant programs level with their rising tuitions. Everywhere else, going to college simply got more expensive.

So, more and more, schools—and their students—turned to loans.

In 1981, for instance, the Massachusetts legislature created a state agency empowered to issue tax-free bonds and use the funds for colleges to make below-market loans to their students. Harvard took advantage of the program to offer fifteen-year loans at 11.5 percent. Meanwhile, the state guaranty agency ran a campaign in schools to educate future collegians about their financing options. Among the materials it distributed to junior high school students—kids who had barely entered puberty—was a pamphlet titled "Everything You've Always Wanted to Know About Repaying Your GSL."

MORE TRANSFORMATIVE EVEN THAN REAGAN'S IMMEDIATE FINANCIAL CUTS was the ideological shift he and his policies represented. He had veered from the New Deal and Great Society notions that the federal government had a role to play in education funding, or that there was societal value in helping citizens gain knowledge, skills, perspective. There would be no twentieth-century land-grant act, no general aid to schools, not even an empty soaring speech about the importance of ensuring educational opportunity for all. Reagan's entire program for higher education was to quietly dismantle it, brick by federally subsidized brick. In place of services, he offered only cuts. There was no there there.

When presented with evidence—in the form of sky-high default rates—that the student aid system wasn't working for students, the Reagan administration chose to make it worse. The American imagination was fixed in a pattern of thought that refused to admit possibilities beyond the familiar, limited options. Student loans were not working, yet alternatives to loans seemed impossible to ponder. For one thing, anything else was assumed to be terribly expensive. So, when it wasn't castigating students as deadbeats, the administration chose to fight student defaults by doing more of what was not working: giving students *more* loans, with fewer protections, over a longer portion of their adult lives.

The Reagan administration argued that paying for college was "the primary responsibility of parents and students." And if they could not afford to do so—and increasingly they could not—the government would help them go into debt, if not get out of it. Congress was only too happy to lend a hand. To complement (and eventually replace) the subsidized loans available to middle-class students, the 1980 reauthorization of the Higher Education Act had offered a new financial instrument.

Families continuing to believe the rhetoric of individual advancement upon which the entire program of student financial aid had been sold to them, who still aspired to send their sons and daughters to the most elite schools to which they were accepted, could now consider PLUS—Parent Loans for Undergraduate Students. It was a program of market-rate loans whose first bill would come due before a family's new collegian made it back home for Thanksgiving. Now parents could borrow an additional $3,000 a year, on top of the $2,500 their freshman could take out. The following year, PLUS expanded to include graduate and independent students in addition to parents; interest rates rose from 9 to 14 percent; and the program was renamed Auxiliary Loans to Assist Students—ALAS. As with every other student aid program, it started out small and got very, very big. The burden of student debt, once the sole province of America's young, would in a few short decades become an intergenerational fiasco.

Although Reagan hadn't created these programs, he had no qualms about expanding them, at one point even threatening to push graduate students out of the GSL program altogether and into ALAS. That change would have increased their interest rates by 5 percent and required them to start paying back their loans while still in school. This proposal failed, but the trend was evident. As middle-class families found themselves squeezed out of the Guaranteed Student Loan Program by Reagan's cuts, they turned to expensive parent loans. "We will carry on at 14 percent," said a father who planned to take out a parent loan to pay for his two kids to attend private colleges. "That's better than the 17 percent I could get with a second mortgage on my house."

Curiously, Bennett's human capital justification for reducing loan subsidies was at odds with the overarching premise of Reaganomics— that preserving income for high earners (via tax cuts) would benefit the economy as money trickled down. By that logic, as college graduates earned more, their extra money would rain down on the less fortunate. Bennett and others justified the cruelty of their policies by stating as fact that student borrowers were the primary beneficiaries of their educations. But they never offered proof that this was actually true, and no one seemed to question them. Evidence that the GI Bill provided a twelvefold return on its initial investment didn't come in until 1988, after all the damage was done.

Here was a great irony. Had Reagan maintained a progressive taxation policy, in which the wealthy were taxed at higher levels, he could have captured the excess benefit supposedly accrued by college graduates without having to resort to an ever-more-byzantine system of loans. The money collected in revenues might then have funded a tuition-free public university system, as it does in nearly every developed nation in the world. This would have had the additional benefit of not punishing those graduates who wound up at the bottom of the curve, unable to earn enough to pay back their loans.

As it was, the student loan policy that Reagan, Stockman, Bell, and Bennett furthered amounted to a *pretax* on presumptive income, something that might or might not ever be earned. This unfairly penalized graduates who simply had bad luck, as well as those who, against their better (financial) judgment, decided to enter low-earning public service careers. Also, the early burden of loans hindered the "entrepreneurial" risk-taking spirit the administration supposedly believed paramount to American success. And by encouraging the acquisition of material success above all else, Reagan's regime fattened the payrolls of corporate law partnerships and Wall Street firms while leaving lacunae in the ranks of earnest, well-meaning public servants.

Practically alone among nations, America eschewed sensible tax policy in favor of an unwieldy mashup of individual funding streams focused increasingly on debt, then punished students for the dysfunction of a system they'd had no part in creating.

In 1976, student loans ate up 21 percent of federal student aid; in 1988, they were at 68 percent, more than two-thirds. By the time Reagan left office, the student aid pendulum had swung irrevocably from grants to loans, particularly for the poor. By 1990, a grant that in 1979 would have covered nearly two-thirds of the cost of a public college would now pay for little more than one-third. With a guaranteed loan, a poor student could almost cover the gap, but they would still need to find a way to finance the last 10 percent of tuition, perhaps by living at home or spending the summers working. Poor students, whose federal grants were covering less and less of their expenses as each year went by, had two choices: drop out or keep borrowing. With everyone telling them they were worth little more than the letters printed on their diplomas, who could blame them for cocooning themselves within a mountain of debt?

For many, the choice was a wise one, a savvy investment in the lives they foresaw. But not for all. For those who'd been lured to the predatory for-profit schools that had sprung up like toadstools during Reagan's tenure, theirs was a mountain built on quicksand.

CHAPTER 7

Grift Revisited

H ow many of you have been ripped off by a trade school?" asked the state assemblywoman at an event she was hosting. All but one of the attendees raised their hands. The representative was not surprised. It was a story she had heard again and again.

The event was meant to be a happy one. The ninety-some residents of a South Central Los Angeles housing project had just graduated from Project Build, a job-training program led personally by their assemblywoman, Maxine Waters. On her visits to the dilapidated projects in her district, Waters had found community members devastated by Reagan's cuts to welfare and other domestic spending programs. As many as half of residents were unemployed, and Waters was constantly fielding requests for help finding work. She suggested job-training programs, but her constituents were disillusioned by years of rejection, and it was difficult to convince them it was worth the effort. One day Waters had an idea. Instead of bringing her constituents to training programs, she could have more impact by bringing the programs to them. In 1985, she held her first set of seminars at Jordan Downs, a drab cinder-block compound at the center of Watts. Over four days, she taught residents how to fill out job applications and brought in local employers to interview them.

But while many of her program graduates soon found work—as typists or medical assistants—others were held back by their pasts. Residents taken in by deceptive trade schools found themselves in debt and out of work. When they inevitably defaulted on their student loans, they lost access to future federal aid. With no more loans and no more Pell Grants, they could not attend even low-cost community colleges to obtain legitimate training. There were more devastating consequences as well: their credit scores plummeted, they lost access to federal housing aid, and their federal tax refunds were garnished.

Meanwhile, no one in Washington, DC, or California state government seemed to care much about the poor, defrauded trade school student. Waters was incensed. If no one else would protect her constituents from collegiate wheeler-dealers, she decided, she would have to do it herself.

Waters had gotten to Watts in 1961, just a few years before the riots. Born in St. Louis and raised in a segregated housing project, she was the fifth of thirteen children, her father gone by the time she was two. Welfare kept the family afloat. As a teenager, Waters bused tables in restaurants that would not serve her. At twenty-one, she left for California with a husband and two young children in tow. To make ends meet, she took a job in a garment factory. Soon she was ascending California's pioneering state college system, earning a degree in sociology from Cal State Los Angeles in 1970. Then she found her way to the Great Society, becoming a teacher and then a parent coordinator with Head Start.

Waters eventually moved into politics, first as a volunteer and then as a staffer on local Democratic campaigns. By 1976, she was representing her district in the California Assembly, where she became known for her hard-charging style and uncompromising moral stands.

Among the targets of her ire were proprietary trade schools.

In the 1980s, California had gotten a reputation as a haven for shady vocational schools—earning the nickname "diploma mill capital of the world." It was a far cry from just a decade earlier, when John Sperling was run out of state and forced to set up shop in lax Arizona. One factor in the expansion was simply the flow of money: Reagan had opened the spigot of unsubsidized loans—under the ALAS program, which he rechristened Supplemental Loans for Students (SLS)—to for-profit schools in 1986, and they had lined up to greedily drink from the tap.

In 1989, Waters took a stand. Her bill in the California Assembly, the Maxine Waters School Reform and Student Protection Act, created a state framework for reining in for-profit bad apples. The legislation required institutions to disclose information about student outcomes and revoked the licenses of poorly performing schools, effectively cutting them off from state and federal funds.

She would soon take her crusade to the nation.

IN THE LATE 1980S, CALIFORNIA WASN'T THE ONLY STATE WITH A PROPRIetary schools crisis. In 1989, Senator Sam Nunn had found himself with a serious case of déjà vu. Not fifteen years on from the 1975 hearings on proprietary school abuses, for-profit schools and the default rates they drove up were back to their relentless expansion. Nunn, now a seasoned legislator in charge of powerful subcommittees, was again fielding reports of outlandish student loan abuses—of precisely the same variety that had plagued students in the 1970s. Student-loan default rates had once again reached crisis levels. During the 1980s, loan volume had more or less doubled, from almost $7 billion in 1983 to more than $12 billion in 1989. But loan defaults had quadrupled, from about $450 million to $2.4 billion. Nearly a third of that came from eighty-nine schools, eighty-four of them proprietary. By 1990, dealing with those defaults—paying back the lenders and chasing down the borrowers—was eating up more than *half* the federal loan program's total annual expenses. Almost half of *that* amount was driven by for-profit trade schools, which served only 22 percent of borrowers but generated 44 percent of defaults.

"We have been down this road before," Nunn fumed as he convened hearings on the issue before the Senate's Permanent Subcommittee on Investigations. And yet, despite all the testimony he'd already gathered in the 1970s, and despite multiple admonishing reports delivered to the Department of Education by the Government Accountability Office— "despite all that," Nunn concluded, "the program's failures seem only to have gotten worse."

"I used to buy the rhetoric that there were just a few bad apples," the president of the Massachusetts Higher Education Assistance Corporation, a major guarantor of federal student loans, had told the subcommittee's investigators. "But then I discovered there were orchards of bad apples." During eight days of hearings, spread out over nearly a year, the senators sampled many of them.

First, there was the case of the American Career Training Corporation (ACT), a secretarial and travel school in Florida. As the subcommittee's staff began to investigate whether proprietary schools were abusing student aid programs, they decided to conduct a case study on a school with high loan volume and picked ACT more or less at random. It was a fair choice, given that ACT had increased its loan volume by nearly 1,400 percent in the three years since it had first gained access to the program. "We found more than we had expected," a subcommittee staff member summarized. That turned out to be an understatement.

"We were not looking for a 'worst-case example,'" the staff member stated. But the investigation's findings "strongly suggest intentional abuse." While school executives earned million-dollar salaries from student aid funds, students suffered. Fewer than 20 percent completed the course, and the investigation found that the school had targeted residents of housing projects and recipients of welfare, admitted ineligible students, and failed to refund those who dropped out. One former employee claimed she had seen the school's president personally falsify students' application forms to ensure they would be approved for federal loans.

Then there was the Culinary School of Washington, accredited by two separate agencies, where students were charged $6,900 for a six-month course in which they were required to cook and serve rancid, moldy food in the cafeteria of the Blue Plains Sewage Treatment Plant. And the accredited nursing assistant school in Florida that taught students in a storefront they entered by climbing through a hole in the drywall of the neighboring porn shop, owned by the proprietor's son. And the schools that hired actors to pose as students, fabricated financial documents, and made up nonexistent students.

But the officials in charge of the loan program seemed set on looking the other way. After one school owner by the name of Tommy Wayne Downs got caught creating fictitious students to take out loans for him, he bought another set of schools and started working the fraud again.

After he was found out for a *second* time, the Department of Education became wary, and the feds eventually indicted him. Asked if he thought the system was rampant with such fraud, Downs replied that it surely was: "I don't think I am that unique," he said. "I am not that smart."

Then there were the less explosive but even more pervasive issues, like the way schools would increase the length of courses to qualify for funding programs and charge higher tuition. By engaging in this "course-stretching," they could extract up to thirty-eight times more money from students than a community college would charge for the same credential. One correspondence school, the committee members learned, had simply doubled the reported length of its course, while changing nothing in the syllabus.

According to state officials from Illinois and Florida, accredited proprietary schools (eligible for federal funds) were of even *lower* quality than nonaccredited ones (reliant on students' out-of-pocket funds, and therefore, good word of mouth). No entity had been removed from the federal accreditors' registry in over a decade, and 97 percent of trade schools were approved for federal money, even though only a quarter of their graduates found jobs in their fields. One school had a withdrawal rate above 50 percent and default rates that edged up toward 75 percent. The department merely took the school in for additional "monitoring" while continuing to funnel $7.5 million in loan money to it, via its students, over the next two years.

Finally, there was the uncomfortable fact that, just as they had in the 1970s, proprietary school recruiters continued to choose their targets precisely. "In the proprietary school business what you sell is 'dreams,' and so 99 percent of my sales were made in the poor, black areas," in places like "welfare offices and unemployment lines, and in housing projects," said Tommy Wayne Downs, who had gotten his start as a recruiter for a truck-driving school in Nashville. Once Downs had encouraged someone to sign up for the school and perhaps accompanied him to a pawn shop to scrape up the money for a down payment, he would have the recruit take him next door and introduce him to the neighbors, so he could work his grift on down the block. He was very good at it: in one three-week period he signed up 180 students, at a commission of $75–$100 a pop—about $35,000 to $45,000 in total, in today's dollars. Another school owner gave a particularly icy summary of the industry's attitude: "I'm a businessman out to make a profit," he said. "I don't care about the well-being of these students."

The subcommittee's staff investigators blamed the government and its move toward deregulation of education-aid policy in the 1970s and '80s. Then, "because of budget constraints," the investigators testified, money for oversight dwindled. Each branch of the Triad was relying on the others for supervision of the program and its actors—as a result, none stepped up to provide it. "We were told that while we may have saved a few million dollars by cutting back on oversight, that action will eventually cost the taxpayers hundreds of millions of dollars lost to fraud and abuse."

The committee was considering a number of fixes. But the proprietary industry wasn't about to go quietly.

Threatened with increased scrutiny or decreased access to government funds (or both), proprietary schools submitted outlandish pleas aimed at maintaining the status quo. "Everyone who cares about educational opportunity for all Americans should be alarmed at the very notion of 'separate but equal' student-aid programs," wrote the head of the National Association of Trade and Technical Schools, the principal accreditor for proprietary vocational schools, in a *Chronicle of Higher Education* op-ed. "At a time when the walls of apartheid are inexorably crumbling in South Africa, it would be tragic if here in America we began to build walls of educational apartheid." (Maxine Waters, who had almost single-handedly pushed California to divest state pension funds from South African businesses in 1986, no doubt found the comparison hard to stomach.)

To its credit, the subcommittee was not buying it either. Its staff report of September 1990 noted that while proprietary schools shared some traits with community colleges—they both enrolled low-income students who attended for short periods of time and borrowed small amounts of money—the for-profits' students had much higher rates of default on those loans. (And while community college students borrowed in low numbers, roughly two-thirds of for-profit students took out loans.) Were the rates high because of the students, the investigators asked, or because of how the schools operated? Their conclusion was bold and stark: it was the schools.

Elizabeth Imholz, a New York legal aid attorney invited to testify before the senators, had urged the subcommittee to take real action—to stop "tinkering with the current system of trade school regulation" and enact bold regulatory reform. She wanted Congress to redefine accreditation, make fraudulent trade schools pay for borrowers' loans, and remove proprietary schools from Title IV programs altogether. And yet, even after observing the failures of the milquetoast fixes of the 1970s, the subcommittee, instead of endorsing strong, unequivocal regulatory reform, still seemed hell-bent on tinkering. Senator Nunn thanked Ms. Imholz for her testimony and then asked her just one question: did she, he wondered, endorse the idea of rejiggering the aid payment schedule from a yearly basis to a quarterly or a monthly one?

In the end, Nunn's committee issued a damning bipartisan report urging "a comprehensive, intensive, and sustained effort to reform the [student loan] program," with twenty-seven specific recommendations, including taking the reins on quality assurance away from in-the-pocket accrediting agencies, limiting the amount of federal aid going to proprietary schools and the kinds of programs eligible for aid, and beefing up the Department of Education's procedures and staffing. But Nunn's colleagues in the House and Senate education committees did not appreciate his homing in on their territory: Ted Kennedy, head of the Senate Labor and Human Resources Committee, reportedly fought Nunn, a conservative Southerner whom he viewed with disdain, "tooth and nail" on proprietary-school reform. In the House, Representative William D. Ford, a Michigan labor stalwart, similarly balked at the idea of government "telling students that one type of school is better than another." They largely ignored the committee's report and its recommendations.

There was another reason for the Democrats' inaction. Although today we might generally think of Democrats as being against for-profit schools and Republicans being for them, this alignment is fairly recent. Up until the 1990s, the two parties' positions on for-profit colleges were flipped. Democrats, blinded by their commitment to "access," were loath to deprive poor young people of educational opportunities. And the Congressional Black Caucus feared that a crackdown on for-profit schools could bring a large number of historically Black colleges and universities under scrutiny; many had high default rates for their own distinct reasons (such as persistent underfunding).

The Republicans, on the other hand, were more concerned with spending. As late as 1987, when loan defaults were approaching $2 billion a year, Reagan's secretary of education, William Bennett, not generally known for his pro-student rhetoric, lambasted the for-profits as "diploma mills designed to trick the poor into taking on federally backed debt" and "milk them for their loan money." He pushed a measure that would cut off schools' access to federal funds if they had loan default rates above 20 percent.

As Bennett tried to tame the beast he had helped create, Democratic trade-school supporters on the education committees in Congress blocked him. They included Senator Pell and Representative Ford, who had attended the Henry Ford Trade School (a nonprofit institution) as a teenager to train as a tool and die maker. In 1988, with Reagan on his way out the door, Montana Democrat Pat Williams cut a deal with George H. W. Bush's incoming education secretary, Lauro Cavazos, to shelve the proposed crackdown. "We won the war," said the head of the for-profits' top lobbying association, as lawmakers seemed poised to mostly ratify the status quo in the next Higher Education Act reauthorization. "The rest of this is minor skirmishes."

That assessment proved to be slightly overoptimistic. The for-profits would indeed win the war, but not before encountering a few more obstacles. If almost no one in Congress or the White House seemed to care much about the plight of students, the for-profits' victims, there were at least a handful of reformers ready to take on the fraudsters. They were small in number, but for a short while they were able to stem the tide.

BENNETT'S IRE TOWARD PROPRIETARY SCHOOLS HAD BEEN A BIT DISINGENU-ous. In fact, much of this crisis had been created and cultivated by Reagan in the final years of his presidency. It was Reagan's 1986 program, Supplemental Loans for Students—which allowed independent students to borrow additional unsubsidized money for school—that was nourishing the for-profits. By 1988, for-profit schools were taking in 64 percent of SLS dollars and churning out 80 percent of the program's defaults. Overall, defaults on SLS loans amounted to nearly a quarter billion dollars a year. But Reagan's legacy of disinvestment, in education as in every other domestic spending category, had not soured the electorate on the Republican Party. In 1988, George Herbert Walker Bush, Reagan's vice president, was elected to succeed him in the White House.

Unlike Reagan, Bush was a staid, classically conservative Republican, not prone to flashy gestures in style or substance. Like more than one of his predecessors, he came into office proclaiming his desire to be an "education president." To prove his bona fides, he assembled a governors' convention to discuss the topic of America's schools. Instead of tuition vouchers, he promoted charter schools, and instead of advancing Reagan's dream of shuttering the Department of Education, he pushed it to begin administering standardized tests to schoolchildren across the nation. Neither of these proposals bore much fruit in his single term in office, but Bush did manage to make his mark on higher education—namely in cracking down on shady trade schools.

In 1989 and 1990, with Republicans still in support of proprietary-school regulation under the banner of deficit reduction, Bush signed budget bills that cut off federal aid to schools with particularly high default rates. By then, the crisis had grown so great that fellow Democrats skeptical of Sam Nunn's investigation had also started to see the light. Montana's Pat Williams admitted that the situation was "beginning to get out of control," becoming a "crisis about to explode." Even the most ardent of the trade schools' advocates began to turn on them. "I've worked on these student-aid programs for twenty-five years," said William Ford, "and I'm not about to see them destroyed by schools abusing this program."

At the end of 1990, another levee broke. The nation's largest guaranty agency, a Kansas-based entity called the Higher Education Assistance Fund (HEAF), collapsed under the weight of bad vocational-school student loans. For the student loan industry, this was as big a scandal as the failure of the nation's savings and loan banks had been a few years earlier. HEAF guaranteed $9 billion in federal loans, nearly a fifth of the entire program, and about a third of those were loans to trade schools, where default rates averaged 30 percent. Among the lenders it guaranteed was a California bank called FITCO that loaned almost exclusively to trade school students. Founded in 1980, FITCO had risen in a few short years to become the second-largest student lender in the country. When FITCO went belly up because of defaults in 1989, HEAF simply couldn't keep up with the payout requests. HEAF's failure threatened a domino collapse and shook confidence in the loan program. In the aftermath, the Department of Education asked Sallie Mae to step in and pick up the pieces—distributing HEAF's portfolio among other guaranty agencies, at an initial loss to taxpayers of more than $200 million.

The for-profit schools crisis was now simply too big to ignore.

In 1991, with the Higher Education Act once again up for reauthorization, legislators got another crack at fixing the system. Only twenty-five years into the guaranteed loan experiment, the student aid system had grown into a byzantine, bureaucratic mess. With each subsequent authorization of the Higher Education Act, more players and regulations and complexity—and money—were added in, resulting in a system that few students could understand, let alone benefit from. A raging default crisis had nearly taken down the nation's student loan program. Students were borrowing more and receiving less genuine aid. And everyone, from lenders to school operators, was looking for a bigger piece of the pie. Students, the ostensible beneficiaries of the system, were to them in fact an obstacle to surmount: the only thing standing between the opportunists and their pot of gold. They had only a few advocates willing to champion their interests and protect them from harm.

Maxine Waters was among the most clear-eyed and unflinching of those advocates. By now she had taken her crusade against for-profit hucksters to the nation. Elected to the House of Representatives in 1991, Waters was the first Black woman to represent California, and she brought the same take-no-prisoners attitude to Congress that she had to the California State Assembly.

Although Waters was not on the powerful House education committee, she was invited to testify at the latest round of the hearings it held every five or so years to hash out changes to the Higher Education Act. As she appeared before the committee, she marshaled all her experience among those snookered by shoddy trade schools in her district. She had boxes of affidavits that she had gathered over four years of meeting with defrauded students. More than almost any other legislator, she was willing to speak frankly about the abuses she saw in the industry. "For many proprietary vocational schools, education is not the end product but an overhead expense," Waters testified. "The more the overhead is reduced, the more the owner gets to pocket."

Waters had some potent reforms in mind, and she outlined them for the committee. She proposed eliminating sales commissions for school recruiters, cutting off schools with high default rates and low job placements, and ensuring that some portion of for-profit schools' students pay their own way. After all, despite school proprietors' loud claim that their businesses were pure expressions of the infallible market, many were in fact almost entirely dependent on federal aid—in other words, they were the ultimate welfare queens. Waters borrowed a rubric from the Veterans Administration: she suggested that no more than 15 percent of a school's revenues come from the federal government.

Waters's proposals were well received by the committee, and when the higher education legislation reached the floor of the House, she added them as amendments, reiterating her clarion call in powerfully emotional terms. "We should not fight for the right of our constituents to be saddled with a debt they cannot pay, or an education they did not receive," she declared, lambasting "the unconscionable ripoff of billions of taxpayer dollars going into [. . .] schools that are not training anybody." To those who cited trade schools as a necessary option for minority students, she had a searing rebuke. "I do not want the owners and the lobbyists of these schools pointing to my community and my people telling me how they are providing opportunity, when in fact they are ripping them off. How many victims must there be before we say enough is enough?"

When the amended bill, passed with bipartisan support, crossed Bush's desk in July 1992, Waters's three big proposals were signed into law. Starting in 1994, no school would be permitted to raise more than 85 percent of its revenues in the form of federal funds. Additionally, proprietary schools would be barred from paying recruiters sales commissions, and schools with student loan default rates over 25 percent for three consecutive years would be excluded from participating in the student loan program. Over the next few years, hundreds of schools, perhaps as many as fifteen hundred—almost all of them proprietary—shut down because of the new rules, and for-profit default rates finally started to fall, dropping to 13 percent in the late 1990s.

LEGISLATORS IN THE 1990S HAD ANOTHER TARGET IN THEIR SIGHTS: ACCRED-itation of for-profit schools. Appalled at the findings of Nunn's commission, which had demonstrated the inadequacies of the Triad and particularly the failings of private accrediting agencies, lawmakers decided to put the onus back on the states. The impetus for this shift had in fact come from the Bush administration, which in its zeal to cut fraud had recommended setting new state parameters for overseeing proprietary vocational programs. Democrats in Congress begrudgingly agreed, and the reauthorization of the Higher Education Act included new regulatory instruments, State Postsecondary Review Entities (SPREs). These gave states more oversight responsibility for the educational institutions they licensed. The SPREs would determine whether an institution was legitimate via a series of criteria—default rates, the portion of revenues coming from federal aid, financial stability, and the correlation of school costs to actual salaries that students would make in the jobs they were being trained for. Any bad apples would be reported to the Department of Education. The legislation also empowered the department to determine what accrediting agencies were required to do and how to take down those that didn't meet certain standards.

The SPREs provided a potent opportunity for states to partner with the federal government to regain the local control that their representatives in Congress and at home had claimed to want for many years. Nevertheless, the states—particularly those having shoddy track records with for-profit schools—turned out to be less than enthusiastic about these enhanced responsibilities. The SPREs required significant investment and effort, and in some cases they threatened powerful local schools providing large numbers of jobs for constituents. Many state officials felt that the federal government had taken too heavy a hand in designing this new partnership. They found the SPRE requirements burdensome, vague, and confusing.

Both for-profit and nonprofit educational institutions saw the new standards as a threat to academic freedom as well as the bottom line. The nonprofits' trade organization, the National Association for Independent Colleges and Universities, began ferociously lobbying against the rules.

The organization was in luck because a new set of Republicans was about to take charge of Congress, and their priorities would differ from those of George H. W. Bush.

The 1992 reauthorization of the Higher Education Act had occurred at a pivot point in American politics. Bush's monotone moderation had not endeared him to voters, who in November again chose a flashy governor, this one a Democrat—Arkansas's slick saxophonist Bill Clinton. They also kept Democrats in control of the House and Senate, instating the first Democratic trifecta since Carter was voted out in 1980.

But just two years later, the Democrats' wave crashed. Republicans gained control of both chambers of Congress for the first time since the 1950s. Right around then, Republicans in Congress started to change their position on proprietary schools. Once their antagonists, Republicans suddenly became the schools' ardent supporters. Political scientist Suzanne Mettler argues that this change of heart was no coincidence. It occurred just as the for-profits—sensing the various knives at their back—kicked their lobbying campaigns into overdrive. In 1991, two of the for-profits' major trade associations merged into the Career College Association, which formed its own PAC and began giving bundles of money to both Democrats and Republicans. A few years later, the University of Phoenix's parent company started its first PAC (of an eventual four). Others followed suit, either forming PACs or donating to those of politicians such as John Boehner, who later became chair of the House education committee.

This new source of potential "patronage" turned Republicans around concerning the sector. "After decades of skepticism toward student aid," Mettler writes, "they suddenly found a political opportunity in it—the means to cater to banks and for-profit colleges that might in turn contribute to their campaigns." No longer were these institutions leeches "'milking' the federal government for profits." Now Republicans "championed them as businesses who embodied the spirit of free enterprise."

With the 1994 midterm elections, Republicans voted in a Speaker of the House, Newt Gingrich, who endorsed this new take on for-profit education. On the campaign trail that summer, he had debuted his Contract with America, a Ross Perot–inspired blueprint for Republicans' legislative plans that took aim at "excessive" federal regulations. The new state education bodies were no exception. After Gingrich took charge of the House, he first defunded the SPREs and then eliminated them altogether. By the time Congress took up the seventh reauthorization of the Higher Education Act a few years later, the Gingrich deregulation machine was unstoppable: gone were rules set in 1992 for accreditors to set standards for tuition and fees, investigate default rates, and make unannounced visits to proprietary schools. For every rein on the industry enacted in the 1992 legislation, there is, just a few years later, a sordid tale of Republican subterfuge. House Republicans in the

1990s set out to dismantle the brakes that reformers like Maxine Waters had just finished installing on a for-profit industry run amok.

For-profit schools did not let this opportunity pass them by. Led by John Sperling's University of Phoenix, they were about to ride the boom times of the 1990s into the financial stratosphere.

After finally receiving regional accreditation from the Higher Learning Commission in 1978, the University of Phoenix became eligible for a massive stream of available federal Title IV student aid funds. Through the next two decades, however, the company continued to take in most of its revenues from private sources—students' out-of-pocket funds and employer tuition programs. Its reputation was decent. Even so, as Phoenix began to expand, Sperling remained unsatisfied. He wanted more. "We can maintain the *status quo*," he said, "or we can continue in the same spirit that got us to where we are." Sperling wanted to take public the parent company created over the University of Phoenix, called Apollo, and grow it to a $100 million company. By the time he got his IPO in 1994, his institution had twenty-eight thousand students and was big enough to rival even the most expansive state university systems. And it had just begun. Thereafter, maintaining a shareholder-pleasing annual growth rate of 25 to 30 percent became a necessity. In the process, students became an afterthought.

Sperling was not alone. In the late 1990s and early 2000s, competitors hot on his heels expanded the field of for-profit education. The American job market was changing, and Americans were desperate to shift with it. As manufacturing flew overseas and high tech rose to the fore, panicked Americans sought opportunities to "upskill" to meet the demands of the new employers. Gone were the in-house training programs of earlier decades. In the Enron '90s, corporations were focused on profits and efficiencies, not employee development. If Americans wanted to keep pace with the good jobs, they would have to train themselves.

Ready and waiting to fill the void were for-profit institutions eager to peddle all the certificates and degrees Americans were told they needed. And unlike the mom-and-pop operations of yore, these institutions were not primarily centers of learning but rather arbiters of high finance—creations of private equity firms and darlings of the stock market. They existed only to serve the bottom line.

It was too late to right the ship. By the time for-profits rebounded in the late 1990s, they formed part of an entire industry that had grown up around higher education—banks, guaranty agencies, accreditors, secondary markets, debt collectors—all driven by a quest for monetary gain. The notion of providing a solid education to students was useful mainly as a marketing pitch—actually providing one would be a drain on the revenue. What had for decades been a side hustle, a discrete grift, had become the logic behind the whole system: grab money, make profits, exploit students.

PART 3

Finance Rules (1996–2007)

FIVE DECADES AFTER THE GI BILL first joined its three strands of inequity—a focus on the individual to the detriment of the polity, exclusion of the already excluded, and a Trojan horse giveaway to the market—they had been braided into an invulnerable steel rope. Meanwhile, the safety net for students was fraying.

By the end of the millennium, students had become the atomized loci not only of politicians' funding but also their judgment. Like the protagonists of a choose-your-own-adventure story with consequences that could never be undone, students were ostensibly vested with the power and responsibility to make choices, deemed either "good" or "bad," that would determine the value of the educational investment that they—and society—had made in them.

If they were lucky enough to have been born wealthy, these young people were almost guaranteed to sail through the American higher education system on calm and pleasant seas, disembarking to a bright and prosperous future. In 1990, 60 percent of children hailing from families with incomes in the top 25 percent made their way to a degree by the age of twenty-four, an increase of 20 percent since 1970. Those from the top half of the income heap received more than three-quarters of all bachelor's degrees, a distribution that has remained remarkably steady in the years since. If there was indeed an education wage premium, it

accrued largely to those already wealthy. But to the poor the seas were
not so kind. Their level of educational attainment in the 1990s had not
budged, stuck since 1970 at a meager 6 percent. They were shut out,
victims of an educational system that left them behind, as potential car-
rion for opportunists and hucksters. Then, if they became the prey of
these "entrepreneurs," the system punished them for their bad sense.

In the meantime, the choppy seas of student aid reform and retrenchment churned on. Reformers could do little more than temper
the excesses of profiteers and bad systems, plugging up holes even as
new (and old) leaks continued to spring, like sailors trying to bail out
a submerged ship to keep it from sinking.

This was the era of the tipping point, when we crossed over into a
system that could no longer be controlled, a piratical flotilla of hucksters, financiers, and bad-faith public servants that would plunder everything in its path.

CHAPTER 8

Iron Triangles

B ill Clinton had become enamored of the idea of a national service bill while on the presidential campaign trail in 1992. He envisioned it as a kind of domestic Peace Corps in which young people would engage in a year or two of civic do-gooding—building homes, cleaning up waterways, tutoring low-income children—in exchange for education funds. To Clinton, the program had the potential to reshape the way Americans paid for college, and he made it a centerpiece of his domestic policy agenda.

Clinton's quest to pass the national service bill appeared oddly quixotic to the moderate Democrat. "This is why I ran for president," he told Eli Segal, the man he tasked with creating the legislation, just a few days after his inauguration. And, to a group of advisers that February: "There is no proposal that means more to me than national service."

Liberal critics charged that the idea had really originated from a policy proposal of the right-leaning Democratic Leadership Council as a way to emphasize loans and eventually choke out the habitually underfunded Pell Grant. Instead of receiving grants, students would borrow. After they graduated, they would perform national service and be rewarded with a stipend to repay their loans. Training and supporting each national service volunteer was projected to cost the government $20,000 a year. On the other hand, the $3.4 billion initially proposed for the national service bill, which would have paid for just 100,000 volunteers by 1997, could instead be used to increase the value of the Pell Grant by up to a third for 5 million students—or even perhaps turn it into a mandated entitlement.

The liberals' critique, it turned out, held some water. As Clinton formulated his national service proposal, he did indeed promote borrowing over other forms of aid. And, more consequentially, he pushed for a major expansion of the government's involvement in the loan program. To pay for his national service bill, he targeted the perceived inefficiencies of the system: the intermediaries. Although the bank-based loan program had been created to reduce government expenditures, by the 1990s subsidizing the middlemen was costing the government $2 billion a year. So Clinton proposed cutting out student lenders and guarantors and instead making all student loans directly from Treasury funds.

A recent change to government accounting made such a direct lending program especially appealing. Prior to 1990, if the Treasury made a loan of $5,000, the budget would record it as a net loss of $5,000 in the year it was given out. But when Congress passed the Federal Credit Reform Act (FCRA), which changed the math: now the federal budget would subtract the amount a borrower was expected to repay over the life of the loan. All of a sudden, a $5,000 loan looked like far less than $5,000 on the balance sheet. Similarly, guaranteed loans now had to account for eventual defaults, so they could no longer be disguised as mostly free money on the federal ledger. As a result, a transition to direct lending for students was projected to save $6.5 billion over five years. Clinton called his new lending program Direct Loans. When he got to the White House in January 1993, he immediately started pushing for a complete shift to this model.

While it still privileged lending, the Direct Loans proposal was in some sense a radical step forward—cutting out actors whose only aim was making money off students. But Clinton hadn't been the first to advocate for this evidently sensible policy. The idea had originated with a Bush education official, and as late as 1992 it remained popular among both Republicans and Democrats eager to trim costs in the student loan program. The 1992 Higher Education Act reauthorization, passed just before Clinton came to office, had contained a provision for a $500 million pilot program for students at a select number of schools. If it went well, supporters hoped, the bank-based Guaranteed Student Loan Program might one day be scrapped altogether, saving the government billions of dollars that could instead be funneled back into student grants.

The students who won the Direct Loans lottery would also be rewarded with a side perk: holders of Direct Loans would be eligible for a new Income Contingent Repayment (ICR) plan, also enacted in 1992, which set their payments at 20 percent of their discretionary income and then canceled the balance after twenty-five years. This was a huge development—it was the first time the student loan program had included a general cancellation provision.* As such, it was an implicit admission that the loan program had grown more punishing to students than even the government was willing to countenance. But this message never got the headline treatment it deserved.

The prospects of both direct lending and the ICR offered, if not a complete reversal of the steady slide into predatory debt financing of education, at least a modicum of relief for students. Under a direct lending program, student borrowers wouldn't have to worry that their loans would be tossed around like hot potatoes, sold from lender to lender, with little requirement that anybody take borrowers' interests into account. They would recover a direct connection with the entity—the federal government—that was ultimately funding their education and would benefit from a variety of federal protections not offered under the bank-based system. And they would have some assurance that if things didn't pan out, their loans would not follow them to the grave.

Paired with Clinton's national service bill, these additions to the options of education finance did suggest some return, however minimal, to a more student-centered outlook on higher education. But each, in different ways, threatened entrenched upholders of the status quo—the kinds of entities that derived their power and money from making sure students couldn't catch a break. And that meant they could not be allowed to succeed.

The first to fail was the national service program. In 1993, Clinton managed to pass a bill creating the new program, called AmeriCorps. It was his first major piece of legislation. To get Republicans on board,

---

* As contrasted with the cancellation programs included in NDEA loans, which relied on fulfillment of certain employment criteria.

he'd had to whittle it down to the bone. In the end, the program allotted $300 million in its first year, enough to fund twenty thousand
volunteers to work in 350 programs around the country. In addition to
a small stipend, after a year of service volunteers would earn an award of
$4,725, which they could apply toward education expenses or use after
the fact to pay down student loans. It was a small win, hardly anything
on the order of the "domestic GI Bill" that Clinton had envisioned, but
it offered a genuinely different model of education funding—one that
harnessed some of the GI Bill's better aspects and gave young Americans
the hint of a way to break free from their chains of debt.

But even after the bipartisan "compromise" required to get this small
program off the ground, in 1995 the Republican majorities in both the
House and Senate voted to eliminate funding for AmeriCorps. Newt
Gingrich called it "coerced voluntarism" and claimed, unpersuasively,
that this program, which constituted 0.03 percent of annual federal
spending, was a threat to a balanced budget. Clinton vetoed the Republicans' bill, leading to a government shutdown. The budget battle was,
as Clinton's chief of staff, Leon Panetta, said, "the first time I've seen
a Congress go out of its way to hurt people in order to implement an
ideological agenda." Eventually the Republicans capitulated, but then
they repeated their defunding attempt the next year. Clinton prevailed
again, but the message was clear: the party of Newt Gingrich would not
hand Clinton anything resembling a win, no matter who benefited.

IN THEIR QUEST TO STYMIE CLINTON'S AGENDA, REPUBLICANS DIDN'T SPARE
direct lending either. Since the program was projected to save money,
their motives here were more patently sinister, the product of an unholy
alliance with student loan financiers.

Clinton's proposed system was a potential death knell for the lenders
and guaranty agencies that relied on student loans and their generous
government subsidies. But the lenders, led by Sallie Mae, the federal
government's own Frankenstein creation, were not about to give up
their government-funded cash cow. In fact, the history—and eventual

failure—of direct lending in the '90s is in many ways the flip side of Sallie Mae's monstrous rise.

In the weeks after Clinton announced his plan for Direct Loans, Sallie Mae's stock plummeted by 40 percent. This was bad news not only for the company but also for its executives, who were by then earning millions of dollars a year. So Sallie and her industry comrades combined forces to respond on two parallel fronts: first, they began to blitz Democrats in Congress with lobbyists to fight Clinton's bill. The lobbying firms took a scorched-earth approach, with direct-mail and on-the-ground campaigns, even an astroturf group called "Ohio Students for Loan Reform." One allegedly passionate Ohio student was paid $7 an hour by a lending company to put up posters on college campuses, place ads in student newspapers, and set up a toll-free hotline for students to express their disdain for direct lending to Ohio senators.

The lobbying campaigns worked, and the bill that finally landed on Clinton's desk in 1993 limited Direct Loans to a voluntary demonstration program capped at 5 percent of the market, with the capacity to increase each year until it hit 60 percent in 1998.

To cover its bases, Sallie Mae also began a push to privatize its way out of the restrictions of its government charter. That way, even if Direct Loans succeeded, the company would still have a path to profit. The Clinton administration came to see authorizing Sallie Mae's privatization plan as a necessary "olive branch" in exchange for direct lending. In 1996, Congress agreed, and Sallie Mae was split into two primary entities: Sallie Mae, a private holding company that could make student loans in its own right, and the Student Loan Marketing Association (SLMA), a subsidiary of the holding company that maintained its secondary market activities. The SLMA was given until 2008 to transfer its assets to Sallie Mae and wind itself out of business entirely. At that point, Sallie Mae would be a fully private profit-making corporation free to pursue business wherever the market took it.

Increasingly, the market took it everywhere, including areas far outside its original brief. According to a Treasury report published in 2006, Sallie Mae's strategy in this wind-down period was "to vertically

integrate and thereby gain control of the entire student loan life cycle."
In the 1990s it began dealing in asset-backed securities, selling student
loans in securitized bundles, not unlike the mortgage-backed securities
that would eventually bring down the housing market and set off the
Great Recession.

Then it began branching out, purchasing guarantors and debt collection agencies such as General Revenue Corporation, which had ties
to John Boehner, the chair of the House Committee on Education and
the Workforce, who later earned distinction as the top recipient of student loan PAC money. Soon it aimed at anything related to student
financing. In the next decade it would acquire UPromise, a leading pur-
veyor of tax-exempt college-savings-plan accounts, allowing it to offer
what it claimed were valuable "financing solutions" to its vast customer
base. Sallie Mae found advantageous deals to be made outside education as well, and it even bought up mortgage lenders and began issuing
mortgage-backed securities. Anything that would help serve the bottom
line was a possible target for the company. "In order for us to do what
we do best," said longtime Sallie Mae executive Albert Lord in 2004,
"our mission [had] to creep."

Among Sallie Mae's most lucrative expansions in this era was getting
into the private loan business. Because of a systematic weakening of
state usury laws beginning in 1980 (one of Jimmy Carter's many acts of
deregulation), caps on private-loan interest rates had all but disappeared.
Sallie Mae and other lenders were subsequently allowed to charge mind-
bogglingly high rates to desperate students and their parents—with
fees, rates on some Sallie Mae private loans ran as high as 28 percent.

Parents and students faced with the widening crevasse between the
unremitting rise in college costs and the relatively stagnant supply of
financial aid capitulated to these unattractive loan options generally because they had nowhere else to turn. Over the next decade, private loans
grew to eat up 20 percent of all student loan money. By 2006, Sallie
Mae was creating $7.7 billion in private loans per year, generating a
third of the market.

Sallie Mae's private loan portfolio also made its collections business an especially profitable side hustle. Many of its usurious private loans were "nontraditional"—aka subprime—marketed to families and students with poor credit ratings and low earnings expectations and those attending for-profit trade schools. A large portion of these borrowers eventually defaulted—in 2008, Sallie Mae's subprime loans, although only 14 percent of its private-loan portfolio, provided 54 percent of the company's charge-offs. But such defaulted loans did not always mean a loss for the company. By the time a bad loan made its way from Sallie Mae the lender to Sallie Mae the collection agency, it had acquired a bewildering premium of additional charges—late-payment fees, delinquency penalties, collections charges, and accrued interest—that could leave it at more than double the original balance. In the early aughts, Sallie Mae was making almost as much on fees and on collections on defaulted loans as it was on the loans themselves. Debt collection alone brought in 18 percent of its revenue in 2005.

By 2006, Sallie Mae was also the holder of more than a quarter of all federal student loan dollars. Its stock value had increased by almost 2,000 percent since the mid-1990s. Its executives made tens of millions of dollars a year, and its CEO, Albert Lord, a man who owned his own eighteen-hole golf course, was worth $30 million. In 2006, Lord's successor, Thomas Fitzpatrick, earned $37 million, making him the best-paid CEO in the country. That year, Sallie Mae's PAC beat out all other finance and credit card companies for the title of most generous campaign donor. The next year, Sallie Mae outspent them all on lobbying as well.

In this period, Sallie Mae came to use lobbying as a cudgel to protect itself from potentially harmful restrictions on its operations and even to expand its money-making capabilities—opening up its war chest to push for everything from lender subsidies to reduced bankruptcy protections for student debtors. The company was catholic with its money, donating to Democrats and Republicans alike, to anyone it deemed likely to support its interests. The strategy paid off. Sallie Mae CEO

Albert Lord wooed John Boehner with private jet rides and golf getaways, to say nothing of the hundreds of thousands of dollars in donations Sallie Mae made to Boehner's PAC over the course of his career. In a 2006 speech to the industry's trade association, the congressman vowed to protect Sallie Mae and other lenders from proposed cuts to their federal subsidies. "Know that I have all of you in my two trusted hands," he said. "I've got enough rabbits up my sleeve to be able to get where we need to."

This was not entirely a surprise—after all, Sallie Mae was mostly beholden to shareholders, particularly after its IPO. "That an entity left to its own devices considers its self-interest first is not exactly a novel idea," noted the 2006 Treasury report. However, "recognizing this fact helps to explain why it was such a challenge to use shareholder-owned [government-sponsored enterprises] to develop, implement and maintain public policy goals."

Sallie Mae was no longer even pretending to be about anything more than profit. And over the course of the 1990s and 2000s, the main victim of its expansion—other than students, of course—was the greatest threat to that profit: Clinton's pet loan program.

At first, in spite of all the lobbying powers lined up against them, Direct Loans was a modest success, and by 1997, it had grown to dominate a third of the student loan market. But Republicans had in fact already written its death warrant.

Clinton's 1993 direct lending law had stipulated that eligible schools were not required to take on Direct Loans: they could choose to stick with the bank-based program instead. Theoretically, they had no reason not to prefer Direct Loans, which was easier to administer, with fewer parties to coordinate, and required less paperwork.

But after the passage of Direct Loans, Republicans repeatedly tried to kneecap it, including by prohibiting the Department of Education from marketing direct lending to schools. This was a boon to lenders like Sallie Mae, who were under no such constraints. They struck up deals with colleges to get them to eschew direct lending and put their names on lists of "preferred lenders" that schools recommended to incoming students. In exchange, lenders brought schools in on profitable lending schemes and treated financial aid administrators to company stock offerings and beachside getaways. They also took over administrative needs, like staffing financial aid call centers, which raised questions about whether they were turning students' calls into marketing opportunities for their own products.

School administrators were all too happy to play along—and as a result students were rarely even presented with Direct Loans. After hitting a peak of 34 percent, direct lending's market share started to drop precipitously; the persuasive tactics of lenders like Sallie Mae had begun to eat away at its success. By 2000, when Clinton had hoped direct lending would dominate student lending, it had dropped to just 25 percent of loan volume. By 2006, it was down to 21 percent, once again lower than Sallie Mae's own share.

Not only did the preferred-lender scheme give Sallie Mae in particular a wider share of the federal loan market, but it also provided the company with opportunities to hawk its lucrative private loan products. These unsavory relationships between colleges and lenders were commonplace until *New York Times* reporter Jonathan Glater covered the story in 2006, spurring a civil investigation by Andrew Cuomo, then New York's attorney general. Sallie Mae ultimately agreed to pay $2 million in a settlement with Cuomo, while admitting no wrongdoing.

It may be unsurprising that a company like Sallie Mae, chartered to make a profit, would spare no effort to extract it. Yet the business model that the company perfected had now spread throughout the lending system. The logic of the student loan program had gotten so twisted that even the supposedly nonprofit actors—state agencies, for instance, that used their loan revenues to fund local college scholarship programs— had been incentivized to tap the veins of American students writ large in order to privilege the subset who resided within their state borders. It was robbing Peter to pay Paul on an absurd, grotesque level. But that was the name of the game now—by the turn of the twenty-first century, no one was immune to the siren song of limitless student-generated revenue.

JON OBERG HAD TAKEN A JOB AT THE DEPARTMENT OF EDUCATION IN 1994, having just fulfilled a lifelong goal. In 1989, after two decades working on higher education policy in both his home state of Nebraska and Washington, DC, Oberg and his family took a sabbatical in Berlin— arriving just before the Wall came down—so that he could complete a doctorate in political science at Freie Universität Berlin.

When they returned to the States, Oberg joined the Department of Education's Office of Legislation and Congressional Affairs, working as a liaison between the department and the House and Senate education committees. His job was to present the department's priorities to these committees. Among the biggest of those priorities at the time was reducing subsidies to lenders, which had grown from necessary enticements into exorbitant cash cows.

At the same time that Republicans in Congress were dismantling the regulatory state that had curbed the worst abuses against American students, they were also permitting sweetheart deals that left student lenders and guarantors raking in millions of taxpayer dollars.

Alongside the commercial lenders that had dominated the student loan industry, a number of ostensibly public-purpose lenders had also gotten in on the action. These were mostly state agencies—nonprofit lenders that funded their loan offerings through less costly tax-free bonds. Because their expenses were lower, they didn't need the same level of subsidy as commercial lenders, whom Congress had wooed through the 1980s with ever-larger special allowance payments (SAPs). So officials created a special category of SAP for these lenders. From 1980 to 1993, these payments had ensured that no matter what happened in the market, nonprofit lenders would achieve a total interest rate of at least 9.5 percent.

When interest rates went down again in the early 1990s, the government lowered SAPs for all lenders and discontinued the 9.5 percent guarantee for the nonprofits. Theoretically, this meant that any new loans issued after this point would be paid at the same rates, no matter the lender. The nonprofits continued, however, to qualify for the SAP on any eligible loans that had been issued prior to 1993 and were still in repayment. And they soon found a way to keep reaping the rewards of those loans ad infinitum.

In 1997, as Congress was gearing up to reauthorize the Higher Education Act, Oberg was tasked with bringing the Clinton administration's wish list of changes up to the Hill. Among the administration's proposed amendments was one to cut off the 9.5 percent subsidies on old loans still in repayment. He met with Sally Stroup, a House staffer working on the education committee under its Republican chair, Bill Goodling. "Looking through the amendments, she saw the one on 9.5 Loans," Oberg told the *Chronicle of Higher Education* years later, "and immediately said, 'Stop right there, take it back, we're not doing that.' It was so abrupt I said, 'What, what, let me explain,' and she said, 'Don't do it, we're not going to accept it.'"

Oberg took the message back, but he remained baffled by Stroup's firm rejection of the SAP amendment. He put the issue to the back of his mind, but he did not forget it.

Not long after the 1998 reauthorization, Oberg moved from the Department of Education's legislative affairs office to its research office. Now in the last years of his career, he hoped to put his doctorate in political science to good use. He was especially interested in analyzing how the student aid programs were functioning: whom they were benefiting, and whom they were hurting.

By this point, Clinton was out. George W. Bush, who came in vowing to restore the "compassionate conservatism" associated with his father's generation, focused little attention on higher—or as his party now referred to it, "postsecondary"—education. His signature education bill, No Child Left Behind, directed its energies exclusively at grades K–12, instituting a nationwide testing regimen and promoting an ideology

of "school choice" that privileged private education models. Most of
Bush's compassion, it soon became clear, was reserved not for American
citizens but for private corporations.

As Bush came to office, Oberg began to produce studies showing that
as schools shifted from need-based aid to merit aid, institutions were
disproportionately loading women, low-income, and minority students
with debt they couldn't repay. And in his view, they were doing it intentionally. "I thought they were discriminating badly," he said. But the
Bush administration "wasn't interested in any of that."

And so Oberg spun his wheels. He thought back on his work trying
to get rid of the 9.5 percent SAP. It had now been ten years since the last
loans to qualify for it had entered repayment. Surely, he thought, the
subsidy ought to be gone by now, right?

But as he began to look into it, Oberg discovered that payouts under
the 9.5 percent SAP had not subsided or even dwindled—they'd actually *gone up*. Oberg was stunned. "How could it possibly be growing?"
he asked himself. "These loans are being paid off."

Determined to figure out what was going on, Oberg started digging
into the nonprofit lenders' financial reports.

That's when he discovered the loophole.

In the years after the 9.5 SAP was discontinued on new loans, market
rates dropped to as low as 3.4 percent. But lenders invented a conve-
nient workaround to keep goosing the rates. The loans that continued to
qualify for the special rate had been financed by nonprofit bonds created
before 1993. To continue billing for the rate on *new* loans, which should
not have qualified, lenders temporarily moved the new loans onto the
ledgers of the old qualifying bonds. This, the lenders claimed, gave the
new loans the coveted status of the old loans and made them eligible for
the higher subsidy. It was as if they had dipped their cheap paper into a
vat of liquid gold.

The lenders' little trick—which, while not strictly speaking illegal,
was not explicitly permitted either—had resulted in hundreds of millions of dollars in excess payments from the federal government. The
Department of Education's inspector general later determined that one

lender alone, Nelnet, had "improperly" received roughly $10 million a month—for a total of nearly $300 million over just two and a half years.

After Oberg discovered the lenders' shenanigans in 2003, just eighteen months before his scheduled retirement, he took the issue up the chain of command. First he notified his supervisor, a Bush appointee named Grover Whitehurst, who instructed him to let it go. "In the 18 months you have remaining," he told Oberg, "I will expect your time and talents to be directed primarily to our business of conceptualizing, competing and monitoring research grants." Officials also rewrote Oberg's job description to prohibit him from continuing to investigate the matter.

But Oberg did not let it go. He continued to alert his higher-ups along with the Department of Education's inspector general, and he even distributed a department-wide memo about the issue in 2003. "I have come across what appears to be significant government waste," he wrote. "I estimate it amounts to about $30,000 per day, perhaps more."

To no avail. For three more years, department officials—including Secretary of Education Rod Paige and his successor, Margaret Spellings, as well as Sally Stroup, who was now the department's assistant secretary for postsecondary education—failed to crack down on the practice, claiming their hands were tied.

Although Stroup had refused any congressional modification to the SAP legislation when Oberg presented it to her back in 1997, she now changed tack as an assistant secretary for the Department of Education. She rejected the Government Accountability Office's call in 2004 for the department to rewrite its regulations. Both she and Spellings argued it was Congress's job to fix the issue with new legislation.

From Oberg's vantage as a political scientist, he questioned whether Stroup's actions were rooted in the dynamics of the education-finance "iron triangle," in which government agencies form close alliances with the entities they regulate. Before joining the House education committee staff in the 1990s, Stroup had directed government affairs for the University of Phoenix, and in the 1980s she had served as chief counsel for the Pennsylvania Higher Education Assistance Agency (PHEAA), a nonprofit guaranty agency. PHEAA had been created in 1963, just a couple of years before the Higher Education Act, by Pennsylvania's General Assembly. Its primary purpose in those years was to administer state grant programs. But as the federal government turned increasingly to state guaranty agencies to manage federal student loans in the 1970s, PHEAA got in on the action. In exchange, the federal Office of Education paid PHEAA 1 percent of each loan it managed; in addition, PHEAA's cut on the money it collected from delinquent loans was between 80 and 100 percent. This then went back to funding Pennsylvania education programs—seemingly a win-win for everyone involved.

Eventually, PHEAA also expanded into lending and began operating as a secondary market for federal student loans. On the loans it issued or purchased in these capacities, it was eligible for the 9.5 percent SAP.

In 2004, Oberg received permission from the Department of Education's ethics division to pursue the SAP matter as an individual, and he took what he'd found to the Government Accountability Office. By this point, Congress had also started taking notice, and both bodies began urging the department to clamp down on the overpayments and recover excess money that had already been paid out. In May 2005, the department's inspector general released an audit report urging the department to recover $36 million in overpayments to a New Mexico lender. But Secretary Spellings, a Bush loyalist going back to his Texas governor days, did not heed the recommendation.

PHEAA also benefited handsomely from the SAP overpayments, allegedly reaping $116.5 million between 2002 and 2006. And it was not eager to let them go. According to Oberg, a 2005 email exchange between PHEAA executives, which was unearthed in a 2017 legal filing, referred to a conversation with Stroup about an impending audit by the Department of Education's inspector general. "She expects that we are high on the IG's list (they are currently at NelNet)," it said. "She said the key point seems to be the need for an unimpeachable link between each loan and the specific bond issue. [. . .] Should we get the notice from the IG, it may be worth having [chief financial officer Tim Guenther] talk to Sally before the IG arrives."

As PHEAA worked its government connections, Nelnet, for its part, was fighting on a parallel front, ramping up efforts to keep its protectors in Congress. As chair of the House Education and Workforce Committee, John Boehner had defended lenders' excessive use of the 9.5 percent subsidy and fought to permit them to keep reaping it. But with the 2006 midterm elections approaching, the party of Boehner was in trouble, and Democrats on the committee had been sharply critical of lenders' actions. That election cycle Nelnet was the largest corporate donor to the National Republican Congressional Committee, and its president and co-CEOs were the committee's top three individual donors.

In September 2006, the inspector general's office released its audit of Nelnet and again urged the department to recover excess payments, in this case $278 million paid between 2003 and 2005. But instead of recouping the lost money, Spellings declared the lenders' overpayments, which Nelnet had pursued under a program it referred to internally as "Project 950," a matter of "confusion" fostered in part by the department. She entered into a settlement that allowed Nelnet to keep the overpayments, so long as it agreed not to submit an *additional* $882 million in projected SAP overcharges over the next several years. As part of the settlement, Nelnet denied any wrongdoing.

Facing sustained pressure and publicity, in early 2007 the Department of Education finally stopped the extra payments, simply by restating its own regulation to lenders, just as Oberg had been urging all along.

But Oberg was not satisfied. "I thought this was absolutely the wrong lesson," he said later. "You don't want the government out there telling its contractors you can make false [. . .] claims, and if we catch you you'll have to stop, but [you] can keep what you've gained, even if it's in the hundreds of millions of dollars."

Secretary Spellings's justification for opposing him did not evince such principled concern for safeguarding the taxpayer. In January 2008, she pooh-poohed the overpayments as constituting a mere fraction of the total loan program. "Just think about it in context," she said, noting that the loan program was by then huge, on the order of hundreds of billions of dollars. In this light, an extra billion dollars to lenders over a few years was practically a rounding error. In other words, at a time when destitute borrowers had fewer rights than ever, when they could be legally pursued to the grave for debts of just a few thousand dollars, the secretary of education was justifying—in fact, explicitly permitting—losses of nearly $1 billion in public funds to greedy lenders.

This was more than Oberg could stomach. In 2007, with no other remedy in sight, he decided to act on his own, opting to file a whistle-blower complaint under the federal False Claims Act. Under the legisla-tion, enacted during the Civil War, private citizens can file suit against federal contractors they suspect of committing fraud against the govern-ment, and whistleblowers are eligible to receive about a quarter of any money recovered. For the next ten years, when Oberg should have been enjoying his retirement, he was instead meeting with lawyers and attend-ing hearings as his case wound its way through various courts. Along the way, most of the nine named lenders settled their suits. Among them was Nelnet, which agreed to pay $55 million in 2010, again without admitting any wrongdoing.

But one of the lenders simply would not let the issue go. PHEAA, Sally Stroup's old employer, fought the case in part by arguing that it was a de facto arm of the Commonwealth of Pennsylvania and therefore had sovereign immunity. The agency took this defense all the way to the Supreme Court. In 2017 the court confirmed that even though PHEAA was a state-chartered benefit corporation—set up in 1963 much like Sallie Mae had been at the federal level a decade later—because it was financially independent of the state and operated nationally, it did not in fact benefit from sovereign immunity.

But that was not the end of Oberg's suit. The case finally made its way to a jury trial in late 2017. In the end, the jury sided with PHEAA, finding that because the department had continued making payments to the agency even after it knew they were improper (in large part be-cause of Oberg's whistleblowing), the fault lay not with PHEAA but with the Department of Education itself.

Finally, the story was over for Oberg. And although his pursuit of justice had taken up a decade of his retirement and ended with a defeat, he didn't regret the time he had put into it. "I was a civil servant. I was being paid by the taxpayer. I wasn't paid to carry anybody's water," he told me. "I took an oath to enforce the constitution and the laws of the country, and if I saw cheating [. . .] I was going to do it, come what may."

But he reflected dimly on the outcome. The whole episode revealed that "a department that was supposed to benefit higher education," he told a reporter in 2018, "has been captured by the interests it's supposed to regulate."

That, in a nutshell, was the story of higher education at the dawn of the twenty-first century. Practically every good thing Bill Clinton—or anyone else—had ever tried to do in higher education had been undone by Republicans in Congress, and any gains had been undermined by the conservative administration that succeeded his. Direct Loans was all but dead, Sallie Mae was an untouchable behemoth, and everyone else in the loan program was aiming not at helping students but getting in on the bottomless treasure chest they represented.

But it wasn't just Republicans who set out to hand the keys of government over to the private sector. Although he'd fought for Direct Loans and national service, Clinton was as infected with the 1990s' obsession with markets and business as anyone else—more than most, even. And before he left office, he too found a way to kick the long-suffering Department of Education—and the students it served—in the knees.

CHAPTER 9

A Bankrupt System

Although Clinton was portrayed by Gingrich and his acolytes as liberal excess incarnate, in fact he was politically much more in line with his Republican predecessors than almost anyone wanted to admit. As he ran for reelection in 1996, for instance, he decided to one-up his rival, Bob Dole, who was proposing a huge income tax cut, by proposing a cut of his own. In 1997, he enacted a long-sought-after Republican goal: tuition tax credits. It would give families the option to deduct $1,500 from their taxes for every child in college—at an annual cost of roughly $5 billion to the government. It was just the type of legislation President Johnson had hoped to fend off by creating the Guaranteed Student Loan Program.

Clinton was a New Democrat, a product and member of the Democratic Leadership Council, a confederation founded in 1985 by conservative Southern Democrats (and funded by such progressive luminaries as the Koch brothers) who wanted to move the party rightward. And as president, he toed a compliantly neoliberal line, with slogans to match. To counter Reagan's "New Federalism," Clinton brought a commitment to "Reinventing Government." By and large, this meant deregulating, privatizing, and window-dressing government services in the decor of the marketplace. The most thoroughgoing of those refurbishments occurred within the Department of Education.

In 1998, amid the pre-Y2K wave of private-sector adulation, Clinton followed through on a reelection campaign promise. He set out to convert the Department of Education's student financial aid office—charged with administering the federal portfolio of student loans, grants, and other monies dedicated to helping students pursue higher education—into Federal Student Aid, the government's first "performance-based organization," or PBO. "We're going to toss out the restrictive rules that keep [federal agencies] from doing business like a business," said Vice President Gore, who had proposed introducing the PBO model, imported from Thatcherite England, as a means of improving "customer" satisfaction and saving costs in a federal government seen as creaky and rule-ridden. He wanted to cut through "all the red tape, personnel rules that keep managers from using people effectively, the budget restrictions that make planning or allocating resources almost impossible." On the 1996 campaign trail, Clinton indicated he might convert hundreds of government offices into PBOs. In the end, only three agencies gained this status: the Patent and Trademark Office, the Air Traffic Organization, and Federal Student Aid (FSA).

Clinton fulfilled the promise to convert FSA with the passage of the 1998 reauthorization of the Higher Education Act. The move enjoyed bipartisan support—unsurprising, given the vitriol that politicians on both sides routinely directed toward the underfunded, supposedly incompetent Department of Education. "Under the legislation that I am proposing today," said California Republican Buck McKeon as he introduced the bill on the House floor, "the department's student financial aid systems would be run more like a business—adopting the best practices from the private sector and focusing on bottom-line results."

As part of the conversion, FSA was given a chief operating officer appointed to a contractually limited term by the secretary of education, as well as a chief financial officer, a chief information officer, and other trappings of the private sector. FSA's COO was given broad hiring and salary-setting power, which was not the case in other government agencies, as well as the discretion to administer performance bonuses—the COO's own salary was prohibited from exceeding only the president's. FSA's charter lists among its goals an improvement in service to students and a reduction in administration costs. It bears watchwords of the late 1990s, such as "accountability," "flexibility," and "information systems."

As a PBO, FSA was responsible for soliciting applications from outside contractors—for instance, for servicers to process payments from Direct Loans borrowers—and overseeing the assignment and distribution of their responsibilities. The Department of Education didn't have much input into this, and FSA did not have to follow the same rules for accessible and competitive bidding that other federal agencies do. Additionally, FSA was housed in a separate building and did not have to share all its data with the rest of the department. One Department of Education official I spoke with referred to its financial decision-making processes as a "black box." The secretary of education was not even able to issue directives for all its activities because it lay outside the chain of command, a positioning that brought distinct benefits to those it dealt with—the companies who contracted with it, that is, but not the students it was meant to serve.

Although applying the rhetoric of corporate efficiency and fiscal stringency may have pleased the neoliberal wonks of the 1990s, the PBO model represented a fundamental paradox for FSA. What, after all, does it mean for a federal agency, whose core mission is to expand poor and middle-class students' access to education, to run like a business? According to Deanne Loonin, a lawyer who advocated for borrowers throughout her career at the National Consumer Law Center and elsewhere, this question represents an unresolvable conflict at the heart of the agency. "FSA is supposed to act on behalf of its customers," she has written, "but there is no single priority group of customers." Are its customers students, their schools, or the banks that lend to them? Each group has different, and often conflicting, interests. FSA's mandate to operate like a private-sector business means it prioritizes areas like "consumer satisfaction" and cost reduction, Loonin emphasizes, while ignoring other "key areas, such as consumer protection."

This conflict, Loonin told me, has been tugging at the student loan program since its inception. "Is it a public program that's meant to be efficient but is focused mostly on public goals and public goods?" she asked. "Or is it a private program that's profit-based and supposed to be all about making sure the government makes some money—or at least doesn't lose money?" Or, as Loonin wrote when she was a staff attorney at the National Consumer Law Center, "In some ways [. . .] student loans are more like social programs. It is unfairly punitive to treat them this way at the outset, but then to focus mostly on the business interest if the borrower gets into trouble."

By transforming government student aid into a performance-based activity, Clinton turned this contradiction into a weapon capable of inflicting maximum damage on vulnerable debtors.

Indeed, by the dawn of the millennium, the long work of transforming students from citizens into sources of revenue was nearly complete. They had been made pawns of the market in the years of the GI Bill, the NDEA, and the Higher Education Act, and then its prey, thrown to the likes of Sallie Mae and John Sperling. Then the American government had made itself over in the image of the private sector, adopting its jargon and practices. Balancing the budget became more important than protecting the down and out. For students, there was no safe harbor. They were mere consumers now, and they would be treated as such.

But then the pendulum swung even farther.

Student debt had inarguably become a millstone for students, set only to weigh heavier in the years to come. Yet public officials still cloaked it in the rhetoric of social welfare. Unwilling to concede that they had given away the candy-store keys to financiers, they refused to change the locks and protect student borrowers. Instead they doubled down and punished them.

It was the worst of all possible worlds.

To understand how this came to be, we have to go back to the 1970s, when legislators first started cracking down on student debtors.

FOR MOST PEOPLE DROWNING IN DEBT, DECLARING BANKRUPTCY IS A LAST, albeit potent, resort. Few undertake this comprehensive and complicated measure to evade only specific debts, for instance, student loans. Yet in the 1970s, frenzied reports emerged in the media, under such headlines as "Study Now, Pay Never," to suggest that recent graduates were abusing bankruptcy protections to avoid ever having to pay a penny on their student loans. In 1973, grandstanding legislators petitioned a recently assembled congressional commission to study the issue. The commission concluded that it was "not aware of any evidence" to suggest that student loan bankruptcies were "significant problems numerically." In fact, in 1972, amid that decade's default crisis, no more than 0.69 percent of student borrowers ended up filing for bankruptcy.

Although it had ruled out the existence of widespread abuse, however, the commission claimed that any that did occur would "discredit the system and cause disrespect for the law." Perhaps more damning, student debt bankruptcies undermined the logic of human capital, which justified education debt in the first place. Since a loan is meant to enable education, which is a profitable investment in the borrower, that person should not, the commission argued, be allowed to evade repayment before testing whether the education they had purchased would in fact pay off, in the form of higher income. So, despite admitting that bankruptcy was a non-problem, the commission recommended revising the law to clamp down on it anyway, as if for good measure.

When legislators met to reauthorize the Higher Education Act in 1976, they took up the commission's suggestion to make federal student loans nondischargeable in bankruptcy for at least five years after the start of repayment. In 1984, Reagan signed a bill that added certain vocational education loans to the mix.

That, for a number of years, was as far as things went, but the Reagan-era budget battles that spilled into the '90s brought bankruptcies back to the chopping block. After budget deficits soared during Reagan's first term—doubling as a percentage of GDP, from 2.5 percent to more than 5 percent—fiscal hawks in Congress tried to clamp down on federal spending. In 1986, Senators Phil Gramm, Warren Rudman, and Ernest Hollings drafted a bill that specified deficit limits for each year until a balanced budget could be achieved. If the yearly limits weren't met, the president would be required to sequester money from other programs. But Gramm-Rudman-Hollings, as the bill became known, left open many new magic-asterisk loopholes that allowed policymakers to play shell games with spending and accrue ever-larger budget deficits.

So in 1990, Congress tried again, passing the Budget Enforcement Act, which set specific spending caps on program categories and created pay-as-you-go (PAYGO), a process that required all federal spending to be offset by equivalent cost cutting somewhere else.

In 1990, the budget cutters took their knives to the already frayed safety net supporting student debtors, stretching their five-year bankruptcy moratorium to seven. A year later, Congress took out the six-year statute of limitations on student loan collections, claiming that a loan's benefits "far outweigh any burden on the student resulting from the Federal Government's ability to collect on the loan over an indefinite period of time." They offered scant evidence to justify such a change, which, Deanne Loonin has pointed out, "placed borrowers in unenviable, rarified company with murderers, traitors, and only a few violators of civil laws. Even rapists are not in this category." For repayment of student loans, unlike any other form of debt, "the government can pursue borrowers to the grave."

But it wasn't until 1998, as Clinton set about reinventing government, that lawmakers decided to really put student debtors in their place.

That year, Vermont senator Jim Jeffords took to the Senate floor to present the conference report that his Committee on Labor and Human Resources had hashed out with the House after two long years of hearings and haggling over the reauthorization of the Higher Education Act. Jeffords acknowledged that because of the new budget constraints, the committee had been forced to make "difficult decisions" to pay for long-sought reductions in student loan interest rates (from 8.25 percent to 7.46 percent) and increases in the maximum Pell Grant. Among these difficult decisions, he conceded, revisions to the bankruptcy provision had generated "particular concern."

In effect, the committee had axed bankruptcy protections altogether, making federal loans nominally nondischargeable in perpetuity. But, Jeffords reassured, this was not really a big deal, since anyone filing for bankruptcy could still qualify for debt cancellation if their loans were deemed an "undue hardship." Never mind that "undue hardship" was not actually defined—leaving its interpretation up to individual bankruptcy judges. In spite of Jeffords's upbeat assessment, judges did not end up taking a very sympathetic position on the subject. One study found that out of more than 200,000 bankruptcy filers with student debt in any given year, only a few hundred—on the order of 0.1–0.2 percent—received debt relief. One woman who tried to get her student loans discharged in bankruptcy proceedings after the 1998 reauthorization reported that "the judge told me not to come back unless I was in a wheelchair."

Congress still was not done going after bankruptcy relief for student debtors. The KO came in 2005, with the Bankruptcy Abuse Prevention and Consumer Protection Act. The overarching goal of the legislation was to make it harder for debtors to receive loan discharges under Chapter 7—or "liquidation"—bankruptcy, and steer them instead to Chapter 13 bankruptcy, which restructures debts and keeps filers paying their creditors.

Among its other restrictions, the 2005 bill closed the last remaining door on bankruptcy protections for student debtors, making even *private* student loans—those funded by profit-gobbling entities like Sallie Mae, at staggering double-digit interest rates—ineligible for discharge. This change, made without even the flimsy ideological basis that had buttressed the bankruptcy reforms for federal student loans, turned private student debt into one of the most onerous types of credit in existence: its prisoners, not only ineligible for any of the special consumer protections offered under federal loans, were now also beholden to their creditors for life.

Removing bankruptcy relief of nearly any kind, for any kind of student debtor, sent a potent message that went beyond talk of budgets and bootstraps. It told students that all parties involved in student lending would get paid, no matter the human cost. There would be no out. This required a new way of looking at education itself. Money to pay for tuition would by necessity have to fund training in a field that promised a high enough income to pay back the loans that had paid the tuition. But who can be sure which fields of work will flourish in the future?

According to this logic, students (and their families) would be mortgaging their futures on something over which they had no control: the future of industries and world economies. How can a student choose the path of education that will best prepare them for something that is unknowable? And if students' plans didn't work out—always a possibility—and they were unable to reset their finances through a protection as basic as bankruptcy, what exactly *were* they supposed to do? It seemed that the politicians, with all their lofty talk of opportunity and access, were in fact more invested in a vision that led to the pillory and the debtors' prison.

With the screws tightened on student borrowers, their advocates conceded precious ground. They had little choice but to accept the terms of the debate that had been set by borrowers' antagonists in the boardrooms of financial corporations and the committees of Congress. They too would treat students as consumers, but they would also help them *as consumers*, deserving of whatever support they could draw from the patchwork scaffolding of federal consumer protections.

These new students-as-consumers found their champion in a Harvard law professor who happened to specialize in bankruptcy law.

The 2005 bankruptcy bill was drafted and supported primarily by Republicans. But it found an unlikely ally in a Democrat from Delaware who sat on the Senate Judiciary Committee. He had introduced the bill in the Senate, and had in fact had a hand in every punitive bankruptcy "reform" going back to the 1970s: that Democrat was Joseph Robinette Biden Jr.

As the 2005 bill circulated, the Senate Judiciary Committee invited the law professor who opposed it, Elizabeth Warren, to testify. At the hearing, she and Biden had a fiery exchange. Biden argued that permitting people to liquidate their debts in bankruptcy merely forced a problem onto creditors that should be addressed by government, through an improved social safety net. "We are going to ask the gas company, the drugstore, the automobile dealer," he said, "to pay for the broken system instead of having the nerve to come and say it is a moral obligation of a nation to pay for that broken system."

Warren agreed, though Biden gave her little room to respond, arguing that her real beef was with usury, not bankruptcy. "But, Senator," she said, exasperated, "if you are not going to fix [the usury] problem, you can't take away the last shred of protection from these families."

Biden basically argued that creating a better social safety net was more important than providing bankruptcy relief, which people would not need if the former goal was met. But as it turned out, neither he nor his fellow Democrats actually went about creating one, for debtors or for anyone else. Instead, they mostly enshrined the existing system, preserving perquisites for the private sector while offering a mirage of improved benefits for citizens. Warren believed that in the absence of that always elusive wider social safety net, the baseline consumer protections guaranteed by government become all the more important. In fact, people have no choice but to rely on them to avoid total financial ruin.

So instead of presenting the debate as one of citizen rights, advocates like Warren turned to a more palatable discourse focused on consumer protection. Americans had long ago given up on expecting that their status as citizens would provide them with benefits (health care, education, protection of the environment) enjoyed in social democracies around the world. Instead, they had been primed, at least as far back as the Reagan years, to accept their role as consumers, whether in relationship to private industry or to the government itself. Warren at the very least wanted to protect them as consumers; Biden prattled about social welfare for American citizens while working behind the scenes to benefit those who profited from them.

But why would a Democrat from Delaware be eager to reward corporate creditors and screw over debtors? Democrats, after all, were the party of Direct Loans, of cutting the banks out of the process, while it was the Republicans who fought tooth and nail to preserve banks' benefits. When Biden's bankruptcy bill came up for debate, Ted Kennedy railed that "this legislation breaks the bond that unites America; it sacrifices Americans to the rampant greed of the credit card industry."

The answer to the Biden enigma lies in the peculiarities of the state he represented. When interstate banking began to spread at the tail end of the Carter years, Delaware became one of two states, along with South Dakota, to permit credit card companies to charge unlimited interest rates to encourage them to plant their headquarters (and jobs) within its borders. By 2005 Biden was as reliant on his adopted state's particular interests as anyone else. His biggest campaign contributor was MBNA, a Delaware-based credit card company that was one of the nation's largest (it is now a subsidiary of Bank of America). It donated more than $200,000 to Biden over the course of his Senate career. Credit card companies were among the strongest proponents of restricting liquidation bankruptcy, since it left them entirely in the lurch. Like private student loan debt, credit card debt is "unsecured": because neither a degree nor a Visa card is tied to any material asset, unlike a car or a house, there is nothing for a creditor to repossess if the debtor defaults.

After the fight with Biden in the Senate, Elizabeth Warren did not go quietly into the DC night. She used her outrage at the policies pushed by people like Biden to propel a political career of her own, founded on building a federal apparatus of consumer protection and preserving the economic well-being of the shrinking American middle class.

But by the time that career would start to take shape, consumers of education would get sold a whole lot more defective merchandise—with no recall yet in sight.

ALONGSIDE THE PATH TO REMOVING BANKRUPTCY PROTECTIONS FROM STU-dent debtors ran a parallel track, which ended in a pot of gold for the sleazy actors who exploited students in the first place: for-profit entities calling themselves schools. They had been chastened somewhat in the early 1990s by Maxine Waters and her allies, but Republican legislators of the late '90s and early aughts were done tamping down on an industry from which investors were reaping such happy returns. It was time to help them operate with nearly absolute impunity once again.

In 1998, legislators deemed that the problem with for-profit schools had been cured, and acted to remove the restrictions that had reined them in. The scoundrels had learned their lesson and been punished enough. "We've seen a fire across the prairie, and that fire has had a purifying effect," said a top for-profit lobbyist. Republican legislators apparently agreed. That year's reauthorization of the Higher Education Act nixed all reference to state oversight agencies (already dismantled), weakened accreditor requirements for monitoring things like default rates, and loosened the definition of default itself, making it easier for problem schools to evade consequences. It also weakened Maxine Waters's 85/15 rule to an almost meaningless 90/10.

But Republican legislators were just getting started. In the George W. Bush administration, student debtors were a target, but for-profit schools were darlings—and they were on the up and up. Their profits were soaring amid unrelenting growth, and the administration was actively assisting the sector in its quest for unrestricted revenues.

Bush had brought with him a clutch of for-profit veterans to staff the Department of Education. Not only was Sally Stroup, Bush's assistant secretary for postsecondary education, a former PHEAA insider, but she had also been the head of government affairs at Apollo Group, the University of Phoenix's parent company. Her deputy had been a consultant for Career College Association, the for-profit lobbying organization. In 2002, Stroup declared that the proprietaries had done a "great job cleaning up their act" and were now "equals to four-year schools."

Now that the excesses of the 1970s and '80s had supposedly been corrected, for-profits were suddenly hailed as valuable innovators, filling a gap in the market that traditional colleges and universities couldn't or wouldn't, by providing skills training and opportunity to the kinds of students the Harvards and Berkeleys wanted nothing to do with. "In our knowledge-based economy," said Buck McKeon, chair of the House education committee, in 2003, "it is more important than ever to remove roadblocks to innovative ideas and methods of providing education." The for-profits' very growth was said to demonstrate their value, validating the supposed demand for online and vocational training of nontraditional students. Meanwhile, traditional schools, from Columbia University to the University of Maryland, got in on the game as well, creating their own for-profit subsidiaries to push online courses to students.

In fact, in the late 1990s and early 2000s, it seemed that almost everyone was blinded by the promise of the schools' expanded "access" and educational "innovations"—even those who had reason to know better. In 2001, the publishing arm of Johns Hopkins University released a supposedly even-handed account of the for-profit boom by Richard S. Ruch, a university professor turned dean of the for-profit school DeVry University. Ruch argued that, while there were of course some downsides to proprietary schools, the profit motive brought to them "a kind of bottom-line discipline," in which "the academic side of the house becomes a tightly managed service operation."

The *Chronicle of Higher Education*, the field's most prominent press outlet, was peppered with articles about the industry's newest and biggest players, issuing gushing reports of soaring stock prices, institutional expansion, and political approval. These accounts featured starry-eyed appraisals from even traditional academics and college administrators, the for-profits' so-called competitors. "They've really made us, as traditional colleges, realize that we may not be serving some markets as well as we thought we were," said one North Carolina community college president.

With their star on the rise, for-profits and their supporters kept hacking away at the regulations that had previously brought them to heel. In 2002, Bush's education secretary, Rod Paige, decided to go after Maxine Waters's 1992 prohibition on incentive sales commissions for school recruiters. Although the ban had resulted in only a handful of sustained violations and settlements, it had taken down a major player. In 2000, department regulators had charged Computer Learning Centers, a publicly traded chain of twenty-five schools, with violating the ban and ordered the company to repay $187 million in federal student aid. Five weeks later, the school shut down and filed for bankruptcy.

For the for-profit industry, this was a bridge too far. They lobbied aggressively to correct it. To remedy the supposed overstep, Paige created a set of "safe harbors" that permitted schools to reward recruiters for high enrollments so long as that wasn't the *only* metric used to determine their pay. In effect, this gutted the incentive pay restrictions, and schools quickly reverted to their boiler-room ways. In 2004, a Department of Education staff report revealed, for instance, that the University of Phoenix was brazenly ignoring recruitment compensation restrictions, and Phoenix agreed to pay a $9.8 million settlement without admitting guilt.

Then, in 2005, John Boehner, the chair of the House education committee, snuck an education provision into a budget bill. His amendment repealed a 1992 rule that said no more than 50 percent of a school's student body could be learning remotely. In the 1990s this had meant taking classes through the mail, but now, Boehner argued, the internet had made such a limitation impractical.

After Boehner removed this cap, online education programs grew from a niche concern to a massive revenue stream for proprietary schools. Within a decade, 60 percent of their students were in online-only programs. And their new business was a big one, about to explode.

BY THIS POINT, JOHN SPERLING WAS NOT THE ONLY ONE OUT TO ESTABLISH A for-profit education empire. He was merely at the leading edge of a great transition—from market-based education to *finance*-driven education. After the University of Phoenix went public, others were close on Sperling's heels: Corinthian, ITT Tech, Kaplan. Each had IPOs in the 1990s, netting tens of millions of dollars and setting off tremendous periods of growth.

Soon, private equity firms also caught wind of the opportunity. In 2003, there were just eighteen for-profits owned by private equity firms; less than a decade later, that number had more than tripled, to sixty-one. For-profit enrollments were also exploding: from a little more than 425,000 in 2000 to 1.7 million in 2012—an increase of more than 300 percent. By contrast, public colleges had grown by just 31 percent.

In the early aughts, the business—for-profit certificate and degree-granting programs ranging from associate to doctorate—was booming. And increasingly the boom could be characterized as a Wall Street versus Main Street match-up. Hardly more than a decade before the University of Phoenix's IPO, the majority of for-profit programs had been mom-and-pop affairs: short-term certificate courses in subjects like cosmetology and truck driving. By the early years of the new millennium, students were attending Fortune 500 chain schools for full-fledged degrees in teaching, medical assisting, business, and psychology. In 2012 there were twenty-one publicly traded for-profit colleges, and less than a quarter of the industry's students attended a mom-and-pop operation; the other 1.3 million went to publicly traded or private-equity-owned schools.

The profits in this new world were beyond belief. One study found that the for-profit industry netted 55 percent profit margins between 2000 and 2012. In other words, for every dollar they took from students, 55 cents went to shareholders, with overall profits maxing out in 2011 at $5 billion. Within a decade of Apollo's IPO, Phoenix's student body had grown tenfold, and thanks to students' easy federal money, the company was bringing in more than $1 billion a year.

It was a win-win for just about everyone involved. The schools' profits came almost exclusively from federal grant and loan monies. The federal government was bankrolling not only their and their investors' windfalls but also those of the financial institutions that did the lending and collecting under the Federal Family Education Loan program (a 1990s renaming of the GSLP). There were really only two groups left out of the bonanza: the public at large, whose tax dollars kept the machine running, and the students who got sacked with the bill.

Then the evidence started coming in, yet again, that the for-profit corporate darlings of the '90s and aughts were no more sophisticated—certainly no more beneficial—than the porn-store computer schools that had preceded them.

In the forty years since Sam Nunn had first taken on for-profit schools, they had only grown stronger. In 1970 there had been only 18,333 students enrolled at degree-granting for-profit schools, less than a quarter of a percent of the total number of college students. By 2009 there were 1.85 million—almost 10 percent of the total. The grift had grown a hundredfold.

"I HAD WORKED IN THE SALES INDUSTRY FOR MANY YEARS," THE ADMISSIONS supervisor stated. "But Ashford [University] had the most aggressive sales floor I have ever seen." The supervisor's employer was putatively an accredited institution that offered a wide variety of bachelor's and advanced degrees; in reality it was effectively a money-printing operation. The school's sordid practices—of which there were many—were revealed in a 2017 lawsuit filed against the institution by the attorney general of California. Among them were the tales of Ashford's salespeople—aka "admissions counselors"—who made hundreds, sometimes even a thousand, cold calls a week. Still their managers berated and taunted them, forcing underperformers to stand all day, jangling keyrings with the ID cards of their fired former colleagues in their faces. Some of them cried; some had mental breakdowns; eventually most quit or were fired. Managers created "lowest performer lists" and then fired the bottom tenth of recruiters. When the salespeople did manage to land a mark, they celebrated by ringing cowbells or flapping plastic hand clappers. "The sales floor had a true boiler room atmosphere," said the supervisor, not unlike that "portrayed in the movie *The Wolf of Wall Street*."

And if they all misled some naive fools in the process, say, a few hundred a month, well, that was just the cost of doing business. It wasn't like they were going to get fired for calling loans "grants" or promising a program would lead to high-paying jobs or guaranteeing that if things didn't work out at the school, any credits earned there would transfer elsewhere (as they almost certainly would not). One Ashford admissions counselor got twenty-five violations in eight months and the managers dished out only a slap on the wrist. The risk of punishment by the company's compliance department was low, but the reward was irresistibly high: admissions counselors got paid by the sale, and the best of them made in the six figures. Recruiters preyed on their marks' naiveté about higher education, convincing them that they couldn't receive their financial aid until well into the semester (when it would be too late to get a refund), lying about what their degrees would qualify them to do, and encouraging them to spend their federal aid funds on things like cars or expensive vacations (against federal law).

Ashford University was owned by Bridgepoint Education, which was backed by Warburg Pincus, a private equity firm. And the secret to its success was a foolproof tactic that for-profit financiers had discovered for getting their business off the ground and gaining access to the all-important stream of federal aid money. The trick was to gobble up existing mom-and-pop proprietary schools—as well as small, financially struggling nonprofits—and to acquire their accreditations, assets as valuable as New York City taxi medallions.

In 2005, Bridgepoint Education, incorporated in California only months before, purchased Franciscan University of the Prairies, a 332-student nonprofit institution in Iowa founded in 1918. Bridgepoint had no interest in the school's Catholic values or low student-to-teacher ratio. What it wanted was Franciscan's regional accreditation, which gave it access to the real golden goose—federal student grant and loan money.

When Bridgepoint bought Franciscan, it got the accreditation, even though it had no educational track record and changed just about everything that had presumably made the school worth going to. The company gutted and eventually closed the Iowa campus and instead began recruiting tens of thousands of online students looking to make something of their lives by going to college through their computers. Within five years, the institution's enrollment had grown by nearly 8,000 percent, to more than 77,000 students, and increased its revenue from virtually nothing to more than $700 million—of which federal funds (including loans, grants, and various Defense Department funds) accounted for 93.7 percent—with 30 percent of that going straight to profit.

Bridgepoint's founder and CEO, Andrew Clark, was well versed in the business model. He had gotten his start as a recruiter for the University of Phoenix in 1992 before ascending through the ranks and leaving the company in 2001 as a regional vice president. He filled out Bridgepoint's executive team with fellow industry cronies from Phoenix, Education Management Corporation (EDMC), and elsewhere.

But for students, the business model was a bust—at Bridgepoint, just as at any number of for-profit giants. With only *seven* full-time faculty for almost 74,000 students, Bridgepoint, like many of its competitors, spent way more on recruiting than it did on instruction. And it showed: only about a quarter of students in any given year went on to get their "diplomas" within six years. Those who did graduate tended to leave with a hefty amount of debt—nearly $35,000 on average. By 2017 almost 20 percent of alumni were unemployed, and of those who had found jobs, almost half didn't do anything related to their degree.

The beneficiaries of Bridgepoint's grift were its shareholders and managing partners. The losers were everybody else. And if theirs wasn't a particularly victimless crime, so what? Nobody cared much about students anyway. "You stop thinking of these students as people," said one recruiting manager.

But it turned out there were groups that still cared, and they were gathering force to take on the Bridgepoints of the world and unmask them for the opportunists they were. Among these were state attorneys general. Five years after California filed suit against Ashford and its parent company, a state superior court judge found that the company had engaged in widespread deception—estimating that over an eleven-year period, its recruiters had spread misinformation in more than 1.2 million calls—and issued more than $22 million in penalties.*

Around the time the for-profits were soaring to the peak of their destructive power, the topic of student debt started growing from a niche issue to a nationwide crisis. Into the void left by a political class that had thrown students to the wolves stepped a whole new cadre of student debt activists and advocates. Starting in the early 2000s, they began to demand a solution to this problem, which had never before

---

* In 2024, an appeals court reduced the penalty by nearly $1 million.

attracted much political attention. Like Elizabeth Warren, most of them approached student debt from a consumer protection angle.

Some of these groups had been around for a long time. The United States Student Association dated back to the 1970s and the Public Interest Research Group, inspired by Nader's Raiders, had a student branch established around the same time. Both had rallied students and borrowers to lobby on behalf of the move to direct lending. But the public took little heed of them, and members of Congress even less.

With the advent of the internet had come the power to quickly draw energy around a cause, and borrowers began to use it to their advantage. In 2005, a disgruntled borrower named Alan Collinge started a website that advocated for the return of bankruptcy relief for student debtors and asked other borrowers to send in their stories. He called his site Student Loan Justice, and it quickly drew hundreds, and then thousands, of responses, some from people who had fled the country to escape their debts or whose family members had committed suicide.

Other groups emerged in this time with demands for more comprehensive change, including the elimination of student debt altogether. The most effective of these was Student Debt Crisis, founded in 2011 by an indebted UCLA graduate named Natalia Abrams.

State attorneys general began taking on student borrower cases and cracking down on predatory schools and lenders as well, and behind them was a cadre of long-suffering consumer-protection lawyers, like Deanne Loonin and her colleagues at the National Consumer Law Center, who had been fighting for preyed-upon borrowers for decades. In 2012, a pair of Loonin mentees cofounded the Project on Predatory Student Lending at Harvard, which took on lawsuits brought by borrowers against for-profit institutions that had defrauded them. A few years later, they were joined by the Student Borrower Protection Center, a nonprofit organization focused on fighting predatory lenders and schools and advocating for improvements to the student loan system.

Together, these advocates effectively banged the drum on protections for student borrowers, bringing massive awareness to the issue. And collectively they have significantly shifted public opinion on what student debt is and how it should be addressed. By generally remaining within a paradigm of consumer rights and protections, however, they did not fundamentally challenge the ideological framework that had made debt-financing of education politically palatable and allowed it to grow to crisis levels. By and large, they worked to optimize the system, rather than tear it down and start anew.

Alongside the ascent of these student debt advocates, Elizabeth Warren's star was also rising, and she would soon add student loans to her list of consumer crises. In 2007, Warren wrote an article for *Democracy* magazine, arguing for the creation of a Financial Product Safety Commission to regulate such products as home mortgages. Its title was "Unsafe at Any Rate," a nod to Nader's 1965 book *Unsafe at Any Speed*, and she intended it to sound the same clarion call to reform. "In a rapidly changing market," she wrote, "customers need someone on their side to help make certain that the financial products they buy meet minimum safety standards. A Financial Product Safety Commission would be the consumers' ally."

She made her case at a particularly opportune moment. Her pitch for protection against financial products like home mortgages coincided with troubling developments in the mortgage industry, which were sending ripples of concern through the global economy. Soon she would be called upon to develop the Consumer Financial Protection Bureau, precisely the regulatory body she was envisioning, and it would advance her consumer protection cause to American student loan borrowers as well as homeowners. After that, she would find her way to the Senate, and then to a presidential campaign that put student debt at the forefront of her political agenda. But before that could happen, the global economy had to completely melt down.

CHAPTER 10

"Borrowers Are the Product"

I n September 2008, the bottom fell out of the American economy. Over the next few months, more than a hundred mortgage lenders went bankrupt, millions of people lost their homes to foreclosure, and the Treasury had to bail out banks, automakers, and others— including Fannie Mae and Freddie Mac, the mortgage-loan counterparts to Sallie Mae—to the tune of almost half a trillion dollars.

This, of course, was the frenzied environment that Barack Obama entered when he took the oath of office in January 2009. And although he is given credit for much of the cleanup that ensued, behind the scenes career government employees were already frantically working to sop up a great deal of the mess. Like Elizabeth Warren, Obama toed a fairly consumerist line on student debt. He aimed to make it less cumbersome and more efficient, to help borrowers manage their payments better, and to expand community college access so fewer people had to go into debt in the first place. But as the person selected to preside over the biggest financial catastrophe since the Great Depression, he was poised to enact a number of more meaningful changes.

The student loan bailout started well before Obama was even elected. Early in the year, it became clear that banks all over the country were out of money. Without some kind of immediate intervention, the lenders warned, they would not have the liquidity to keep loaning to college students in the following school year. Given how many students were by this point reliant on student loans, this would have had unimaginably dire consequences for higher education. According to David Bergeron, then a director of policy and budget development at the Department of Education, it would have meant the closing that fall of "every tuition-dependent college and university in the United States."

In other words, just about all of them.

So the Department of Education hurriedly worked out a plan to buy up more than $110 billion in loans from private banks at premium rates, in some instances paying the loan balance plus $75 per loan. That way, the banks would have a major influx of funds that would permit them to keep making more loans to students. In essence, this was Sallie Mae on steroids. According to Bergeron, the bailout represented a phenomenally good deal for the banks—so good that it actually made the government look bad for not negotiating better terms with the battered, limping financial institutions—which nevertheless complained that they were getting a raw deal.

As the financial crisis dragged on and Obama entered the picture, momentum grew for more reform to the bank-based student lending system. Obama aimed to get rid of it entirely and appointed Robert Shireman as deputy undersecretary of education to make it happen. In the early 1990s, as a staffer for Illinois senator Paul Simon, Shireman had been instrumental in developing and promoting the legislation that created direct lending, and he later joined the Clinton administration as an education policy adviser. He was an expert at working the politics: he got the Office of Management and Budget to estimate the savings of a shift to Direct Loans at $47 billion over a decade. Not long after, the Congressional Budget Office came out with an even better number: $87 billion. In a time of financial meltdown, such blockbuster savings practically neutralized Republicans' arguments against the shift.

In September 2009, the Student Aid and Fiscal Responsibility Act (SAFRA) easily passed the House by a vote of 253 to 171. If it had sailed as easily through the Senate, it would have made major changes to the financial aid system, even in addition to eliminating the bank-based loan program. Under SAFRA, banks and guaranty agencies, cut out of lending, would have been allowed to compete for contracts to service loans (collecting and managing loan payments for the department). Forty billion dollars of the projected savings generated from this shift would have gone toward making the Pell Grant an entitlement, meaning it wouldn't "run out" every year, regardless of whether poor students had their need met; it would be guaranteed in full for every student who qualified. And it would have indexed the grants to the Consumer Price Index, so that their value would no longer be entirely beholden to legislators' feelings of magnanimity; they would automatically increase when the cost of living did. Additionally, the bill would have set aside several more billions for Obama's pet projects, such as boosting funds to community colleges and increasing national enrollment and graduation rates.

By the time Obama and the House had turned their attention to direct lending in the fall, the Senate was more interested in passing a health care bill, and legislators put SAFRA on the back burner. This allowed lobbyists for the bank-based system—notably those employed by Sallie Mae, which spent more than $4 million lobbying against direct lending in 2009—time to turn the tide against the reform. The lobbying blitz was effective, transforming even some Democrats into turncoats. By November, even though the Democrats controlled the Senate with a filibuster-proof sixty-vote majority, SAFRA was in peril.

Then, in January, the former *Cosmopolitan* pinup—and Republican— Scott Brown shocked just about everyone by winning Ted Kennedy's former Senate seat in an upset special election after the senator's death in August 2009. Now the Democrats were one vote shy of even the possibility of a filibuster-proof bloc. This put both health care and student aid reform at dire risk, and the only possible way to pass either bill would be to package them together in a budget-reconciliation bill, requiring only a simple majority.

Fortunately for the Democrats, they'd already gotten a head start on SAFRA; without it, they wouldn't have been able to afford the Affordable Care Act (ACA). The savings from the shift to direct lending made the ACA possible. But in the six months since SAFRA's passage by the House, many schools had already been driven to Direct Loans by the banks' austerity, which had preemptively reaped some of the projected savings of the legislation. The Congressional Budget Office reestimated SAFRA's cost savings down from $87 billion to $61 billion. That meant an even greater share of the savings from direct lending would have to go to paying for the health-care bill—$19 billion, all told. As a result,

Obama's pet reforms were out, as was the plan to make the Pell Grant an entitlement. In the end, the bill passed by only a scant 56–43 margin.

Nevertheless, by July 1, 2010, Clinton's old dream was finally realized: all new federal loans were to be made under the Direct Loans program. This was a monumental reform, one that had eluded legislators for decades. After nearly fifty years during which banks had been given the run of the federal aid store, the government had at last kicked them out—or so it seemed at the time. This was not only a way of reclaiming federal money, in the form of squandered bank subsidies; it also opened up increased protections for students and accountability from their lender, which was now, on paper and in practice, the federal government.

For the student-loan middleman organizations—the lenders and guarantors who made and managed the loans—the prospect of a change to Direct Loans was no more welcome than it had been under Clinton. It would take a big chunk out of their revenue streams at a time when government money was just about all they could count on. They lobbied hard against the move. But their power had waned since their heyday in the 1990s.

The collapse of the world's financial system in 2008 and 2009 was so complete that it tempered the banks' iron-clad hold on the student lending system—at least briefly. As had happened many times before in the history of the student aid program, starting with the GI Bill, a national crisis allowed the previously unimaginable to be considered. To use the term preferred by the political scientist Suzanne Mettler, a "policy window" opened, suddenly shifting what had been deemed politically possible, or even conceivable. The banks were now—at least nominally—out of the student loan business.

In this case, the window provided a chance to stem the student loan system's longstanding abuse of students for simply believing education would bring them a better life. Taking the banks out of the system was a good step, a big one, but as is often the case, the reform did not go far enough. The lobbying of vested interests was too intense and the path to success too narrow, ultimately making it impossible to fully cut out the cancer of private finance. And so it soon grew back.

Perhaps to mollify the lenders and guarantors, the Department of Education decided to contract out the management of its burgeoning Direct Loans portfolio. In June 2009, it announced that it had offered loan-servicing contracts to four organizations: Great Lakes, FedLoan Servicing, Nelnet, and Navient. All had been heavily invested in the Federal Family Education Loan (FFEL) program: Navient, for instance, was the servicing arm of Sallie Mae, and FedLoan Servicing was a creation of the Pennsylvania Higher Education Assistance Agency (PHEAA). Their contracts to service Direct Loans—there were already 9 million of them, and more made every day—guaranteed a massive, and captive, source of revenue. This drove the priorities of these organizations further away from serving students. Because the servicers' revenue was fixed, every minute spent helping students cost them money they could not make up elsewhere. They had cemented their status as vested interests, motivated to make money off students rather than help them.

Now these vested financial interests were not just sanctioned by the federal government but also contracted to do its bidding.

DIRECT LOANS WAS NOT THE ONLY BILL CLINTON EDUCATION POLICY PIPE dream to be resurrected in the decade after he left office. In 2007, legislators created a program that showcased the more hopeful aspects of American education funding—while also exposing its colossal aptitude for dysfunction.

Although it had seemed as though Clinton's plan to exchange national service for money toward the cost of higher education had died in the early 1990s, along with universal health care and essentially any other ambitious legislation he might have envisioned passing with a hostile Republican Congress, a few Democratic legislators had refused to give up on the idea. In June 2007, Representative John Sarbanes, a Maryland Democrat, picked up the baton with a bill to provide loan forgiveness after ten years for people working in government or nonprofit jobs. Sarbanes's bill was soon absorbed into a larger budget-reconciliation bill, the College Cost Reduction and Access Act, which would pay for itself through $42 billion in cuts to lender subsidies over a decade and add money to the Pell Grant. It also created a new income-based repayment (IBR) plan for Direct Loans. IBR improved on the old ICR plan by cutting borrowers' payments from 20 percent to 15 percent of discretionary income and reducing the total loan period to twenty years, after which any remaining debt would be canceled. "Yes, we know the cost of education has gone up," said Ted Kennedy on the Senate floor in 2007. "Help is on its way."

The bill easily passed the Democrat-controlled House and Senate and was reluctantly signed by President George W. Bush, who had threatened to veto it. Democrats were exultant. Several referred to the bill as the largest, most important education assistance legislation since the GI Bill. Sarbanes declared that the Public Service Loan Forgiveness (PSLF) program he'd authored would give "students and recent graduates the chance to make career decisions based on their passions rather than on their pocketbooks."

The evidence suggested their pocketbooks needed the help. At the time, Senator Tom Harkin noted, nearly a quarter of college students at public schools and more than a third of those at private schools graduated with too much debt to afford living on a public school teacher's starting salary. Yet in spite of the bill's title, the College Cost Reduction and Access Act didn't do anything to solve the problem of spiraling college costs, the cause of borrowers' heavy debt. And for white-collar professionals, the debt was about to get a lot heavier: in 2005, Congress had expanded eligibility for the PLUS (Parent Loan for Undergraduate Students) program that had existed since 1990. Starting in 2006, graduate students, like parents, would be allowed to borrow up to the full cost of their program. In the years that followed, the median Grad PLUS balance nearly tripled, from $21,800 in 2007 to $57,000 in 2019, and graduate students came to account for 47 percent of all federal loan dollars.

And while the creation of PSLF offered some hope of relief, it did not fully relieve participants of their burden. According to one estimate, participants in PSLF would pay back as much as 91 percent of their original loan amount before their debts were eliminated.

But PSLF did accomplish something important. It permitted people to consider a meaningful career of service that did not promise the bloated salaries of the private sector. Students could be assured that this choice would not drive them to financial ruin through onerous student debt. "Young people want to get involved. Young people want to make a difference in people's lives," said Ted Kennedy, and the forgiveness program offered them a powerful message: "if you want to give something back, we are going to make it possible."

The passage of PSLF should have been a celebratory moment for additional reasons as well—for the first time in half a century, legislation supported the idea that higher education could be about more than a market investment in a student's personal future. Instead, given the right incentives and supports, a college degree could be a stepping stone toward a more humane, caring, and functional American society.

But the celebration didn't last long.

The first problem with PSLF was that almost no one knew it existed. After Bob Shireman joined the Department of Education in 2009, he discovered that virtually nothing was being done to inform borrowers about PSLF, or help them qualify for it. Shireman says he "begged" the department "to create a process to tell people whether they're in public service employment or not," but until 2012, five years after the start of the program, a form didn't even exist for borrowers to submit to find out if they were on the right track. To maintain their repayment plan, they had to send in yearly tax forms, but beyond that, borrowers just had to trust that the Department of Education would eventually come through for them.

The next issue, ironically, concerned the private sector. Even as Jon Oberg was exposing PHEAA for overbilling the Department of Education, Federal Student Aid (FSA) was giving PHEAA a huge new volume of guaranteed business. In 2012, FSA assigned all PSLF accounts to

FedLoan Servicing, PHEAA's new servicing arm. If a borrower sent in Shireman's PSLF tracking form, and the department determined it met all the program's criteria, the loans would automatically be transferred to FedLoan.

PHEAA was already a major player in the federal loan program. So it made some sense that it was among the four contractors chosen to continue on as a servicer of federal loans and then picked to handle the PSLF program (other servicers were also given contracts for specific programs). And after 2012 it was sitting pretty. Over the next six years, FedLoan gained servicing rights to about a third of all federal student debt. For every loan that it serviced, it earned up to $1.90 per month. Multiplied by a few million borrowers, FedLoan's take amounted to more than $100 million per year. In 2017, the company took home $195 million from the Department of Education. By 2019, because of its sweetheart contracts, PHEAA had racked up $1.3 billion in servicing fees from the federal government.

Oberg's lawsuit against the 9.5 lenders had shined a light on the revolving door between PHEAA and the federal government, which continued long after his dispute was resolved. In addition to the Department of Education's Sally Stroup, who had spent more than a decade as PHEAA's chief counsel, there was Matthew Sessa, who had led PHEAA's bid to win the PSLF contract in 2012. In 2014, he was hired as deputy COO at FSA. In 2018, Trump's education secretary, Betsy DeVos, named Kathleen Smith, a longtime education staffer in the Department of Education as well as Congress and lobbying groups, to succeed him at FSA. In 2019, she left the department to take an executive role at PHEAA, leading federal relations.

But even before PHEAA created FedLoan, there was plenty of reason to question whether PHEAA was acting entirely in the public interest. In 2007, investigations by news outlets had revealed that the agency had given out $2.5 million in bonuses to executives that year and spent almost $1 million between 2000 and 2005 on board retreats that included $150 cigars and falconry lessons. In 2007, the CEO, Richard Willey, made nearly $500,000: his $181,000 bonus that year was more than the Pennsylvania governor's salary. Amid the fallout from a newspaper exposé, Willey resigned.

The problems at FedLoan did not disappear with Willey. As FedLoan started taking on the portfolio of PSLF borrowers in 2012, many began complaining of unsolvable problems. Borrowers reported servicing issues, such as FedLoan's failure to correctly count their payments; another issue was FedLoan pushing borrowers into unnecessary forbearances—in which payments are deferred but interest accumulates—that did nothing to advance them toward loan forgiveness.

"I've never missed a payment," one borrower, a woman named Leigh McIlvaine, told me in 2017. But because of the company's delays in recertifying her income each year, she said, "I have found it absolutely impossible to get those twelve qualifying payments within one year." As a result, she said, what is supposed to be a ten-year program requires at least eleven to complete.*

McIlvaine experienced more dramatic problems as well. After she applied to switch to a more generous repayment plan in 2016, FedLoan erroneously issued her a bill for $1,200, then reported her to credit bureaus for not paying it. Just as she was interviewing for a new job, she discovered that her credit score had dropped nearly three hundred points. The company took a full year to resolve the issue.

"And the problem is, you can't switch out of it," McIlvaine told me. "If you are working toward Public Service Loan Forgiveness, you must use FedLoan Servicing."†

In addition to experiencing errors and poor customer service from FedLoan, PSLF borrowers faced an arcane system of confusing payment pathways and bad information. For instance, under direct lending, borrowers had several repayment plan options: among them were

---

* McIlvaine's loans were ultimately forgiven in 2020.
† In 2021, PHEAA announced that it would not seek to renew its servicing contract. The Department of Education subsequently transferred borrowers' accounts to other servicers; the PSLF servicing contract was assigned to the Missouri Higher Education Loan Authority (MOHELA).

the Standard Repayment Plan for Direct Consolidation Loans and the 10-Year Standard Repayment Plan. Only one of them qualified for PSLF, a distinction that most borrowers would be unlikely to know. The increasing bureaucratization of student aid itself was partly to blame for such ambiguities; the shift to direct lending, with its multiple repayment plans and reliance on private contractors to guide borrowers, did nothing to simplify the situation. The maddening impossibility of figuring out one's status in the PSLF maze mirrored the experience of trying to deal with student loans in general, through any number of servicers.

The path toward debt forgiveness was perilous, and it was easy for borrowers to fall off track without even realizing it.

Other servicers contributed to the PSLF borrowers' difficulties. Many who wanted to get into the program were misled about their eligibility and status by their existing servicers—who would of course lose the loan, and its guaranteed income stream, if it was transferred to FedLoan. Unaware of the peculiarities of the program requirements, borrowers often had no idea that they needed to consolidate old FFEL loans into Direct Loans and switch to an income-driven repayment plan to qualify; presumably they would have discovered this if they'd been given the option to formally apply for entry into the program. But instead, when asked, servicers merely reassured them that they were already on the track toward debt forgiveness, thus leading borrowers to make functionally worthless, unqualifying payments for years.

The only real recourse students had was to complain to their servicer or take the issue to their state attorney general or the Consumer Financial Protection Bureau (CFPB), the new government agency that Elizabeth Warren had dreamed in up 2007. The agency had created the position of student loan ombudsman to take consumer complaints, keep statistics on lender and servicer issues, and help borrowers find relief when they'd been wronged. Leigh McIlvaine had turned to the CFPB when FedLoan reported her as delinquent to credit bureaus, and its ombudsman ultimately helped her restore her rating.

The CFPB also produced research to demonstrate the growing crisis in federal student loan servicing. In a June 2017 report, the CFPB wrote that "servicing breakdowns" for PSLF borrowers "may cause delays or dead ends that can cost them thousands of dollars [. . .] or render a borrower's loans entirely ineligible for PSLF, even after a decade of qualifying public service." One borrower cited in the report, a public school employee, had been repeatedly assured by FedLoan of eligibility for PSLF. "I have been paying for 4 years and was misled by this company completely," the borrower complained. "Recently, I called to check in around this, and was informed that I WAS NOT in the loan forgiveness program."

A few months later, in October 2017, the first cohort of borrowers in the program became eligible for debt forgiveness. This too should have been a moment of celebration for those sunk by debt. Yet out of the 28,000 people who submitted applications for debt relief under PSLF over the next year, only 96 received it. The program had an effective failure rate of 99.7 percent. A decade after scores of borrowers had begun paying into the program, many were only marginally closer to their goal of being debt-free. And some were even more in debt than they had been when they started.

BUT THE ISSUES WEREN'T JUST WITH FEDLOAN OR PSLF. BORROWERS ACROSS the board experienced problems with the new Direct Loans system. This mostly had to do with their government-contracted loan servicers, which eventually numbered more than a dozen. But perhaps borrowers' issues shouldn't have come as much of a surprise. After all, for them, not much had changed. "From the customer perspective," averred one Department of Education official interviewed by Suzanne Mettler at the time of the switch to direct lending, "students will barely know the difference. It is a government program, like before, and run by private actors, like before."

This was not reassuring. In effect, the change to Direct Loans—loans that were serviced by the same poorly performing companies that had managed the old program—had merely transferred a private sector problem to the government. And borrowers now had even less choice in the matter. Before, they might have been able to consolidate their loans with a new lender. But now their servicer was chosen by the Department of Education, and they were not permitted to shop around. The consequences were grim.

Servicers—beholden to the profit margins dictated by their contracts—did not have a lot of incentive to act in the interests of their "customers." Their money, after all, didn't come from borrowers—it came from the federal government, and it was contractually guaranteed. As they began acquiring old FFEL and new Direct Loans accounts, these companies started receiving money from the government for every loan they serviced. The Department of Education paid them from $1.90 a month for loans in good standing to 50 cents for those that hadn't been paid in almost a year. So if a borrower fell into financial trouble and called up a servicer to learn about options for relief, servicers often failed to inform them about many of the new Direct Loans benefits available to them, such as reduced payments under IBR or Pay as You Earn (PAYE), another new Obama repayment plan that cut payments even further. These were complicated options, requiring paperwork and administrative follow-up. It was much easier for servicers, instead, to quickly place a borrower in forbearance, which would pause all payments but allow interest to continue accruing on their accounts.

Eric Fink, a law professor who wrote about servicers in 2014, asked what incentive servicers really had to spend thirty minutes on the phone with a borrower about to slide off a cliff. Those thirty minutes represented several dollars lost in call-center employee wages (FedLoan customer service reps, for instance, then started at about $11.50 an hour), an amount the company wouldn't recoup from their contracted fees for more than four months, even if the call was successful in getting the borrower to pay. It was actually cheaper for them, at least in the short term, to put a struggling borrower into forbearance. For this, they received $1.73 per month. (In 2014, the contracts were updated to tweak the pricing scheme, and the federal government increased payments for loans in active repayment.)

But this cavalier attitude could have serious consequences for borrowers. If and when a debtor did manage to move into a new, more beneficial repayment plan, the interest that had accrued under their forbearance period would capitalize and be added to the principal, thus altering the borrower's debt-to-income ratio (important for things like renting an apartment or buying a house) and expected payoff timeline, and their time in forbearance wouldn't count as progress toward loan forgiveness.

In essence, Johnson's initial 1965 compromise on loans—intended to thwart the push for tuition tax credits, which Clinton had put back on the table—had grown into what Fink, the law professor, characterized as the worst of public-private partnerships: the government had begun forcing borrowers to deal with private companies they didn't get to pick, which regarded them as a captive source of revenue. With direct lending, what should have been a huge accomplishment became yet a new way for government to obstruct its own role in people's lives through its sublimation into the private sector—a process Suzanne Mettler calls the "submerged state." "Reformers," she writes, "neglected to fashion new policies in ways that would help reestablish the bond between citizens and government. They willingly agreed to establish direct lending through delivery mechanisms that bear resemblance to those of the old bank-based system, making government's role less than clear." Instead, most people—even those directly affected by it—weren't even aware of the huge shift that student aid had just undergone.

In this respect, the switch to Direct Loans had a curious consequence. Now, instead of producing profits for banks, the returns on student loans went straight to the government and its contractors. If anything, the transition to direct lending—in spite of Republicans' dire warnings about its portending a sinister turn to socialism—actually demonstrated how beholden even the most well-meaning of government programs had become to the dictates of the free market's profit motive. As Rohit Chopra, who was the CFPB's first student loan ombudsman and is now directing the agency, put it to me in 2018: "We didn't design the student loan system to be a profit center for the government." But it grew into a "program that has been chowing down billions of dollars of profits." For

Deanne Loonin, this drift toward the profit motive highlighted the fundamental contradiction at the heart of the student aid program, which had long split its mission between helping students and saving money. "If we believe in education as a public good," she said, "then we haven't created a system that supports that."

And where was education in all this? The initial goal of the student aid program was to make it easier for straitened low- and middle-income students to afford a college degree because, as a nation, we believed that was mutually beneficial for individuals and society. This motive had been lost in a morass of cynical disputes about the federal budget and political posturing over personal responsibility. Students and the degrees they sought for themselves and the country were no longer placed at the forefront of decisions about higher education. Instead, they became figures on a ledger aimed at enriching private contractors and reducing the federal deficit.

Chopra put it more bluntly: "The most important thing to remember," he said, "is borrowers are not the customer. Borrowers are the product."

But a set of newcomers to the conversation on student debt were about to enter the scene, and they would soon push the discourse on student loans into a new, almost unthinkably radical realm.

PART 4

Debtors Unite (2008–)

THE FINANCIAL CRISIS HAD OPENED up two distinct pathways toward solving a student-financing system that had become, almost everyone agreed, unmanageable. Liberal consumer advocates chose a tried-and-true route: they treated students as the consumers they had become. Having capitulated to the terms of the debate set by financial institutions as well as their partners on the ground—craven, cynical politicians like Ronald Reagan, John Boehner, Bill Clinton, and Joe Biden—advocates like Elizabeth Warren positioned themselves to demand, if not radical change to the system, at least some semblance of a protective scaffolding for student borrowers.

But this was not enough—it could never be enough. Accepting students as consumers would mean that even the most well-intentioned advocates could be no more than doorstops pushing back on exploitive financial institutions, for-profit schools, and antipathetic legislators eager to further disinvest from the collective mission of education.

There was one group of people who recognized this—the student debtors themselves. As the global economy melted down and yet nothing really seemed to change, they began to see through the fiction of patient, incrementalist progress via a feeble American regulatory apparatus. Instead of accepting the crumbs of consumer protection offered through direct lending and the CFPB, they chose to ask for the whole pie.

In the wake of the Great Recession, a national movement of debtors coalesced—atomized, sold for parts, and left to financial death by
their own government, they had finally had enough. In 2011 groups of
people angry with the inequities of the American economy and disappointed by the Obama administration's seeming willingness to let corrupt financial institutions off the hook, even as they shoved millions
of Americans into the street, traveled from across the country to Wall
Street, the belly of the beast. The protesters who formed Occupy Wall
Street—student debtors, victims of foreclosure, members of the missing
middle class—were angry, and they were beaten down, but they had one
thing going for them: they had nothing left to lose.

And as they joined together, they found they could become their
own font of collective power. Once a source of shame and regret, their
debts became the source of a group identity. To be a college student
now meant, for most Americans, being a debtor: more than two-thirds
of college graduates had taken out loans for their degrees. The burden
lifted, and in its wake came not just relief, but almost a kind of pride—
they were finally choosing action over shameful despair, they were calling bullshit on a system that had punished them for doing everything
right, they were demanding what they and everyone else deserved. Now
bound together, they no longer relied on the legitimacy of presidents
or members of Congress, or even advocates. They would take action
directly, and they would accept nothing less than everything.

CHAPTER 11

The Collective Debtor

I n the summer of 2007, around the time American economy watchers were first starting to sound the alarm about a looming crisis, Thomas Gokey had just graduated from the School of the Art Institute of Chicago. He was thinking about how much his degree had cost him. His diploma was a simple piece of paper, but it came with a price tag of thousands of dollars—dollars that were themselves pieces of paper, transmitted to him in the form of student loans, which he now owed to the federal government. While chewing on this thought, he had an idea for a project that would occupy him for much of the next year. He obtained a letter of permission from the Treasury Department's Bureau of Engraving and Printing to go to a Federal Reserve bank of his choice and pick out some shredded bills from its stores of mutilated currency. One day, he walked over to the Federal Reserve Bank of Chicago, five blocks from the Art Institute, and asked for some money.

"Nobody had ever seen this letter before," he told me. "They made phone calls that kept going higher and higher and higher." Finally, the bank's vice president came down and took Gokey on a tour of the building. The mutilated money was kept several floors below, past a labyrinth of security checkpoints. At last, he entered a big, open room that resembled a vast warehouse. "You could look in any direction, and you couldn't see the back wall. It was just filled, floor to ceiling, with clear plastic trash bags of shredded money."

Gokey asked the vice president for a specific amount: the equivalent of $49,983, the sum of debt he'd incurred to go to the Art Institute. The bank executive gathered up a stack of the shredded bills, put them on a scale, and measured out the requested dollars by weight.

Once home with his mutilated money, Gokey undertook the painstaking process of pulping the bills and reassembling them into paper sheets, which he planned to sell off to interested collectors. It was a clever plan: he would make an artwork serve as a means of settling his debt—thereby using his degree to pay off the cost of getting it. He called the work *Total Amount of Money Rendered in Exchange for a Master's of Fine Arts Degree to the School of the Art Institute of Chicago, Pulped into Four Sheets of Paper.*

Over the next few years, Gokey exhibited *Total Amount of Money* on the walls of galleries from the Midwest to the United Kingdom. He calculated the value of each square inch at $4.22, each square foot at $607.70. "I sold some," he told me, "but not a lot."

By September 2011, as collective student debt was edging toward $1 trillion, Gokey had moved to New York for a job as an adjunct instructor of art at Syracuse University. He found working for the university perplexing. He was making a pittance as an adjunct, and yet his students were all paying exorbitantly for the privilege of his instruction. "I got really concerned about my students, who were in way more debt than I was," he said. Gokey has a soft Midwestern tone of voice, sounding curious and engaged while somehow speckled with sadness. "I was very confused about where the money went," he said. "Why does it work this way? Why can't it work differently?"

While teaching at Syracuse, Thomas Gokey heard about a protest movement in New York City that was coalescing around many of the issues that had been on his mind for years. It was called Occupy Wall Street. Gokey felt called to be a part of it, but *Total Amount of Money* had just been accepted to the annual ArtPrize exhibit in Grand Rapids, Michigan—an art fair founded by Rick DeVos, son of Betsy, who helps fund it. "And I thought, You know, these things always fizzle. I'm gonna show up, it's going to fizzle, and then I'm going to miss this opportunity."

But when Gokey got to Michigan, Occupy Wall Street was still on his mind, and he began attending meetings of the satellite encampment that had sprung up in Grand Rapids. When ArtPrize 2011 ended, in early October, he traveled back to New York and made his way to the main Occupy encampment, at Zuccotti Park. Almost immediately, he said, "a switch flipped in my brain. It was like, wait a second, what if we all stopped paying our debt? What if we organized a debt strike? This is how we're going to gain leverage over Wall Street."

At the time, no major politicians were talking about canceling student debt. Nor were even the most left-leaning voices in Congress then particularly concerned with student debt. But on the ground at Zuccotti Park, debt was among the most popular and incendiary topics. "When the occupation of Zuccotti began," wrote the debt scholar and anthropologist David Graeber in 2014, "we discovered that the largest contingent by far were debt refugees."

Gokey didn't discover the student debt working group until after the park was cleared, in November. He had been splitting time between Syracuse and New York City and returned to the city for an Occupy-affiliated protest at the New York Stock Exchange, where he was among hundreds arrested. After his release, he was briefly stranded in New York, sleeping in churches while waiting to get his belongings back from the police. He heard about an event the following week, the launch of a student debtors' "pledge of refusal" organized by the Occupy Student Debt Campaign. Signatories would commit to stop paying their debts if a million others also did so. Finding himself still in the city, Gokey decided to attend.

Back in Syracuse, Gokey had already become active on InterOccupy, the internal network of the Occupy organizers. Also loitering was David Graeber, who would sometimes email the other Occupiers with strange, esoteric ideas. Some of them went over Gokey's head, like the suggestion of buying up personal debts that were sold on the secondary market. "When I read the email at first, I didn't understand any of it," Gokey said. "I didn't believe it; it seemed too good to be true—that we could buy and abolish someone's debt for pennies on the dollar."

Intrigued, Gokey started lurking on debt buyers' internet forums. Delinquent debts are often sold by their initial lender and wind up on the secondary market, bundled in tranches with other debts and traded for a fraction of their total value. Gokey thought if he could cobble together $5,000, he'd have enough to buy up to $1 million of debt. It could be another art project. He spent the next nine months researching how to go about it.

Eventually he started calling debt buyers. "Normally, it's a waste of time for them to do a deal that's, like, under $30,000. And so I kept saying: Will you sell me just like $50 worth of debt just so I can learn how to do this? And they would just hang up on me." The buyers were aggressive, all of them men, none of them willing to engage with the thought experiment Gokey was presenting: "Just a total group of jerks." The calls never lasted longer than a minute.

One of the buyers ran his own website, with tips for getting into the field—finding good debt to buy, avoiding scams, and so forth. He was one of the people who had hung up on Gokey—several times. But then, weirdly, the buyer started g-chatting him late at night. Sometimes he would talk about his family, sometimes the industry, and sometimes he would spew crazy anti-Semitic conspiracies. At last, Gokey persuaded this guy to sell him a small amount of debt: $14,000 worth in exchange for $446, a not-insignificant portion of Gokey's total assets.

Months earlier, Gokey had told some of the other Occupy Student Debt Campaign members about his debt-buying plans. Among them was Ann Larson, an early member of the group, to whom he'd mentioned it at the "pledge of refusal" event back in November.

"I just remember thinking: this person is insane," Larson told me. "It was like one of these things when somebody's talking to you, and you just want to slowly back away." But once she understood the implications of Gokey's proposal, she went down the rabbit hole herself. The pledge of refusal had abjectly failed, garnering only a few thousand signatures. The group now wanted to pivot, to find a way to bail out individuals, just as the government had bailed out the banks. When Gokey came to them with his research into debt buying, they realized he'd hit on something that could gain them publicity and build momentum for more structural change.

At the time, there were just a few core members: among them Gokey, the sociologist Andrew Ross, Graeber, a graduate student at the New

School named Pam Brown, the writer and filmmaker Astra Taylor, and Taylor's frequent artistic collaborator, Laura Hanna. Now referring to themselves as Strike Debt, they worked on launching Gokey's debt-buying project, which they'd started calling the Rolling Jubilee. The organizing took different forms: collaborators gathered to hash out logistics at Brown's apartment and Ross's New York University office, and Larson worked on building a website.

The Rolling Jubilee launched via a livestreamed telethon in 2012, on the one-year anniversary of the eviction from Zuccotti Park. Taylor and Hanna hoped to raise $50,000, but the project quickly went viral and collected almost $200,000 before the event even started. At the close of the telethon, they'd raised nearly $300,000, enough to abolish several million dollars of delinquent debt. "At the end, there was all this confetti, and I just had, like, sweat dripping down my forehead," Taylor said. "Because I was like, That's [$300,000] that we have to spend ethically, and we've promised not to pay ourselves a cent. And we've promised to have it be perfectly audited by professionals and be perfectly transparent. And it was a huge amount of work."

The group first targeted medical debt, purchasing $15 million owed by about two thousand people. They sent the debtors they relieved a letter, announcing their windfall. All told, Strike Debt bought up $30 million worth of personal medical and private student loan debt and simply made it disappear.

But amid the success of the Rolling Jubilee, some in Strike Debt began to question the project. "What to do with the money became a huge problem," Brown told me. Giving it to debt collectors, who would simply use it to buy more debt, risked boosting precisely the predatory system Strike Debt was trying to undermine. Some members suggested the money should instead go to more positive endeavors, like creating land trusts in Detroit, and that race should be centered. Unable or unwilling to move beyond this disagreement, the collective essentially disbanded.

It would take a new fight, focused on predatory for-profit colleges, to reignite the movement that Strike Debt had begun. The primary target

of the group's new campaign was, implausibly, a company founded in
the 1950s to sell bows and arrows; it had grown to become the nation's
biggest for-profit education chain.

IN 1954, A RESTLESS ENTREPRENEUR NAMED JOHN J. MCNAUGHTON WAS
looking for new business ventures. Born in Canada, McNaughton had
grown up in sunny Southern California—his mother's chosen exile after Dad lost the family house in a poker game. In his late twenties he
formed an advertising company with a couple of friends. Among their
clients was Frederick's of Hollywood, the racy lingerie store, which was
blazing a mail-order trail to dominate its market and make millions.
McNaughton and his partners wanted in on the mail-order game. First
they had to find a product. For reasons lost to time, they chose bamboo
bows and arrows from Japan. They called their business the Malibu Archery Company. At first the joint was a side hustle, but soon their little
archery company began to grow.

From bamboo bows, McNaughton curiously redirected the company
into schools. Under the moniker North American School of Conserva-
tion, he began offering correspondence courses to foresters who wanted
to train as fire spotters. Then he branched off into other subjects: au-
tomotive repair, drafting, painting. In 1961, when the company's value
hit $3 million, he renamed it National Education Corporation (NEC)
and took it public, using the $300,000 in proceeds from the IPO to
buy up some other vocational schools—in aeronautics, broadcasting,
electronics, computer programming. As McNaughton's company grew
throughout the 1970s, it kept gobbling up businesses, which became
subsidiaries, expanding its brief. By the end of the 1980s, NEC comprised eighty-nine schools and was worth $450 million.

The company's success would not last. In the early 1990s, NEC had
just concluded a decade-long spree of speculative acquisitions. Now,
amid increased public scrutiny on for-profit schools, including accusa-
tions of fraud at NEC, the company suddenly found itself on the rocks
financially.

By this point, McNaughton had retired, and the company's new president claimed that an "increasingly restrictive regulatory environment," the result of the reforms Maxine Waters had championed, was making it impossible to turn a profit. "This business doesn't look as promising as it did four or five years ago," he said. "We no longer want to be in it." In fact, NEC was sinking under the weight of its own failure. In the late 1980s, nearly half its schools had student loan default rates above 20 percent; of those, half were over 30 percent, and several topped 50 percent. At one point, more than three-fifths of graduates from an NEC school in Atlanta were unable to repay their debts. Because of the reforms in the 1990 budget bill and the 1992 reauthorization of the Higher Education Act, NEC schools had been restricted from receiving federal funds because of default rates that topped 30 percent. NEC's stock prices had fallen by 80 percent, and the board decided to break the company up and scrap it for parts. In 1994, the company announced that it would sell off its entire trade school division.

But that wasn't quite the end of NEC. In 1995, five former executives teamed up to purchase and revive sixteen of the company's schools in Irvine, California. They rebranded their spinoff under a new name: Corinthian Colleges. After a few quiescent years, J. J. McNaughton's monster would go on to ruin yet more dreams.

ABOUT A YEAR AFTER THE BREAKUP OF STRIKE DEBT, LUKE HERRINE, A LAW student who had helped the group organize events, got a call from Larson and Hanna. Under a new name, the Debt Collective, Larson and Hanna and several of the other original Strike Debt members were working with California-based students of Everest College, a subsidiary of Corinthian Colleges. In the years since the post-NEC rebranding of the school, Corinthian had gone public and eaten up dozens of other for-profit chains to become the biggest proprietary school system in the country.

Unfortunately, with the gift of hindsight, not to mention hundreds of millions of dollars in legal payouts, it turned out that the main ways proprietary schools like Corinthian racked up all that profit was by misrepresenting their programs and ruining the lives of those they claimed to be saving.

By 2014, Corinthian's students were accusing the company of fraud and protesting the debts they had incurred to attend. They alleged that the school had signed loan applications for them without their knowledge, inflated job and salary figures to lure students to its worthless programs, and committed various other schemes. Around this time, the Consumer Financial Protection Bureau and multiple state attorneys general, led by Kamala Harris, then the attorney general of California, filed suit against the chain for predatory practices.

One of the students making those claims was Nathan Hornes, who called enrolling at Everest, in 2010, "the dumbest decision" he'd ever made. Immediately, he said, he knew something was amiss. He said instructors would suddenly quit or get fired for trying to warn the students away. Replacement teachers would be sourced from former, or even current, students. Sometimes, he said, a class period consisted of playing Monopoly or hangman on the chalkboard.

Two years in, Hornes tried to transfer out—to the University of Southern California, Cal State, even to other for-profit schools such as Argosy and the University of Phoenix—but no school would accept his credits. So he decided to stick it out. A few months after graduation the school called him to say he owed them $700 a month on private loans he'd taken out. He did not recall ever taking out any loans and quickly called up the school's financial aid representatives. When Hornes and his sister had enrolled, the school had helped him fill out a Free Application for Federal Student Aid (FAFSA), the government form that since 1992 has been the official means of securing federal financial aid. But, he said, he hadn't ever signed the financial aid forms. The school, it turned out, had done that for him. Now he owed $68,000.

Hornes had already decided to start organizing against Corinthian. He sent out a call to meet up with a handful of other students at a coffee shop just down the street from the campus, to figure out how to fight back. The group, which grew to 150 within a few weeks, decided to file a class-action lawsuit.

When members of the Debt Collective learned of the students' plan from a news story, they saw an opportunity for something big. They started contacting the students and talking to them about how they might organize a debt strike. The students wanted to sue the school, but, like Hornes, they had signed arbitration agreements preventing them from taking legal action, and most of their student loan debt was issued by the federal government, not the school itself. "Your target is the US Department of Education in Washington, DC," the organizers told them. "It was their job to make sure this didn't happen to you."

At the time, Debt Collective organizers weren't especially familiar with the history of education-aid legislation, but after Larson and Hanna contacted Herrine, he began scrutinizing the text of the 1965 Higher Education Act. Eventually he came across an item that intrigued him: a line added in the 1992 reauthorization, which stated that students who had been defrauded or misled by their schools could assert a "borrower defense to repayment" and have their federal loans canceled. Herrine was excited. It seemed to him that he had found precisely what he was looking for.

He called up Hanna and Larson and told them he thought they could "find a way to get these debts canceled with some organizing and some creative strategy." The Debt Collective started bringing together Corinthian borrowers through a Facebook group. In the meantime, Herrine reached out to Deanne Loonin and Robyn Smith, her colleague at the National Consumer Law Center, to find out if the borrower defense provision could apply to the Corinthian students' debts. They said it could; indeed, they had fought—mostly unsuccessfully—for years to get the department to use it for their own clients. But in all the time that the borrower defense provision had been on the books, only a handful of people had managed to benefit from it.

Because the department had never really planned for this provision to be employed on a large scale (or perhaps at all), there was no internal process for applying it. So the group set about creating one themselves—designing an application for loan relief, which they could collect from borrowers and submit directly to the Department of Education. Then they created a website and began collecting submissions.

To apply more pressure, the Debt Collective organizers also decided to launch a formal debt strike. "These borrowers aren't paying anyway—they'll say they're striking," Herrine said. "Why not turn inability and unwillingness to pay into a collective action?"

Student borrowers—so long betrayed by their leaders, who had for decades sold them down the river in the name of budget balancing or private profits—had now decided they were tired of waiting for government action. From here on out, they would take it themselves.

With some grant money they had received, the Debt Collective flew the small group of students, now called the Corinthian 15, to San Francisco, where they roomed together in an Airbnb. Legal experts at the East Bay Community Law Center in Berkeley conducted a know-your-rights training about loan default, and at night everyone shared their debt stories. "It was just a deeply powerful and emotional space, where people were able to talk about the pain of having debt for the first time," Herrine said. "To me, these are the moments in organizing that are the most amazing, where you see people have this experience of being like, 'Oh, this is not my fault.'"

The efforts of the debt strikers started drawing attention. By December 2014, the idea of using borrower defense had reached Senator Warren, who called on Obama's secretary of education, Arne Duncan, to use it to cancel the Corinthian students' debts. At first he deflected, but as the pressure mounted, he began, reluctantly, to respond to the debtors' demands.

BETWEEN THE BEGINNING AND END OF BARACK OBAMA'S PRESIDENCY, THE American love affair with for-profit education ended, or at least took a break. Obama's administration was in many ways instrumental in this shift. The Consumer Financial Protection Bureau, under Elizabeth Warren's watchful eye and guidance, took up the banner of policing the industry. And because of pressure from groups like the Debt Collective, Obama's Department of Education began issuing regulations that finally targeted the issues that had been plaguing students at for-profit schools since the GI Bill.

The administration's first line of attack was to take the sector to task for not fulfilling its core promise: providing students with jobs.

In 2009, the Department of Education set about defining a vague requirement that had been inserted into the Higher Education Act in 1976. It stated that vocational programs receiving federal funds must provide "training to prepare students for gainful employment in a recognized occupation." But there was no agreed-upon metric for determining what made employment "gainful" nor an occupation "recognized." Until the Obama administration took the issue up, schools were asked merely to check a box on their applications for federal funds, assuring that they met the requirement, which was never audited. For-profit apologists liked to argue that *any* employment should count, even if a student merely returned to the job they'd had before attending a school. Obama's officials who disagreed faced a difficult task: Who could say what "gainful employment" meant, anyway? And how should that be measured?

Although Congress writes the text of amendments to the Higher Education Act, defining the parameters of its rules and enforcement mechanisms is a task left to the Department of Education. By law, when the department seeks to issue certain new regulations based on the statute, it must go through a long and grueling process known as negotiated rulemaking.

In May 2009, the department published a notice stating that it intended to negotiate new regulations, including one that would deal with gainful employment. The next month, DeVry, University of Phoenix, and other for-profit schools flooded the department's public hearings with their employees and students, all talking about how great the schools were. At the final hearing, Deanne Loonin, the borrower legal advocate, tried to push back. Of the hundreds of proprietary school students she had represented in her decades-long career, she said, not a single one had ever managed to get a job in the field for which they were supposedly trained.

After the hearings, the department convened meetings in late 2009 and early 2010. The participants represented a broad swath of so-called stakeholders—students, nonprofit and for-profit schools, accreditors, state officials, and consumer advocates, as well as the Department of Education's own negotiator. When the group failed to reach consensus on the gainful employment rule, the department ultimately wrote its own, which it finally published in June 2011. In order to continue receiving funds for vocational programs, the rule stated, schools would have to demonstrate that former students were not paying more than 30 percent of their discretionary income toward their loans *or* that at least 35 percent of students were considered to be in repayment on their debts (these metrics were considered proxies for employment). The department determined that under these guidelines, approximately 5 percent of programs, all of them at for-profit schools, would fail the tests.

The Obama administration's stance on gainful employment had sent a signal to the for-profits, and they interpreted it as a declaration of war. They believed the administration was out to get them, and worse, to kick them while they were down. But the for-profits were not about to surrender.

As the department was finalizing its gainful employment rule, Congress was also once again going after the for-profit sector. In 2010, Tom Harkin, chair of the Senate's education committee, began a two-year investigation into for-profit schools. His committee took particular aim at the schools' recruitment practices. These practices, by and large, focused on finding pain and inflicting more of it.

In one recruitment training document uncovered by the investigation, ITT Tech illustrated its preferred technique via a still frame from the 1976 movie *Marathon Man*, in which a fugitive ex-Nazi dentist played by Laurence Olivier tortures Dustin Hoffman's character by drilling mercilessly into his teeth. "FIND OUT WHERE THEIR PAIN IS," read the caption. Similarly, the Washington Post–owned company

Kaplan instructed recruiters to "keep digging until you uncover their pain, fears, and dreams. [. . .] If they discuss the life they can't give their family because they don't have a degree, you will dramatically increase your chances of gaining a commitment from the student!"

Other tactics were less probing but just as manipulative. Apollo's manual offered standard responses to potential objections from prospective recruits. "Why would you not want to invest in yourself?" they might ask. Or, if a prospect brought up the school's exorbitant cost (running up to $67,000 for a degree in business), they might wheedle, "When your degree hangs on the wall in a few years [. . .] will you tell your friends and family you bought the cheapest degree you could find?" Once the prospect started to relent, the recruiter would pounce. Before the aspiring student had time to talk to a financial aid counselor or visit the physical campus, if there even was one, the recruiter would wrench an enrollment from them.

Harkin's assessment of the sector was scathing. He declared for-profits expensive, exploitative, and concerned only with their own profits. The typical for-profit school in 2010 employed three times as many recruiters as it did career services staff. In some cases, schools had *no* career services staff. "They are not focused on the success of their students," Harkin declared.

A number of these schools were held by private equity firms like Goldman Sachs. In 2011, one Goldman-backed chain took in more than $350 million in Pell Grant funds and made a little more than that in profit. At a time when the federal government was refusing to help unemployed, down-on-their-luck, and defrauded borrowers, it was bailing out banks like Goldman Sachs twice over: they had already benefited from billions of dollars in Great Recession recovery funds, and now they were scooping up ill-begotten federal student aid via failing for-profit colleges.

Fifteen of the schools Harkin's team investigated were publicly traded. These schools received, on average, 86 percent of their revenues from federal sources, right up to the line of what was legal. One of the ways they did this, Harkin found, was by recruiting veterans. In the years after World War II, legislators reinvented the GI Bill several times to reward veterans of later conflicts, like the Vietnam and Iraq wars, and to adapt to the evolving military, which had become an all-volunteer force in the 1970s. A loophole in the 90/10 rule for proprietary schools allowed them to count Defense Department monies, including GI Bill funds, as non-federal money. In 2009, a Bloomberg News reporter uncovered a tactic used by Ashford University recruiters. They were targeting a wounded warriors unit at Camp Lejeune, signing up veterans with brain injuries who couldn't remember which classes they were taking. Each veteran was a lucrative prospect, allowing schools to gobble up yet more federal funds.

And gobble they did. By 2010, Harkin found, for-profits were taking in a third of all GI Bill education funds. But even more shocking, federal money flowing to for-profit schools accounted for 25 percent of *all* federal student aid and 47 percent of eventual loan defaults. This, in spite of the fact that the schools enrolled little more than 10 percent of all American college students.

So what happened to all the extra money for-profits took in? Harkin's investigation found that for-profits spent nearly a quarter of all revenues on marketing and recruiting and often paid their executives multimillion-dollar salaries, far above the average rates for public or nonprofit university presidents. Students' money enriched every corner of the for-profit industry except one: quality of instruction.

In short, a simple equation sums up the for-profit ethos at this time: charge as much as federal student aid will supply, and cut costs to the bone. Everything in the middle could be harvested as profit. For-profit education was an industry on the dole.

The benefits were not passed along to students. Back in 1987, Reagan's second-term education secretary, William Bennett, had theorized that college costs rose largely in relation to supplies of federal aid—in other words, the more students were allotted in Pell Grants or student loans, the greater the incentive for institutions to capture that aid by raising their rates. Evidence to support the "Bennett hypothesis" has been mixed over the years. But it's spot on for one sector of higher education.

It turns out that when for-profit institutions gain access to federal financial aid monies, they celebrate by raising tuitions by almost *exactly* the amount of aid their students have been awarded. In some cases, this amounts to a 500 percent markup over the local public institution. And their students are not getting their money's worth.

In 2010, for-profit schools graduated about a fifth of all associate's degree students, about 200,000 students a year. In 2012, two economists, Stephanie Riegg Cellini and Latika Chaudhary, found that graduates of proprietary associate's programs did increase their earnings by about 4 percent for each year of school they completed. But this boost did not rise above their own costs of attending—for instance, the student loans they took out. Even with the wage boost, students still came out behind. Most would have been better served by opting for "a lower-cost community college."

Cellini also co-authored another sweeping study of for-profits, which found that students of for-profit certificate programs were slightly less likely to hold a job than their counterparts in public programs. In 2015, a separate study found that job applicants got just as many call-backs by listing *no* educational experience on their résumés as they did by listing for-profit credentials.

When for-profit grads did find employment, Cellini found, they earned about a tenth less than the public program certificate holders. In fact, these for-profit students were actually *worse off* than if they hadn't gone to school at all. When taking into account their debt loads, for-profit graduates were projected to *lose* about $1,200 on their educational "investments" over the course of their lifetimes.

AFTER HARKIN'S HEARINGS, FOR-PROFITS' METEORIC RISE FINALLY CRESTED and reversed direction. Between the economy's return to life* and the

---

* Trade schools typically do better in recessions, when the unemployed go seeking new skills.

"attacks" lobbed at the for-profit industry by the Obama administration, the for-profit industry looked like a bubble that had finally burst, a sector on the decline. Between 2010 and 2011, for-profit enrollments fell for the first time in fifteen years, and chains across the country were freezing costs and dropping outposts by the hundreds. But the for-profits were about to start fighting back.

Immediately after the Obama administration issued its new regulations in 2011, the Association of Private Sector Colleges and Universities, a proprietary-schools group, sued the Department of Education. The organization argued that all the parameters the rule defined—about how much discretionary income students paid and whether they were in repayment at all—were arbitrary and capricious. In an embarrassing blow to the department and the administration, a district judge agreed in June 2012, a year after the gainful employment rule was finalized and before it had even been implemented.

So the administration was back to square one. Rulemaking negotiations resumed and continued over the next two years, yet again with no consensus. In the end, the department published a watered-down rule that left almost no one happy. It dropped any mention of repayment and punished schools only if students failed the debt-to-income test. It had taken more than five years of "negotiating" and numerous legal battles to arrive at a rule that imposed minimal restrictions on an industry that had been repeatedly identified as predatory and rent-seeking, with few ensuing consequences, over more than a half century.

Meanwhile, the Department of Education remained hesitant to provide meaningful relief to the students who had been cheated by the schools it had failed to regulate.

That was of little comfort to the schools' former students, who were drowning in debt for degrees that, no one could any longer dispute, were worth little more than the paper they were printed on. With the department brought low by for-profit schemery, borrowers had almost no one to turn to.

There was nothing left to do but take the reins themselves.

Once the Corinthian debt strike had garnered some press, the Debt

Collective harnessed it for a bigger push to cancel the borrowers' debts en masse. They got the attention of Rohit Chopra, then the student loan ombudsman at the Consumer Financial Protection Bureau. In March, Chopra set up a meeting among Debt Collective organizers, Corinthian borrowers, and officials from the Education and Treasury departments. Luke Herrine had brought a red-painted cardboard box filled with debt-relief applications, and at the end of the meeting he slammed it down on the table.

In response, the Department of Education was initially evasive and noncommittal. But increased media coverage began to focus public scrutiny on its inaction. Eventually, the Debt Collective managed to persuade an education official to provide a department email address, permitting borrowers to send their applications for relief directly to their creditor.

Then, in the middle of the debt-strike campaign, something huge happened. Corinthian filed for bankruptcy. As it collapsed, the Department of Education focused not on helping defrauded students, but on recouping as much of its own money as possible. Meanwhile, borrowers' debt-relief applications began flooding in. "With abundant evidence of fraud available at both the federal and state levels," the *New York Times* editorial board chided in September 2015, "it's perplexing that the federal government has not promptly granted loan forgiveness for at least some of the people with complaints."

Finally, several months after the Debt Collective launched its campaign, Secretary Arne Duncan announced that students of Corinthian and other provably fraudulent schools, like ITT Tech, would get relief under borrower defense. But it took more than a year for the department to hash out the terms of the new regulation, and the rules, finalized in October 2016, weren't set to go into effect until the next summer. Just a month before the 2016 election, Elizabeth Warren sent a searing letter to then Secretary of Education John King, noting that the department was still aggressively collecting on nearly eighty thousand delinquent Corinthian loans.

Then, in November, came yet another deus ex machina.

Donald Trump won the election, and he came to office with, if not a

well-reasoned policy agenda, a firm commitment to undermining everything his predecessor had accomplished. This extended even to Obama's
wishy-washy actions on for-profit schools.

To accomplish the turnabout, Trump nominated Betsy DeVos, the
billionaire school-choice activist from Michigan, as his secretary of education. Republicans, who had pretended to be shocked by Trump's
campaign-trail rhetoric, now mostly capitulated to his requests. DeVos
was in, and she filled her department with an unprecedented stock of
for-profit industry insiders. The new education secretary, whose great
mission was dismantling the public education system, made undoing
the requirements of gainful employment and borrower defense top priorities. In March 2017, just weeks before schools' first gainful employment compliance deadline, DeVos announced that she would delay
implementing the rule. In 2019, she repealed it altogether.

DeVos was even harsher with provably defrauded students. In a 2017
speech, she incorrectly claimed that under Obama's borrower defense
rules, "all one had to do was raise his or her hands to be entitled to so-
called free money." Soon she declared that she would agree to approve
borrower claims from for-profit students cheated out of their money
and dreams only "with extreme displeasure." Then she stopped processing any claims at all. Judges repeatedly ruled against the administration
in lawsuits brought by state attorneys general and Harvard's Project on
Predatory Student Lending, and ultimately DeVos failed to completely
circumvent the process. By the end of her time in office, she had managed to stall on providing defrauded borrowers with relief, but her ene-
mies had won the war of public opinion, and they were about to expand
the pot of potential "free money" beyond her worst nightmares.

AFTER ALL THE YEARS OF HAMMERING AWAY AT POLITICIANS AND THE PUBLIC
at large about student loan debt, not even the most ardent debt-
cancellation advocates could have anticipated the shift that was set off
by the arrival of the coronavirus on America's cruise-ship docks in early
2020. As with almost every other part of American life, the business

(and rhetoric) of student loans was dramatically altered by the depredations of the virus as it swept across the country.

Perhaps ironically, it was Trump's actions during the early months of the pandemic that would pave the way for Biden to use executive action on student debt cancellation. As the American economy shuddered to sleep, with unemployment rates shooting to 15 percent, Congress acted quickly to wake it back up. In March 2020, legislators passed the CARES Act, a $2 trillion stimulus bill that paused payments and stopped interest accrual on all federal loans held by the Treasury (as distinct from old bank-based loans still held by commercial lenders, which were ineligible). The initial pause was set to last through September, but when it became clear that the pandemic would be nowhere near over by then, Trump extended it through the end of his term.

This was not an insignificant gift: borrowers were permanently spared tens of billions of dollars in payments under the moratorium. Yet, on its way out, Trump's administration tried to slam the door shut on further relief. In a memo, DeVos argued that canceling student debt by executive action would be unconstitutional. In a video conference with staff, she urged lifers in the Department of Education to "be the resistance."

Presumably DeVos was displeased at relieving people of debts because the idea goes against small-*c* conservative principles of fiscal responsibility. Students should be more financially literate, conservatives argue. But this ethos implies that young people are largely to blame for incurring huge debts in an absolutely impenetrable system of student finance. And, it further implies, should students find their "credentials" deemed useless after their schools have gone bankrupt or shut down in disgrace, it is in fact the students who are at fault for not better vetting these "schools." Never mind that all the while, recruiters were showering them with lies and false promises to fulfill their career dreams.

DeVos and her minions raised other objections to debt relief. Blanket student debt forgiveness, even for borrower defense applicants with proven claims, "would be abandoning our duty to be good stewards of tax dollars," said a Department of Education press secretary in 2019. But there is irony buried deep within this argument. The department had itself recognized that the practices of schools like Corinthian and ITT Tech—whose operations it was in effect bankrolling—were fraudulent. So, over the decades when students were racking up federal loans to attend them, it was the department, and the Treasury, and by extension the elusive "taxpayer," who were funding those loans, and thus they *themselves* were being defrauded.

In other words, the debt that borrowers owed to the Department of Education, the department in turn owed back to taxpayers. Requiring borrowers to make the federal government whole on bad loans that *it* gave out and guaranteed is essentially loan forgiveness in reverse. It's asking borrowers to relieve a debt that the government never should have incurred in the first place. After all, if individual students are expected to see through the falsehoods and fairy-tale promises made by for-profit school recruiters, shouldn't a cabinet-level arm of the federal government, fortified with thousands of experts and regulators and accreditors and an annual budget in the billions, be at least a little bit more prepared to cut through the same bullshit?

And if the students of for-profit schools—institutions engaged in mind-boggling levels of fraud—had miscalculated the worth of *their* future earnings, how could any student be expected to see through the nuanced financial equations behind even respected institutions of learning? When the burden of vetting a trillion-dollar industry depends upon the bets students have made against their own futures, something has gone very, very wrong.

In many ways, the arrangement looks much more like a Ponzi scheme—with student borrowers ultimately left holding the bag—than a system of student aid.

And by the end of Trump's term in office, more and more people were seeing that system for the scam that it had become.

AFTER LUKE HERRINE APPROACHED DEANNE LOONIN AND ROBYN SMITH ABOUT borrower defense, the pair had submitted a memo on behalf of the Corinthian borrowers. In it, they dropped something of a bombshell for the debt strikers. They argued that there would be no legal barrier to adopting the policy, because the Higher Education Act also allowed for executive action to "compromise, modify, or waive" *any* federal student loan.

This provision was news to Luke Herrine, but when he realized it existed—in fact, it had been in the Higher Education Act from the moment it was signed into law in 1965—he wondered why it wasn't being used more broadly. Perhaps, he thought, this provision could be used to cancel *all* student debt, not just the debts of defrauded for-profit students. Herrine believed that by using a power akin to a prosecutor's discretion to waive pretrial detention, the Department of Education could voluntarily forgo its collection of an individual borrower's federal student loan debt.

This idea hit at a crucial political juncture: the cusp of a presidential primary that would serve to elevate a number of leftist policy proposals, including student debt relief. Herrine was soon in touch with Julie Margetta Morgan, a longtime advocate of student debt relief. Then at the Roosevelt Institute, Morgan asked Herrine to write a white paper on the legal grounds for broad debt cancellation for the Great Democracy Initiative, a left-leaning policy shop that she had cofounded.

A few months later, Morgan was a policy adviser on Elizabeth Warren's presidential campaign and, lo and behold, the senator soon announced a student loan cancellation policy relying on the provision Herrine had written about. Warren had become more radical on student debt as the years (and her political career) went on, and she was now calling for the cancellation, by executive action, of up to $50,000 per borrower. This was surpassed only by Bernie Sanders's proposal—to cancel it all. Because both Warren and Sanders were calling for student debt relief, each of the other Democratic contestants was forced to address the issue, albeit often pathetically: before becoming Biden's VP pick, Kamala Harris tweeted out her support for $20,000 in cancellation "for Pell Grant recipients who start a business that operates for three years in disadvantaged communities."

Suddenly the rhetoric of student loan "forgiveness" was everywhere.

House Democrats wanted it. Sociologists and economists penned op-eds urging cancellation as a means of reducing the racial wealth gap, noting that in the twenty-first century Black college graduates, who borrow roughly 50 percent more than white graduates, have fallen even farther behind.

Among those who backed cancellation, $10,000 and $50,000 emerged as the headline figures. Supporters of the $10,000 figure argued that it was targeted to benefit the majority of borrowers currently in default (who are disproportionately Black and paradoxically tend to have lower balances, often because they never completed their degrees). They were countered by researchers like sociologist Louise Seamster, who found that $50,000, with phase-outs for higher earners, would leave about 80 percent of current borrowers debt-free while doing more to close the racial wealth gap.*

It was a remarkable development. Although student loans had previously been taken for granted as a net benefit, basically everyone now conceded that there was a glaring problem with student indebtedness in the United States. By this point, more than 44 million Americans held debt, on average almost $40,000, for a total of more than $1.7 trillion. Newspapers and magazines touted the stories of down-on-their-luck borrowers with six-figure debt and no career prospects; public servants locked out of federal relief programs by bureaucratic incompetence and negligence; students scammed by for-profit schools and shady lenders. It was undeniable that the student loan program was in crisis.

And then Donald Trump was voted out, and Joe Biden was in the White House. On the campaign trail, Biden had offered some milquetoast assurances that he would address the issue, canceling perhaps $10,000 of debt. And after the election, he vowed to address the question "immediately." But he never seemed totally convinced that student debt was actually a serious problem.

Throughout the early months of his presidency, Biden offered con-

---

* Because of inflation, the amount has since gone up.

tradictory statements about how much debt cancellation he supported or whether he supported it at all. At a town hall in early 2021, he said that canceling "debt for people who have gone to Harvard and Yale and Penn" would come at the expense of early-education programs for poor children. In fact, less than 0.5 percent of American students attend an Ivy League school, and those who do generally aren't saddled with huge loan balances. Only 3 percent of Harvard undergrads take out any federal loans at all.

Yet as Biden began his term, advocates of cancellation continued pushing him to take up the mantle. In February 2021, several members of Congress, including Maxine Waters, called on him to cancel $50,000 for all borrowers, a move that was supported by dozens of organizations and individuals, including the NAACP, the American Medical Student Association, and a third of all state attorneys general. Chuck Schumer urged him to address the issue via executive order, "with the flick of a pen."

Cancellation, proponents argued, would be good policy, however it was achieved, providing an overall stimulus to the economy. One study, by Bard College's Levy Economics Institute, estimated that it would direct as much as $1 trillion over a decade away from debt repayment into consumer spending. It would allow people to make choices currently foreclosed by their debts, such as buying homes, getting married, having children, and going into lower-paying public service positions. It would also help redress the racial wealth gap.

Finally, debt relief would be a major component in a revamping of higher education finance itself, so that our higher education system, like the vast majority of those in the developed world, would no longer finance itself through the indenture of its young people.

Faced with activist pressure, Biden started coming around too, reluctantly endorsing a plan to cancel $10,000 for most borrowers. As he took office, he immediately extended the Trump administration's payment pause, eventually stretching it to October 2023. Meanwhile, he asked both the Education and Justice departments to draft a memo advising him as to whether he had the authority to cancel debt by executive action. And then he simply never released the memo.

Finally, more than a year and a half into his first term, Biden decided to act. In August 2022, he released a plan to cancel between $10,000 and $20,000 of federal student loan debt for nearly every borrower.

It was not what the advocates had pushed for—it wasn't enough, it wouldn't undo the predatory system that had built up over more than six decades, and crucially, it wouldn't survive the scrutiny of the conservatives on the Supreme Court—but it was a remarkable development nonetheless. In little more than a decade, radical debt abolitionists had taken a laughably pie-in-the-sky ask and transformed it into the only sane response to a brutally efficient machine of inequity and exploitation. Through sheer force of will, they had even made it into the law of the land.

After a half century of being taken for a ride by lenders, schools, shams, and even their own government, students were set to see material returns on the bottomless community debt chest they'd been told it was their civic duty to pay into and a mark of personal failing that they had to do so at all.

For all 44 million of them, Biden's cancellation action was a small step, but one that was finally moving in the right direction.

But, naturally, it couldn't last.

As students and borrowers expressed jubilation and disbelief that student debt relief was finally on the table, a group of conservative antagonists were seeding lawsuits around the country to try to stop it. They invariably had little legitimate claim to oppose the program, but that didn't stop federal judges from siding with them. Soon they would get to press their case to the highest court in the land.

CHAPTER 12

Biden Time

S COTUS, can you hear us?" the woman at the lectern shouted, repeating herself for emphasis. "Debt relief is legal! Debt relief is just! And debt relief is necessary!" The nine berobed men and women in the building behind her could not, of course, hear her, nor were they there to listen to what she or anyone else out in the cold had to say. When a man with a bullhorn led a chant of "Whose court? Our court!" a short while later, he was engaging the crowd in what might most accurately be termed an exercise in magical thinking.

It was the last day of February 2023, and the Supreme Court was hearing challenges to President Biden's debt forgiveness plan. Immediately after Biden had announced it, conservative critics of loan forgiveness had come out of the woodwork to challenge it in courts across the country. Most of the challenges were quickly dismissed, but eventually, two cases made their way to the top rung of the American legal system.

Inside the courthouse, Elizabeth Prelogar, the country's solicitor general, was imploring the justices to spare student debtors, who, following a three-year respite, would soon be required to resume their monthly tithing to the student loan tarpit. If they did not, she warned, tens if not hundreds of thousands of Americans would sink into delinquency and default, their economic future imperiled for years, perhaps entire lifetimes. But the justices—six of them, anyway—heard only the sound of dollar bills flying from the Treasury's vaults into the hands of undeserving elites.

The challengers had barely a leg to stand on. The statute was clear as day. It allowed the secretary of education to "waive or modify" student loans in times of war or national emergency—more or less without limit.

But the six conservatives on the bench saw in the challenges a grand opportunity to slap a Democratic presidential administration on the wrist for, in their view, availing itself of power beyond its branch. Through an act of semantic sorcery, they sliced the words "waive" and "modify" beyond recognition, finally rendering them impotent. The issue of student debt relief, at a cost estimated at $400 billion over thirty years, was, they decided, simply too big for the president to decide. This was, in their term of art, a "major question" to be resolved only by Congress, which had of course generated the law they had just neutered.

In other words, the decision was spurious, but its power final. In the days after it came down, the Biden administration announced that it would try again, this time under the authority offered by the Higher Education Act, a process that would surely drag on for months, if not years, and would undoubtedly be subject to myriad legal challenges itself. In the meantime, payments would resume, borrowers would default, and in the weeks and months to come, the semestral hordes of eighteen-year-olds would matriculate into colleges charging tens of thousands of dollars a semester, to which the only response available was debt.

For now, the status quo had won. Debt relief was not to be.

BEHIND THE SCENES, MORE SUBTLE YET MEANINGFUL CHANGES WERE AFOOT. While Biden was dithering over a debt-relief plan at the beginning of his term, his secretary of education, Miguel Cardona, had already begun to act. In June 2022, he announced that the department would forgive the debts of all students who attended Corinthian Colleges schools going back to 1995, more than half a million of them. In the months that followed, he discharged federal loans hanging over the heads of thousands more—former students of ITT Tech, Ashford University, the University of Phoenix, and more.

In October 2022, the Biden administration reconfigured PSLF to provide forgiveness to all those disqualified by servicer errors and bureaucratic potholes. When Biden had entered office, only 7,000 public service employees had received relief. Within weeks of Cardona's announcement, 40,000 people found themselves suddenly set free of thousands of dollars of debt. By 2023, that number was up to more than 600,000—a total of $42 billion in relief.

Cardona also set about reorganizing the very mechanism of federal loan repayment. He introduced a new plan, Saving on a Valuable Education (SAVE), that reduced payments and stopped borrowers from being buried under infinitely accruing interest. And he ensured that people who paid consistently would be eligible for forgiveness under an income-driven repayment plan, even if they hadn't signed up for one. Subsequent adjustments to borrowers' accounts relieved $56.7 billion from nearly 800,000 borrowers who had been locked into their debts because their loan servicers had miscounted payments, or simply because no one ever told them they might qualify for relief.

These changes brought neither the acclaim nor the scrutiny that broad-based cancellation had, but in some ways they were more powerful. Unlike the COVID relief plan shot down by the court, which would have affected only the borrowers of today, Cardona's changes to repayment would ripple out to help borrowers tomorrow and the day after.

They were estimated to cost the government more than $475 billion over a decade—more than the forgiveness plan the Supreme Court shot down, in only a third of the time.

After the Supreme Court's decision, Biden said that he would continue to pursue broad-based cancellation, under the cumbersome process of negotiated rulemaking. In the meantime, in late February 2024, he announced that he would immediately cancel $1.2 billion for 150,000 borrowers enrolled in SAVE. The move received headline treatment, but in fact it was extremely targeted—affecting only those borrowers who had taken out less than $12,000 and already paid on their loans over ten years. Then, in April, the Biden administration released a draft of its cancellation plan: a new set of regulations would eliminate excess interest charges for borrowers and cancel the debts of those who had been in repayment for twenty or twenty-five years or who had attended since-discredited institutions. Immediately, conservatives vowed to fight the plan in court.

And of course, significant as these modifications have been, they do not solve the fundamental issue: an advanced degree is still a de facto requirement for most white-collar employment. And, except in rare instances, it is a requirement that costs money—a lot of money, more every year, and more than most people have.

As long as that's the case, student debt will continue to be inevitable, holding Americans back—especially those who arrive at the starting gate already hobbled by America's centuries-old policies of oppression.

Those who object to canceling student debt usually point to income quintiles: people with large quantities of debt—that is, people who went to graduate school—are more likely to earn high incomes. Some critics even argue that cancellation would be "regressive," that it would give the biggest boost to high earners and those privileged enough to go to college in the first place. Conservatives often cite the unfairness of forgiveness for those who saved for college or already paid off their debts (a critique that could be levied against all progress)—or the burden on the "taxpayer," as though student debt isn't itself a regressive tax (paid with interest) imposed upon those who can't afford to pay outright.

And what is the taxpayer burden, anyway? Because student loans represent money already spent, forgiving them would have no effect on the national debt, although it would raise the annual budget deficit, which takes into account the expected repayment on those loans. (This amount is already limited by the Department of Education's own estimates that a third of the student loan portfolio is junk—in other words, uncollectible.) To account for this shortfall in their presidential campaign plans, Bernie Sanders had proposed taxing Wall Street trades, and Elizabeth Warren had rolled out an "ultra-millionaire tax."

There are also reasons to question the idea that loan cancellation would primarily benefit the already privileged. Amid the debate, the economist Darrick Hamilton and public health scholar Naomi Zewde touted a plan to fully cancel all student debt. Their analysis focused on the fact that Black Americans lag behind their white counterparts far more in *wealth* than *income*, and they emphasized "the added burden that a long history of discriminatory policy places on borrowers of color." Black Americans, who typically start out with one-eighth the family wealth of their white classmates, must take on debt in higher numbers. Then, if they wish to overcome persistent racial and gender wage gaps, Black and female borrowers must credentialize to higher levels than their white male counterparts—perhaps needing an expensive grad degree just to start at a bachelor's-level salary. In other words, their degrees cost more and are worth less.

But something important has shifted in the decade or two since these debates began: the American populace, conditioned for half a century to view education debt as "good debt," a commodity synonymous with that of education itself, has begun to recognize it for what it really is—an unshakable burden, a sinking stone tied to the ankles of generation after generation.

Already we are seeing some curious corollaries to this realization. Young people are eschewing college in greater numbers, choosing to try their hand at endeavors less time and cost intensive. College enrollment, which peaked in 2010, is down from 18 million to 15 million. According to a 2023 *Wall Street Journal* poll, the majority of Americans now view a college degree as "not worth the cost."

Increasingly colleges themselves are seeing it this way as well. In recent decades, they have cut entire departments and eliminated untold numbers of faculty, turning instead to underpaid adjuncts and fellowship-reliant graduate students. While institutions pour money into supposedly lucrative (and costly) fields of study like computer engineering and the hard sciences, they starve the inexpensive subjects, like English, which, contrary to popular belief, actually *bring in* money to institutions.

This state of affairs is patently unsustainable—as indicated not just by declining enrollments but also by recent waves of contingent-laborer uprisings. Adjuncts and grad students have begun to organize, and unionize, to demand their due. On the one side are those who see education as a unit to monetize, on the other a moral, even spiritual pursuit—a social good. Between them is a seemingly unbridgeable gulf.

At the heart of these competing views of education is the concept of "value." For most of contemporary American history, the question has been one of material gain. Although a college degree may be costly, it will be worth it, or pay off, in higher wages down the line. The experience may also be personally enriching, but this is usually viewed as a bonus.

Thus, if a university education has lost "value" in recent years, this is only because we have been conditioned to treat it as a consumer product. Going back to the GI Bill—and magnified in the years and policies since—the federal government has advanced a vision of education as a product you *buy* rather than a transformation you *undergo*. This corruption of education has been so thorough that it has infected the lower grades as well, in a public school system that is overrun with a lexicon of metrics and "choice." Everything leading up to college is about getting into college, which is about getting the most bang for your buck—as measured not by knowledge or societal progress or any other such utopian outcome, but simply and wholly by the amount of money it yields. It is, at heart, a matter of pure arithmetic.

Yet this approach more or less undermines the very concept of a university as a vast, self-replicating repository of knowledge, in that it requires always chasing the next lucrative field and abandoning the rest. Right now this is STEM, but that can't last, a reality that the die-hard consumerists don't seem to appreciate. If everyone learns to code, coding ceases to be lucrative, a trend we are already witnessing. Society evolves, and it's difficult to predict what it will elevate and what it will discard. This is a big ask even for professional prognosticators adept at playing the employment stock market, and it is extraordinarily cruel to ask of eighteen-year-olds. We are essentially telling teenagers to toss the dice on their own lives and then punishing them if they make the "wrong" choices or, god forbid, follow their own interests instead.

Even the well-meaning advocates of student-loan borrowers are stuck within Nader's framework of "consumer" advocacy, which is pragmatic but offers little hope of utopian overhaul. It does not attempt to reframe the narrative around the value of higher education or society's collective responsibility for it, but rather takes for granted that it is a product of fundamentally individual risk and reward (albeit one necessitating regulation and oversight). This is what makes a group like the Debt Collective, which has the courage and the gall to demand no less than everything, so intriguing.

And yet, despite glimmers of progress, the outlook remains mostly grim. We have mostly squandered the opening presented by COVID with programs of targeted relief that may or may not deliver on their promises and won't solve the underlying issue. It is unclear what the next crisis will be, or when it will come. Perhaps student debt itself will generate a crisis worthy of its own reparation. Whatever the case, if we are ever to dismantle the status quo and reshape our education system in an image worthy of the name, we must be ready to seize whatever opening comes our way.

BETWEEN THE CONGRESSIONAL HEARINGS OF 1952, 1975, AND 1990, SEVERAL evocative claims appeared and reappeared, yet were not fully examined. Only when viewed in aggregate do they collectively offer glimmers of an alternative future. For instance: witnesses and legislators repeatedly stated that although student aid abuses were most egregious at proprietary schools, the same rot was festering at a lower level in the public and nonprofit sectors as well. Yet the lawmakers and government officials provided scant evidence of this. They made emphatic pronouncements about the value and benefit that some, nay many, for-profit schools were providing to their students and the public at large, lest anyone get the idea they had it out for the sector. Yet they provided no real evidence of this either.

Were they to scrape beneath the surface of these claims, they might have come up with some sweeping questions about the overall system: if public and nonprofit schools are indeed subject—in miniature—to the same corrupting influences that are proprietary schools' oxygen, then perhaps there's something wrong with those influences themselves. And if there really are proprietary schools that offer a valuable product, why must they rely almost entirely on a massive federal subsidy to survive? Shouldn't they, above all others, live or die by the market?

Most infuriating, the testifying senators and Department of Education auditors and accreditors and school administrators referred again and again to the notion of risk: specifically, the inherent risk posed to lenders by a cohort of borrowers not yet old enough to purchase an alcoholic beverage. They discussed only glancingly the much greater risk that students themselves assume by taking on debt at a time when, by definition, they do not have the means to pay it back and their future prospects for doing so are often little more than a mirage in the desert.

For some reason, the officials never seemed to stop and think about how little sense this makes. They recognized that some number of defaults were going to happen and the taxpayer was just going to have to eat them. Yet they paused only briefly to consider what each default would mean for the person experiencing it: the hounding by collection agents at home and work, the melting of credit, the humiliation and lost time. These individuals became casualties of the program, of no greater significance than the dollars they could not repay.

The experts never seemed to see what was staring them right in the face: perhaps these are the riskiest borrowers for a reason? As in, they're most risky because they are *most at risk*. And if that's the case, it's functionally immoral to lend to them in the first place. After all, it wouldn't make any sense to, say, give out loans for million-dollar homes to unemployed people with bad credit. We've played out that thought experiment empirically: it ended quite badly. Yet the same risk matrix that drove the 2008 foreclosure crisis has been an issue with college students for decades—with ever-increasing stakes year after year, Senate hearing after Senate hearing. Student borrowers are, in essence, subprime.

Again and again, the people in charge of the loan program somehow missed the most obvious conclusion: it's bad, actually. Nowhere along the line did anyone stop to say, This program is a nightmare. Let's shut it down.

The outright fraud of unscrupulous for-profit schools merely highlights this insidious apparatus of inequity, deceit, and anguish. They took our national obsession with individualism and value and metastasized it into a program of gargantuan government-sponsored grift. Though they may appear to be an outlier, a bag of bad apples in a barrel of good, ev-erything wrong with for-profits is indeed present in nonprofit and public institutions to at least some degree. All of them are siphoning federal dollars and indebting students in the process.

Let's call this what it is: corporate welfare. And yet it's even worse than that. Instead of distributing the cost for that welfare across the tax base, we've insisted it fall directly into the laps of the individuals exploited by it. And until very recently we've given them almost no way out from under that burden—be it via bankruptcy or borrower defense. If the burden on the taxpayer is the greatest issue here, then shouldn't Congress be at least a little bit concerned with the people who are actu-ally getting away with the taxpayers' money? Say, for instance, those like Jack D. Massimino, who made millions as the CEO of Corinthian Col-leges and was made to pay back only $80,000 when the company went down the tube, taking all its former students with it?

In the meantime, as we propped up the grifters, we lost sight of the myriad community benefits of education (like better health and civic engagement, in addition to higher tax revenues). Almost invariably, if there is a community benefit to be had, it will be better generated by a well-resourced public option. Profit itself—intended to enrich lucky individuals—is largely incompatible with the very idea of community.

This is, essentially, the Debt Collective's perspective. The group starts from the premise that financing higher education by asking the non-wealthy to take on increasingly unmanageable levels of debt is wrong. Education ought to be a right of citizenship in a wealthy, humane, democratic society. Its effects—intellectual, financial, cultural, social, or otherwise—are not limited to enhancement of the individual receiving it. They benefit us all by creating an astute citizenry and a populace whose members are well matched to their interests and labor goals. Therefore, education ought to be provided as a public good. Student debt shouldn't exist in the first place.

They're right. It's time—beyond time—to design a better system.

It would be nice to think that we could create one merely by writ-ing letters to senators and heckling Joe Biden at campaign rallies. But if the history of student debt reveals anything, it's that a major shift will come only in a moment of crisis. In order to make use of that crisis, whatever it is, we must be ready with big ideas for radical change. And we must work together, organize in even greater numbers, to demand that America finally deliver on the bargain it has made with its young people for nearly a century.

CHAPTER 13

Past Due

I n the realm of big ideas for higher education, there is one that looms above all others—decoupling "education" from "job training." In other words, we must try to unlearn the notion that an education is the necessary means to a job, wealth, and socioeconomic standing and dismiss this idea from educational theory and practice. There is nothing wrong with learning skills for work. But teaching them should be the task of employers, job-training programs, specialized (ideally public) vocational and professional programs. Bachelor's degrees should not stand in for workplace development. A college education should be about learning—a time for exploring ideas and finding what it means to be a member of a society. And that opportunity should be available to everyone.

To effect this shift, we must also change how we treat the acquisition of education—to understand it not as an individual consumer commodity but rather as a public good. This will require not only a major ideological renovation, but also massive material investment in constructing a national infrastructure for public higher education. We must make free public college an option for everyone who wants it and can benefit from it.

But, as we have seen, one major reason why federal funding for higher education has proven so hard to come by over the decades is that a certain breed of American legislator (and constituent) fears it as a precursor to "federal control" of education. They find this idea abhorrent for reasons ranging from the vile (racism) to the understandable (America is a big country with many kinds of social-organizing mechanisms that have specific, sometimes divergent needs). The provision of education is not enumerated in the Constitution, they say, and so it should not be a responsibility of the federal government, but rather a baton for state and local government to pick up.

But there is one glaring problem with this philosophy: it doesn't work. Before the middle of the twentieth century, state and local government often did not pick up the baton. And in the absence of strong national involvement in education, standards varied so widely that it was impossible to determine what, for instance, a high school diploma actually meant; in Des Moines and Spokane, it might signify different things. College entrance requirements were similarly heterogeneous, as were faculty credentials (the PhD was by no means a common requirement until well into the twentieth century). The quality of education represented by a college diploma was nearly impossible to judge on its face. Until the latter part of the twentieth century, education in America was a hodgepodge of mostly low-quality offerings, particularly for students from the lower rungs of the economy.

As higher education developed along the lines established by wealthy philanthropists and free-market economic priorities, the enterprise came to be seen as an individualist affair, rather than a cooperative one. Students were market actors, consumers, in pursuit of a financial good that would benefit them personally; their education might benefit the country as well, but only incidentally.

It should come as no surprise that this system led to a distribution of education and its benefits that highly privileges the wealthy and leaves the poor mostly hung out to dry—with little opportunity, except to accrue insurmountable debt. In fact, it is almost more remarkable that, for a few brief moments, forces of equity—the GI Bill, the Pell Grant—managed to edge toward even a partial leveling of the playing field.

Essentially, because a deal was struck at the founding of the country to keep the federal government a macro- rather than a micromanager of higher education, we collectively abdicated our role as safeguards of the educational system, its quality, its offerings, the equity of its access, and its purpose. Those qualities were given over to university administrators and professors—the experts—to the states, and to private enterprise.

In this light, would federal control really have been so bad?

For one answer to this question, we can look to other countries, where national governments really do control higher education. This is largely the case in Europe, which built up university offerings—and standards—in the early part of the twentieth century, usually organized under one central ministry of education. Let's take France, for example.

There is no question that public education in France is regimented to a degree that would be unthinkable here in America. Almost all children attend public school, which begins as early as age two. Children progress through a standard, generalized curriculum until high school. Then they are sorted into a number of tracks, based on their interests and abilities: literature, economics, science. At the end of high school students must submit to a comprehensive battery of written and oral exams, the *baccalauréat*, to receive their diploma. This allows them entry into a public French university. Usually they attend a school near where they live, although a small cadre of exceptional students are admitted into a set of elite public schools known as the *grandes écoles*. At university students spend three years—largely endured in massive lecture courses, with grades determined by performance on a single end-of-semester exam—toward the equivalent of a bachelor's degree, known as the *licence*.

Students who do not wish to enter the university can choose alternate tracks after the twelfth grade—they might opt for a vocational school that prepares them to enter the workforce more quickly. These institutions are also public and almost entirely tuition-free.

All of this is funded by the national purse. In fact, France's postwar constitution, ratified in 1946, guarantees free higher education. Nevertheless, French and EU citizens pay a small annual fee, about $190—*per year*. When right-leaning French politicians—from Nicolas Sarkozy to Emmanuel Macron—have proposed scrapping this system and introducing American-style tuition, mass protests and nationwide strikes have ensued. Macron learned this in early 2022, when he hinted that he would introduce a tuition model. "We cannot remain forever in a system in which higher education is free for almost all students," he said. He was met with a barrage of public outcry and eventually backed off.

But of course, French education isn't really free. France has personal income tax rates that reach up to nearly 50 percent for high earners. Its tax revenues, at 46 percent of GDP, are almost double ours. Everyone pays into the system.

Still, the French model, like all others, has its drawbacks. Among the latter include the fact that only about 25 percent of the population has a bachelor's degree or higher, versus 39 percent in the United States. College students are often disaffected and neglected, with little individual attention or support; French university housing tends to be drab and isolating; and there is little in the way of a campus "community" after the American model. The system is not perfect. But it's hard to imagine that aping the financing model of the United States would be the answer to any of its putative problems.

America is not France, nor even England, where a public university education costs half what it would in America. We will likely never have the centralized university model of the Continent, whether such a thing would even be desirable.

So what can we do to return education to a source of both personal and societal well-being, one in which people of all ages learn for enrichment and citizenship, not just employment and status?

I HAVE A FEW PROPOSALS:

First, we need a massive new investment in public higher education, on both the federal and state level. There are some prior examples to show the way. The 1972 reauthorization of the Higher Education Act introduced the State Student Incentive Grant (SSIG) program, by which the federal government provided matching funds for states to establish student grant programs. It endured the budget hacks of the 1980s (and was renamed LEAP) but died a death of defunding in the upheavals of the Obama administration. Although it was a relatively small program aimed at individual students, on the order of $65 million per year, it provided a crucial incentive for states to continue funding public higher education.

After that incentive was taken away, in 2010, state investment in higher education plummeted. Between 2008 and 2018, states decreased their spending on students by 13 percent, an overall drop of $6.6 billion after inflation. Over the same period, public universities increased tuition and fees by nearly 50 percent. Student debt was the only thing left to bridge the gap.

The LEAP program offers a model for how we might go about establishing a mechanism of what Jon Oberg calls "cooperative federalism." Imagine that instead of funding student grants, the Department of Education funded state college and university systems instead. The feds might offer an annual pot of money, conditioned on state matching and "maintenance of effort" (i.e., continued investment). They might also set upper limits on student fees and even establish labor standards for adjuncts and graduate students.

This would undoubtedly be greeted with horror by university administrators, who would shout about the threat of incursion into their academic freedom. But a financial imperative need not cross the iron curtain into academic standards. As long as the firewall was maintained, with the federal government providing a desperately needed infusion of funds, states would have little room to complain.

Another, more controversial, solution takes on private schools.

Why should Harvard and Yale—or even Reed and NYU, where I went to school—benefit to such a great degree from the largesse of the federal government, via Pell Grants and student loans? According to Federal Student Aid, nonprofit private institutions receive more than one-third of all federal grant and loan disbursements, despite enrolling only one-sixth of all undergraduate students.

If these schools are going to receive such a heavy federal investment, there's no reason the money shouldn't come with strings attached. They should face public standards and regulations, just like their public counterparts. In fact, if they're going to receive so much public money, they should *be* public. Private colleges and universities should be given an option: either stop accepting public funds or stop being private.

It's unlikely that Harvard or Yale, which could afford the hit, would take the bait. They would remain private, and exclusive—perhaps even more so. And undoubtedly, some small private colleges without huge endowments would choose to close altogether rather than become public.

Critics would cry out about the two-tiering of American education; private schools would be the exclusive province of wealthy elites, with everyone else relegated to state universities. *But this is already the case.* Wealthy students are much more likely than poor ones to attend elite schools. If their parents are in the top 1 percent of earners, they are 1.5 times more likely to go to Harvard than poor kids who matched them on the SAT. At Georgetown, their odds are nearly triple. (Public universities tend to skew in the opposite direction.) Legacy applicants make up a tenth to a quarter of college admissions at top schools—at Harvard, a third. Meanwhile, only 16 percent of Harvard's 2025 freshmen are Black.

The Ivy League will always be a machine for burnishing the status of those who don't really need it in the first place. I say this as a person who received degrees from two prestigious, albeit not Ivy-level, private schools. My college experience opened my eyes to a wealth of knowledge and perspective that quite literally changed my life. I would not trade it for the world.

But I would change it for a system in which *everyone* had the same opportunity. In which even community college students were encouraged to study and learn—not for money, but just for the sake of it.

Imagine what could be done with all the taxpayer money we currently use to subsidize the Ivy League's members. Imagine how much more we could do for UC Berkeley, or SUNY, or Boise State University. Imagine if every graduating high school senior had a quality college or university within commuting distance from their home. What a fundamental shift this would offer our higher education system—and society itself.

Finally, we have to eliminate the cancer of for-profit higher education once and for all. There is simply no reason that proprietary schools should receive virtually limitless pools of federal money, with very few strings attached and minimal accountability.

In fact, they should receive none.

For-profit-eers like to claim that they deserve their subsidized money, because, unlike nonprofit and public institutions, they pay taxes on their revenue. As well they should! In fact, what they pay taxes on is almost exclusively tax-funded money. They are merely rendering back unto Caesar the very smallest portion of what was already Caesar's to begin with.

The bottom line is that for-profit schools should be allowed—*at most*—merely to exist. If individual states want to shore them up, fine, that's their problem. But societally, we should have no obligation nor interest in subsidizing them. And to do so on the backs of their students is unconscionable. Throw the proprietary schools into the waters of their beloved free market and let them sink or swim by their own lifeboats.

But what about the claim that at least some of these schools perform an important function—that they provide employees for new industries, and do so more nimbly and responsively than the public sector can? Dubious. And if there really is, as officials from Barack Obama to Betsy DeVos like to remind us, an important national interest in ensuring that the populace is well trained for emerging technologies and labor demands, then it should rightly be the role of government to ensure that this interest is met. This is exactly what government is for! Right now workforce-training funds—of which there are not many—travel a complicated distribution system that is much harder for schools and beneficiaries to access than federal student loans. What an inexcusable travesty this is.

In the language so dear to the cheerleaders of student aid, government needs to *invest* more in the education of its citizens if it wants to reap the benefits of their increased productivity. And not by funneling taxpayer funds through third-rate entrepreneurs regulated with all the strength of a friendship bracelet, but through public provision. We don't have to go the way of France or Germany and track twelve-year-olds into lifelong careers to get there. Instead, let us simply fund community colleges, fund public vocational institutions—and fund them generously. Let us insist that states substantially match federal dollars, and make them commit to keeping tuitions low or nonexistent.

This is not merely a question of the economic health of our society. It's also about equity, and racial and economic and gender justice. We have for too long thrown the most marginalized members of our society to the wolves of profit and debt, and it's time to truly level the playing field.

And, finally, it's about health, literally. It's going to take a staggering amount of investment for us to achieve the technological breakthroughs and labor realignments necessary to turn around (or at least slow) the ship on climate change, and prepare for the *next* global pandemic. Who do we really want to entrust with the responsibility for making that investment—Elon Musk? Jeff Bezos? the CEO of the University of Phoenix?

To put it mildly: yikes.

THERE IS MUCH MORE TO THE TOPIC OF STUDENT DEBT—TO SAY NOTHING OF higher education finance—than could fit in a single book, and I have had to leave a great deal out of this one. In particular, I have omitted countless examples of the kinds of fraud, malfeasance, and incompetence that permeate all corners of student borrowing.

For instance, even as the Biden administration began surgically mending the student loan repayment system, and the pull and power of for-profit schools waned after the scandals of the Obama years, these arenas have continued to breed scandals that reveal the unsalvageability of the loan program writ large.

Loan servicers, although brought somewhat to heel, continue to provide stunningly shoddy service to their borrower "customers." In October 2023, for instance, MOHELA admitted that it had miscalculated nearly 300,000 borrowers' payments, overcharging borrowers right as they reentered repayment after a three-year reprieve.

As the federal bureaucracy proliferates repayment plans and forgiveness programs for borrowers to benefit by, con artists fill the information vacuum left by poor-performing government contractors. On the internet, scammers try to scrape dollars from unsuspecting borrowers to sign them up for free federal payment programs. At best, these borrowers pay money for access to something they could have gotten for free from their loan servicer.

And although for-profit schools have started to wane, wherever there is federal money there will be avenues for grift, and con artists will always find them. As the for-profit moniker has become something of a scarlet letter, many schools have turned to a new strategy: removing the stigma by converting into nonprofit institutions. This permits them to renovate their image, and boast of newfound values.

In most cases, this is just a clever shell game. In 2020, for instance, the public University of Arizona acquired the for-profit Ashford University from Zovio, the company that owned it, then gave Ashford a new name: University of Arizona Global Campus (UAGC). The University of Arizona then contracted management of UAGC out to Zovio, and students attending UAGC, a fully online "school," unwittingly paid some of their fees to a company that had collapsed to widespread fraud charges only a few years earlier.*

Grand Canyon University similarly converted itself into a nonprofit, run by Grand Canyon Education, Inc.; Purdue bought Kaplan University (previously owned by the Washington Post Company) and rebranded it Purdue Global.

Now even John Sperling's great monstrosity, the University of Phoenix, is getting in on the game. Since for-profits began their great decline in the 2010s, the school has faced dwindling admissions—down almost 80 percent from its 2010 high of 470,000—and the private equity firm that owns it has been on the hunt for a new buyer. In 2023, the University of Idaho announced that it was creating a nonprofit corporation to buy Phoenix and run it as a nonprofit, reinvesting any potential revenues in "strategic initiatives." Senators Richard Blumenthal, Dick Durbin, and Elizabeth Warren urged the University of Idaho to reconsider the acquisition, which, they warned, "could cause great harm to students and taxpayers not only in Idaho but also across the country."

---

* UAGC terminated its contract with Zovio in 2022.

Although the University of Idaho deal would keep Phoenix under nonprofit management, many other "nonprofit" conversions outsource their programs to for-profit corporations run by the same people, who continue to reap their outrageous revenues. The new boss is—literally— the same as the old boss. And students continue to receive an exorbitant, subpar education for which they must turn to debt financing.

Genuinely nonprofit—and even public—institutions are not immune from such malign incentives. Many schools, seeing the virtually endless revenues to be extracted from graduate programs, have developed master's programs that can only be described as cash cows. Because students can take out an almost unlimited amount of student loan money to attend graduate programs, schools are incentivized to charge whatever they can get.

More and more, they are also turning to online education—the mode pioneered by for-profits—to reap these dollars at a discount. Online programs are up at schools across the country, especially for graduate programs (up 37 percent since 2020). Some of them, like Southern New Hampshire University (SNHU), a private institution that until recently boasted just a few thousand students, have surpassed the 100,000-matriculants mark. SNHU estimates costs for its online-only undergraduate programs at roughly $10,000 a year. Nearly 50,000 of its students benefit from the Pell Grant.

It remains to be seen if here, as ever, students will suffer the cost for the sake of administrative and technological "innovation."

I HAVE HAD THE PRIVILEGE OF BUILDING A BIRD'S-EYE VIEW OF THIS GRO-tesque system while I researched and wrote this book over the past four-plus years. And from my vantage, the circuitous route by which we arrived at today's student debt lava pit calls to mind a lesson delivered by the late anthropologist (and debt abolitionist) David Graeber in his 2015 book, *The Utopia of Rules*: "The ultimate, hidden truth of the world is that it is something that we make, and could just as easily make differently." So much of legislation, when you take a close look at it, depends on more or less arbitrary factors. In the case of financial aid policy, those factors included the personalities and power plays of legislators and presidents, the intransigence of Southern Democrats over segregation and liberal Democrats' willingness to placate them, sudden shifts in national and global politics, and world-historical crises. A good deal of our higher education system, as with much of America itself, came about by accident.

The Higher Education Act of 1965, the law that set in legislative stone the mechanisms of our college funding system, depends no more on some grand design for college completion and affordability than it does the pettiness of individuals and the unknowability of the future. Throughout the history of higher education legislation in the United States, there have been tantalizing moments when a push for free college seemed no more or less absurd than the notion of free high school. Along the way, there were voices pushing to turn higher education into a right of citizenship, suggesting, in essence, that there was another way to make the world, a better one, and we really ought to have considered it.

So why didn't we? Again, mostly arbitrary factors—politics and personalities and crises.

Perhaps less arbitrary, at least in the present day, are the ideological underpinnings of our system. America has always been wedded to a morality of individual responsibility and accomplishment, particularly for the poor, and this is as true in education as in anything else. Time and again, members of Congress proved unwilling to brook the notion of offering needy students a "free ride." Instead, these students were made to work, and to borrow.

This ideological framework has only recently begun to crumble, and only because the financial system that both undergirds and feeds on it has itself collapsed multiple times in the past two decades—another series of world-historical events. But public opinion isn't auto-generating: the gradual realization that our current financing system is untenable and the moral imperative for debt-free education have not emerged without a huge amount of sustained effort, in large part by citizen-activist organizations such as Student Debt Crisis Center,* Student Loan Justice, and perhaps most powerfully, the Debt Collective. They were derided at first, but now their ideas are mainstream. More than anything, it is their example that shows the way forward, offering an antidote to the petty arbitrariness of national politics: if we want to overcome the complacency and venal self-interest of Congress, we must provide something more powerful—an unflinching moral position and an unyielding commitment to it. This is far more important than coming up with the perfect means test or the wonkiest equity calculus. It is only by making—and winning—the case that education is a right that we will ever convince those in charge to distribute it as such, by virtue not of privilege but citizenship.

This, in any event, is what I have come to believe. Although, like all the others I have spoken with about their student debt over the past several years, I am not what anyone would call a disinterested party.

When I graduated from Reed College in 2005, I had a little more than $20,000 in student loan debt. At the time this seemed an impossible amount, which I would never repay (indeed, nearly twenty years later, my undergraduate loan balance hovers around $5,000).

College, for me, was a life-changing experience. It opened my eyes to entire worlds of thought—quantum physics, post-structuralism, Proust. My way of approaching the world is different because of my education. And yet it left me with apparently very little to offer the professional world. For the next couple of years, I worked low-paying jobs—as a parking lot attendant, an assistant English teacher in rural France, a grunt at a twenty-four-hour Kinko's in Portland, Oregon—never making more than $10 an hour. Between rent, health insurance premiums, and my $125 monthly student loan payment, I was left with less than $500 a month to spend on food, transportation, and everything else.

A few years later, I began applying to graduate schools in New York.

---

* Student Debt Crisis changed its name to Student Debt Crisis Center in 2021.

I was twenty-four and casting about, not sure where I wanted to go or who I wanted to become. On nights and weekends I took filmmaking classes at a local nonprofit. I tried to write fiction. I vaguely wanted to move to New York, but I had no sense of how I would find a job in the city. All I really knew was that I could not stay in Portland, working meaningless low-paying jobs and living in cheap rental houses with half a dozen friends who were similarly ground down. I have often joked, darkly, that I wasn't sure I would survive many more years in Portland. Was it a joke though, really?

Eventually, I decided to attend a global journalism master's program at NYU. I did not, at that time, realize that terminal master's programs are cash cows for their institutions, funding undergraduate scholarships and PhD fellowships. When I initially balked at the cost of NYU, the head of the journalism department contacted me directly, offering a one-semester tuition scholarship. Then I was put in touch with another professor. I asked him how most students financed the program's costs, given NYU's exorbitant tuition (about $35,000 a year in 2008). "Well," he said sheepishly, "most of them take out student loans."

I had grown up on the edge of poverty, on food stamps, inventing excuses to absent myself from school events because I didn't want to burden my mom with the expense. I was petrified of returning there. Ironically, because of student loan funds, my years in school have been the only ones in my life to offer a respite from otherwise constant and crippling financial anxiety.

This is the lure of capitalism: when you have faced privation, even mild (as mine certainly was), you long for the relief of not having to ruthlessly budget for every need, or even the occasional desire. Although I continued to live rather frugally while in graduate school, the pool of loan money deposited into my bank account at the beginning of each semester brought a sense of relief I have never experienced before or since. It was, I knew even then, a luxury I could not really afford, but at twenty-four, the prospect of two years of freedom from financial panic—even if they ensured I would never experience such serenity again—was one I was apparently powerless to resist.

And then, two years later, I graduated with another $100,000 added to my debt ledger, and no great prospects for paying it off.

WHAT SHOULD I HAVE DONE INSTEAD? I HAVE OFTEN HAD THIS THOUGHT, AND the answers are fairly plain. Most obviously, I shouldn't have gone to grad school; I should have gone to a cheaper grad school; I should have threatened to drop out; I should have actually dropped out; I should have moved back in with my mom; and I most definitely should *not* have spent the year after graduating living on my leftover loan funds while I interned at various low-paying literary magazines. And when a five-month, full-time, unpaid stint at *Harper's Magazine* resulted in a job offer the next fall, I should not have let go of my $42,000 fact-checker's salary from *Self* magazine and taken an $11,000 pay cut for the same job at *Harper's*. Finally, once at *Harper's*, a 501(c)(3) nonprofit, I should have done everything in my power to remain employed there, in spite of a crushingly dysfunctional work environment and poverty-level wages, so that, in late 2021, after ten years, I might have benefited from the relief offered by the Public Service Loan Forgiveness program.

In short, I have made a lot of mistakes. Reading the paragraph above, it seems as if I've made exactly the wrong decision at literally every turn. The blame for my situation is almost too easy to place on my shoulders. But I always return to my time in Portland, and the knowledge that I deserved more than what I found on offer there (as everyone does). I fundamentally believed that more education would solve my problems, even if I wasn't sure exactly how. "Student loan debt is good debt," said my mom, by then a social worker, who had only that year paid off her own student loans, thanks to a small inheritance from a recently deceased aunt.

It is of course hard—impossible?—in retrospect to untangle outcomes from the disastrous choices that led to them. To look back through the crystal ball and see everything clearly again. Had I not attended graduate school, I would never have worked at *Harper's*, which, in spite of everything, was the most fulfilling job I've ever had. More consequentially, I would not have met a new colleague there in 2014, who would eventually become my husband and the father of my two children. I would not have written a feature article for *Mother Jones* in 2018 inspired by my firsthand knowledge of the troubles facing the Public Service Loan Forgiveness program. Had I not written that piece, I would have had nothing on which to base the proposal for a book about the history of the student loan program. In short, you would not be reading these words. Would I be better off? That's an unanswerable question. I would not give up my husband or my sons or the life we have together for anything. And yet I find it inconceivable that my husband and I will be able to offer our children the same educational opportunities we had. So I guess I—and they—will have to live with the decisions that led me here.

But of course I wish that I, and all the other people who bought into the American promise of higher education, did not have to face the already uncertain future with an unshruggable weight of debt across our backs. In writing this book, I was confronted with mountains of evidence that there is nothing natural or inevitable about the financial straits our country, its legislators, and their policies have placed us in. We all deserve something better, and with enough hope and fight, I believe we can get it.

ACKNOWLEDGMENTS

I first started delving into the history of student debt in 2017, while writing a feature article about the Public Service Loan Forgiveness program for Wes Enzinna, then an editor at *Mother Jones*. I'm grateful to him and to everyone who helped bring that story to the world—especially Clara Jeffery, who made it a cover story, as well as research director Nina Liss-Schultz and fact-checker Olivia Exstrum, who combed that article down to the last pica.

Eventually my husband, Henry Freedland, persuaded me to work up a book proposal and introduced me to Mel Flashman, who agreed to be my agent. Mel was integral to this book's existence: she helped me shape the proposal and then worked tirelessly to find a good editor for it. That editor was Kate Napolitano, whose punk-rock enthusiasm for the book never waned, even after she departed HarperCollins in 2022.

Stuart Roberts stepped in to fill Kate's shoes, and I am tremendously grateful to him and to editorial assistant Chelsea Herrera for pushing me to rethink and reorganize the manuscript, helping me to sharpen its focus and stitch together a narrative from nearly a century of sprawling, technical policy history. Susanna Brougham's masterful line edit improved the manuscript beyond words. I am also grateful to the publisher's design team and to its production department, who wrangled my absurd quantity of endnotes.

I am immensely thankful as well to Paco Alvarez, who fact-checked an early draft of the book, saving me from countless embarrassing errors. (Any that remain are, of course, my own doing.)

Many other people helped make this book a reality during a period of my life that included a cross-country move, the births of two spirited children, a global pandemic, and much more. At the top of the list are all those who graciously loaned their time, their stories, and their expertise. In particular, I want to thank borrowers Leigh McIlvaine, Jordan Long,

Pam Hunt, Nathan Hornes, Brandon Isaacs, Michelle Quintero-Millan, Jamie Rudert, Kate Voigt, Haylee Adamson, Samantha Mangino, Sanders Fabares, Rebekah Valorn, Richelle in South Los Angeles, Victoria Weiley, and Kate Schweizer. I received invaluable information on a variety of student aid topics from Jon Oberg, David Bergeron, David Madzelan, Julie Margetta Morgan, Rohit Chopra, Seth Frotman, Mike Pierce, Bob Shireman, Mark Kantrowitz, and many others. I am also thankful to Thomas Gokey, Astra Taylor, Luke Herrine, Ann Larson, Winter Casuccio, Laura Hanna, Hannah Appel, Pam Brown, Andrew Ross, Braxton Brewington, and Alexis Goldstein for providing me with on-the-ground oral histories of Occupy Wall Street, the Debt Collective, and the fight for debt cancellation. I am thankful to Deanne Loonin, Robyn Smith, Eileen Connor, and Toby Merrill for schooling me on student loan law, and for spending their careers fighting for borrowers. Thank you also to Natalia Abrams, Eric Fink, Louise Seamster, Thomas Shapiro, Dominique Baker, Marshall Steinbaum, Jonathan Glater, Persis Yu, Alan Collinge, Will Hubbard, Jennifer Esparza, Isaac Bowers, Kate Kennedy, and many, many others.

I am also grateful to the writers and reporters who have covered this issue before me, and upon whose work I relied to produce my own. Beat reporters like Danielle Douglas-Gabriel, Jillian Berman, Andrew Kreighbaum, Erica Green, Tara Bernard Siegel, Ron Lieber, and Josh Mitchell generated many of the primary sources that helped me build a narrative of recent policy history. The book-length accounts of Seth Rosenfeld, Suzanne Mettler, Ira Katznelson, Kathleen Frydl, Elizabeth Tandy Shermer, John Thelin, and others were invaluable in shaping my own understanding of the historical record.

As I embarked on this project, colleagues, friends, and family offered assignments, listening ears, and sometimes housing. Emily Cooke commissioned two articles for *The New Republic*, which offered crucial opportunities (and funds) to stay abreast of student loan policy. Anthony Lydgate and Britt Harwood provided extremely valuable feedback on a completed draft of the manuscript. Ben Platt offered wise and reassuring counsel on the editorial process. Carine Ernoult updated my twenty-year-old recollections of France's educational system. Allison Moseley and Celeste Broderick patiently listened to me gripe, as did Tay Wiles and Chase Munson, who were the ideal neighbors to ride out a global pandemic with.

Thank you also to my friends and former colleagues at *Harper's Magazine*, especially Emily Stokes, Sam Stark, Jacob Gross, Joe Kloc, Jeremy Keehn, Rafil Kroll-Zaidi, Ben Gottlieb, and the aforementioned Anthony Lydgate. Collectively you taught me to recognize good writing and gave me the confidence to believe I might someday produce it. Thank you to Lewis H. Lapham for referring to me as "good news" and asking after the book's progress. Thank you to the whole Freedland extended family for helping to materially support the book, whether by putting me up on reporting trips (Seth, both Amys, and Jeff) or watching my children (Rich, Nanette, Melanie, and Matt).

None of this would have been possible without the lifelong encouragement and support of my parents, Deanah Messenger and John Liebenthal. I was a shy, bookish, nonconfrontational child, but through repeated exposure to rallies, marches, and rants, my mom succeeded in giving me an appetite for social justice. My dad was my first writing teacher, and his advice to "just write the worst thing you can" still helps me find the courage to finish terrible first drafts. Both have always pushed me to continue learning and trying new things.

Finally, there is one person to whom I owe more gratitude than everyone else combined: my husband, Henry, who functioned as a shadow editor, therapist, cheerleader, and practically a cowriter on this project from its inception to the final draft.

Very little in my life made sense to me in June of 2014. I lived in a tiny room in a decrepit rent-stabilized Brooklyn apartment; I was lonely, bored, underpaid, insecure and unhappy at my job, broke, deep in debt, rather lost. I had always joked (to myself, despondently) that I was just waiting for a miracle to fall into my lap. The miracle appeared that July, when Henry appeared one day at my workplace to occupy the office next to mine. (Thank you to Rafil Kroll-Zaidi and Chantal Clarke, our accidental shadchonim.) It feels borderline folkloric, not to mention pathetic, to suggest that Henry turned my life around, yet it is difficult for me not to view it that way. None of what has followed in subsequent years would have been possible without him. I would never have believed I had what it takes to write a book without Henry's encouraging me—cajoling, practically—to give it a shot. His is the most wonderful form of support: he believes in others to the fullest extent of their potential, and he offers generously of his time and his talents to make sure they attain it. In my case, this has amounted to a far more capacious faith in my abilities than I hold for myself. Everyone should be as lucky as I am to have someone like him in their life, not only to offer support for professional ambitions and personal dreams, but also to demonstrate what true friendship and love can look like.

Because of Henry, I now also live with two small humans who look very much like Henry. I can't say that *they* personally offered much in the way of help getting this book to print, but having them has clarified what I think education is for and why it is important. I hope that neither of them ever has to know what it feels like to be ears-deep in debt for pursuing curiosity. And even more, I hope that both can emerge from the educational systems they join with a sense of who they are and how they want to be in the world, not merely the ways they plan to make money. Asa and Elian, thank you, just for being.

NOTES

Introduction

1 *Jordan Long should have:* Jordan Long, telephone conversations with the author, September 5, 2019, and January 12, 2023, and interview, Hayward, California, April 19, 2023.

2 *wealthiest Black man:* Audra D. S. Burch, Alan Blinder, and Ron Lieber, "A Pledge to Pay Morehouse College Students' Debt Prompts Elation, Envy, and a Host of Questions," *New York Times*, May 22, 2019, https://www.nytimes.com/2019/05/22/us/robert-smith-morehouse-college-student-loan-debt.html; "About Robert F. Smith," Robert F. Smith, https://robertsmith.com/about-robert-f-smith/.

2 *"We all have":* Robert F. Smith, "Billionaire Robert F. Smith Pays Debt of Graduates: 135th Commencement at Morehouse College," Morehouse College, May 19, 2019, YouTube, 35:55, https://youtu.be/-P1CcRphVnM.

Part 1: The Era of Missed Opportunities (1941–1971)

11 *New Deal agency:* "Security Work and Relief Policies: Report of the Long-Range Work and Relief Policies to the National Resources Planning Board" (Washington, DC: Social Security Administration, April 1, 1943), 461, https://www.ssa.gov/history/reports/NRPB/NRPBreport.html.

1. The GI Bill of Goods

13 *extremely generous benefit:* Edward Humes, *Over Here: How the GI Bill Transformed the American Dream* (New York: Diversion Books, 2006), chap. 1, Kobo.

13 *the Marshall Plan:* Kathleen J. Frydl, *The GI Bill* (New York: Cambridge University Press, 2009), 3.

13 *the number of men:* Suzanne Mettler, introduction to *Degrees of Inequality: How the Politics of Higher Education Sabotaged the American Dream* (New York: Basic Books, 2014), Kobo.

13 *the bill expired:* Because some veterans were surely planning to resume their studies after the war regardless of federal assistance, there remains some debate about how many more got bachelor's degrees than would have without the bill. Glenn Altschuler and Stuart M. Blumin, *The GI Bill: A New Deal for Veterans* (New York: Oxford University Press, 2009), chap. 4, Kobo; Suzanne Mettler, *Soldiers to Citizens: The GI Bill and the Making of the Greatest Generation* (New York: Oxford University Press, 2005), 107–14; John Bound and Sarah E. Turner, "Going to War and Going to College: Did World War II and the G.I. Bill Increase Educational Attainment for Returning Veterans?," *Journal of Labor Economics* 20, no. 4 (October 2002): 784–815.

14 *a turning point:* Mettler, *Soldiers to Citizens*, 87–88.

14 *"This legislation created":* Ira Katznelson, *When Affirmative Action Was White* (New York: W. W. Norton & Company, 2005), 113.

14 *"extraordinarily large payoff":* "A Cost-Benefit Analysis of Government Investment in Post-Secondary Education Under the World War II GI Bill," Joint Economic Council, Subcommittee on Education and Health, December 14, 1988, cited in *Improving*

Access to Preschool and Postsecondary Education, Hearings Before the Subcommittee on Education and Health of the Joint Economic Committee, 100th Cong. 12–23 (1988), https://files.eric.ed.gov/fulltext/ED338323.pdf.

14 *through the eighth grade:* Michael S. Katz, "A History of Compulsory Education Laws," *Phi Delta Kappa,* Fastback Series 75 (1976): 22.

14 *none but the wealthiest:* John R. Thelin, *A History of American Higher Education,* 3rd ed. (Baltimore: Johns Hopkins University Press, 2019), 24–25.

15 *"One important reason":* Frydl, *The GI Bill,* 24.

15 *Women, pushed out:* "Undergraduate Enrollment," National Center for Education Statistics, March 2023, https://nces.ed.gov/programs/coe/indicator/cha/undergrad-enrollment; *Deeper in Debt: Women and Student Loans* (American Association of University Women, 2021), https://www.aauw.org/resources/research/deeper-in-debt/.

16 *the family wealth:* Neil Bhutta et al., "Disparities in Wealth by Race and Ethnicity in the 2019 Survey of Consumer Finances," FEDS Notes, Board of Governors of the Federal Reserve System, September 28, 2020, https://www.federalreserve.gov/econres/notes/feds-notes/disparities-in-wealth-by-race-and-ethnicity-in-the-2019-survey-of-consumer-finances-20200928.html; Chris Geary, "College Pays Off: But by How Much Depends on Race, Gender, and Type of Degree," *Education Policy* (blog), New America, March 1, 2022, https://www.newamerica.org/education-policy/edcentral/college-pays-off/.

16 *frauds and scams:* Frydl, *The GI Bill,* 186.

16 *"bad-looking mob":* "Anacostia Camp No More," *New York Times,* July 29, 1932, 1; John P. Roche, "Eisenhower Redux," *New York Times,* June 28, 1981, sec. 7, 12; Herbert Hoover, "Statement About the Bonus Marchers," July 28, 1932, The American Presidency Project, transcript, https://www.presidency.ucsb.edu/documents/statement-about-the-bonus-marchers; Eric Rauchway, *Why the New Deal Matters* (New Haven: Yale University Press, 2021), 15–24.

17 *even greater moment:* For an expanded version of this counterfactual scenario, see Mettler, *Soldiers to Citizens,* chap. 1; Frydl, *The GI Bill,* 138–40.

17 *lost their opening:* Frydl, 128–33.

18 *a mere 2 percent:* Mettler, *Soldiers to Citizens,* 80–81.

18 *openly applied quotas:* Altschuler and Blumin, *The GI Bill,* chap. 5; Mettler, *Soldiers to Citizens,* chap. 9.

18 *unyielding commitment:* Frydl, *The GI Bill,* 110–16, 121–22, 126–44.

19 *white supremacy:* Associated Press, "John Rankin Dies; Ex-Legislator, 78," *New York Times,* November 26, 1960, 86; Davis R. B. Ross, *Preparing for Ulysses* (New York: Columbia University Press, 1969), 21–24; Katznelson, *When Affirmative Action Was White,* 123–28.

19 *diminishing Black veterans:* Altschuler and Blumin, *The GI Bill,* chap. 3; Frydl, *The GI Bill,* 89–94, 121–22, 134–38.

19 *no more equitable:* David H. Onkst, "'First a Negro . . . Incidentally a Veteran': Black World War Two Veterans and the GI Bill of Rights in the Deep South," *Journal of Social History* 31, no. 3 (Spring 1998): 517–43.

19 *less than one-third:* "A Half-Century of Learning: Historical Census Statistics on Educational Attainment in the United States, 1940 to 2000: Table 3," US Census Bureau, 2015, https://www.census.gov/data/tables/time-series/demo/educational-attainment/educational-attainment-1940-2000.html.

20 *41 percent of Black:* Mettler, *Soldiers to Citizens,* 29.

20 *married white recruits:* Katznelson, *When Affirmative Action Was White,* 101.

20 *six units designated:* George Q. Flynn, "Selective Service and American Blacks During World War II," *The Journal of Negro History* 69, no. 1 (Winter 1984): 14–25.

20 *more than a million:* Humes, *Over Here,* chap. 8.

20 *mostly to service roles:* Katznelson, *When Affirmative Action Was White*, 106–8; Mettler, *Soldiers to Citizens*, chap. 2.

20 *in separate barracks:* Matthew F. Delmont, *Half American: The Epic Story of African Americans Fighting World War II at Home and Abroad* (New York: Viking, 2022), chap. 6, Kobo.

20 *Black troops were aghast:* Christopher S. Parker, *Fighting for Democracy: Black Veterans and the Struggle Against White Supremacy in the Postwar South*, Princeton Studies in American Politics: Historical, International, and Comparative Perspectives (Princeton, NJ: Princeton University Press, 2009), 94; Delmont, *Half American*, chap. 15.

20 *to develop skills:* Katznelson, *When Affirmative Action Was White*, chap. 4.

21 *92 percent:* Onkst, "'First a Negro . . . Incidentally a Veteran.'"

21 *single Black college:* Bound and Turner, "Closing the Gap or Widening the Divide," 152–53.

21 *mere 12 percent:* Bound and Turner, "Closing the Gap or Widening the Divide," 6n4.

22 *White Americans with:* Mettler, *Soldiers to Citizens*, 211.

22 *a "double V":* Delmont, *Half American*, introduction; Humes, *Over Here*, chap. 8; Katznelson, *When Affirmative Action Was White*, 86, 88; Ira Katznelson and Suzanne Mettler, "On Race and Policy History: A Dialogue About the G.I. Bill," *Perspectives on Politics* 6, no. 3 (September 2008): 519–37, https://www.jstor.org/stable/20446759.

22 *"I spent three":* "The Blinding of Isaac Woodard," *American Experience* (Boston: WGBH, March 30, 2021), https://www.pbs.org/wgbh/americanexperience/films/blinding-isaac-woodard/#transcript; DeNeen L. Brown, "A Black WWII Veteran Was Beaten and Blinded, Fueling the Civil Rights Movement," *Washington Post*, March 31, 2021, https://www.washingtonpost.com/history/2021/03/31/isaac-woodard-truman-integration-military/; Audra D. S. Burch, "Why a Town Is Finally Honoring a Black Veteran Attacked by Its White Police Chief," *New York Times*, February 8, 2019, https://www.nytimes.com/2019/02/08/us/sergeant-woodard-batesburg-south-carolina.html; Theodore R. Johnson, "Presidents, Race, and the Military, in the 1940s and Now," *New York Times*, July 26, 2018, https://www.nytimes.com/2018/07/26/magazine/military-desegregation-trump-truman.html.

23 *"Goddamn it":* Rolundus R. Rice, *Hosea Williams: A Lifetime of Defiance and Protest* (Columbia: University of South Carolina Press, 2021), 35–38.

23 *degree in chemistry:* Rice, *Hosea Williams*, 42; Ernie Suggs, "Hosea Williams: 1926–2000—A Lieutenant of the Civil Rights Movement," *Atlanta Journal-Constitution*, November 17, 2000, https://www.ajc.com/news/obituaries/hosea-williams-1926-2000-a-lieutenant-of-the-civil-rights-movement/MAVJHQA2VFHV5P4O2FEOJPFUNM/.

24 *haughty, scornful eye:* Robert M. Hutchins, "The Threat to American Education," *Collier's*, December 30, 1944; "Conant Suggests GI Bill Revision," *Harvard Crimson*, January 23, 1945, https://www.thecrimson.com/article/1945/1/23/conant-suggests-gi-bill-revision-pentering/.

24 *to school full-time:* Mettler, *Soldiers to Citizens*, 103–5.

24 *more than 2 million:* Because some veterans were surely planning to resume their studies after the war regardless of federal assistance, there remains some debate about how many more got bachelor's degrees than would have without the bill. Mettler, *Soldiers to Citizens*, 107–14; Bound and Turner, "Going to War and Going to College."

24 *"are the most mature":* Charles J. V. Murphy, "GIs at Harvard," *Life*, June 17, 1946, 17.

25 *5,600 had sprung up:* Altschuler and Blumin, *The GI Bill*, 377–82.

25 *pilfered annually for lessons:* For a full list of examples gathered by a 1950 congressional report, see *Report on Education and Training Under the Servicemen's Readjustment Act, as Amended* (Washington, DC: Administrator of Veterans' Affairs, February 8, 1950),

114–61; Albert Q. Maisel, "What's Wrong with Veterans' Schools?," *Collier's*, May 1, 1948, 25.

25 *"Veterans, come"*: Homer A. Ramey, "Let's Stop Abuses in Veterans' Schools," *Collier's*, May 8, 1948, 27.

25 *shoe shop owner*: Onkst, "'First a Negro . . . Incidentally a Veteran,'" 525–26.

25 *never completed: General Accounting Office Report of Survey—Veterans' Education and Training Program* (Washington, DC: General Accounting Office, 1951), 4, 7, 9–10, 12.

25 *the 85–15 rule*: David Whitman, "Truman, Eisenhower, and the First GI Bill Scandal," The Century Foundation, January 24, 2017, https://tcf.org/content/report/truman-eisenhower-first-gi-bill-scandal/.

27 *disturbed by the story*: Brown, "A Black WWII Veteran Was Beaten and Blinded."

27 *threatening to bolt*: Delmont, *Half American*, conclusion.

27 *an uncooperative Congress*: "Executive Order 9981: Desegregation of the Armed Forces (1948)," National Archives, accessed December 20, 2023, https://www.archives.gov/milestone-documents/executive-order-9981.

27 *delaying full integration*: "EO 8891 Lesson Plan," Truman Library, accessed December 8, 2023, https://www.trumanlibrary.gov/sites/default/files/EO%208891%20Lesson%20Plan.pdf.

27 *free higher education: Higher Education for American Democracy* (Washington, DC: President's Commission on Higher Education, December 1947), 36–38, 67–70.

28 *Southern Democrats: Higher Education for American Democracy*, 30–36; Frydl, *The GI Bill*, 338–48.

28 *last great stop*: Kathleen Frydl makes this point forcefully in her introduction to *The GI Bill*. See especially p. 24.

2. Reading, Writing, and *Sputnik*

30 *"Why and how"*: "Sputnik I," *CBS Special Report*, October 6, 1957, posted July 21, 2023, YouTube, https://youtu.be/dO33bvFbUCU?si=EZDgIXyARSStVFp0.

30 *artificial space satellite*: Robert A. Divine, *The Sputnik Challenge* (New York: Oxford University Press, 1993), xiii.

30 *lagging behind*: Joel H. Spring, *The Sorting Machine Revisited: National Educational Policy Since 1945* (New York: Longman, 1989), 22.

30 *average American teenager*: Robert Divine notes, however, that only one-third of Russians went on to high school, and even fewer made it to university. *The Sputnik Challenge*, 53, 66.

30 *keep the United States*: Spring, *The Sorting Machine Revisited*, 7–8, 18; Divine, *The Sputnik Challenge*, 52; Barbara Barksdale Clowse, *Brainpower for the Cold War: The Sputnik Crisis and National Defense Education Act of 1958* (Westport, CT: Greenwood Press, 1981), 3.

31 *"Sputnik has made"*: Quoted in Divine, *The Sputnik Challenge*, 159.

31 *"For decades, we"*: *Scholarship and Loan Program: Hearings Before the Subcomm. on Special Educ. of the Comm. on Educ. and Lab.*, House of Representatives, 85th Cong. 1–2 (1958) (statement of Rep. Carl Elliott, Chair of the House Subcomm. on Special Educ.).

32 *three to two*: *Scholarship and Loan Program, Hearings Before the Subcomm. on Special Educ. of the Comm. on Educ. and Lab.*, House of Representatives, 85th Cong. 34 (1958) (statement of Ralph C. M. Flynt, Dir. of Higher Educ. Programs Branch, Dep't of Health, Educ., and Welfare).

32 *"Everywhere we went"*: Carl Elliott Sr. and Michael D'Orso, *The Cost of Courage: The Journey of an American Congressman* (New York: Doubleday, 1992), 148.

32   *a nut about books:* Elliott Sr. and D'Orso, *The Cost of Courage*, 3, 13–14, 17.
32   *headed to Tuscaloosa:* Elliott Sr. and D'Orso, *The Cost of Courage*, 44; Wil Haygood, "Twilight of a Southern Liberal," *Boston Globe*, February 29, 1989; Gigi Douban, "How an Alabama Congressman Got the Government to Help Pay for College" (WBHM, June 8, 2018), https://wbhm.org/2018/alabama-congressman-got-government-help-pay-college/.
32   *"Education [. . .] had always":* Elliott Sr. and D'Orso, *The Cost of Courage*, 166.
33   *In his first year:* Barksdale Clowse, *Brainpower for the Cold War*, 52.
33   *"a politically paranoid":* Elliott Sr. and D'Orso, *The Cost of Courage*, 129.
33   *"Sometimes people can":* Elliott Sr. and D'Orso, *The Cost of Courage*, 148.
33   *"While most of":* Elliott Sr. and D'Orso, *The Cost of Courage*, 149–50.
33   *who saw kismet:* Virginia Van der Veer Hamilton, *Lister Hill: Statesman from the South* (Chapel Hill: University of North Carolina Press, 1987), 222.
34   *"John, I want":* "Stewart E. McClure: Chief Clerk, Senate Committee on Labor, Education, and Public Welfare (1949–1973)," Oral History Interviews, December 8, 1982, to May 3, 1983, transcript, Senate Historical Office, Washington, DC, 114, https://www.senate.gov/about/oral-history/mcclure-stewart-e-oral-history.htm.
34   *"You know, I've been":* Elliott Sr. and D'Orso, *The Cost of Courage*, 152–54.
34   *a live dog:* Alex Wellerstein, "Remembering Laika, Space Dog and Soviet Hero," *New Yorker*, November 3, 2017, https://www.newyorker.com/tech/annals-of-technology/remembering-laika-space-dog-and-soviet-hero.
34   *"Just then," Elliott recalled:* Elliott Sr. and D'Orso, *The Cost of Courage*, 154.
34   *"large baby crops":* Scholarship and Loan Program, Hearings Before the Subcomm. on Special Educ. of the Comm. on Educ. and Lab., House of Representatives, 85th Cong. 2–5, 18 (1958) (statement of John A. Perkins, Undersec'y of Health, Educ., and Welfare).
35   *the one tool:* Black Americans in Congress: 1870–2007 (Washington, DC: Office of History and Preservation, US House of Representatives, 2008), 261, 300–307, https://www.govinfo.gov/content/pkg/GPO-CDOC-108hdoc224/pdf/GPO-CDOC-108hdoc224.pdf; Wil Haygood, *King of the Cats: The Life and Times of Adam Clayton Powell Jr.* (New York: Houghton Mifflin Company, 1993), 191–93; Lee A. Daniels, "The Political Career of Adam Clayton Powell," *Journal of Black Studies* 4, no. 2 (December 1973): 115–38; Thomas A. Johnson, "A Man of Many Roles," *New York Times*, April 5, 1972.
36   *led filibusters:* Van der Veer Hamilton, *Lister Hill: Statesman from the South*, 236.
36   *moving "too fast":* Elliott Sr. and D'Orso, *The Cost of Courage*, 181.
36   *after the crisis:* "President Asks $1.3 Billion for Schools in Four Years," *CQ Almanac 1957*, 13th ed. (Washington, DC: Congressional Quarterly, 1958), http://library.cqpress.com/cqalmanac/cqal57-1346657; "Eisenhower on Air: Says School Defiance Has Gravely Harmed Prestige of U.S.," *New York Times*, September 25, 1957, late city edition.
37   *"I'd like to know":* Divine, *The Sputnik Challenge*, 5–11, 18–42, 165; Barksdale Clowse, *Brainpower for the Cold War*, 10, 25–27.
37   *a resounding "Flopnik":* Divine, *The Sputnik Challenge*; John Uri, "60 Years Ago: Vanguard Fails to Reach Orbit," National Aeronautics and Space Administration, December 6, 2017, accessed December 23, 2023, https://www.nasa.gov/history/60-years-ago-vanguard-fails-to-reach-orbit/.
37   *eroded trust:* Divine, *The Sputnik Challenge*, 58–60, 76–77, 82–93, 157–58; Barksdale Clowse, *Brainpower for the Cold War*, 3, 9; Wayne J. Urban, *More Than Science and Sputnik* (Tuscaloosa: University of Alabama Press, 2010), 20–21.
37   *didn't have the money:* Divine, *The Sputnik Challenge*, 57, 163; Scholarship and Loan Program, Hearings Before the Subcomm. on Special Educ. of the Comm. on Educ. and

Lab., House of Representatives, 85th Cong. 42–46 (1958) (statement of Ralph C. M. Flynt).

37 *"But when a Soviet"*: Bess Furman, "Senate Gets Plea for Language Aid," *New York Times*, March 16, 1958, 60.

37 *a "turncoat"*: This phrase was the title of a chapter in Meerloo's 1956 book about brainwashing, *The Rape of the Mind*. Joost A. M. Meerloo, "Pavlov's Dogs and Communist Brainwashers," *New York Times Magazine*, May 9, 1954, 9; Christopher Loss, *Between Citizens and the State* (Princeton, NJ: Princeton University Press, 2014), 136–37.

38 *only forty thousand*: Divine, *The Sputnik Challenge*, 157–58; National Defense Education Act of 1958, S. 3187, 85th Cong. (1958).

38 *narrow their bill*: Divine, *The Sputnik Challenge*, 57–58, 163–64; Barksdale Clowse, *Brainpower for the Cold War*, 91, 95.

38 *"I invented that"*: McClure, Oral History Interviews, 117.

38 *even by Eisenhower*: Barksdale Clowse, *Brainpower for the Cold War*, 102; Divine, *The Sputnik Challenge*, 158.

39 *low-interest loans*: Barksdale Clowse, *Brainpower for the Cold War*, 130, 163.

39 *115,450 students*: Pamela Ebert Flattau et al., *The National Defense Education Act of 1958: Selected Outcomes* (Washington, DC: Institute for Defense Analyses, March 2006), II-2.

39 *correctly predicted*: Divine, *The Sputnik Challenge*, 165–66.

39 *schoolhouse steps*: Thomas D. Snyder, ed., *120 Years of American Education: A Statistical Portrait*, National Center for Education Statistics, Table 9, "Enrollment in Regular Public and Private Elementary and Secondary Schools, by Grade Level: 1869–70 to Fall 1992," 36, https://nces.ed.gov/pubs93/93442.pdf; Barksdale Clowse, *Brainpower for the Cold War*, 71, 124–25; Divine, *The Sputnik Challenge*, 55–56.

40 *"a satellite"*: Barksdale Clowse, *Brainpower for the Cold War*, 88–89; "Education, Change the Thinking," *Time*, November 25, 1957, https://content.time.com/time/subscriber/article/0,33009,891861-1,00.html

41 *"to serve the interests"*: Spring, *The Sorting Machine Revisited*, vii–x.

42 *seal his own fate*: Ronald Smothers, "After 26 Years, a Lawmaker's Fight Is Recognized as a Profile in Courage," *New York Times*, May 28, 1990, sec. 1; "Elliott, Carl," Encyclopedia of Alabama, accessed May 4, 2023, https://encyclopediaofalabama.org/article/carl-elliott/; Wolfgang Saxon, "Carl Elliott, 85, Congressman from Alabama," *New York Times*, January 12, 1999, sec. C; "Election Called Blow to Wallace; GOP Gains in Alabama Also Cause for Trouble," *New York Times*, November 8, 1964, 84.

42 *"America's future success"*: Scholarship and Loan Program, Hearings Before the Subcomm. on Special Educ. of the Comm. on Educ. and Lab., House of Representatives, 85th Cong. 1–2 (1958) (statement of Rep. Carl Elliott).

3. The Education President

44 *lacquered billfish*: Michael Beschloss, "Kennedy, L.B.J., and a Disputed Deer Hunt," *New York Times*, August 15, 2014, https://www.nytimes.com/2014/08/16/upshot/kennedy-lbj-and-a-disputed-deer-hunt.html.

44 *"Look, we've got to"*: Hugh Davis Graham, *The Uncertain Triumph: Federal Education Policy in the Kennedy and Johnson Years* (Chapel Hill: University of North Carolina Press, 1984), chap. 3, Kobo; "The 89th Congress," Association of Centers for the Study of Congress, accessed December 26, 2023, https://congresscenters.org/great-society-congress/exhibits/show/89th-congress; Julian E. Zelizer, *The Fierce Urgency of Now: Lyndon Johnson, Congress, and the Battle for a Great Society* (New York: Penguin Books, 2015), chap. 1, Kobo.

45 *famous Johnson "treatment"*: Robert Dallek, *Flawed Giant* (New York: Oxford Univer-

sity Press, 1998), chaps. 1 and 4, Kobo; Lyndon Baines Johnson, *The Vantage Point: Perspectives of the Presidency, 1963–1969* (New York: Holt, Rinehart, and Winston, 1971), 137.

45 *"an almost hypnotic"*: Quoted in Robert A. Divine, "Assessing Lyndon Johnson," *The Wilson Quarterly* 6, no. 3 (Summer 1982): 142–50.

45 *one of Kennedy's*: "Civil Rights Act (1964)," National Archives, accessed December 26, 2023, https://www.archives.gov/milestone-documents/civil-rights-act.

45 *"a nut on education"*: Merle Miller, *Lyndon: An Oral Biography* (New York: G. P. Putnam's Sons, 1980), 407.

46 *3.6 million young*: *Characteristics of American Youth*, Series P-23, no. 30 (Washington, DC: US Census Bureau, February 6, 1970); "Sputnik Spurs Passage of the National Defense Education Act," US Senate, accessed January 18, 2024, https://www.senate.gov/artandhistory/history/minute/Sputnik_Spurs_Passage_of_National_Defense_Education_Act.htm.

47 *"He just believed"*: Miller, *Lyndon*, 407.

47 *due in September*: Robert Caro, *The Years of Lyndon Johnson: The Path to Power* (New York: Knopf, 1982), 163–67, 225.

47 *"five other teachers"*: Caro, 167.

47 *quit his teaching job*: Caro, *The Path to Power*, 206–14; Caro, *The Years of Lyndon Johnson: Master of the Senate* (New York: Knopf, 2002), 1035.

48 *set of task forces*: Eric Pace, "Edwin H. Land Is Dead at 81; Inventor of Polaroid Camera," *New York Times*, March 2, 1991, sec. 1; Alex S. Jones, "Hedley Donovan Is Dead at 76; Retired Chief Editor of Time Inc.," *New York Times*, August 14, 1990, sec. B; Robert McG. Thomas Jr., "Stephen J. Wright, 85; Led in Education for Blacks," *New York Times*, April 19, 1996, sec. B; Graham, *The Uncertain Triumph*, 56–57.

48 *"roam imaginatively"*: Philip C. Kearney, "The 1964 Presidential Task Force on Education and the Elementary and Secondary Education Act of 1965" (dissertation, University of Chicago, 1967), 77.

48 *"Every child must"*: Robert E. Hawkinson, "Presidential Program Formulation in Education: Lyndon Johnson and the 89th Congress" (dissertation, University of Chicago, 1977), 80; Dallek, *Flawed Giant*, chap. 2; *Higher Education Act of 1965, Hearings Before the Special Subcomm. on Educ. of the Comm. on Educ. and Lab.*, House of Representatives, 89th Cong. 110 (1965) (statement of Francis Keppel, Comm'r of Education); Lyndon B. Johnson, "Lyndon B. Johnson Message to Congress on Education," January 12, 1965, "Education" folder, Box 1, Senate Comm. on Educ. and Lab., 89th Congress, Records of the US Senate, RG 46, National Archives, accessed March 10, 2022, http://acsc.lib.udel.edu/items/show/43.

49 *worked like magic*: Marjorie Hunter, "House Approves School-Aid Bill; G.O.P. Is Rebuffed," *New York Times*, March 26, 1965, 1, 18; Marjorie Hunter, "Senate Passes School Aid Bill with No Change," *New York Times*, April 10, 1965, 1, 12; Marjorie Hunter, "Debate on School Aid: Democrats Concede Bill's Imperfections, but Hope to Improve on It Next Year," *New York Times*, April 2, 1965, 22.

49 *the college-bound population*: *Hearings Before the Special Subcomm. on Educ. of the Comm. on Educ. and Lab.*, House of Representatives, 89th Cong. 28, 80 (1965) (statement of Anthony J. Celebrezze, Sec'y of Health, Educ., and Welfare; statement of Francis Keppel); Elizabeth Tandy Shermer, *Indentured Students: How Government-Guaranteed Loans Left Generations Drowning in College Debt* (Cambridge, MA: Belknap Press of Harvard University Press, 2021), 165–68, 188–89; Graham, *The Uncertain Triumph*, chap. 3; "1964 Outside Task Force on Education," Task Force Reports, Box 1, iv, LBJ Presidential Library and Museum, Austin, TX.

50 *a nude swim*: José Chávez, "Presidential Influence on the Politics of Higher Education: The Higher Education Act of 1965" (dissertation, University of Texas at Austin,

1975), 79–80; Dallek, *Flawed Giant*, chap. 4; David G. McComb, Douglass Cater Oral History Interview I, April 29, 1969, LBJ Presidential Library, 5–6, http://www .lbjlibrary.net/assets/documents/archives/oral_histories/cater/CATER01.PDF.

50 *foot soldiers:* Kearney, "The 1964 Presidential Task Force," 275–76; *Hearings Before the Special Subcomm. on Educ. of the Comm. on Educ. and Lab.*, House of Representatives, 89th Cong. 64–65, 138, 452 (1965) (statement of Francis Keppel).

50 *academic libraries:* Graham, *The Uncertain Triumph*, chap. 3; *Higher Education Act, Hearings Before the Special Subcomm. on Educ. of the Comm. on Educ. and Lab.*, House of Representatives, 89th Cong. 10–11 (1965) (statement of Rep. Edith Green, Chair of the Special Subcomm. on Educ.).

51 *"Many, many incomes":* Elmer O. Cappers, "The Massachusetts Higher Education Loan Plan," *Industry* (July 1957), quoted in Cong. Rec. A6100–A6101 (appendix, July 29, 1957) (statement of Rep. Thomas J. Lane); Shermer, *Indentured Students*, 159, 166.

51 *up sixfold:* Allan Carter, "Tax Reliefs and the Burden of College Costs," American Council on Education, quoted in *Higher Education Act of 1965, Hearings Before the Special Subcomm. on Educ. of the Comm. on Educ. and Lab.*, House of Representatives, 89th Cong. 48–53 (1965).

51 *"It is clear that":* *Higher Education Act of 1965, Hearings Before the Special Subcomm. on Educ. of the Comm. on Educ. and Lab.*, House of Representatives, 89th Cong. 28, 39, 41, 399 (1965) (statement of Francis Keppel; statement of Anthony J. Celebrezze).

52 *loan guarantee fund:* *Higher Education Act of 1965, Hearings Before the Special Subcomm. on Educ. of the Comm. on Educ. and Lab.*, House of Representatives, 89th Cong. 281 (1965) (statement of Allen D. Marshall, President, United Student Aid Funds, Inc.).

52 *by commercial banks:* "College Aid," *CQ Almanac 1964*, 20th ed., 265–67 (Washington, DC: Congressional Quarterly, 1965), http://library.cqpress.com/cqalmanac /cqal64-1304332.

52 *had escaped legislators:* Hawkinson, "Presidential Program Formulation in Education," 155; *Higher Education Act of 1965, Hearings Before the Special Subcomm. on Educ. of the Comm. on Educ. and Lab.*, House of Representatives, 89th Cong. 13, 28, 82 (1965) (statement of Rep. Edith Green; statement of Anthony J. Celebrezze; statement of Francis Keppel); Howard A. Glickstein, "Federal Educational Programs and Minority Students," *The Journal of Negro Education* 38, no. 3 (Summer 1969): 313nn47–48.

53 *"This goose can":* *Higher Education Act of 1965, Hearings Before the Special Subcomm. on Educ. of the Comm. on Educ. and Lab.*, House of Representatives, 89th Cong. 57, 80 (1965) (statement of Rep. Sam Gibbons; statement of Francis Keppel).

53 *tuition tax credits:* Chávez, "Presidential Influence on the Politics of Higher Education," 90; Hawkinson, "Presidential Program Formulation in Education," 163–64; "Republican Party Platform of 1964," The American Presidency Project, July 13, 1964; *Higher Education Act of 1965, Hearings Before the Special Subcomm. on Educ. of the Comm. on Educ. and Lab.*, House of Representatives, 89th Cong. 48 (1965) (statement of Francis Keppel).

53 *tax-credit scheme:* Marjorie Hunter, "Wider School Aid Urged at Capital," *New York Times*, January 6, 1965, 17; Graham, *The Uncertain Triumph*, chap. 3; Hawkinson, 167–68, 171–72; Chávez, "Presidential Influence on the Politics of Higher Education," 89–91; *Hearings on H.R. 15067, Before the Special Subcomm. on Educ. of the Comm. on Educ. and Lab.*, House of Representatives, 90th Cong. 477 (1967) (statement of Dr. John W. Oswald, Chairman of the Legis. Comm. of the Nat'l Ass'n of State Univs. and Land-Grant Colls.).

54 *seem unreasonable:* Graham, *The Uncertain Triumph*, chap. 3; Lawrence Gladieux and Thomas Wolanin, *Congress and the Colleges* (Lexington, MA: D. C. Heath and Company, 1976), 41; Chávez, "Presidential Influence on the Politics of Higher Education," 181.

54 *loan-guarantee programs:* Shermer, *Indentured Students*, 166–67; Mettler, *Degrees of Inequality*, chap. 2.

54 *an appealing model:* Shermer, *Indentured Students,* 165; *Higher Education Act of 1965, Hearings Before the Special Subcomm. on Educ. of the Comm. on Educ. and Lab.*, House of Representatives, 89th Cong. 17–18, 44, 84, 294 (1965) (statement of Rep. Edith Green; statement of Anthony J. Celebrezze; statement of Francis Keppel; statement of Allen D. Marshall).

54 *enticing venture: Higher Education Act of 1965, Hearings Before the Special Subcomm. on Educ. of the Comm. on Educ. and Lab.*, House of Representatives, 89th Cong. 683, 689, 693 (1965) (statement of Keith G. Cone, American Bankers Association); Shermer, *Indentured Students,* 187; Mettler, *Degrees of Inequality*, chap. 2.

55 *For every dollar: Higher Education Act of 1965, Hearings Before the Special Subcomm. on Educ. of the Comm. on Educ. and Lab.*, House of Representatives, 89th Cong. 281–84 (1965) (statement of Allen D. Marshall).

55 *"has made a friend": Higher Education Act of 1965, Hearings Before the Special Subcomm. on Educ. of the Comm. on Educ. and Lab.*, House of Representatives, 89th Cong. 283 (1965) (statement of Allen D. Marshall).

56 *"Reliance on loans": Higher Education Act of 1965, Hearings Before the Special Subcomm. on Educ. of the Comm. on Educ. and Lab.*, House of Representatives, 89th Cong. 310, 460 (1965) (statement of Maurice Heartfield, Director of Student Financial Aid, George Washington University; statement of Homer D. Babbidge, American Council on Education).

56 *be made free: Higher Education Act of 1965, Hearings Before the Special Subcomm. on Educ. of the Comm. on Educ. and Lab.*, House of Representatives, 89th Cong. 412, 574–75 (1965) (statement of Rep. Edith Green; statement of Ralph Mansfield, Bd. Member, Americans for Democratic Action).

57 *"The best way": Hearings on S. 600, Before the Subcomm. on Educ. of the Comm. on Lab. and Pub. Welfare*, Senate, 89th Cong. 990 (1965) (statement of Andrew J. Biemiller, Dir. of the Dep't of Legis., American Federation of Labor and Congress of Industrial Organizations).

57 *a "free ride": Hearings on S. 600, Before the Subcomm. on Educ. of the Comm. on Lab. and Pub. Welfare*, Senate, 89th Cong. 107, 1380 (1965) (statement of Anthony J. Celebrezze; statement of Jerome E. Leavett, Executive Assistant Professor of Education, Portland State College).

57 *former schoolteacher: Higher Education Act of 1965, Hearings Before the Special Subcomm. on Educ. of the Comm. on Educ. and Lab.*, House of Representatives, 89th Cong. 286, 412 (1965) (statement of Rep. Edith Green); Shermer, *Indentured Students,* 171, 181, 187–88.

57 *"I must say": Higher Education Act of 1965, Hearings Before the Special Subcomm. on Educ. of the Comm. on Educ. and Lab.*, House of Representatives, 89th Cong. 287 (1965) (statement of Rep. Edith Green).

58 *strike it entirely:* Shermer, *Indentured Students*, 181, 188, 340n2; Chávez, "Presidential Influence on the Politics of Education," 117–19, 162, 166.

58 *bankers on board:* Shermer, *Indentured Students*, 190–92; Chávez, "Presidential Influence on the Politics of Education," 121–24, 136–38; Graham, *The Uncertain Triumph*, chap. 3.

58 *selling socks:* "President: Higher Education Act," University Archive Digital Exhibitions, Texas State University, https://exhibits.library.txstate.edu/s/univarchives/page

/lbj-higher-education-act; "LBJ on Campus: School Days," University Archive Digital Exhibitions, Texas State University, https://exhibits.library.txstate.edu/s/univarchives /page/school-days; "Students: Lyndon Johnson's School Days," *Time*, May 21, 1965, https://content.time.com/time/subscriber/article/0,33009,901708-1,00.html.

58 *"that a high school senior":* "Remarks at Southwest Texas State College upon Signing the Higher Education Act of 1965," The American Presidency Project, November 8, 1965, https://www.presidency.ucsb.edu/documents/remarks-southwest-texas-state -college-upon-signing-the-higher-education-act-1965.

59 *"far-reaching effect":* Hearings on S. 600, Before the Subcomm. on Educ. of the Comm. on Lab. and Pub. Welfare, Senate, 89th Cong. 267 (1965) (statement of Francis Keppel).

59 *subsidizing banks:* Hearings on S. 600, Before the Subcomm. on Educ. of the Comm. on Lab. and Pub. Welfare, Senate, 89th Cong. 120–22, 1271–72, 1290 (1965) (statement of Sen. Ralph Yarborough; statement of Blue Carstenson, National Farmers Union; statement of Charles A. Moore, Americans for Democratic Action).

60 *urban chaos:* Rick Perlstein, *Nixonland: The Rise of a President and the Fracturing of America* (New York: Scribner, 2008), chap. 1, Kobo; Graham, *The Uncertain Triumph*, 130–31; Dallek, *Flawed Giant*, chaps. 4, 8.

60 *Gulf of Tonkin:* Zelizer, *The Fierce Urgency of Now*, chap. 5.

61 *"Thus," wrote political:* Larry Berman, *Planning a Tragedy: The Americanization of the War in Vietnam* (New York: W. W. Norton & Company, 1982), 146.

61 *waffled his way:* Berman, *Planning a Tragedy*, 145–47; Graham, *The Uncertain Triumph*, 130, 181; Dallek, *Flawed Giant*, chap. 8.

61 *"We talked about":* Graham, *The Uncertain Triumph*, 168–74.

62 *down to the bone:* Graham, *The Uncertain Triumph*, 181–84; Dallek, *Flawed Giant*, chap. 8.

62 *"I happen to believe":* Graham, *The Uncertain Triumph*, 191; *Hearings on S. 3098 and S. 3099, Before the Subcomm. on Educ. of the Comm. on Lab. and Pub. Welfare*, Senate, 90th Cong. 303 (1968) (statement of Sen. Ralph Yarborough).

62 *"I do not intend":* Hearings on S. 3098 and S. 3099, Before the Subcomm. on Educ. of the Comm. on Lab. and Pub. Welfare, Senate, 90th Cong. 479 (1968) (statement of Sen. Wayne Morse, Chair of the Subcomm. on Educ.).

62 *$10 million less:* "Congress Votes $18.6 Billion in Labor-HEW Funds," *CQ Almanac 1968*, 24th ed., 06-593-6-603 (Washington, DC: Congressional Quarterly, 1969), http://library.cqpress.com/cqalmanac/cqal68-1281936.

62 *Johnson finally asked:* Graham, *The Uncertain Triumph*, 181–82, 186–90; Eileen Shanahan, "Senate Supports Slash in Spending as Tax-Rise Price," *New York Times*, March 27, 1968, 1, 73; *Hearings Before the Subcomm. on Educ. of the Comm. on Lab. and Pub. Welfare*, Senate, 90th Cong. 856–57 (1968) (statement of Sen. Wayne Morse).

62 *"vastly greater funding":* Hearings on H.R. 15067, Before the Special Subcomm. on Educ. of the Comm. on Educ. and Lab., House of Representatives, 90th Cong. 4, 20, 685 (1967) (statement of Harold Howe II, Comm'r of Education; statement of Allen D. Marshall); *Hearings on S. 3098 and S. 3099, Before the Subcomm. on Educ. of the Comm. on Lab. and Pub. Welfare*, Senate, 90th Cong. 387 (1968) (statement of Charles E. Walker, Exec. Vice President, American Bankers Association).

63 *"Helping disadvantaged students":* Hearings on H.R. 15067, Before the Special Subcomm. on Educ. of the Comm. on Educ. and Lab., House of Representatives, 90th Cong. 410 (1967) (statement of Dr. John W. Oswald).

63 *"Indeed," they claimed:* Hearings on H.R. 15067, Before the Special Subcomm. on Educ. of the Comm. on Educ. and Lab., House of Representatives, 90th Cong. 409–57, 473 (1967) (statement of Dr. John W. Oswald).

65   *in whatever way:* Roger L. Geiger, *American Higher Education Since World War II: A History* (Princeton, NJ: Princeton University Press, 2019), chap. 5, Kobo.

4. Market Actors

69   *"four years on":* Gerard J. De Groot, "Ronald Reagan and Student Unrest in California, 1966–1970," *Pacific Historical Review* 65, no. 1 (February 1996): 119; Seth Rosenfeld, *Subversives: The FBI's War on Student Radicals, and Reagan's Rise to Power* (New York: Farrar, Straus and Giroux, 2012), 115–16.

71   *hoped the trouble:* Rosenfeld, *Subversives*, 182, 191–97; Jo Freeman, "The Berkeley Free Speech Movement and the Mississippi Sovereignty Commission," *Left History* 8, no. 2 (Spring 2003): 135–44.

71   *"beatniks, radicals":* Associated Press, "Reagan 'Knifepoint' Story Denied by Alleged Source," *Independent* (Long Beach, CA), February 20, 1969, A-4, https://www.news papers.com/newspage/17595324/; Rosenfeld, *Subversives*, 324; De Groot, "Ronald Reagan and Student Unrest," 111, 115–16.

71   *at the forefront:* Critics have noted, however, that almost half of the $500 million for colleges and universities went to the University of California system, even though it enrolled far fewer students than the other two systems. "A Master Plan for Higher Education in California, 1960–1975," California State Department of Education (Sacramento, 1960), 14, 46, 146, 152–54; "Analysis of the 1967–1968 Budget Bill: Education," California Legislative Analyst's Office, February 24, 1967, 293–94, https://lao.ca.gov/analysis/1967/08_education_1967.pdf.

72   *shone a spotlight:* Melinda Cooper, *Family Values: Between Neoliberalism and the New Social Conservatism* (New York: Zone Books, 2017), 215–57; Gladieux and Wolanin, *Congress and the Colleges*, 21–23.

72   *to make napalm:* Edgar Z. Friedenberg, "The University Community in an Open Society," *Daedalus* 99, no. 1 (Winter 1970): 56–74.

73   *"The hall was entirely":* Rosenfeld, *Subversives*, 320–22.

73   *the governor's power:* De Groot, "Ronald Reagan and Student Unrest," 112–13.

73   *before and after:* Rosenfeld, *Subversives*, 374–79; De Groot, "Ronald Reagan and Student Unrest," 124.

74   *"Once the dogs":* De Groot, "Ronald Reagan and Student Unrest," 117; Rosenfeld, *Subversives*, 464.

74   *a liberal benefit:* De Groot, "Ronald Reagan and Student Unrest," 125.

74   *"subsidizing intellectual curiosity":* De Groot, "Ronald Reagan and Student Unrest," 115, 119, 123.

74   *"those who are there":* De Groot, "Ronald Reagan and Student Unrest," 125.

74   *in boom years:* Christopher Newfield, *The Great Mistake: How We Wrecked Public Universities and How We Can Fix Them* (Baltimore: Johns Hopkins University Press, 2016), 42–43, 55–56, 156–57; Michael Fabricant and Stephen Brier, *Austerity Blues* (Baltimore: Johns Hopkins University Press, 2016), chap. 3, Kobo.

74   *a "student charge":* The regents instituted the fee starting in 1970, at $150 a year for undergraduates and $180 for graduate students. "Higher Education," in *Analysis of the Budget Bill of the State of California for the Fiscal Year July 1, 1971, to June 30, 1972,* Legislative Analyst's Office, California State Legislature (March 1971), 843, https://lao.ca.gov/analysis/1971/12_higher_ed_1971.pdf; De Groot, "Ronald Reagan and Student Unrest," 123; UPI, "'Tuition' Out, 'Charges' In," *Desert Sun* (Palm Springs, CA), September 1, 1967, 1, https://cdnc.ucr.edu/?a=d&d=DS19670901.2.6-; William Trombley, "UC Split on How to Handle Reagan," *Los Angeles Times*, September 11, 1967, /https://s3.documentcloud.org/documents/23719067/19670911 -regents-reagan.pdf.

75 *"If it takes"*: UPI, "Reagan: If It Takes a Bloodbath," *Berkeley Daily Gazette*, April 8, 1970.

75 *"When dissent turns"*: Robert B. Semple Jr., "Nixon Says Violence Invites Tragedy," *New York Times*, May 5, 1970, 17; "At War with War," *Time*, May 18, 1970, 6–14, https://time.com/vault/issue/1970-05-18/page/24/; Geiger, *American Higher Education Since World War II*, chap. 5.

75 *more than four hundred:* Robert Luckett, "50 Years Ago, Police Fired on Students at a Historically Black College," *New York Times*, May 14, 2020, https://www.nytimes.com/2020/05/14/opinion/Jackson-state-shooting-police.html; Nancy K. Bristow, "Remembering the Jackson State Tragedy," *The Nation*, May 4, 2020, https://www.thenation.com/article/politics/jackson-state-shootings-fifty/; Amanda Miller, "May 1970 Student Antiwar Strikes," Mapping American Social Movements Project, University of Washington, accessed December 29, 2023, https://depts.washington.edu/moves/antiwar_may1970.shtml.

75 *for a crackdown:* Hope Chamberlin, *A Minority of Members: Women in the U.S. Congress* (New York: Praeger, 1973), 251–58; "Green, Edith Starrett," History, Art, and Archives, US House of Representatives, accessed December 29, 2023, https://history.house.gov/People/Detail/14080.

75 *more than thirty states:* Bruce R. Hopkins and John H. Myers, "Governmental Response to Campus Unrest," *Case Western Reserve Law Review* 22, no. 3 (1971): 408–69, https://scholarlycommons.law.case.edu/cgi/viewcontent.cgi?article=2846&context=caselrev.

75 *nation's major issues:* Gladieux and Wolanin, *Congress and the Colleges*, 24–25; *Campus Unrest*, Report of the President's Commission on Campus Unrest (Washington, DC, 1970), https://files.eric.ed.gov/fulltext/ED083899.pdf.

75 *had persuaded him:* Gladieux and Wolanin, *Congress and the Colleges*, 63–64, 145.

76 *one of the most:* John Brademas, "Higher Education and the 87th Congress," *Higher Education* 17, no. 7 (April 1961), Office of Education, Department of Health, Education and Welfare, 7; Gladieux and Wolanin, *Congress and the Colleges*, 133–34, 253.

76 *"If she doesn't get"*: Hopkins and Myers, "Governmental Response to Campus Unrest," 408, 437; Gladieux and Wolanin, *Congress and the Colleges*, 118–19; Hope Chamberlin, *A Minority of Members*, 253.

76 *Federal support:* Gladieux and Wolanin, *Congress and the Colleges*, 21–22; Michael Mumper, *Removing College Price Barriers: What Government Has Done and Why It Hasn't Worked* (Albany: State University of New York Press, 1996), 40; Earl F. Cheit, *The New Depression in Higher Education* (New York: McGraw-Hill Book Company, 1971), 3–12, 133.

77 *"The only place"*: Gladieux and Wolanin, *Congress and the Colleges*, 21–23, 36–38, 49–54; Douglas Martin, "Earl Cheit, Prescient Educator, Dies at 87," *New York Times*, August 13, 2014, https://www.nytimes.com/2014/08/14/us/earl-cheit-prescient-educator-dies-at-87.html.

77 *"fiscal responsibility"*: Gladieux and Wolanin, *Congress and the Colleges*, 61; Richard Nixon, "Special Message to the Congress on the Administration's Legislative Program," September 11, 1970, American Presidency Project, UC Santa Barbara, https://www.presidency.ucsb.edu/documents/special-message-the-congress-the-administrations-legislative-program.

77 *further convert:* Richard Nixon, "Special Message to the Congress on Higher Education," March 19, 1970, American Presidency Project, UC Santa Barbara, https://www.presidency.ucsb.edu/documents/special-message-the-congress-higher-education-0; Gladieux and Wolanin, *Congress and the Colleges*, 70–71, 254; Shermer, *Indentured Students*, 211–12; Fabricant and Brier, *Austerity Blues*, chap. 3.

77 *legislators felt compelled:* Gladieux and Wolanin, *Congress and the Colleges,* 72–74, 75–78, 127.

78 *ski-lodge placemat:* Gladieux and Wolanin, *Congress and the Colleges,* 90–91; Shermer, *Indentured Students,* 209.

78 *wealthy diplomat's son:* William H. Honan, "Claiborne Pell, Patrician Senator Behind College Grant Program, Dies at 90," *New York Times,* January 1, 2009, https://www .nytimes.com/2009/01/02/us/politics/02pell.html; Mettler, *Degrees of Inequality,* chap. 2; Gladieux and Wolanin, *Congress and the Colleges,* 85–86.

78 *rather than supplant:* Gladieux and Wolanin, *Congress and the Colleges,* 90–91; *Report on Higher Education,* Office of Education, US Department of Health, Education, and Welfare (Washington, DC, March 1971), 73–74.

79 *points of disagreement:* Gladieux and Wolanin, *Congress and the Colleges,* 132, 138, 163, 196.

79 *"Inherently we are":* *Hearings on H.R. 32, H.R. 5191, H.R. 5192, H.R. 5193, and H.R. 7248, Before the Special Subcomm. on Educ. of the Comm. on Educ. and Lab.,* House of Representatives, 90th Cong. 876 (1971) (statement of Rep. Edith Green).

79 *middle-class white:* *Report on Higher Education,* (March 1971), 45.

79 *got virtually nothing:* This was a big blow to Edith Green, the institutions' primary advocate; her few wins included, curiously, an irrelevant anti-busing measure she tacked onto the student aid bill and the nondiscrimination provision Title IX. Gladieux and Wolanin, *Congress and the Colleges,* 172, 186–89, 193–95.

79 *the bill it amended:* Gladieux and Wolanin, *Congress and the Colleges,* 230.

79 *$19 billion:* Gladieux and Wolanin, *Congress and the Colleges,* 96–108; Mettler, *Degrees of Inequality,* chap. 2; *2017–2018 Federal Pell Grant End-of-Year Report, Table 1: Federal Pell Grant Program: Summary of Statistics for Cross-Year Reference,* Federal Pell Grant Program Annual Data Reports, Department of Education, accessed December 29, 2023, https://www2.ed.gov/finaid/prof/resources/data/pell-data.html.

80 *public college costs:* Michael Mumper and Jeremy Anderson, "Maintaining Public College Affordability in the 1980s: How Did the States Do?," *Journal of Education Finance* 19, no. 2 (Fall 1993): 183–99, https://www.jstor.org/stable/40703828; Michael Mumper, "The Transformation of Federal Aid to College Students: Dynamics of Growth and Retrenchment," *Journal of Education Finance* 16, no. 3 (Winter 1991): 315–31, https://www.jstor.org/stable/40703899.

80 *secondary student-loan:* Mettler, *Degrees of Inequality,* chap. 2.

80 *stop making waves:* Gladieux and Wolanin, *Congress and the Colleges,* 226–28.

81 *"education as an investment":* Theodore W. Schultz, "Capital Formation by Education," *Journal of Political Economy* 68, no. 6 (December 1960): 571.

81 *benefits the individual:* Cooper, *Family Values,* 219; Milton Friedman, "The Role of Government in Education," in *Capitalism and Freedom* (Chicago: University of Chicago Press, 2020), Kobo.

81 *"Since most of":* "A Better Tuition Aid Plan," *New York Times,* February 13, 1978.

81 *"campus rebels":* Milton Friedman, "'Free' Education," *Newsweek,* February 14, 1967, 86, quoted in "The Collected Works of Milton Friedman," eds. Robert Leeson and Charles G. Palm, Hoover Institution, October 25, 2012, https://miltonfriedman .hoover.org/internal/media/dispatcher/214000/full; Mike Konczal, *Freedom from the Market* (New York: The New Press, 2021), chap. 8, Kobo.

82 *"Should higher education":* *Toward a Long-Range Plan for Federal Financial Support for Higher Education* (Washington, DC: US Department of Health, Education, and Welfare, January 1969), iii–iv.

82 *"unlike houses and cars":* *Toward a Long-Range Plan,* 23, 32; Gladieux and Wolanin, *Congress and the Colleges,* 49–54; Martin, "Earl Cheit, Prescient Educator, Dies at 87."

83 *quasi-public quasi-private: Lessons Learned from the Privatization of Sallie Mae* (Washington, DC: US Department of the Treasury, Office of Sallie Mae Oversight, March 2006), 101–2, Appendix 1, 4; "Sallie Mae Plans New Borrowing," *New York Times*, May 8, 1981, D4; *Hearings on Reauthorization of the Higher Educ. Act and Related Measures, Before the Subcomm. on Postsecondary Educ. of the Comm. on Educ. and Lab.*, House of Representatives, 96th Cong. 10–11 (1979) (statement of Alfred B. Fitt, Congressional Budget Office).

83 *"When we first":* Edwin L. Dale Jr., "U.S. Student-Loan Unit Schedule Stock Offering," *New York Times*, July 17, 1973, 53, 58; Peter J. Howe, "Cashing In on Student Loans," *Harvard Crimson*, February 22, 1984, https://www.thecrimson.com /article/1984/2/22/cashing-in-on-student-loans-pstudent/.

83 *"If Harvard thinks":* Howe, "Cashing In on Student Loans"; *Lessons Learned*, Appendix 3-A, 7.

83 *found its footing:* "Student-Loan Agency Reports a Profit," *New York Times*, April 7, 1976, 63; "Sallie Mae Plans Market Borrowing," *New York Times*, March 10, 1981, D9; "Sallie Mae Plans Sale of Notes," *New York Times*, January 15, 1982, D8; *Lessons Learned*, 64.

84 *"Do good":* *Lessons Learned*, Appendix 3-A, 2.

84 *"The New Debtor Class":* Michael C. Jensen, "Students: The New Debtor Class," *New York Times*, January 8, 1978, sec. 13, 1.

84 *"going to create":* Edward B. Fiske, "Students' Debt Rise Stirs Fear," *New York Times*, July 6, 1978, C20; *Hearings on H.R. 32, H.R. 5191, H.R. 5912, H.R. 5193, and H.R. 7248, Before the Special Subcomm. on Educ. of the Comm. on Educ. and Lab.*, House of Representatives, 92nd Cong. 711–12 (1971) (statement of Rep. James H. Scheuer).

84 *"If [students] are unable":* *Hearings on H.R. 32, H.R. 5191, H.R. 5912, H.R. 5193, and H.R. 7248, Before the Special Subcomm. on Educ. of the Comm. on Educ. and Lab.*, House of Representatives, 92nd Cong. 662 (1971) (statement of Harry J. Drolet, American Bankers Association).

85 *had borne out:* "U.S. Would Consolidate Student Aid Plans," *New York Times*, March 21, 1979, D15; Jensen, "Students: The New Debtor Class."

85 *staggering 12 percent:* Michael Quint, "Sallie Mae at 10—Profitable and Competitive," *New York Times*, March 20, 1983, F8; Winston Williams, "Education: Large Banks Remain Wary of Loan Program for Parents," *New York Times*, July 13, 1982, C1.

85 *less expensive alternative:* Mumper, "The Transformation of Federal Aid to College Students," 319–20.

85 *top off lenders: Hearings on Reauthorization of the Higher Educ. Act and Related Measures, Before the Subcomm. on Postsecondary Educ. of the Comm. on Educ. and Lab.*, House of Representatives, 96th Cong. 9–10 (1979) (statement of Alfred B. Fitt).

86 *another reauthorization: Hearings on H.R. 32, H.R. 5191, H.R. 5912, H.R. 5193, and H.R. 7248, Before the Special Subcomm. on Educ. of the Comm. on Educ. and Lab.*, House of Representatives, 92nd Cong. 2 (1971) (statement of Rep. William D. Ford, Chair of the Comm. on Educ. and Lab.).

86 *"The time is here":* Jensen, "Students: The New Debtor Class."

86 *took out $5 billion:* The GSLP accounted for $2.8 billion of this total. *Hearings on S. 1839, Before the Subcomm. on Educ., Arts, and Human. of the Comm. on Lab. and Human Resources*, Senate, 96th Cong. 143–45, 153 (1979) (statement of David S. Mundel, Congressional Budget Office); Timothy D. Naegele, "The Guaranteed Loan Program: Do Lenders' Risks Exceed Their Rewards?," *Hastings Law Journal* 34, no. 3 (January 1983): 602.

86 *"gigantic business": Hearings on Reauthorization of the Higher Educ. Act and Related*

Measures, Before the Subcomm. on Postsecondary Educ. of the Comm. on Educ. and Lab., House of Representatives, 96th Cong. 3–4, 12–13, 20 (1979) (statement of Alfred B. Fitt).

86 *"It has become": Hearings on Reauthorization of the Higher Educ. Act and Related Measures, Before the Subcomm. on Postsecondary Educ. of the Comm. on Educ. and Lab.,* House of Representatives, 96th Cong. 33 (1979) (statement of Rep. William D. Ford).

87 *who needed aid:* Michael Quint, "Policy May Curtail Student Loans," *New York Times,* December 21, 1983, D1; *Hearings on Reauthorization of the Higher Educ. Act and Related Measures, Before the Subcomm. on Postsecondary Educ. of the Comm. on Educ. and Lab.,* House of Representatives, 96th Cong. 920 (1979) (statement of Charles Saunders, American Council on Education).

87 *make loans interest-free: Hearings on Reauthorization of the Higher Educ. Act and Related Measures, Before the Subcomm. on Postsecondary Educ. of the Comm. on Educ. and Lab.,* House of Representatives, 96th Cong. 530–33, 538–58 (1979) (statement of Rep. Neal Smith; statement of Rep. Andrew Maguire).

87 *"served the nation": Hearings on Reauthorization of the Higher Educ. Act and Related Measures, Before the Subcomm. on Postsecondary Educ. of the Comm. on Educ. and Lab.,* House of Representatives, 96th Cong. 910, 927–28 (1979) (statement of Charles Saunders).

88 *directly to students:* Leonard Sloane, "Personal Finance: Buying Time on Those Student Loans," *New York Times,* June 12, 1983, F11; Erin Dillon, *Leading Lady: Sallie Mae and the Origins of Today's Student Loan Controversy* (Education Sector Reports, May 2007), 4.

88 *$8.3 billion:* "Sallie Mae Is Planning Sale of Stock to Public," *New York Times,* July 26, 1983, D9; "Sallie Mae Arranging Sale of 6 Million Shares," *New York Times,* September 14, 1983, D12; "Sallie Mae Is Offering 10 Million Shares at $20," *New York Times,* September 22, 1983, D10.

88 *"support vital national": Hearings on Reauthorization of the Higher Educ. Act and Related Measures, Before the Subcomm. on Postsecondary Educ. of the Comm. on Educ. and Lab.,* House of Representatives, 96th Cong. 677 (1979) (statement of E. T. Dunlap, Chairman of the Board, Student Loan Marketing Association).

88 *liberal arts carried:* Geiger, *American Higher Education Since World War II,* chap. 4.

89 *everybody's mind:* Geiger, *American Higher Education Since World War II,* chaps. 4 and 6. See also Mettler, *Degrees of Inequality,* chap. 2.

89 *"very well off":* Geiger, *American Higher Education Since World War II,* chap. 6.

89 *battle for free tuition:* Geiger, *American Higher Education Since World War II,* chap. 6; Larry Van Dyne, "The New York Tragedy," *Chronicle of Higher Education,* September 13, 1976; Fabricant and Brier, *Austerity Blues,* chap. 3.

5. Profits and Loss

91 *John Sperling was:* John Sperling, *Rebel with a Cause* (New York: John Wiley and Sons, 2000), 24–25, 32–39.

92 *"The lesson was simple":* Sperling, *Rebel with a Cause,* 56.

92 *$26,000 nest egg:* Sperling, *Rebel with a Cause,* 71.

92 *students really wanted:* Sperling, *Rebel with a Cause,* 59, 68.

92 *good financial condition:* Sperling, *Rebel with a Cause,* 68–70.

93 *running his courses:* Sperling, *Rebel with a Cause,* 72–76.

93 *packed up and moved:* Kevin Kinser notes that Sperling's "colorfully told" account of his run-in with WASC deviates somewhat from the facts: Sperling's claim that WASC had categorically refused to accept IPD because of its for-profit status was

undermined by the fact that WASC had already accredited two other for-profit schools at the time it rejected IPD, suggesting that "it was the nontraditional structure and unique academic model of the University of Phoenix rather than its profit-making status that caused such a ruckus." Kevin Kinser, *From Main Street to Wall Street: The Transformation of For-Profit Education*, ASHE Higher Education Report 31, no. 5 (2006), 103–4; Sperling, *Rebel with a Cause*, 76–100.

93 *entrepreneurs saw:* Thelin, *A History of American Higher Education*, 41.

94 *"The earliest form":* Robert F. Seybolt, *Source Studies in American Colonial Education: The Private School*, Bureau of Educational Research, College of Education, University of Illinois–Urbana, Bulletin no. 28 (1925): 35; Robert F. Seybolt, "The Private Schools of Seventeenth-Century Boston," *The New England Quarterly* 8, no. 3 (September 1935): 418–24.

94 *nearly a quarter million:* A. J. Angulo, *Diploma Mills* (Baltimore: Johns Hopkins University Press, 2016), chap. 1, Kobo.

94 *fly-by-night schemes:* Angulo, *Diploma Mills,* chap. 1.

95 *didn't make the grade:* Angulo, *Diploma Mills,* chap. 2; David W. Breneman, Brian Pusser, and Sarah E. Turner, eds., *Earnings from Learning: The Rise of For-Profit Universities* (Albany: State University of New York Press, 2006), 5; Robert Bocker Stevens, *Law School: Legal Education in America from the 1850s to the 1980s* (Chapel Hill: University of North Carolina Press, 1983; repr., Union, NJ: Lawbook Exchange Ltd., 2001), 170.

95 *vocational training:* Larry Van Dyne, "The FISL Factories," *Chronicle of Higher Education,* August 4, 1975, 4–5.

95 *between 1920 and 1980:* Breneman, Pusser, and Turner, eds., *Earnings from Learning,* 35–36.

95 *expanded a 1946 act:* National Defense Education Act of 1958, Pub. L. 85-864, 72 Stat. 1580 (1958); Vocational Education Act of 1946, 20 U.S.C. §§ 15i–15ggg (1958).

96 *"Fewer than half":* John D. Pomfret, "President Signs Scenic Road Bill," *New York Times,* October 23, 1965, 28; Lyndon B. Johnson, "Statement by the President upon Signing the National Vocational Student Loan Insurance Act," October 22, 1965, American Presidency Project, UC Santa Barbara, https://www.presidency.ucsb.edu/documents/statement-the-president-upon-signing-the-national-vocational-student-loan-insurance-act.

96 *vocational loan bill:* David Whitman, "Vietnam Vets and a New Student Loan Program Bring New College Scams," The Century Foundation, February 13, 2017, https://tcf.org/content/report/vietnam-vets-new-student-loan-program-bring-new-college-scams/; Van Dyne, "The FISL Factories," 4–5; Breneman, Pusser, and Turner, eds., *Earnings from Learning,* chap. 1.

96 *enrollment was up:* For Profit Higher Education: The Failure to Safeguard the Federal Investment and Ensure Student Success, vol. 1, part I (Comm. on Health, Educ., Lab., and Pensions, Senate, July 30, 2012), 132–33; Charles G. Burck, "Education for the World of Work II: School Where Students Pay to Learn Paying Jobs," *Fortune,* December 1975, quoted in *Guaranteed Student Loan Program, Hearings Before the Permanent Subcomm. on Investigations of the Comm. on Gov't Operations,* Senate, 94th Cong. 586 (1975).

96 *"Public educators":* Sperling, *Rebel with a Cause,* 101.

97 *"A new breed":* Sylvia Kronstadt, "Student Loans: How the Government Takes the Work out of Fraud," *Washington Monthly,* November 1, 1973, quoted in *Family Contribution Schedule for the Basic Educational Opportunity Grant Program, Hearing Before the Subcomm. on Educ. of the Comm. on Lab. and Pub. Welfare,* Senate, 93rd Cong. 211–18 (1973).

98 *"have become"*: Robert D. Peck, *Proprietary Schools and Educational Planning: A Staff Report* (Salem, OR: Educational Coordinating Council, October 1970), 6; Dan Rottenberg, "Failing the Teacher: Many Computer Schools Charged with Offering a Useless Education," *Wall Street Journal*, June 10, 1970.

98 *"Because the government"*: Kronstadt, "Student Loans."

98 *known scam artist:* The hearing testimony contains entertaining examples of Braneff's many colorful autobiographical tales, which include the assertion that he had been a soldier of fortune hired (unsuccessfully) to assassinate Patrice Lumumba. *Guaranteed Student Loan Program, Hearings Before the Permanent Subcomm. on Investigations of the Comm. on Gov't Operations*, Senate, 94th Cong. 50–54 (1975) (statement of John J. Walsh, Investigator, Permanent Subcomm. on Investigations).

98 *"He talked a beautiful"*: *Guaranteed Student Loan Program, Hearings Before the Permanent Subcomm. on Investigations of the Comm. on Gov't Operations*, Senate, 94th Cong. 80, 127 (1975) (statement of Ulla Wallin Peters; statement of O. A. Dameron).

98 *proprietary career schools: Undergraduate Enrollment and Completion Among Minorities* (Washington, DC: Congressional Budget Office, February 1992), xiii, https://www.govinfo.gov/content/pkg/GOVPUB-Y10-PURL-gpo45189/pdf/GOVPUB-Y10-PURL-gpo45189.pdf.

99 *"She told me that"*: *Guaranteed Student Loan Program, Hearings Before the Permanent Subcomm. on Investigations of the Comm. on Gov't Operations*, Senate, 94th Cong. 202–3, 206 (1975) (statement of Enrique E. Ponce).

99 *his instructor was drunk: Guaranteed Student Loan Program, Hearings Before the Permanent Subcomm. on Investigations of the Comm. on Gov't Operations*, Senate, 94th Cong. 210 (1975) (affidavit of Frank R. Alejandre).

99 *half of the defaults:* Nearly twenty years later, an investigator for the Government Accountability Office found almost exactly the same figures. Chester E. Finn Jr., "Washington in Academe We Trust: Federalism and the Universities, The Balance Shifts," *Change* 7, no. 10 (Winter 1975/1976), 24–29, 63; Adam Looney and Constantine Yannelis, "A Crisis in Student Loans? How Changes in the Characteristics of Borrowers and in the Institutions They Attended Contributed to Rising Loan Defaults," *Brookings Papers on Economic Activity* (Fall 2015), 1–68; Joel Best and Eric Best, *The Student Loan Mess: How Good Intentions Created a Trillion-Dollar Problem* (Berkeley: University of California Press, 2014), 58; Kronstadt, "Student Loans."

100 *a startling rise:* By 1975, they were up to $134 million. *Family Contribution Schedule for the Basic Educational Opportunity Grant Program, Hearing Before the Subcomm. on Educ. of the Comm. on Lab. and Pub. Welfare*, Senate, 93rd Cong. 110 (1973).

100 *more collections agents: Proprietary Vocational Schools, Hearings Before a Subcomm. of the Comm. on Gov't Operations*, House of Representatives, 93rd Cong. 76 (1974) (statement of Lawrence T. Graham, Minority Pro. Staff, Comm. on Gov't Operations).

100 *"We can't be held"*: Kronstadt, "Student Loans," 213, 216.

100 *"Default rates soared"*: *Guaranteed Student Loan Program, Hearings Before the Permanent Subcomm. on Investigations of the Comm. on Gov't Operations*, Senate, 94th Cong. 329–30, (1975) (statement of William O. Goodman, Texas Attorney General's Office).

100 *"quite disturbing"*: *Guaranteed Student Loan Program, Hearings Before the Permanent Subcomm. on Investigations of the Comm. on Gov't Operations*, Senate, 94th Cong. 413, (1975) (statement of Phillip H. Battersall, Am. Bankers Assoc'n).

101 *"Of course we knew"*: Van Dyne, "The FISL Factories"; *Guaranteed Student Loan Program, Hearings Before the Permanent Subcomm. on Investigations of the Comm. on Gov't Operations*, Senate, 94th Cong. 323–29 (1975) (statement of William O. Goodman).

101 *"We can't throw"*: Mike Tharp, "Costly Lesson: Charges of Fraud Hit Student-Loan

Program Backed by Government," *Wall Street Journal*, June 30, 1975; John H. Allan, "Loans to Students Now Total $8 Billion," *New York Times*, November 16, 1975, 446; *Hearings on Reauthorization of the Higher Educ. Act and Related Measures, Before the Subcomm. on Postsecondary Educ. of the Comm. on Educ. and Lab.*, House of Representatives, 96th Cong. 925 (1979) (statement of Charles Saunders, Vice President, Am. Council on Educ.).

102 *federal officials:* Nicholas M. Horrock, "Former Aide Charges Rep. Flood Sold His Influence for $100,000," *New York Times*, January 28, 1978; Wendell Rawls Jr., "Rep. Flood Had Secret Ties to Haiti While Pushing U.S. Aid to Duvalier," *New York Times*, February 5, 1978; Richard D. Lyons, "Daniel Flood, 90, Who Quit Congress in Disgrace, Is Dead," *New York Times*, May 29, 1994, sec. 1, 34; Bruce Keppel and Bill Sing, "Officer of Firm That Got Contract Had '77 Conviction," *Los Angeles Times*, August 7, 1982, 33, 36.

102 *Braneff also entered: Guaranteed Student Loan Program, Hearings Before the Permanent Subcomm. on Investigations of the Comm. on Gov't Operations*, Senate, 94th Cong. 107–19 (1975) (statement of O. A. Dameron).

102 *bank branch in Phoenix: Guaranteed Student Loan Program, Hearings Before the Permanent Subcomm. on Investigations of the Comm. on Gov't Operations*, Senate, 94th Cong. 44–45, 157, 159, 168, 170 (1975) (statement of John J. Walsh; statement of LaVern J. Duffy, Assistant Counsel, Permanent Subcomm. on Investigations).

102 *affected surprise: Guaranteed Student Loan Program, Hearings Before the Permanent Subcomm. on Investigations of the Comm. on Gov't Operations*, Senate, 94th Cong. 157–64 (1975) (statement of Lavern J. Duffy).

103 *still billing: Guaranteed Student Loan Program, Hearings Before the Permanent Subcomm. on Investigations of the Comm. on Gov't Operations*, Senate, 94th Cong. 45, 170, 290–91 (1975) (statement of John J. Walsh; statement of Sen. Sam Nunn; statement of Kenneth Kohl, Assoc. Comm'r, Off. of Guaranteed Student Loans, Off. of Educ.).

103 *federal, state, and independent:* Terese Rainwater, "The Rise and Fall of SPREs: A Look at Failed Efforts to Regulate Postsecondary Education in the 1990s," *American Academic* 2 (March 2006): 108.

104 *"it was common": Proprietary Vocational Schools, Hearings Before a Subcomm. of the Comm. on Gov't Operations*, House of Representatives, 93rd Cong. 125, 133 (1974) (statement of Peter P. Muirhead, Dep. Comm'r, Bureau of Postsecondary Educ., Off. of Educ.); *Summary Report of the House Select Committee to Investigate the Educational, Training, and Loan Guaranty Programs Under G.I. Bill* (Washington, DC: House of Representatives, June 1951), 3; Antoinette Flores, "Hooked on Accreditation: A Historical Perspective," Center for American Progress, December 14, 2015, 2–3.

104 *In 1952:* Whitman, "Truman, Eisenhower, and the First GI Bill Scandal."

104 *"accredit a ham sandwich":* Quoted in Kinser, *From Main Street to Wall Street*, 109.

105 *"A pile of money": Proprietary Vocational Schools, Hearings Before a Subcomm. of the Comm. on Gov't Operations*, House of Representatives, 93rd Cong. 56, 60, 180 (1974) (statement of Dr. Harold Orlans, Sr. Research Assoc., Acad. of Pub. Admin. Found.).

105 *"Consumers may predictably":* The *Boston Globe's* Spotlight team published a searing set of articles about abuses by ITT Tech in early 1974, a full forty years before the school was cut off from federal funds and went bankrupt, taking tens of thousands of students with it. "ITT Tech Watches Profit, Puts Quality Training in Back Row," *Boston Globe*, March 26, 1974, 20; Eric Wentworth, "For Thousands, Accreditation Has Spelled Deception," *Washington Post*, June 26, 1974.

106 *"Some recruiters": Proprietary Vocational Schools, Hearings Before a Subcomm. of the Comm. on Gov't Operations*, House of Representatives, 93rd Cong. 57 (1974) (statement of Dr. Harold Orlans).

108 *national "curse": Proprietary Vocational Schools, Hearings Before a Subcomm. of the Comm. on Gov't Operations,* House of Representatives, 93rd Cong. 8, 42 (1974) (statement of Rep. Jerry L. Pettis; statement of Joan Z. Bernstein, Deputy Dir., Bureau of Consumer Prot., Fed. Trade Comm'n).

108 *"I do not happen":* David Whitman, "Vietnam Vets and a New Student Loan Program Bring New College Scams," The Century Foundation, February 13, 2017, https://tcf.org/content/report/vietnam-vets-new-student-loan-program-bring-new-college-scams/; *Proprietary Vocational Schools, Hearings Before a Subcomm. of the Comm. on Gov't Operations,* House of Representatives, 93rd Cong. 49 (1974) (statement of Joan Z. Bernstein).

108 *loan records:* Commissioner of Education Terrel Bell testified that staff were transitioning to a computer record system and had files out to key them in. The Office of Education also disputed the finding of lost promissory notes, claiming that they had been preserved via microfiche, and that no payment would be made without at least a copy of the original note on file. *Guaranteed Student Loan Program, Hearings Before the Permanent Subcomm. on Investigations of the Comm. on Gov't Operations,* Senate, 94th Cong. 19–20, 565 (1975) (statement of James D. Martin, Deputy Dir., Manpower and Welfare Div., Gen. Acct. Off.; Appendix, exhibit no. 113).

109 *the Defense Department's: Guaranteed Student Loan Program, Hearings Before the Permanent Subcomm. on Investigations of the Comm. on Gov't Operations,* Senate, 94th Cong. 164 (1975) (statement of John J. Walsh).

109 *what schools did: Guaranteed Student Loan Program, Hearings Before the Permanent Subcomm. on Investigations of the Comm. on Gov't Operations,* Senate, 94th Cong. 68–74 (1975) (statement of Joan Z. Bernstein).

109 *"A good many officials": Guaranteed Student Loan Program, Hearings Before the Permanent Subcomm. on Investigations of the Comm. on Gov't Operations,* Senate, 94th Cong. 17, 55 (1975) (statement of John J. Walsh; statement of James D. Martin).

109 *"If the Government": Guaranteed Student Loan Program, Hearings Before the Permanent Subcomm. on Investigations of the Comm. on Gov't Operations,* Senate, 94th Cong. 1 (1975) (statement of Sen. Sam Nunn).

109 *"Students will make":* Evan Jenkins, "Truth in Advertising Takes on Colleges," *New York Times,* November 14, 1976, 422.

110 *discharged in bankruptcy:* John A. E. Pottow, "The Nondischargeability of Student Loans in Personal Bankruptcy Proceedings: The Search for a Theory," *Canadian Business Law Journal* 44, no. 2 (2007): 245–78; Caspar W. Weinberger, "Reflections on the Seventies," *Journal of College and University Law* 8, no. 4 (1981–82): 455; Best and Best, *The Student Loan Mess,* 60–61; Looney and Yannelis, "A Crisis in Student Loans?," 46.

110 *much more palatable:* Weinberger, "Reflections on the Seventies," 456.

6. The Reagan Regression

111 *something of a hayseed:* David A. Stockman, *The Triumph of Politics: The Crisis in American Government and How It Affects the World* (New York: Harper and Row, 1986; Coronet Books, 1987), 106–7. Citations refer to the Coronet edition.

111 *up to 7.5 percent:* Diane N. Westcott and Robert W. Bednarzik, "Employment and Unemployment: A Report on 1980," *Monthly Labor Review,* Bureau of Labor Statistics (February 1981): 4–14; John M. Berry, "Prime Rate Is Raised to a Record 21%," *Washington Post,* December 17, 1980, https://www.washingtonpost.com/archive/politics/1980/12/17/prime-rate-is-raised-to-a-record-21/63c4be2d-4eb1-4e88-a229-0e1273601837/.

112 *dire predictions:* William Greider, "The Education of David Stockman," *The Atlantic*, December 1981, https://www.theatlantic.com/magazine/archive/1981/12/the-education-of-david-stockman/305760/; Stockman, *The Triumph of Politics*, 100–102.

112 *"coast-to-coast":* David A. Stockman, "Avoiding an Economic Dunkirk," reprinted in John Greenya and Anne Urban, *The Real David Stockman* (New York: St. Martin's Press, 1983), 257; Stockman, *The Triumph of Politics*, 66.

112 *"White House aides":* Greenya and Urban, *The Real David Stockman*, 12, 236, 239; Lois Romano, "Stockman's Life Beyond the Bottom Line," *Washington Post*, May 24, 1983, https://www.washingtonpost.com/archive/lifestyle/1983/05/24/stockmans-life-beyond-the-bottom-line/0edcd981-3f38-45e9-8bea-ef60704f46c1/.

112 *even the generals:* Robert G. Kaiser, "Reagan's Defense Spending Could Turn into Economic Nightmare," *Washington Post*, April 4, 1981, https://www.washingtonpost.com/archive/politics/1981/04/25/reagans-defense-spending-could-turn-into-economic-nightmare/f99243fa-89ca-44d6-9104-ca4281fd7251/; John R. Gist, "The Reagan Budget: A Significant Departure from the Past," *PS* 14, no. 4 (Autumn 1981): 738–46, https://www.jstor.org/stable/418697; James R. Anderson, "Bankrupting America: The Impact of President Reagan's Military Budget," *International Journal of Health Services* 11, no. 4 (1981): 623–29, https://www.jstor.org/stable/45130983.

113 *he chipped away:* Thomas B. Edsall, "Oct. 1, 1981: That Day Is Finally Here—Reagan's Budget Cuts Begin," *Washington Post*, October 1, 1981, https://www.washingtonpost.com/archive/politics/1981/10/01/oct-1-1981-that-day-is-finally-here-reagans-budget-cuts-begin/c4872e17-43c4-46a6-8d4e-6804027678c0/; Stockman, *The Triumph of Politics*, 130–32, 141–42.

113 *fantasy math:* Greenya and Urban, *The Real David Stockman*, 87, 97; Stockman, *The Triumph of Politics*, 132–33, 142, 166, 177–78.

113 *"The idea that's been":* Greenya and Urban, *The Real David Stockman*, 76.

113 *more than $35 billion:* Martin Tolchin, "House and Senate Give Final Votes of Approval to Reagan Budget Cuts," *New York Times*, August 1, 1981, sec. 1, 7.

113 *spared the ax:* "Defense Budget Increases: How Well Are They Planned and Spent?," General Accounting Office, April 13, 1982, 1, https://www.gao.gov/assets/plrd-82-62.pdf.

113 *"pulled the revenue":* Cited in Deborah A. Verstegen and David L. Clark, "The Diminution in Federal Expenditures for Education During the Reagan Administration," *Phi Delta Kappan* 70, no. 2 (October 1988): 134–38; Sheldon Danziger and Robert Haveman, "The Reagan Administration's Budget Cuts: Their Impact on the Poor," *Focus* 5, no. 2 (Winter 1981–82): 13–16, https://www.irp.wisc.edu/publications/focus/pdfs/foc52.pdf; Robert D. Plotnick, "Changes in Poverty, Income Inequality, and the Standard of Living in the United States During the Reagan Years," *International Journal of Health Services* 23, no. 2 (1993): 347–58, https://www.jstor.org/stable/45131666.

114 *the "truly needy":* Ronald Reagan, "Address to the Nation on the Economy—February 1981," February 5, 1981, Ronald Reagan Presidential Library and Museum, February 5, 1981, https://www.reaganlibrary.gov/archives/speech/address-nation-economy-february-1981.

114 *giant glowing target:* Marjorie Hunter, "Cuts in U.S. Aid to Education to Have Wide Impact," *New York Times*, April 3, 1981, A1.

114 *slashed Pell Grants:* "An Analysis of President Reagan's Budget Revisions for Fiscal Year 1982," Congressional Budget Office, March 1981, A-44–A-45, https://www.cbo.gov/sites/default/files/97th-congress-1981-1982/reports/82-cbo-020.pdf; Tom Mirga, "College Groups Protest 50% Cuts in Student Aid," *Education Week*, February 10, 1982, https://www.edweek.org/education/college-groups-protest-50-cuts-in-student-aid/1982/02.

114 *"Why should some":* Greider, "The Education of David Stockman."
114 *"If any of your children":* Paul Gross, "Money," *House & Garden* 152, no. 2 (February 1980): 48, 52, 54, 59; Lawrence E. Gladieux, "What Has Congress Wrought?," *Change,* October 1980, quoted in 126 Cong. Rec. S33570–S33574 (daily ed., December 11, 1980).
115 *He reversed:* Edward B. Fiske, "Reagan Record in Education: Mixed Results," *New York Times,* November 14, 1982, sec. 12, 1; Edward B. Fiske, "Public College Students to Bear Most of Cuts in Guaranteed Loan Program," *New York Times,* August 23, 1981, sec. 1, 64; Gene I. Maeroff, "After 20 Years, Educational Programs Are a Solid Legacy of Great Society," *New York Times,* September 30, 1985, B7.
115 *on the Pell Grant:* Although spending was reduced by roughly $100 million over the previous year, according to the American Council on Education, an additional $500 million would have been required to meet full student need. "Student Aid in the Reagan Administration: Fact Sheet," American Council on Education, October 1984, https://eric.ed.gov/?id=ED253123; Fiske, "Reagan Record in Education: Mixed Results."
115 *more than $100,000:* Fiske, "Public College Students to Bear Most of Cuts in Guaranteed Loan Program"; Edward B. Fiske, "After the Federal Cutbacks, a New Era in Paying for College," *New York Times,* November 15, 1981, sec. 12, 1.
115 *"I do not accept":* Econ. Outlook for the Second Budget Resol., Hearings Before the Comm. on the Budget, House of Representatives, 97th Cong. 397 (1981) (statement of David A. Stockman, Dir. of the Off. of Mgmt. and Budget).
116 *just paid off:* Greenya and Urban, *The Real David Stockman,* 13; Curtis Wilkie, "Student Stockman Had Loan Troubles," *Boston Globe,* February 19, 1981, 12; Jack W. Germond and Jules Witcover, "A Loan Lecture," *Boston Globe,* October 23, 1981, 15.
116 *dropped by $2 billion:* Associated Press, "Study Finds Significant Drop in Financial Aid for Students," *New York Times,* January 16, 1984, B10.
116 *largest ever recorded:* Edward Cowan, "Deficit in Reagan Budget at Record $110.7 Billion," *New York Times,* October 27, 1982, D1.
116 *grow the economy:* Michael A. Urquhart and Marilyn A. Hewson, "Unemployment Continued to Rise in 1982 as Recession Deepened," *Monthly Labor Review,* Bureau of Labor Statistics, February 1983, https://www.bls.gov/opub/mlr/1983/02/art1full.pdf; Steven R. Weisman, "Reaganomics and the President's Men," *New York Times,* October 24, 1982, sec. 6, 26.
116 *"the assault on":* Lewis F. Powell Jr., "Powell Memorandum: Attack on Free Enterprise System," August 23, 1971, Lewis F. Powell Jr. Papers, Washington and Lee University School of Law Scholarly Commons, 2, 6, 10, 24–25, https://scholarlycommons.law.wlu.edu/powellmemo/1.
117 *conservative dominance:* Gregg Easterbrook, "Ideas Move Nations," *The Atlantic,* January 1986, https://www.theatlantic.com/past/docs/politics/polibig/eastidea.htm; Lewis H. Lapham, "Tentacles of Rage," *Harper's Magazine,* September 2004.
117 Mandate for Leadership: Phil Gailey, "Heritage Foundation Disappointed by Reagan," *New York Times,* November 22, 1981, sec. 1, 34.
118 *"None of us really":* Greider, "The Education of David Stockman."
118 *50 percent reduction:* Mirga, "College Groups Protest 50% Cuts in Student Aid."
118 *"chipped away unrelentingly":* The Impact of the President's Fiscal Year 1988 Higher Educ. Proposals on the State of Tenn., Hearings Before the Comm. on the Budget, Senate, 100th Cong. 15 (1987) (statement of Andrew Spooner, Univ. of Tenn.–Memphis); Deborah A. Verstegen and David L. Clark, "The Diminution in Federal Expenditures for Education During the Reagan Administration," 134–38.
119 *by another name:* The Impact of the President's Fiscal Year 1988 Higher Educ. Proposals on the State of Tennessee, Hearings Before the Committee on the Budget, US Senate,

100th Cong. xvi (1987) (statement of Andrew Spooner); "Consumer Price Index, 1913–," Federal Reserve Bank of Minneapolis, accessed December 29, 2023, https://www.minneapolisfed.org/about-us/monetary-policy/inflation-calculator/consumer-price-index-1913-.

119 *Social Security benefits:* Fiske, "After the Federal Cutbacks."

119 *percentage-point increase:* Leslie Maitland Werner, "Study Voices Fear That Student Debt Will Burden Lives," *New York Times*, December 29, 1986, A1.

119 *loan applications dropped:* Joseph Michalak, "Education: Interest Rate Dip Expected to Fuel a Dramatic Rise in Student Loans," *New York Times*, September 6, 1983, C1.

119 *"If you're paying":* "To Some Students, College Is a Lesson in High Debt," *New York Times*, February 19, 1981, B11; Laurie Johnston, "The $10,000-a-Year College Education Has Arrived," *New York Times*, February 19, 1981, B1; UPI, "Around the Nation: Private Colleges Report Drop in Freshmen," *New York Times*, November 16, 1981, A14; Associated Press, "Private Colleges Report Drop of 3.8% in Freshman Classes," *New York Times*, October 31, 1982, sec. 1, 62.

120 *"that wants to invest":* Marjorie Hunter, "Students Issue Plea to Spare Aid Budget," *New York Times*, April 4, 1981, A15; Marjorie Hunter, "Students Lobby in Capital Against Cuts in U.S. Loans," *New York Times*, March 2, 1982, D22; "Campus Activities Focus on Student Loans Issue," *New York Times*, May 17, 1982, D15; Fiske, "After the Federal Cutbacks."

120 *his two terms:* Greg Schneider and Renae Merle, "Reagan's Defense Buildup Bridged Military Eras," *Washington Post*, June 9, 2004, https://www.washingtonpost.com/wp-dyn/articles/A26273-2004Jun8.html; Greider, "The Education of David Stockman"; Daniel Yergin and Joseph Stanislaw, "Reaganomics," excerpt from *Commanding Heights*, PBS, 1998, https://www.pbs.org/wgbh/commandingheights/shared/minitext/ess_reaganomics.html.

120 *borrowing more than:* Leslie Maitland Werner, "Loan Cost Shift to Students Is Sought," *New York Times*, January 2, 1987, A14; Mumper, "The Transformation of Federal Aid to College Students."

120 *"Student Loans":* Associated Press, "Students at Black Colleges Hit Hard by Grant Cuts," *New York Times*, April 1, 1987, A19; Maitland Werner, "Study Voices Fear"; Edward B. Fiske, "Student Debt Reshaping Colleges and Careers," *New York Times*, August 3, 1986, sec. 12, 34.

121 *"There is a lot":* Edward B. Fiske, "Education: College Freshman Better in Basics," *New York Times*, March 20, 1984, C1; Edward B. Fiske, "Higher Education's New Economics," *New York Times*, May 1, 1983, sec. 6, 46; Reginald Stuart, "Black Colleges Survive, but Students Are Fewer," *New York Times*, February 1, 1984, A18; Gene I. Maeroff, "The Class of '84 Is Another Disappointment for Blacks," *New York Times*, June 10, 1984, sec. 4, 8; Bernard W. Harleston, letter to the editor, *New York Times*, February 18, 1984, sec. 1, 22.

121 *"the path to higher":* Johannah S. Cornblatt, "In Face of Reagan Cuts, Low-Income Admissions Drop," *Harvard Crimson*, June 4, 2007, https://www.thecrimson.com/article/2007/6/4/in-face-of-reagan-cuts-low-income/; Fiske, "Student Debt Reshaping Colleges and Careers."

122 *"excessive loans":* Associated Press, "'Excessive' Student Debt Is Cited," *New York Times*, September 17, 1985, A15; Frank Newman, *Higher Education and the American Resurgence* (Princeton, NJ: Carnegie Foundation for the Advancement of Teaching, 1985), 77–78.

122 *everything was business: The American Freshman: National Norms for Entering College Freshmen—Fall 1970*, ACE Research Reports 5, no. 6 (Washington, DC: American Council on Education, 1970), 41; Alexander W. Astin, Kenneth C. Green, Wil-

liam S. Korn, and Mary Jane Maier, *The American Freshman: National Norms for Fall 1984* (Los Angeles: Cooperative Institutional Research Institute, 1984), 48.

122 *"the age of the entrepreneur":* "Transcript of Speech by the President at St. John's University," *New York Times,* March 29, 1985, B4.

122 *"an eight-year moratorium":* Fiske, "Student Debt Reshaping Colleges and Careers."

123 *"They prefer safe classes":* Ernest L. Boyer, "Higher Education: How Professors See Their Future," *New York Times,* August 18, 1985, sec. 12, 36.

123 *"These are not draconian":* Anthony Lewis, "Abroad at Home: Depleting Our Capital," *New York Times,* February 11, 1982, A35; William Robbins, "College Presidents Assail Cuts in Education Budget," *New York Times,* February 16, 1982, B8; Edward B. Fiske, "Bell Assails Criticism of Plan to Cut Student Aid as Unjust," *New York Times,* May 4, 1982, A29.

123 *"stereo divestiture":* Associated Press, "Bennett Sees 'Divestiture' of Cars, Stereos," *Los Angeles Times,* February 11, 1985, https://www.latimes.com/archives/la-xpm-1985-02-11-mn-4317-story.html; Ezra Bowen, "The Secretary of Controversy: William Bennett," *Time,* May 20, 1985, https://content.time.com/time/subscriber/article/0,33009,956353,00.html.

123 *into a frenzy:* Edward B. Fiske, "Pain Relievers for Tuition Headaches," *New York Times,* October 31, 1982, sec. 4, 9; Edward B. Fiske, "As Tuitions Rise, Colleges Adopt Banks' Role," *New York Times,* April 14, 1986, A1.

123 *"I've never seen":* Eric N. Berg, "Borrowing to Pay for Your Education," *New York Times,* May 20, 1984, sec. 12, 42; Edward B. Fiske, "College Offers Financial Aid to Middle-Class and Wealthy," *New York Times,* November 12, 1983, sec. 1, 1; Edward B. Fiske, "Colleges Struggle to Cope with U.S. Aid Cuts," *New York Times,* February 16, 1982, A1.

124 *twenty-year decline: Youth Indicators, 2005,* Indicator 1: Number of Young Persons, National Center for Education Statistics, July 2005, https://nces.ed.gov/programs/youthindicators/index.asp.

124 *picking budget options:* Dena Kleiman, "For Some, Hard Times Limit College Dreams," *New York Times,* April 29, 1982, A1; Fiske, "Higher Education's New Economics."

124 *emphasizing their value:* Edward B. Fiske, "Colleges Seek to Replace Loan Funds Cut by U.S.," *New York Times,* October 11, 1981, sec. 1, 26.

124 *Bennington College topped:* Warren T. Brookes, ". . . Why So Costly?," *New York Times,* August 28, 1986, A23; Associated Press, "7% Rise Reported in College Tuition for 1988–89," *New York Times,* August 7, 1988, sec. 1, 22.

125 *Family income:* "Median Family Income in the United States," Federal Reserve Bank of St. Louis, accessed September 20, 2023: https://fred.stlouisfed.org/series/MEFAINUSA646N.

125 *they couldn't help it:* Fred M. Hechinger, "About Education: Rise in College Costs Challenged," *New York Times,* December 9, 1986, C11; Paul E. Gray, letter to the editor, *New York Times,* March 9, 1987, A14.

125 *ability to pay:* John Thelin, "The 50-Year Path That Left Millions Drowning in Student Loan Debt," *Washington Post,* September 13, 2022, https://www.washingtonpost.com/made-by-history/2022/09/13/50-year-path-that-left-millions-drowning-student-loan-debt/; Susan Chira, "Wesleyan to Bar Some Poor Because of Reduced U.S. Aid," *New York Times,* February 8, 1982, A1.

125 *"We always get tears":* Kleiman, "For Some, Hard Times Limit College Dreams."

125 *"It's like a sailing":* Edward B. Fiske, "Colleges Turning More to Aid Based on Merit, Not on Need," *New York Times,* April 25, 1983, A1.

126 *"We're now in":* Fiske, "Higher Education's New Economics."

126 *"It's like buying":* Edward B. Fiske, "About Education: No-Need Scholarships," *New*

York Times, September 4, 1984, C1; Edward B. Fiske, "Minority Enrollment in Colleges Is Declining," *New York Times*, October 27, 1985, sec. 1, 1.

126 *"Even though the money"*: Fiske, "Minority Enrollment in Colleges Is Declining."

126 *"You can't put"*: Samuel G. Freedman, "Yale Students Worry over Rising Fees," *New York Times*, February 23, 1982, B1.

126 *flip burgers*: Fiske, "Student Debt Reshaping Colleges and Careers"; Leslie Maitland Werner, "Education: College Cost Burden on Family Called Stable," *New York Times*, August 26, 1986, C1; "History of Federal Minimum Wage Rates Under the Fair Labor Standards Act, 1938–2009," US Department of Labor, accessed September 13, 2023, dol.gov/agencies/whd/minimum-wage/history/chart; Francis X. Clines, "Reagan's Wish Is No Minimum Wage for Youths," *New York Times*, February 10, 1983, A24; Kristi Tanner, "Accurate but Misleading: Trump on Black Youth Unemployment," *Detroit Free Press*, August 13, 2016, https://www.freep.com/story/opinion/contributors/raw-data/2016/08/13/donald-trump-black-youth-unemployment/88614252/.

127 *"People ought to cultivate"*: Christopher Wellisz, "Can Financial-Aid Searchers Find You Money?," *New York Times*, November 15, 1981, sec. 12, 39; Daniel F. Cuff, "School Costs May Require New Tactics," *New York Times*, September 29, 1985, sec. 12, 34; Fiske, "Student Debt Reshaping Colleges and Careers."

127 *"Education has become"*: Fiske, "Higher Education's New Economics."

127 *bewilderingly complex*: *Lessons Learned*, 13–14, 72, 141.

128 *never even been audited*: Robert Pear, "Watch Urged on U.S. Loan Agencies," *New York Times*, August 16, 1990, D1.

128 *Reagan was known*: Binyamin Appelbaum, foreword to Milton Friedman, *Capitalism and Freedom* (Chicago: University of Chicago Press, 2020).

128 *"It is only sensible"*: Maitland Werner, "Loan Cost Shift to Students Is Sought"; Maitland Werner, "Study Voices Fear."

129 *"The prospect of heavy"*: Maitland Werner, "Study Voices Fear"; Maitland Werner, "Loan Cost Shift to Students Is Sought"; Peter Passell, "Lend to Any Student," *New York Times*, April 1, 1985, A20.

129 *"More loan money"*: Allan W. Ostar, "Rising Tide of Public College Costs," *New York Times*, October 4, 1983, A26; Leslie Maitland Werner, "Education Chief Urges Aid Change," *New York Times*, November 20, 1986, B13.

130 *"flies in the face"*: Edward B. Fiske, "Bell Assails Reagan's Proposal to Cut Student Aid," *New York Times*, April 14, 1985, sec. 1, 31.

130 *"new federalism"*: B. Drummond Ayres Jr., "Reagan Reaffirms Determination to Cut Federal Aid Even Further," *New York Times*, November 22, 1981, sec. 1, 1.

131 *"Even the Russians"*: "Sound and Fury over Taxes," *Time*, June 19, 1978, https://content.time.com/time/subscriber/article/0,33009,919742,00.html; Burt A. Folkart, "Paul Gann Dies; Tax-Crusading Prop. 13 Author," *Los Angeles Times*, September 12, 1989, https://www.latimes.com/archives/la-xpm-1989-09-12-mn-2212-story.html; Ben Christopher, "Why Do We Keep Voting on This? Exploring Prop. 13's 'Tax Revolt Family Tree,'" CalMatters, October 21, 2020, https://calmatters.org/politics/2020/10/prop-13-family-tree/.

131 *any other state*: Michael Mumper and Jeremy Anderson, "Maintaining Public College Affordability in the 1980s: How Did the States Do?," *Journal of Education Finance* 19, no. 2 (Fall 1993): 183–99, https://www.jstor.org/stable/40703828.

131 *state spending*: Mumper and Anderson, "Maintaining Public College Affordability," 192.

131 *"balance wheel"*: Mary P. McKeown and Daniel T. Layzell, "State Funding Formulas for Higher Education: Trends and Issues," *Journal of Education Finance* 19, no. 3 (Winter 1994): 320, https://www.jstor.org/stable/40703858; Jennifer A. Delaney

and William R. Doyle, "State Spending on Education: Testing the Balance Wheel over Time," *Journal of Education Finance* 36, no. 4 (Spring 2011): 343–68, https://www.jstor.org/stable/23018116; Mumper and Anderson, "Maintaining Public College Affordability," 184.

132 *development officer:* Edward B. Fiske, "State Colleges Seeking Share of the Philanthropic Pie," *New York Times,* July 29, 1986, A1.

132 *officials' hand-wringing:* Mumper, "The Transformation of Aid to College Students," 327; Mumper and Anderson, "Maintaining Public College Affordability," 198.

132 *"Everything You've Always":* Fiske, "College Offers Financial Aid to Middle-Class and Wealthy"; Fiske, "Student Debt Reshaping Colleges and Careers."

133 *as deadbeats:* Scott Carlson, "When College Was a Public Good," *Chronicle of Higher Education,* November 27, 2016, https://www.chronicle.com/article/when-college-was-a-public-good/.

133 *"the primary responsibility":* Fiske, "Public College Students to Bear Most of Cuts in Guaranteed Loan Program."

134 *intergenerational fiasco:* Deborah Rankin, "Your Money: Aid for Parents of Students," *New York Times,* November 29, 1980, B30.

134 *"We will carry on":* Robert Pear, "Reagan Threatens Graduates' Loans," *New York Times,* January 31, 1982, sec. 1, 28; Joseph Michalak, "Students' Parents Rush to Get Loans," *New York Times,* October 11, 1981, sec. 1, 26.

135 *more than one-third:* Cooper, *Family Values,* 243; Janet S. Hansen, "Student Assistance in Uncertain Times," *Academe* 74, no. 5 (September–October 1988): 28; Mumper, "The Transformation of Federal Aid to College Students."

7. Grift Revisited

137 *Project Build:* Ronald Brownstein, "The Two Worlds of Maxine Waters: Mastering the Back Rooms of Sacramento, Battling Despair on the Streets of L.A.," *Los Angeles Times,* March 5, 1989, https://www.latimes.com/archives/la-xpm-1989-03-05-tm-7-story.html.

138 *Reagan had opened:* David Whitman, "When George H. W. Bush 'Cracked Down' on Abuses at For-Profit Colleges," The Century Foundation, March 9, 2017, https://tcf.org/content/report/president-george-h-w-bush-cracked-abuses-profit-colleges/; "Congress Moves to Stem Student-Loan Losses," *CQ Almanac 1989,* 45th ed., (Washington, DC: Congressional Quarterly, 1990), 189–91, http://library.cqpress.com/cqalmanac/cqal89-1138449.

138 *Her bill:* Calif. Educ. Code §§ 94850–94882 (Justia 2005) (passed Sept. 20, 1989), https://law.justia.com/codes/california/2005/edc/94850-94882.html.

139 *generated 44 percent: Abuses in Federal Student Aid Programs, Report Made by the Permanent Subcomm. on Investigations of the Comm. on Governmental Affs.,* Senate, 102nd Cong. 2 (May 17, 1991).

139 *"We have been": Abuses in Federal Student Aid Programs, Hearings Before the Permanent Subcomm. on Investigations of the Comm. on Governmental Affs.,* Senate, 101st Cong. 13 (1990) (statement of Sen. Sam Nunn, Chair of the Permanent Subcomm. on Investigations).

139 *"despite all that": Abuses in Federal Student Aid Programs, Hearings Before the Permanent Subcomm. on Investigations of the Comm. on Governmental Affs., Part 4,* Senate, 101st Cong. 4 (1990) (statement of Sen. Sam Nunn).

139 *"I used to buy": Abuses in Federal Student Aid Programs, Hearings Before the Permanent Subcomm. on Investigations of the Comm. on Governmental Affs.,* Senate, 101st Cong. 21 (1990) (statement of David B. Buckley, Chief Investigator, Permanent Subcomm. on Investigations).

140   *"We found more than": Abuses in Federal Student Aid Programs, Hearings Before the Permanent Subcomm. on Investigations of the Comm. on Governmental Affs.*, 101st Cong. 54–56 (1990) (statement of David B. Buckley).

140   *"intentional abuse": Abuses in Federal Student Aid Programs, Hearings Before the Permanent Subcomm. on Investigations of the Comm. on Governmental Affs.*, 101st Cong. 177–199 (1990) (statement of Permanent Subcomm. staff).

140   *personally falsify: Abuses in Federal Student Aid Programs, Hearings Before the Permanent Subcomm. on Investigations of the Comm. on Governmental Affs.*, 101st Cong. 88–89 (1990) (statement of Brenda Ann Brandon, former employee of American Career Training School).

140   *moldy food: Abuses in Federal Student Aid Programs, Hearings Before the Permanent Subcomm. on Investigations of the Comm. on Governmental Affs., Part 2*, Senate, 101st Cong. 3, 153 (1990) (statement of Sen. Sam Nunn; statement of Permanent Subcomm. staff).

140   *neighboring porn shop: Abuses in Federal Student Aid Programs, Hearings Before the Permanent Subcomm. on Investigations of the Comm. on Governmental Affs., Part 2*, Senate, 101st Cong. 161, 311 (1990) (statement of Permanent Subcomm. staff); *Abuses in Federal Student Aid Programs, Report Made by the Permanent Subcomm. on Investigations of the Comm. on Governmental Affs.*, Senate, 102nd Cong. 19–20 (May 17, 1991).

141   *"I don't think": Abuses in Federal Student Aid Programs, Hearings Before the Permanent Subcomm. on Investigations of the Comm. on Governmental Affs., Part 2*, Senate, 101st Cong. 29 (1990) (statement of Tommy Wayne Downs).

141   *increase the length: Abuses in Federal Student Aid Programs, Hearings Before the Permanent Subcomm. on Investigations of the Comm. on Governmental Affs.*, Senate, 101st Cong. 33–38 (1990) (statement of James B. Thomas Jr., Inspector Gen., Dep't of Educ.); *Abuses in Federal Student Aid Programs, Report Made by the Permanent Subcomm. on Investigations of the Comm. on Governmental Affs.*, Senate, 102nd Cong. 12 (May 17, 1991).

141   *even* lower *quality: Abuses in Federal Student Aid Programs, Hearings Before the Permanent Subcomm. on Investigations of the Comm. on Governmental Affs., Part 2*, Senate, 101st Cong. 113–14, 166–68, 205–6 (1990) (statement of Samuel L. Ferguson, Fla. Dep't of Educ.; statement of Permanent Subcomm. staff; statement of James B. Thomas); *Abuses in Federal Student Aid Programs, Report Made by the Permanent Subcomm. on Investigations of the Comm. on Governmental Affs.*, Senate, 102nd Cong. 16 (May 17, 1991); Katherine Boo, "Beyond Beauty Schools," *Washington Monthly*, March 1991, https://washingtonmonthly.com/magazine/march-1991/beyond-beauty -schools/.

141   *"In the proprietary": Abuses in Federal Student Aid Programs, Hearings Before the Permanent Subcomm. on Investigations of the Comm. on Governmental Affs., Part 2*, Senate, 101st Cong. 25, 175 (1990) (statement of Tommy Wayne Downs); *Abuses in Federal Student Aid Programs, Report Made by the Permanent Subcomm. on Investigations of the Comm. on Governmental Affs.*, Senate, 102nd Cong. 12–13 (May 17, 1991).

142   *"I'm a businessman": Abuses in Federal Student Aid Programs, Report Made by the Permanent Subcomm. on Investigations of the Comm. on Governmental Affs.*, Senate, 102nd Cong. 10–11 (May 17, 1991).

142   *"because of budget": Abuses in Federal Student Aid Programs, Hearings Before the Permanent Subcomm. on Investigations of the Comm. on Governmental Affs., Part 2*, Senate, 101st Cong. 25, 157–58 (1990) (statement of Permanent Subcomm. staff); *Abuses in Federal Student Aid Programs, Hearings Before the Permanent Subcomm. on Investigations of the Comm. on Governmental Affs.*, Senate, 101st Cong. 129 (1990) (statement of Permanent Subcomm. staff).

142 *"Everyone who cares"*: Stephen J. Blair, "Congress Should Reject 'Separate but Equal' Aid Programs," *Chronicle of Higher Education*, March 7, 1990, quoted in *Abuses in Federal Student Aid Programs, Hearings Before the Permanent Subcomm. on Investigations of the Comm. on Governmental Affs.*, Senate, 101st Cong. 417 (1990).

142 *pushed California:* Helena Andrews-Dyer and R. Eric Thomas, *Reclaiming Her Time* (New York: Dey Street, 2020), chap. 4, Kobo.

142 *was not buying it: Abuses in Federal Student Aid Programs, Hearings Before the Permanent Subcomm. on Investigations of the Comm. on Governmental Affs.*, Part 2, Senate, 101st Cong. 146 (1990) (statement of Permanent Subcomm. staff).

143 *roughly two-thirds:* Charlotte J. Fraas, *Proprietary Schools and Student Financial Aid Issues: Background and Policy Issues, Congressional Report for Congress* (Washington, DC: Congressional Research Service, August 1990), CRS-15.

143 *take real action: Abuses in Federal Student Aid Programs, Hearings Before the Permanent Subcomm. on Investigations of the Comm. on Governmental Affs.*, Part 2, Senate, 101st Cong. 55–60 (1990) (statement of Elizabeth Imholz, Esq., Dir., Consumer Unit, S. Brook. Legal Servs.).

143 *"a comprehensive, intensive": Abuses in Federal Student Aid Programs, Report Made by the Permanent Subcomm. on Investigations of the Comm. on Governmental Affs.*, Senate, 102nd Cong. 34–40 (May 17, 1991); Mettler, *Degrees of Inequality*, chap. 3.

143 *"telling students"*: Mettler, *Degrees of Inequality*, chap. 3.

144 *two parties' positions:* David Whitman, "The Reagan Administration's Campaign to Rein in Predatory For-Profit Colleges," The Century Foundation, February 13, 2017, https://tcf.org/content/report/reagan-administrations-campaign-rein-predatory-profit-colleges/; Barbara Vobejda, "Bennett to Expel Schools from Loan Program If Too Many Students Default," *Washington Post*, November 5, 1987, https://www.washingtonpost.com/archive/politics/1987/11/05/bennett-to-expel-schools-from-loan-program-if-too-many-students-default/c8bf978e-6158-4b41-8380-541a05d6e850/.

144 *"We won the war"*: Mettler, *Degrees of Inequality*, chap. 3; Matt Schudel, "Rep. William D. Ford of Michigan Dies at 77," *Washington Post*, August 15, 2004, https://www.washingtonpost.com/archive/local/2004/08/15/rep-william-d-ford-of-michigan-dies-at-77/aba3657f-7333-4932-ac0d-45f3947d4b77/; Whitman, "When President George H. W. Bush 'Cracked Down'"; "Henry Ford College History," Henry Ford College: https://www.hfcc.edu/history; Whitman, "The Reagan Administration's Campaign"; Jason Deparle, "Trade Schools Near Success as They Lobby for Survival," *New York Times*, March 25, 1992, sec. A, 1.

145 *quarter billion dollars: Supplemental Student Loans: Who Borrows and Who Defaults* (Washington, DC: General Accounting Office, October 17, 1989); Fraas, *Proprietary Schools and Student Financial Aid Issues*; Whitman, "When President George H. W. Bush 'Cracked Down.'"

145 *flashy gestures:* Jack Schneider, "George H. W. Bush Laid the Foundation for Education Reform," The Conversation, December 3, 2018, https://theconversation.com/george-h-w-bush-laid-the-foundation-for-education-reform-108018.

146 *"beginning to get"*: "Congress Moves to Stem Student-Loan Losses," *CQ Almanac 1989*, 45th ed. (Washington, DC: Congressional Quarterly, 1990), 189–91, http://library.cqpress.com/cqalmanac/cqal89-1138449.

146 *"I've worked on these"*: "Congress Moves to Stem Student-Loan Losses," *CQ Almanac 1989*.

147 *"For many proprietary"*: Whitman, "When George H. W. Bush 'Cracked Down'"; *Hearings on the Reauthorization of the Higher Educ. Act of 1965: Program Integrity, Before the Subcomm. on Postsecondary Educ. of the Comm. on Educ. and Lab.*, House of Representatives, 102nd Cong. 52 (1991) (statement of Rep. Maxine Waters).

147 *"We should not fight"*: 138 Cong. Rec. H6850 (daily ed., March 25, 1992) (statement of Rep. Waters).

148 *finally started to fall:* Whitman, "When George H. W. Bush 'Cracked Down.'"

148 *onus back on the states:* Whitman, "When George H. W. Bush 'Cracked Down.'"

149 *Any bad apples:* Antoinette Flores, "Hooked on Accreditation: A Historical Perspective," Center for American Progress, December 14, 2015, 8, https://www.american progress.org/article/hooked-on-accreditation-a-historical-perspective/.

149 *ferociously lobbying:* Rainwater, "The Rise and Fall of SPREs," 113–14.

150 *schools' ardent supporters:* Mettler, *Degrees of Inequality*, chap. 3.

150 *"After decades":* Mettler, *Degrees of Inequality,* chap. 1.

150 *Republican subterfuge:* In 2008, with the eighth (and most recent) reauthorization, legislators watered the standards down even more, giving more power to accreditors and institutions to define their own performance metrics and less to the secretary of education to set standards for them to adhere to. A 2015 *Wall Street Journal* investigation found that accreditors were often more worried about things like campus aesthetics than graduation or loan default rates. In the Higher Learning Commission's 2011 review of West Virginia's Bluefield State College (a public institution), the site visitors admonished the school for its difficult-to-read electronic signage but did not note that it had not graduated more than a quarter of its students since 2006. "Sometimes, I feel that we're doing more harm than good," said one HLC accreditor. Andrea Fuller and Douglas Belkin, "The Watchdogs of College Education Rarely Bite," *Wall Street Journal*, June 17, 2015, https://www.wsj.com/articles/the-watchdogs-of -college-education-rarely-bite-1434594602; Flores, "Hooked on Accreditation."

151 *"We can maintain":* Sperling, *Rebel with a Cause*, 165–66.

151 *Thereafter, maintaining:* Sperling, *Rebel with a Cause,* 174.

151 *in-house training:* Peter Cappelli, "What Employers Really Want? Workers They Don't Have to Train," *Washington Post*, September 5, 2014, https://www.washington post.com/news/on-leadership/wp/2014/09/05/what-employers-really-want-workers -they-dont-have-to-train/.

Part 3: Finance Rules (1996–2007)

154 *those already wealthy:* Tom Mortensen, "Unequal Family Income and Unequal Opportunity for Higher Education" (PowerPoint presentation, 36th Student Financial Aid Research Network Conference, Atlanta, GA, June 7, 2019), https://www.pell institute.org/downloads/sfarn_2019-Mortenson.pdf.

8. Iron Triangles

155 *"This is why I ran":* Steven Waldman, *The Bill: How the Adventures of Clinton's National Service Bill Reveal What Is Corrupt, Comic, Cynical—and Noble—About Washington* (New York: Viking, 1995), 43–44, 46–47.

155 *to emphasize loans:* Waldman, *The Bill,* 3–4, 39–43; Paul West, "Clinton Outlines $7.4 Billion National Service Plan," *Baltimore Sun*, March 2, 1993.

155 *$20,000 a year:* Some supporters, however, projected a positive return on the investment, of up to $2.88 per dollar spent. Waldman, *The Bill,* 21; Kathleen Kennedy Townsend, letter to the editor, *Baltimore Sun*, August 21, 1993.

155 *the Pell Grant:* Waldman, *The Bill,* 48–49, 61, 81.

156 *changed the math: CBO Staff Memorandum: An Explanation of the Budgetary Changes Under Credit Reform* (Washington, DC: Congressional Budget Office, April 1991).

156 *transition to:* While it had been started as a pilot program under George H. W. Bush, Republicans quickly soured on the idea. Waldman, *The Bill,* 19–20, 74–75.

157 *The first to fail:* Waldman, *The Bill,* 238–39, 243, 252; Jim Zook, "Senate Gives Final Approval to National-Service Plan," *Chronicle of Higher Education,* September 15, 1993, https://www.chronicle.com/article/senate-gives-final-approval-to -national-service-plan/.

158 *"domestic GI Bill":* Waldman, *The Bill,* 9.

158 *funding for AmeriCorps:* "Bowling for Virtue," *Newsweek,* January 22, 1995, https:// www.newsweek.com/bowling-virtue-182106; Catherine S. Manegold, "Clinton's Favorite, AmeriCorps, Is Attacked by the Republicans," *New York Times,* March 31, 1995, A25; Brian Knowlton, *International Herald Tribune,* "Republicans Reject New Shutdown," *New York Times,* January 15, 1996, https://www.nytimes.com /1996/01/15/IHT-republicans-reject-new-shutdown.html.

159 *Sallie Mae's stock:* Eric Konigsberg, "Sallie Maen't," *New Republic,* July 12, 1993, 15–16; *Lessons Learned,* 27–28.

159 *"Ohio Students":* Michael Weisskopf, "Simon Attacks Lobbying by Student Loan Industry," *Washington Post,* March 26, 1993, https://www.washingtonpost.com/archive /politics/1993/05/26/simon-attacks-lobbying-by-student-loan-industry/f12f67dc -840f-405c-8c97-8f51eeb45e87/; Stephen Burd, "Should Borrowers Fear a Student-Loan Behemoth? Sallie Mae's Top 10," *Chronicle of Higher Education,* August 11, 2000, A24, https://www.chronicle.com/article/Should-Borrowers-Fear-a/24205; Thomas J. DeLoughry, "Legislators Question Student-Aid Conflicts," *Chronicle of Higher Education,* February 19, 1992, https://www.chronicle.com/article/legislators -question-student-aid-conflicts/.

159 *capped at 5 percent: Lessons Learned,* 22.

159 *two primary entities: Lessons Learned,* 47; Erin Dillon, *Leading Lady: Sallie Mae and the Origins of Today's Student Loan Controversy* (Education Sector Reports, May 2007), 6–7.

159 *"to vertically integrate": Lessons Learned,* v, 9.

160 *student loan PAC money:* Alan Collinge, *The Student Loan Scam: The Most Oppressive Debt in U.S. History—and How We Can Fight Back* (Boston: Beacon Press, 2009), 30–32.

160 *"In order for us": Lessons Learned,* 10, 13–14, 83–85, 141; Dawn Kopecki, "Sallie Mae Completes Privatization 4 Years Early," *Wall Street Journal,* December 30, 2004: https://www.wsj.com/articles/SB110433510316112008; "Sallie Mae to Acquire UPromise," InsideARM, September 12, 2006, https://www.insidearm.com /news/00000789-sallie-mae-to-acquire-upromise/.

160 *mind-bogglingly high:* Mehrsa Baradaran, "Credit, Morality, and the Small-Dollar Loan," *Harvard Civil Rights–Civil Liberties Law Review* 55, no. 1 (2020), 99–100; Collinge, *The Student Loan Scam,* 9–13.

160 *third of the market:* Jonathan D. Glater, "Greater Scrutiny on Colleges and Ties to Lenders," *New York Times,* February 3, 2007, https://www.nytimes.com/2007/02/03 /education/03loans.html; Deanne Loonin, *The Sallie Mae Saga: A Government-Created, Student Debt Fueled Profit Machine* (Boston: National Consumer Law Center, January 2014), 5–10.

161 *the company's charge-offs:* Alejandro Lazo, "Sallie Mae Forecasts Surge in Defaults," *Washington Post,* January 23, 2009: https://www.washingtonpost.com/wp-dyn /content/article/2009/01/22/AR2009012203631.html; Collinge, *The Student Loan Scam,* 4–5, 38; Dillon, *Leading Lady,* 10–12; *Lessons Learned,* 84–86; Bethany McLean, "When Sallie Met Wall Street," *Fortune,* December 26, 2005, https://archive .fortune.com/magazines/fortune/fortune_archive/2005/12/26/8364649/index.htm.

161 *eighteen-hole golf course:* Dillon, *Leading Lady,* 10; Suzanne Mettler, *The Submerged State: How Invisible Government Policies Undermine American Democracy* (Chicago: University of Chicago Press, 2011), 25; Mettler, *Degrees of Inequality,* chap. 2;

Alexander Zaitchik, "Protesters' New Front," *Salon*, April 23, 2012, https://www
.salon.com/2012/04/23/protesters_furious_new_front/; Steven Pearlstein, "In a Fight
to His Finish at Sallie," *Washington Post*, January 11, 2008, https://www.washington
post.com/wp-dyn/content/article/2008/01/10/AR2008011003785.html.

162   *"Know that I have"*: James B. Steele and Lance Williams, "Who Got Rich off the
Student Debt Crisis?," Reveal, June 28, 2016, https://revealnews.org/article/who-got
-rich-off-the-student-debt-crisis/.

162   *its death warrant: Lessons Learned*, 84; McLean, "When Sallie Met Wall Street";
Collinge, *The Student Loan Scam*, 9–12.

162   *prefer Direct Loans: Lessons Learned*, 39.

162   *kneecap it:* "Student Loan History," New America, https://www.newamerica.org
/education-policy/topics/higher-education-funding-and-financial-aid/federal
-student-aid/federal-student-loans/federal-student-loan-history/; Robert Shireman,
"Straight Talk on Student Loans," Research and Occasional Papers Series, Center
for Studies in Higher Education, October 1, 2004, https://escholarship.org/content
/qt1vq388vv/qt1vq388vv.pdf.

162   *deals with colleges: Lessons Learned*, 84; Jonathan D. Glater, "Lenders Pay Universities
to Influence Loan Choice," *New York Times*, March 16, 2007, https://www.nytimes
.com/2007/03/16/education/16loans.html; Jonathan D. Glater, "Colleges Hiring
Lenders to Field Queries on Aid," *New York Times*, March 29, 2007, https://www
.nytimes.com/2007/03/29/education/29loans.html; Marcia Clemmitt, "Student Aid:
Will Many Low-Income Students Be Left Out?," *CQ Researcher*, January 25, 2008, 156,
https://library.cqpress.com/cqresearcher/document.php?id=cqresrre2008012503.

163   *lending schemes:* Megan Barnett, Julian E. Barnes, and Danielle Knight, "Big Money
on Campus," *U.S. News & World Report*, October 19, 2003.

163   *Sallie Mae's own share:* McLean, "When Sallie Met Wall Street"; Thomas H. Stanton,
"The Life Cycle of the Government-Sponsored Enterprise: Lessons for Design and
Accountability," *Public Administration Review* 67, no. 5 (2007), 837–45, http://www
.jstor.org/stable/4624638; SLM Corporation, *Form 10-K 2006* (Reston, VA: SLM
Corporation, 2006), 15.

163   *Glater covered the story:* Jonathan D. Glater, "Offering Perks, Lenders Court Colleges'
Favor," *New York Times*, October 24, 2006, https://www.nytimes.com/2006/10/24
/education/24loans.html; Jonathan D. Glater, "Greater Scrutiny on Colleges
and Ties to Lenders," *New York Times*, February 3, 2007, https://www.nytimes
.com/2007/02/03/education/03loans.html; Jonathan D. Glater, "Cuomo Investi-
gates Colleges and Ties to Lenders," *New York Times*, February 1, 2007, https://www
.nytimes.com/2007/02/01/nyregion/01inquiry.html; Jonathan D. Glater, "New York
to Take Action over Steering of Students to Lender," *New York Times*, March 23,
2007, https://www.nytimes.com/2007/03/23/us/23loans.html.

163   *admitting no wrongdoing:* Amit R. Paley and Tomoeh Murakami Tse, "Student
Loan Giant Sallie Mae Settles in N.Y. Conflict-of-Interest Probe," *Washington
Post*, April 12, 2007, https://www.washingtonpost.com/wp-dyn/content/article
/2007/04/11/AR2007041101326_pf.html.

164   *the Wall came down:* Jon Oberg, telephone conversation with the author, October 19,
2023.

164   *no matter what:* Paul Basken, "After $600-Million Is Lost to Lender Loophole, U.S.
Seeks $15-Million Back," *Chronicle of Higher Education*, January 28, 2008: https://
www.chronicle.com/article/after-600-million-is-lost-to-lender-loophole-u-s-seeks
-15-million-back-441/; *Federal Family Education Loan Program: Statutory and Regulatory Changes Could Avert Billions in Unnecessary Charges*, GAO-04-1070 (Washington, DC: Government Accountability Office, September 2004), 14, https://www
.gao.gov/assets/gao-04-1070.pdf.

165 *discontinued the 9.5:* Kelly Field, "Department Approves 7 Lenders' Bids to Remain Eligible for 9.5-Percent Returns," *Chronicle of Higher Education*, February 6, 2008, https://www.chronicle.com/article/department-approves-7-lenders-bids-to-remain-eligible-for-9-5-percent-returns-475/.

165 *"Looking through":* Paul Basken, "'Captured by the Interests It's Supposed to Regulate': A Whistle-Blower's Grim Assessment of the Ed. Dept.," *Chronicle of Higher Education*, January 9, 2018, https://www.chronicle.com/article/captured-by-the-interests-its-supposed-to-regulate-a-whistle-blowers-grim-assessment-of-the-ed-dept/

165 *whom they were hurting:* Oberg, telephone conversation with the author, October 19, 2023.

165 *No Child Left Behind:* Alyson Klein, "No Child Left Behind: An Overview," *Education Week*, April 10, 2015, https://www.edweek.org/policy-politics/no-child-left-behind-an-overview/2015/04.

166 *"I thought they were":* Oberg, telephone conversation with the author, October 19, 2023.

166 *"How could it possibly":* Oberg, telephone conversation with the author, October 19, 2023.

166 *liquid gold:* Greg Winter, "Legal Loophole Inflates Profits in Student Loans," *New York Times*, September 22, 2004, sect. C1, https://www.nytimes.com/2004/09/22/business/legal-loophole-inflates-profits-in-student-loans.html; John Hechinger and Anne Marie Chaker, "Did Revolving Door Lead to Student Loan Mess?," *Wall Street Journal*, April 13, 2007, https://www.wsj.com/articles/SB117642836964868636; Jon Oberg, "Highest Praise, Part III," *Three Capitals* (blog), December 2017, http://viewfromthreecapitals.blogspot.com/2017/12/highest-praise-part-iii.html; Jon Oberg, "One Last Post on Student Loans, Then . . . ," *Three Capitals* (blog), December 2017, http://viewfromthreecapitals.blogspot.com/2017/12/one-last-post-on-student-loans-then.html.

167 *"improperly" received:* "Special Allowance Payments to Nelnet for Loans Funded by Tax-Exempt Obligations" (Chicago: US Department of Education Office of Inspector General, September 2006), 1.

167 *Oberg's job description:* Sam Dillon, "Whistle-Blower on Student Aid Is Vindicated," *New York Times*, May 7, 2007: https://www.nytimes.com/2007/05/07/washington/07loans.html.

167 *"I have come across":* Amit R. Paley, "Confusion Cited in Overpayments to Student Lenders," *Washington Post*, October 20, 2007, https://www.washingtonpost.com/wp-dyn/content/article/2007/10/19/AR2007101902607_pf.html.

167 *changed tack:* Dillon, "Whistle-Blower on Student Aid Is Vindicated."

167 *House education committee:* Hechinger and Chaker, "Did Revolving Door Lead to Student Loan Mess?"; "Sally L. Stroup—Assistant Secretary for Postsecondary Education," Department of Education, accessed August 11, 2022, https://www2.ed.gov/print/about/offices/list/ope/stroup.html; Ryann Liebenthal, "The Incredible, Rage-Inducing Inside Story of America's Student Debt Machine," *Mother Jones*, September/October 2018, https://www.motherjones.com/politics/2018/08/debt-student-loan-forgiveness-betsy-devos-education-department-fedloan/.

168 *clamp down on:* Jon Oberg, "Iron Triangles, Part I," *Three Capitals* (blog), December 2017, http://viewfromthreecapitals.blogspot.com/2017/12/pubad-101401.html; *Federal Family Education Loan Program: Statutory and Regulatory Changes Could Avert Billions in Unnecessary Charges, GAO-04-1070* (Washington, DC: Government Accountability Office, September 2004), https://www.gao.gov/assets/gao-04-1070.pdf.

168 *did not heed:* Kelly Field, "Lender Allowed to Keep Federal Overpayment of $278 Million," *Chronicle of Higher Education*, February 2, 2007, Government and Politics

53, no. 22, A18, https://www.chronicle.com/article/lender-allowed-to-keep-federal
-overpayment-of-278-million/.

168   *$116.5 million:* Oberg, "Iron Triangles, Part I"; Liebenthal, "The Incredible, Rage-
Inducing Inside Story."

168   *2005 email exchange: United States ex rel. Oberg v. Pennsylvania Higher Educ. Assistance
Agency,* No. 1:07-CV-00960, Ex. 833-3 (E.D. Va. 2017).

169   *keep reaping it:* "The Loophole's Loophole," editorial, *Washington Post,* July 18,
2005, https://www.washingtonpost.com/wp-dyn/content/article/2005/07/17/AR
2005071700803.html

169   *largest corporate donor:* "Follow the Money: Nelnet Campaign Contributions," *Higher
Ed Watch* (blog), New America, https://www.newamerica.org/higher-education
/higher-ed-watch/follow-the-money-nelnet-campaign-contributions/; Stephen Burd,
"Report on Student-Loan Provider's Gift to Republicans Comes at Politically In-
opportune Time," *Chronicle of Higher Education,* November 7, 2006, https://www
.chronicle.com/article/report-on-student-loan-providers-gift-to-republicans-comes
-at-politically-inopportune-time/.

169   *In September 2006:* "Special Allowance Payments to Nelnet for Loans Funded by Tax-
Exempt Obligations" (Chicago: US Department of Education Office of Inspector
General, September 2006), 1–2.

169   *matter of "confusion":* Paley, "Confusion Cited in Overpayments to Student Lenders."

169   *"I thought this was":* Basken, "'Captured by the Interests It's Supposed to Regulate.'"

169   *"Just think about it":* Basken, "After $600-Million Is Lost to Lender Loophole."

170   *whistleblower complaint:* Basken, "Captured by the Interests It's Supposed to Regulate."

170   *pay $55 million:* Dillon, "Whistle-Blower on Student Aid Is Vindicated"; Paul
Basken, "After 10 Years in Court, a Student-Loan Whistle-Blower Fights His Last
Battle," *Chronicle of Higher Education,* December 5, 2017, https://www.chronicle
.com/article/after-10-years-in-court-a-student-loan-whistle-blower-fights-his-last
-battle/; Danielle Douglas-Gabriel, "The Student Loan Scandal That Just Won't Die,"
Washington Post, October 21, 2015, https://www.washingtonpost.com/news/grade
-point/wp/2015/10/21/the-student-loan-scandal-that-just-wont-die/.

170   *sovereign immunity:* Liebenthal, "The Incredible, Rage-Inducing Inside Story."

170   *not with PHEAA:* Jon Oberg, "Moving On to More Questions about Student Loans,"
Three Capitals (blog), December 2017, http://viewfromthreecapitals.blogspot.com
/2017/12/moving-on-to-more-questions-about.html

171   *"I was a civil servant":* Oberg, telephone conversation with the author, October 19,
2023.

171   *"a department that was":* Basken, "Captured by the Interests It's Supposed to Regulate."

9. A Bankrupt System

172   *a cut of his own:* Mettler, *Degrees of Inequality,* chap. 2; Christian Gonzalez and Mark
P. Kneightley, *Higher Education Tax Credits: An Economic Analysis* (Washington, DC:
Congressional Research Service, March 4, 2009), 1, 6.

172   *a New Democrat:* Robert Dreyfuss, "How the DLC Does It," *American Prospect,* December 19, 2001, https://prospect.org/features/dlc/; Waldman, *The Bill,* 3–4; Garry
Wills, "The Clinton Principle," *New York Times,* January 19, 1997, https://www
.nytimes.com/1997/01/19/magazine/the-clinton-principle.html.

172   *"performance-based organization":* "Government's First Performance-Based Organization Created," *Government Executive,* October 14, 1998, https://www.govexec.com
/federal-news/1998/10/first-performance-based-organization-created/4680/.

173 *"from doing business like a business":* David Osborne, "Bureaucracy Unbound," *Washington Post,* October 13, 1996, https://www.washingtonpost.com/archive /lifestyle/magazine/1996/10/13/bureaucracy-unbound/db6fccb3-c049-4d0d-92e4 -268170ff9513/; Al Gore, "Governing in a Balanced Budget World" (speech, National Press Club, Washington, DC, March 4, 1996), https://govinfo.library.unt.edu /npr/library/speeches/272e.html.

173 *a means of improving "customer" satisfaction:* Charmaine Jackson, *The Office of Federal Student Aid: The Federal Government's First Performance-Based Organization* (Washington, DC: Congressional Research Service, October 2, 2003), CRS-2, https:// www.everycrsreport.com/files/20031002_RL32098_f441bc9e1667e0133e1883cd fe0d7a4c4d39a39d.pdf.

173 *only three agencies:* Ben Miller and Jason Delisle, *Ensuring Accountability and Effectiveness at the Office of Federal Student Aid* (Washington, DC: Center for American Progress; American Enterprise Institute, May 2019), 7, https://www.americanprogress .org/wp-content/uploads/sites/2/2019/04/FederalStudentAid-report.pdf.

173 *"Under the legislation":* Miller and Delisle, *Ensuring Accountability and Effectiveness,* 6.

173 *the private sector:* Higher Education Act of 1965, 20 U.S.C. § 1018 (2000), https:// www.law.cornell.edu/uscode/text/20/1018#.

174 *"black box":* David Bergeron, telephone conversation with the author, June 20, 2018; Miller and Delisle, *Ensuring Accountability and Effectiveness,* 16–21, 29–30.

174 *"FSA is supposed to":* Deanne Loonin and Persis Yu, *Pounding Student Loan Borrowers: The Heavy Costs of the Government's Partnership with Debt Collection Agencies* (Boston: National Consumer Law Center, September 2014), 4, 20, https://studentloan borrowerassistance.org/wp-content/uploads/2013/05/report-sl-debt-collectors.pdf.

174 *"Is it a public program":* Deanne Loonin, telephone conversation with the author, June 19, 2018.

174 *"In some ways":* Deanne Loonin, *No Way Out: Student Loans, Financial Distress, and the Need for Policy Reform* (Boston: National Consumer Law Center, June 2006), 30, https://www.nclc.org/wp-content/uploads/2023/04/nowayout.pdf.

175 *"Study Now, Pay Never":* Quoted in Loonin, *No Way Out,* 28.

176 *"not aware of":* Report of the Commission on the Bankruptcy Laws of the United States, H.R. Doc. No. 93-137, Part I, 93rd Cong. 73–74, 170 (1973).

176 *0.69 percent: Report of the Commission on the Bankruptcy Laws,* Part I, 178–79n5; Xiaoling Ang and Dalié Jiménez, "Private Student Loans and Bankruptcy: Did Four-Year Undergraduates Benefit from the Collectability of Student Loans?," in Brad J. Hershbein and Kevin M. Hollenbeck, eds, *Student Loans and the Dynamics of Debt* (Kalamazoo, MI: Upjohn Institute Press, 2015), 180, https://research.upjohn.org /up_press/231/.

176 *"discredit the system": Report of the Commission on the Bankruptcy Laws,* Part I, 170.

176 *logic of human capital: Report of the Commission on the Bankruptcy Laws of the United States,* Part II, 140.

176 *at least five years: Report of the Commission on the Bankruptcy Laws,* Part I, 11–12.

176 *vocational education loans:* Stanley Tate, "Student Loan Bankruptcy Law: How We Got Here," *Tate Law* (blog), January 21, 2024, https://www.tateesq.com/learn /student-loan-bankruptcy-law-history.

177 *equivalent cost cutting:* Megan Suzanne Lynch, *Statutory Budget Controls in Effect Between 1985 and 2002* (Washington, DC: Congressional Research Service, July 1, 2011), 1–2, 9–10.

177 *"far outweigh any burden":* Glenn E. Roper, "Eternal Student Loan Liability: Who Can Sue Under 20 U.S.C. § 1091a?," *Brigham Young University Journal of Public Law* 20, no. 1 (2005): 43–44; 137 Cong. Rec. S13764 (daily ed., June 6, 1991).

177 *"placed borrowers"*: Loonin, *No Way Out*, 4, 6.

177 *"difficult decisions"*: 144 Cong. Rec. S11071–S11075 (daily ed., September 29, 1998) (statement of Sen. Jeffords).

178 *a few hundred*: This study, however, claims that the vast majority of these non-discharges occurred because borrowers, led by attorneys, media reports, and creditors to believe the cause already lost, did not even attempt to seek relief on their student loans within their bankruptcy proceedings. Jason Iuliano, "The Student Loan Bankruptcy Gap," *Duke Law Journal* 70, no. 3 (December 2020): 498, 525.

178 *"the judge told me"*: Collinge, *Student Loan Scam*, 14–15.

179 *"We are going to ask"*: Bankruptcy Reform, Hearing Before the Comm. on the Judiciary, Senate, 109th Cong. 31 (2005) (statement of Sen. Biden).

180 *"But, Senator"*: Bankruptcy Reform, Hearing Before the Comm. on the Judiciary, Senate, 109th Cong. 33 (2005) (statement of Elizabeth Warren).

181 *biggest campaign contributor*: And at the same time Biden was working to advance the company's interests, his son Hunter was either an MBNA employee or consultant. Tim Murphy, "House of Cards," *Mother Jones*, November/December 2019, https://www.motherjones.com/politics/2019/11/biden-bankruptcy-president/; Mike McIntire and Serge F. Kovaleski, "An Everyman on the Trail, with Perks at Home," *New York Times*, October 1, 2008, https://www.nytimes.com/2008/10/02/us/politics/02finances.html.

182 *"We've seen a fire"*: Stephen Burd, "The Subprime Student Loan Racket," *Washington Monthly*, November 1, 2009, https://washingtonmonthly.com/2009/11/01/the-subprime-student-loan-racket-2/.

182 *"great job cleaning up"*: Elizabeth F. Farrell, "A Common Yardstick?," *Chronicle of Higher Education*, August 13, 2003, https://www.chronicle.com/article/a-common-yardstick/.

182 *"In our knowledge-based"*: Dan Carnevale, "Republicans in U.S. House Push to Ease Regulations on For-Profit Colleges," *Chronicle of Higher Education*, September 12, 2003, https://www.chronicle.com/article/republicans-in-u-s-house-push-to-ease-regulations-on-for-profit-colleges/; Goldie Blumenstyk, "Temple U. Shuts Down For-Profit Distance-Education Company," *Chronicle of Higher Education*, July 20, 2001, https://www.chronicle.com/article/temple-u-shuts-down-for-profit-distance-education-company/.

183 *"a kind of"*: Richard S. Ruch, *Higher Ed, Inc.* (Baltimore: Johns Hopkins University Press, 2001), 16–17.

183 *"They've really made"*: Stephen Burd, "For-Profit Trade Schools Win New Respect in Congress," *Chronicle of Higher Education*, September 4, 1998, https://www.chronicle.com/article/for-profit-trade-schools-win-new-respect-in-congress/.

183 *a major player*: Anne Marie Borrego, "How a Computer-Training Chain Crashed in Plain Sight," *Chronicle of Higher Education*, February 16, 2001, https://www.chronicle.com/article/how-a-computer-training-chain-crashed-in-plain-sight.

184 *lobbied aggressively*: Stephen Burd, "For-Profit Colleges Praise a Shift in Attitude at the Education Department," *Chronicle of Higher Education*, November 9, 2001, https://www.chronicle.com/article/for-profit-colleges-praise-a-shift-in-attitude-at-the-education-department/.

184 *"safe harbors"*: David Whitman, "The GOP Reversal on For-Profit Colleges in the George W. Bush Era," The Century Foundation, June 7, 2018, https://tcf.org/content/report/gop-reversal-profit-colleges-george-w-bush-era/.

184 *$9.8 million settlement*: Whitman, "The GOP Reversal."

184 *more than tripled*: Charlie Eaton et al., "The Financialization of U.S. Higher Education," *Socio-Economic Review* 14, no. 3 (July 2016): 19.

185 *55 percent profit:* Eaton, "The Financialization of U.S. Higher Education," 20.

186 *1.85 million:* David J. Deming, Claudia Golding, and Lawrence F. Katz, "The For-Profit Postsecondary School Sector: Nimble Critters or Agile Predators?," *Journal of Economic Perspectives* 26, no. 1 (Winter 2012): 140; Mettler, *Degrees of Inequality,* chap. 1.

186 *"I had worked in":* Notably, Ashford advertised that its programs would prepare students for social work, teaching, and nursing careers, even though it did not have the necessary accreditation to meet state licensing or certification requirements for those professions. *California v. Ashford University, LLC, and Bridgepoint Education, Inc.,* Complaint, November 29, 2017.

186 *"lowest performer lists":* California v. Ashford University, Statement of Decision, March 3, 2022, 10.

187 *straight to profit:* California v. Ashford University, Complaint, 5–6; *For Profit Higher Education: The Failure to Safeguard the Federal Investment and Ensure Student Success, Part I, Maj. Staff Report,* Health, Educ., Lab., and Pensions Comm., Senate, 112th Cong. 296–97 (2012).

188 seven *full-time faculty: For Profit Higher Education, Part II,* 295; *California v. Ashford University,* Complaint, 7–8, 29–30.

188 *"You stop thinking":* California v. Ashford University, Complaint, 10.

188 *widespread deception:* California v. Ashford University, Decision, 8, 43.

189 *Student Loan Justice:* Collinge, *The Student Loan Scam,* xii–xiii.

190 *"In a rapidly changing":* Elizabeth Warren, "Unsafe at Any Rate," *Democracy,* no. 5 (Summer 2007), https://democracyjournal.org/magazine/5/unsafe-at-any-rate/.

10. "Borrowers Are the Product"

191 *"every tuition-dependent college":* David Bergeron, phone conversation with author, June 20, 2018.

192 *Sallie Mae on steroids:* Mettler, *The Submerged State,* 74.

192 *the early 1990s:* The extent of Shireman's influence on Direct Loans is detailed in Steven Waldman's 1995 book, *The Bill.* For a shorter summary, see Doug Lederman, "Mission Accomplished," Inside Higher Ed, May 17, 2010, https://www.inside highered.com/news/2010/05/18/mission-accomplished.

192 *neutralized Republicans' arguments:* Mettler, *Degrees of Inequality,* chaps. 4 and 5; Mettler, *The Submerged State,* 69–88.

193 *Obama's pet projects:* Not all of Obama's desired student aid reforms were so progressive. He had also pushed hard on including a new set of tuition tax credits—worth $2,500 a year—in the February 2009 stimulus bill. Mettler, *Degrees of Inequality,* chap. 5.

193 *SAFRA was in peril:* Mettler, *Degrees of Inequality,* chap. 5.

193 *made the ACA possible:* Mettler, *The Submerged State,* 82–83; Mettler, *Degrees of Inequality,* chap. 5.

194 *deemed politically possible:* Mettler, *Degrees of Inequality,* chap. 5.

195 *loan-servicing contracts:* Prior to this, there had been just one contractor responsible for all Direct Loans accounts: ACS, a subsidiary of Xerox. It was notoriously unpopular with borrowers and the department, and was later found to have committed egregious errors—and outright fraud—that greatly harmed borrowers. No one was particularly sad to see its influence diluted after the shift to full direct lending, and in 2013, it was dropped altogether. "Broken Promises: The Untold Failures of ACS Servicing," Student Borrower Protection Center, October 2020, https://protect borrowers.org/wp-content/uploads/2020/12/Broken-Promises_ACS-12_9.pdf.

195 *9 million:* "Federal Student Aid Portfolio Summary," Federal Student Aid, accessed March 10, 2024, https://studentaid.gov/data-center/student/portfolio.

196 *"Yes, we know":* Liebenthal, "The Incredible, Rage-Inducing Inside Story."

196 *Democrats were exultant:* For examples, see 153 Cong. Rec. H7530 (daily ed., July 11, 2007); John Sarbanes, letter to the editor, *New York Times*, February 1, 2008, https://www.nytimes.com/2008/02/01/opinion/lweb01ivies.html.

196 *teacher's starting salary:* 153 Cong. Rec. S9539 (daily ed., July 19, 2007) (statement of Rep. Harkin).

196 *a lot heavier:* Beth Akers et al., *A Framework for Reforming Federal Graduate Student Aid Policy* (The Century Foundation, December 8, 2023), https://tcf.org/content/report/a-framework-for-reforming-federal-graduate-student-aid-policy/.

197 *"Young people want":* 153 Cong. Rec. S9536 (daily ed., July 19, 2007) (statement of Sen. Kennedy).

197 *"begged" the department:* Robert Shireman, phone conversation with the author, February 26, 2018.

198 *reason to question:* Erica L. Green and Stacy Cowley, "Broken Promises and Debt Pile Up as Loan Forgiveness Goes Astray," *New York Times*, November 28, 2019, https://www.nytimes.com/2019/11/28/us/politics/student-loan-forgiveness.html.

198 *falconry lessons:* Jack Wagner, *Pennsylvania Higher Education Assistance Agency: A Special Performance Audit for the Period of July 1, 2005, Through June 30, 2007*, Pennsylvania Department of the Auditor General, August 2008, https://www.paauditor.gov/Media/Default/Reports/spePHEAA081908.pdf; Jan Murphy, "PHEAA Awards Six-Figure Bonuses to Top Execs," August 22, 2007, https://blog.pennlive.com/patriotnews/2007/08/pheaa_awards_sixfigure_bonuses.html.

199 *many began complaining:* Ron Lieber, "Your Student Loan Servicer Will Call You Back in a Year. Sorry," *New York Times*, April 12, 2019, https://www.nytimes.com/2019/04/12/your-money/public-service-loan-forgiveness.html.

199 *"I've never missed":* Leigh McIlvaine, interview with the author, November 29, 2017.

199 *repayment plan options:* "What Is Considered a Qualifying Repayment Plan for Public Service Loan Forgiveness?," Federal Student Aid, accessed March 9, 2024, https://studentaid.gov/help-center/answers/article/qualifying-repayment-plan-for-pslf.

200 *functionally worthless:* Ron Lieber, "A $350 Million Fund Helps Many Public Servants. Meet the Ones Left Out," *New York Times*, April 6, 2018, https://www.nytimes.com/2018/04/06/your-money/public-servants-student-loans.html; Danielle Douglas-Gabriel, "Watchdog Blasts Education Department for Sloppy Oversight of Loan-Servicing Contractors," *Washington Post*, February 14, 2019, https://www.washingtonpost.com/education/2019/02/14/watchdog-blasts-education-department-sloppy-oversight-loan-servicing-contractors/.

200 *help borrowers find relief: Strengthening the Student Loan System to Better Protect All Borrowers* (Washington, DC: Department of Education, October 1, 2015), https://www2.ed.gov/documents/press-releases/strengthening-student-loan-system.pdf.

201 *96 received it:* Stacy Cowley, "28,000 Public Servants Sought Student Loan Forgiveness. 96 Got It," *New York Times*, September 27, 2018, https://www.nytimes.com/2018/09/27/business/student-loan-forgiveness.html.

201 *"From the customer perspective":* Mettler, *The Submerged State*, 86; Marian Wang, "Student Loan Borrowers Dazed and Confused by Servicer Shuffle," ProPublica, April 23, 2012, https://www.propublica.org/article/student-loan-borrowers-dazed-and-confused-by-servicer-shuffle.

202 *they received $1.73:* Eric M. Fink and Roland Zullo, *Federal Student Loan Servicing: Contract Problems and Public Solutions* (Elon, NC: Elon University, 2014); Liebenthal, "The Incredible, Rage-Inducing Inside Story."

203 *into the private sector:* Mettler, *The Submerged State*, 70, 85.

203 *"We didn't design"*: Rohit Chopra, telephone conversation with the author, February 27, 2018.

204 *"If we believe"*: Loonin, telephone conversation with the author, June 19, 2018.

Part 4: Debtors Unite (2008–)

206 *more than two-thirds*: Sarah Wood, "How Much Student Loan Debt Does the Average College Graduate Have?," *US News & World Report*, September 22, 2023, https://www.usnews.com/education/best-colleges/paying-for-college/articles/see-how-student-loan-borrowing-has-changed.

11. The Collective Debtor

207 *his degree had cost him*: Thomas Gokey, interview with the author, November 5, 2020.

209 *"When the occupation"*: David Graeber, *Debt: The First 5,000 Years*, rev. ed. (Brooklyn, NY: Melville House, 2014), 397.

210 *"I just remember"*: Ann Larson, telephone conversation with the author, November 12, 2020.

211 *"At the end"*: Astra Taylor, telephone conversation with the author, December 11, 2020.

211 *"What to do with"*: Pam Brown, telephone conversation with the author, March 16, 2021.

212 *lost the family house*: Elaine Woo, "John J. McNaughton; Founded Vocational Education Programs," *Los Angeles Times*, October 28, 2000, https://www.latimes.com/archives/la-xpm-2000-oct-28-me-43581-story.html.

212 *McNaughton curiously*: Eric Schine, "Founder of National Education Corp. to Retire: McNaughton-Led Firm Tapped Demand for Home Study, Vocational Schools," *Los Angeles Times*, February 10, 1988, https://www.latimes.com/archives/la-xpm-1988-02-10-fi-28052-story.html.

212 *on the rocks financially*: The NEC story is full of bizarre wrinkles: in this era, Dianne Feinstein's husband, Richard Blum, owned a 20 percent stake in NEC through his investment firm, and Feinstein's opponent in her 1994 Senate campaign, Michael Huffington (then the husband of Arianna Huffington), implied that she had privileged the "fraud-ridden" schools to benefit her husband. Andrea Adelson, "Market Place: Election Attacks Are the Least of National Education's Problems," *New York Times*, November 8, 1994, D10; Whitman, "When President George H. W. Bush 'Cracked Down'"; Kinser, *From Main Street to Wall Street*, 44–45, 50–51.

213 *"This business doesn't look"*: Greg Johnson, "National Education Will Sell Training Centers, Lay Off 40," *Los Angeles Times*, June 29, 1994, https://www.latimes.com/archives/la-xpm-1994-06-29-fi-9993-story.html.

213 *its own failure*: Gregory Crouch, "National Education Corp.: U.S. Asks for Plan on Student Loan Defaults," *Los Angeles Times*, August 15, 1989, https://www.latimes.com/archives/la-xpm-1989-08-15-fi-662-story.html.

213 *Because of the reforms: Hearings on the Reauthorization of the Higher Educ. Act of 1965: Program Integrity, Before the Subcomm. on Postsecondary Educ. of the Comm. on Educ. and Lab.*, House of Representatives, 102nd Cong. 250 (1991) (testimony of Ted Sanders, Deputy Undersec'y, Department of Education).

213 *They rebranded*: Kinser, *From Main Street to Wall Street*, 44–45.

213 *Herrine, a law student*: Luke Herrine, telephone conversation with the author, October 10, 2020.

213 *eaten up dozens*: Jessica Glenza, "The Rise and Fall of Corinthian Colleges and the Wake of Debt It Left Behind," *The Guardian*, July 28, 2014, https://www.theguardian

.com/education/2014/jul/28/corinthian-colleges-for-profit-education-debt-investigation.

214 *Kamala Harris:* The California suit, filed in 2013, resulted in a $1 billion judgment against Corinthian in 2016: State of California Department of Justice, "Attorney General Kamala D. Harris Obtains $1.1 Billion Judgment Against Predatory For-Profit School Operator," press release, March 23, 2016, https://oag.ca.gov/news/press-releases/attorney-general-kamala-d-harris-obtains-11-billion-judgment-against-predatory.

214 *"the dumbest decision":* Nathan Hornes, telephone conversation with the author, January 13, 2021.

215 *"Your target is":* Larson, telephone conversation with the author, November 12, 2020.

215 *he began scrutinizing:* Herrine, telephone conversations with the author, October 10, 2020, and November 20, 2020.

215 *"find a way":* Herrine, telephone conversation with the author, October 10, 2020.

215 *They said it could:* Robyn Smith, telephone conversation with the author, March 10, 2021.

216 *"These borrowers aren't":* Herrine, telephone conversation with the author, October 10, 2020.

216 *"It was just a deeply":* Herrine, telephone conversation with the author, October 10, 2020.

216 *reached Senator Warren:* Sen. Elizabeth Warren et al., to Arne Duncan, letter, December 9, 2014, https://www.warren.senate.gov/files/documents/2014%2012%209%20Corinthian%20Letter.pdf.

217 *be measured:* Federal Register 75, no. 142 (July 26, 2010): 43,657.

218 *not a single one:* "Public Regional Hearing on Negotiated Rulemaking," Department of Education, Philadelphia, June 22, 2009, transcript, 184, https://www2.ed.gov/policy/highered/reg/hearulemaking/2009/transcript-phila.pdf.

218 *would fail the tests:* "Program Integrity: Gainful Employment; Proposed Rule," Department of Education, July 26, 2010, https://www.federalregister.gov/documents/2010/07/26/2010-17845/program-integrity-gainful-employment#p-145.

218 *recruitment practices:* 157 Cong. Rec. S600–S602 (daily ed., February 7, 2011) (statement of Sen. Harkin).

218 *"FIND OUT WHERE": For Profit Higher Education: The Failure to Safeguard the Federal Investment and Ensure Student Success, Part I, Maj. Staff Report,* Health, Educ., Lab., and Pensions Comm., Senate, 112th Cong., 16, 60.

219 *school's exorbitant cost: For Profit Higher Education, Part I,* Health, Educ., Lab., and Pensions Comm., Senate, 112th Cong. 38, 63–64 (2012).

219 *"They are not focused":* 157 Cong. Rec. S602 (daily ed., February 7, 2011) (statement of Sen. Harkin); *For Profit Higher Education, Part I,* 2, 8, 63.

219 *more than $350 million:* 157 Cong. Rec. S602 (daily ed., February 7, 2011) (statement of Sen. Harkin); *For Profit Higher Education, Part I,* 2, 8, 63.

219 *86 percent: For Profit Higher Education, Part I,* 3.

220 *wounded warriors:* Daniel Golden, "For-Profit Colleges Target the Military," *Bloomberg Businessweek,* December 30, 2009, https://www.bloomberg.com/news/articles/2009-12-30/for-profit-colleges-target-the-military.

220 *nearly a quarter: For Profit Higher Education, Part I,* 3, 15, 167.

220 *the "Bennett hypothesis":* Stephanie Riegg Cellini and Claudia Goldin, "Does Federal Student Aid Raise Tuition? New Evidence on For-Profit Colleges," National Bureau of Economic Research, working paper 17827, http://www.nber.org/papers/w17827.

221 *came out behind:* Stephanie R. Cellini and Latika Chaudhary, "The Labor Market Returns to a For-Profit College Education," *Economics of Education Review* 43, no. 6 (December 2014): 125–40.

221   no *educational experience:* Rajeev Darolia et al., "Do Employers Prefer Workers Who Attend For-Profit Colleges? Evidence from a Field Experiment," *Journal of Policy Analysis and Management* 34, no. 4 (Fall 2015): 881–903.

221   *projected to* lose: Stephanie Riegg Cellini and Nicholas Turner, "Gainfully Employed? Assessing the Employment and Earnings of For-Profit College Students Using Administrative Data," National Bureau of Economic Research, working paper 22287, January 2018, http://www.nber.org/papers/w22287.

222   *enrollments fell:* Doug Lederman, "Higher Ed Shrinks," Inside Higher Ed, October 9, 2012, https://www.insidehighered.com/news/2012/10/10/enrollments-fall-first-time-15-years.

222   *it had even been:* Goldie Blumenstyk and Charles Huckabee, "Ruling on 'Gainful Employment' Gives Each Side Something to Cheer," *Chronicle of Higher Education,* July 2, 2012, https://www.chronicle.com/article/judges-ruling-on-gainful-employment-gives-each-side-something-to-cheer/.

222   *had almost no one:* Kelly Field, "In the Final 'Gainful Employment' Rule, a Key Measure Vanishes," *Chronicle of Higher Education,* October 30, 2014, https://www.chronicle.com/article/in-the-final-gainful-employment-rule-a-key-measure-vanishes/.

223   *cardboard box:* Herrine, telephone conversation with the author, October 10, 2020.

223   *"With abundant evidence":* "Speedy Help for Victims of College Fraud," editorial, *New York Times,* September 26, 2015, https://www.nytimes.com/2015/09/27/opinion/sunday/speedy-help-for-victims-of-college-fraud.html.

223   *a searing letter:* Sen. Elizabeth Warren et al., to John B. King Jr., letter, September 29, 2016, https://www.warren.senate.gov/files/documents/2016-9-29_Letter_to_ED_re_Corinthian_data.pdf.

224   *repealed it altogether:* Brian E. Frosh et al., to Elisabeth DeVos, letter, July 18, 2018, https://oag.ca.gov/system/files/attachments/press_releases/GE%20Comment%20-%20July%202018%20Third%20Delay%20of%20Disclosures_0.pdf; Andrew Kreighbaum, "DeVos Issues Final Repeal of Gainful Employment," Inside Higher Ed, July 1, 2019, https://www.insidehighered.com/quicktakes/2019/07/02/devos-issues-final-repeal-gainful-employment.

224   *"all one had to do":* Cory Turner, "Betsy DeVos Overruled Education Dept. Findings on Defrauded Student Borrowers," NPR, December 11, 2019, https://www.npr.org/2019/12/11/786367598/betsy-devos-overruled-education-dept-findings-on-defrauded-student-borrowers.

225   *$2 trillion stimulus bill:* Kelsey Snell, "What's Inside the Senate's $2 Trillion Coronavirus Aid Package?," NPR, March 26, 2020, https://www.npr.org/2020/03/26/821457551/whats-inside-the-senate-s-2-trillion-coronavirus-aid-package.

225   *"be the resistance":* Allison Quinn, "Betsy DeVos Pleads with Staffers to 'Be the Resistance' Under Biden: Report," Daily Beast, December 16, 2020, https://www.thedailybeast.com/betsy-devos-pleads-with-staffers-to-be-the-resistance-under-biden-report-says.

225   *"to be good stewards of tax dollars":* Turner, "Betsy DeVos Overruled Education Dept. Findings."

226   *submitted a memo:* Ryann Liebenthal, "The Long Fight to Cancel Student Loans," *New Republic,* April 19, 2021, https://newrepublic.com/article/161883/biden-student-loans-debt-cancel.

227   *news to Luke Herrine:* Herrine, telephone conversation with the author, October 10, 2020.

227   *write a white paper:* Herrine, telephone conversation with the author, October 10, 2020; Luke Herrine, *An Administrative Path to Student Debt Cancellation* (Great Democracy Initiative, December 2019), https://rooseveltinstitute.org/wp-content

/uploads/2021/08/GDI_Administrative-Path-to-Student-Debt-Cancellation_201912
.pdf.

227 *become more radical:* Rebecca Morin, "Warren Says She Would Cancel Student
Debt on Day 1, Citing Legal Authority of Department of Ed.," *USA Today,* January 14, 2020, https://www.usatoday.com/story/news/politics/elections/2020/01/14
/election-2020-elizabeth-warren-says-she-cancel-student-loan-debt-first-day-in
-white-house/4460802002/.

227 *"for Pell Grant recipients":* Kamala Harris (@KamalaHarris), "Yesterday I announced
that, as president," Twitter, July 27, 2019, https://twitter.com/kamalaharris/status
/1155305122911723526.

228 *the racial wealth gap:* Raphaël Charron-Chénier et al., "A Pathway to Racial Equity:
Student Debt Cancellation Policy Designs," *Social Currents* 9, no. 1 (February 2022):
1, https://doi.org/10.1177/23294965211024671.

229 *"debt for people who":* Annie Nova, "Biden Questions Why Yale or Harvard Graduates Should Get Loans Forgiven: But Few Borrowers Attend Elite Schools," CNBC,
February 19, 2021, https://www.cnbc.com/2021/02/19/very-small-share-of-student
-loan-borrowers-attended-elite-colleges-.html.

229 *Harvard undergrads:* "College Scorecard: Harvard University," Dept. of Education,
accessed January 23, 2024, https://collegescorecard.ed.gov/school/?166027-Harvard
-University.

229 *"with the flick of a pen":* "Joint Statement: Coalition Applauds Bicameral Resolu-
tion Calling on Biden to Cancel $50K of Student Debt," Americans for Financial
Reform, February 4, 2021, https://ourfinancialsecurity.org/2021/02/joint-statement
-coalition-applauds-bicameral-resolution-calling-on-biden-to-cancel-50k-of-student
-debt/; Maura Healey et al., to Sen. Chuck Schumer et al., letter, February 19, 2021,
https://ag.ny.gov/sites/default/files/multistate_letter_in_support_of_administrative
_student_debt_cancellation_final.pdf; Annie Nova, "Schumer Pressures Biden to
Bypass Congress to Cancel $50,000 in Student Debt per Borrower," CNBC, Decem-
ber 7, 2020, https://www.cnbc.com/2020/12/07/schumer-calls-on-biden-to-cancel
-50000-in-student-debt-per-borrower.html.

229 *as much as $1 trillion:* Scott Fullwiler et al., *The Macroeconomic Effects of Student Debt
Cancellation* (Annandale-on-Hudson, NY: Levy Economics Institute of Bard College,
February 2018), https://www.levyinstitute.org/pubs/rpr_2_6.pdf.

229 *to draft a memo:* Danielle Douglas-Gabriel, "Pelosi Says Biden Has No Authority
to Cancel Student Loans on His Own," *Washington Post,* July 28, 2021, https://
www.washingtonpost.com/education/2021/07/28/pelosi-student-loan-forgiveness/;
Michael Stratford, "Dozens of Democrats Demand Biden Release Legal Memo on
Student Debt Cancellation," *Politico,* January 26, 2022: https://www.politico.com
/news/2022/01/26/democrats-biden-memo-student-debt-cancellation-00002193.

12. Biden Time

231 *"SCOTUS, can you":* People's Rally for Student Debt Cancellation, February 28,
2023, video, https://www.cancelmystudentdebt.org/peoples-rally-livestream.

231 *spare student debtors: Biden v. Nebraska et al.,* no. 22-506, oral arguments, February 28, 2023, transcript, https://www.supremecourt.gov/oral_arguments/argument
_transcripts/2022/22-506_k53l.pdf.

232 *Biden was dithering:* "Borrower Defense Updates," Federal Student Aid, accessed
January 23, 2023, https://studentaid.gov/announcements-events/borrower-defense
-update.

233 *$42 billion in relief:* Department of Education, "Education Department Announces
Permanent Improvements to the Public Service Loan Forgiveness Program and

One-Time Payment Count Adjustment to Bring Borrowers Closer to Forgiveness," October 25, 2022, https://www.ed.gov/news/press-releases/education-department -announces-permanent-improvements-public-service-loan-forgiveness-program -and-one-time-payment-count-adjustment-bring-borrowers-closer-forgiveness; Ka- meron McNair, "The Biden Administration Has Forgiven $42 Billion in Student Loan Debt for Borrowers in Public Service," CNBC, May 8, 2023, https://www .cnbc.com/2023/05/08/biden-admin-has-forgiven-42-billion-dollars-in-student -loan-debt-via-pslf.html; https://www.insidehighered.com/news/2022/10/26/biden -administration-unveils-permanent-fixes-public-service-program.

233 *relieved $56.7 billion:* Shirin Ali and Mark Joseph Stern, "Biden's Plan B on Student Loan Forgiveness Is a Massive and Improbable Success," *Slate,* February 23, 2024, https://slate.com/news-and-politics/2024/02/student-loan-forgiveness-biden-plan -since-supreme-court-decision.html.

233 *the forgiveness plan:* Stacy Cowley, "Analysis Says Biden's New Student Debt Plan Could Cost $475 Billion," *New York Times,* July 19, 2023, https://www.nytimes .com/2023/07/19/business/biden-student-loans-repayment.html.

233 *continue to pursue:* Mark Joseph Stern, "Joe Biden's New Student Debt Relief Plan Might Actually Work This Time," *Slate,* July 11, 2023, https://slate.com/news-and -politics/2023/07/joe-biden-new-student-debt-plan-supreme-court-analysis.html; "Biden-Harris Administration Approves $1.2 Billion in Loan Forgiveness for Over 150,000 SAVE Plan Borrowers," Department of Education, February 21, 2024, https://www.ed.gov/news/press-releases/biden-harris-administration-approves-12 -billion-loan-forgiveness-over-150000-save-plan-borrowers; Annie Nova, "Biden Administration Releases Formal Proposal for New Student Loan Forgiveness Plan," CNBC, April 17, 2024, https://www.cnbc.com/2024/04/17/biden-administration -releases-new-student-loan-forgiveness-proposal.html.

234 *"ultra-millionaire tax":* Elizabeth Warren, Warren for Senate, accessed January 23, 2024, https://elizabethwarren.com/plans/ultra-millionaire-tax.

234 *"the added burden":* Naomi Zewde and Darrick Hamilton, "What Canceling Student Debt Would Do for the Racial Wealth Gap," *New York Times,* February 1, 2021, https://www.nytimes.com/2021/02/01/opinion/student-debt-cancellation-biden .html; Andrew Kreighbaum, "Student Debt Reinforces the Racial Wealth Gap, Study Finds," Inside Higher Ed, September 25, 2019, https://www.insidehighered.com /quicktakes/2019/09/26/student-debt-reinforces-racial-wealth-gap-study-finds.

235 *"not worth the cost":* Douglas Belkin, "Americans Are Losing Faith in College Educa- tion, WSJ-NORC Poll Finds," *Wall Street Journal,* March 31, 2023, https://www.wsj .com/articles/americans-are-losing-faith-in-college-education-wsj-norc-poll-finds -3a836ce1.

235 *money to institutions:* Newfield, *The Great Mistake,* 93–100.

239 *pay back only $80,000:* Michael Hiltzik, "SEC Gives Former Execs of Corinthian Col- leges, a Massive Scam, Slaps on the Wrist," *Los Angeles Times,* March 6, 2019, https:// www.latimes.com/business/hiltzik/la-fi-hiltzik-corinthian-college-sec-20190306 -story.html.

13. Past Due

243 *free higher education:* Hannah Thompson, "Macron Hints at End of Free University Access in France," *Connexion,* January 18, 2022, https://www.connexionfrance.com /French-news/Macron-hints-at-end-of-free-university-access-in-France; "Le Coût des Études Supérieures en France," Campus France, accessed January 23, 2024, https:// www.campusfrance.org/fr/cout-etudes-superieures-france-frais-inscription.

243 *nationwide strikes:* Francois Murphy, "French Students Take to Streets as Protest Grows,"

Reuters, November 8, 2007, https://www.reuters.com/article/us-france-students
/french-students-take-to-streets-as-protest-grows-idUSL0854584020071108.

243 *"We cannot remain":* Thompson, "Macron Hints at End of Free University Access in France."

244 *Everyone pays into:* Valentine Marie, "Taxes in France: A Guide to the French Tax System," Expatica, January 9, 2024, https://www.expatica.com/fr/finance/taxes/a -guide-to-taxes-in-france-101156/; Tax Policy Center *Briefing Book*, https://www .taxpolicycenter.org/briefing-book/how-do-us-taxes-compare-internationally.

244 *versus 39 percent:* Michael Rajski et al., "The Problem with French Universities," European Horizons, accessed January 23, 2024, https://voices.uchicago.edu/euchicago /the-problem-with-french-universities; *Education at a Glance 2021: OECD Indicators* (OECD, September 16, 2021), https://www.oecd-ilibrary.org/docserver/b35a14e5 -en.pdf.

244 *a few proposals:* My suggestions draw on similar models of reform proposed by others. For instance, education-equity scholar Sara Goldrick-Rab has outlined plans for the federal government to provide funding for two years of college at public institutions and partner with states to enhance investments in institutional aid. See Sara Goldrick-Rab and Nancy Kendall, *Redefining College Affordability: Securing America's Future with a Free Two-Year College Option* (Washington, DC: Lumina Foundation, 2014), https://www.luminafoundation.org/files/publications/ideas_summit/Redefining _College_Affordability.pdf; Sara Goldrick-Rab, *Paying the Price: College Costs, Financial Aid, and the Betrayal of the American Dream* (Chicago: University of Chicago Press, 2016), chap. 10, Kobo; Sara Goldrick-Rab et al., "Making College Affordable," in *Reinventing Financial Aid: Charting a New Course to College Affordability*, eds. Andrew P. Kelly and Sara Goldrick-Rab (Cambridge, MA: Harvard Education Press, 2014), 191–205.

244 *death of defunding:* Marie Bennett, "LEAP Fact Sheet," National Association of State Student Grant and Aid Programs, November 2008, https://www.nassgap.org/wp -content/uploads/LEAP-Fact-Sheet-2008-Color-Nov-08.pdf.

244 *state investment:* Michael Mitchell, Michael Leachman, and Matt Saenz, "State Higher Education Funding Cuts Have Pushed Costs to Students, Worsened Inequality," Center on Budget and Policy Priorities, October 24, 2019, https://www .cbpp.org/research/state-budget-and-tax/state-higher-education-funding-cuts-have -pushed-costs-to-students.

245 *more than one-third:* "Award Year Summary by School Type," Title IV Program Volume Reports, Federal Student Aid, accessed March 10, 2024, https://studentaid.gov /data-center/student/title-iv; "Characteristics of Postsecondary Students," National Center for Education Statistics, accessed March 10, 2024, https://nces.ed.gov /programs/coe/indicator/csb/postsecondary-students.

246 *Harvard's 2025 freshmen:* Carlos Moreno, "How Ending Legacy Admissions Can Help Achieve Greater Education Equity," ACLU, April 12, 2022, https://www.aclu .org/news/racial-justice/how-ending-legacy-admissions-can-help-achieve-greater -education-equity; Aatish Bhatia and Claire Cain Miller, "Explore How Income Influences Attendance at 139 Top Colleges," *The Upshot* (blog), *New York Times*, https:// www.nytimes.com/interactive/2023/09/11/upshot/college-income-lookup.html.

248 *miscalculated nearly 300,000:* Tara Siegel Bernard, "More Than 400,000 Student Loan Borrowers Had Wrong Monthly Payments," *New York Times*, October 16, 2023, https://www.nytimes.com/2023/10/16/your-money/student-loans-save-mistakes .html.

249 *clever shell game:* Natalie Schwartz, "University of Arizona Global Campus Terminates Contract with Zovio," Higher Ed Dive, August 1, 2022, https://www

.highereddive.com/news/university-of-arizona-global-campus-terminates-contract-with-zovio/628603/; Bernard, "More Than 400,000 Student Loan Borrowers."

249   *to buy Phoenix:* Kevin Richert, "Two Days in May: Inside the Frenzied Rush to Approve—and Oppose—the Phoenix Purchase," Idaho Ed News, December 20, 2023, https://www.idahoednews.org/top-news/two-days-in-may-inside-the-frenzied-rush-to-approve-and-oppose-the-phoenix-purchase/; "University of Idaho Phoenix Affiliation FAQ," University of Idaho, December 1, 2023, https://www.uidaho.edu/president/university-of-phoenix-affiliation; Katherine Knott, "Senate Democrats Question Idaho Plan to Buy University of Phoenix," Inside Higher Ed, September 12, 2023, https://www.insidehighered.com/news/quick-takes/2023/09/12/senate-democrats-question-idaho-deal-buy-university-phoenix.

250   *online education:* Tuition and Financial Aid, Southern New Hampshire University, accessed January 23, 2024, https://www.snhu.edu/tuition-and-financial-aid/online; Lauren Coffey, "'Dynamic, Uncertain Moment' for Online Learning," Inside Higher Ed, August 15, 2023, https://www.insidehighered.com/news/tech-innovation/teaching-learning/2023/08/15/report-suggests-online-learning-has-yet-peak.

250   *"The ultimate, hidden truth":* David Graeber, *The Utopia of Rules: On Technology, Stupidity, and the Secret Joys of Bureaucracy* (Brooklyn, NY: Melville House, 2015), 89.

251   *free high school:* Scholars generally date the movement for mass, free, public secondary education from about 1910 to 1940. Claudia Goldin and Lawrence F. Katz, *The Race Between Education and Technology* (Cambridge, MA: The Belknap Press, 2008).

251   *made to work:* Mettler, *Degrees of Inequality*, chap. 2.

253   *$35,000 a year: New York University Bulletin: 2008–2010* (New York: NYU Leonard N. Stern School of Business), 67, https://w4.stern.nyu.edu/uc/advising/SternUGBulletin.pdf.

INDEX

ABOUT THE AUTHOR

RYANN LIEBENTHAL is a writer and editor living in Oakland, California, who has reported widely on the student loan crisis. She has written for *Mother Jones*, *n+1*, and *The New Republic* and was previously an editor at *Harper's Magazine*.